D0083333

WITHDRAWN

ARMAND-JEAN DE RANCÉ
ABBOT OF LA TRAPPE

1. Rancé: the portrait surreptitiously made by Rigaud, acting for Saint-Simon, and drawn from memory (1696)

ARMAND-JEAN DE RANCÉ

ABBOT OF LA TRAPPE

His Influence in the
Cloister and the World

BY

A. J. KRAILSHEIMER

CLARENDON PRESS · OXFORD
1974

Oxford University Press, Ely House, London W.1

GLASGOW   NEW YORK   TORONTO   MELBOURNE   WELLINGTON
CAPE TOWN   IBADAN   NAIROBI   DAR ES SALAAM   LUSAKA   ADDIS ABABA
DELHI   BOMBAY   CALCUTTA   MADRAS   KARACHI   LAHORE   DACCA
KUALA LUMPUR   SINGAPORE   HONG KONG   TOKYO

ISBN 0 19 815744 4

© *Oxford University Press 1974*

*Printed in Great Britain by
William Clowes & Sons, Limited, London, Beccles and Colchester*

Acknowledgements

THIS is in some ways not the book I wanted to write. When I began it seemed that the basic material was already well known, and that the real task was to interpret it afresh. Then there came a stage when it looked as though there would be no end to the new material that I was discovering, and certainly not enough time to examine it properly. Finally, when the sources began to trickle rather than pour, the most urgent problem became one of presentation and selection. I think I now know the answers to my original questions, but I am sure that until others can look at the same evidence they will not even ask the right questions. The Bibliography, especially of manuscript sources, tells its own story, of journeys always against the clock, of exhaustive written inquiries, followed eventually by piles of photocopies, and as for the printed sources, only those who try to check that part of the Bibliography on this side of the Channel will appreciate what that represents.

Clearly none of this work could have been done without the kindness and generosity of many people. It is a real pleasure to acknowledge their help. Among those who answered sometimes importunate requests for information I would mention M. Jean Mesnard, M. Bruno Neveu, Père Paul Auvray, archivist of the Oratorian house at Montsoult (now removed to Paris), dom Guy Oury, O.S.B., of Solesmes, M. Jean Lebrun, a young researcher working in the same field, Dr. Robert Shackleton, Bodley's Librarian, who even lent me one of his own precious books, and M. Michel Castaing, of Charavay in Paris, for great courtesy to someone who could never afford the price of a Rancé autograph.

Librarians and archivists who have supplied information and then photocopies, sometimes free of charge, often helped by saving me a journey. I would particularly like to express my thanks to H.M. the Queen, who graciously permitted the Royal Librarian, Mr. Robert Mackworth-Young, to supply me with copies of the Stuart Papers, to M. Irénée Noye, of Saint-Sulpice, for unearthing and having copied papers of whose existence he was not at first aware, to Mlle S. Montagne, of Clermont-Ferrand, for detailed answers to complicated questions, to M. P. Campagne, then acting librarian at Poitiers, for an extraordinarily generous gift of photocopies, and to M. André Gazier for going to such trouble in procuring me copies from his library of Port-Royal. In three places the warmth of the welcome and extent of the help went far beyond what a visitor has a right to expect; at Troyes Mlle F. Bibolet and M. A. Morin, at Utrecht Dr. A. J. van de Ven and at Annecy Sister Marie-Agathe (who even secured episcopal authority for me to enter the enclosure) have put me heavily in their debt.

There is no space here to list all the other individuals and libraries who have been of assistance, but my gratitude to them is no less real. To two communities, however, I owe a debt which words cannot adequately express. First to my own college of Christ Church, both officially to the Governing Body, for most generous contributions to my expenses, and then to my individual colleagues, whose patience, wisdom, and learning continue to sustain me. Lastly to the abbot and monks of la Trappe, who not only put at my entire disposal their priceless archives, but who have completely accepted the stranger in their midst and given him a second home. If I name only the abbot, dom Gérard Guérout, the librarian, Père Lucien Aubry, and the archivist, Père Eric de Jessé, it is in accordance with professional courtesies, not because I am unmindful of my other friends at la Trappe. I hope that these two great houses will forgive the imperfections of this work and accept it as the best tribute I have to offer to godliness and good learning—and boundless kindness.

A.J.K.

Contents

List of Plates

Abbreviations

THE following abbreviations have been used for convenience in the footnotes:

A	Bibliothèque de l'Arsenal, MS.
AE	Archives du Ministère des Affaires Étrangères, France, MS.
BN	Bibliothèque Nationale, MS. fonds français (unless otherwise stated)
CF	Clermont-Ferrand, Bibliothèque Municipale et Universitaire, MS.
DBF	*Dictionnaire de biographie française*
G	Grenoble, Bibliothèque Municipale
GC	*Gallia Christiana*
M	Bibliothèque Mazarine, MS.
MC	Minutier Central
P	Poitiers, Bibliothèque Municipale, MS. Fontaneau 65
PR	Bibliothèque de la Société de Port-Royal, MS.
SG	Bibliothèque de Sainte-Geneviève, MS.
SP	Stuart Papers, Windsor Castle
SS	Bibliothèque de Saint-Sulpice
T	Troyes, Bibliothèque Municipale, MS.
TA	La Trappe, *Lettres originales*
TB	La Trappe, *Lettres à imprimer* (page references)
TC	La Trappe, *Lettres de piété*
TD	La Trappe, *Lettres diverses*
U	Utrecht, *ancien fonds d'Amersfoort*, MS. PR
Vis	Annecy, Archives du monastère de la Visitation

Gonod	*Lettres de Rancé*, ed B. Gonod, 1846
Muguet	*Lettres de piété*, Muguet, 1701/2

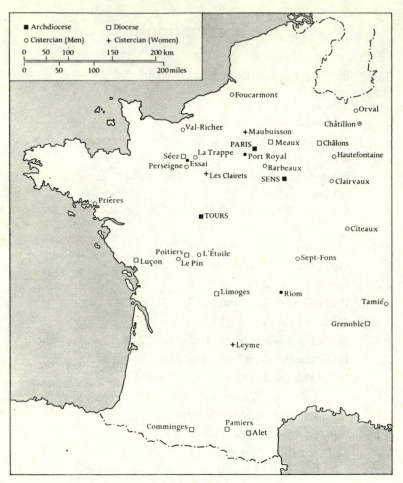

Places mentioned in the text

Introduction

THE abbé de Rancé is hardly an unknown figure, but most people who have heard of him, or the Trappists, turn out to have astonishingly little real information, and much of that is wrong. Three biographies appeared within twenty years of his death in 1700, and the still authoritative work of Dubois which came out rather more than a century ago is in fact an edited version of a fourth early eighteenth-century life.[1] None of these so-called lives is readily available, not even the two massive tomes of Dubois, with the result that general knowledge about Rancé, such as it is, derives from Chateaubriand's *Vie de Rancé* (1844), a highly romanticized, partly autobiographical study, which owes its fame more to its author than its subject, and from Henri Bremond's brilliantly perverse *L'Abbé Tempête* (1929), which, with cavalier disregard for evidence, presents a masterly and entertaining caricature of a Rancé as remote from historical reality as that of Chateaubriand. Perhaps even odder is general ignorance about la Trappe. Those who associate Trappists with Cistercians at all often seem surprised to learn that the name derives from the happily still flourishing abbey which Rancé reformed but did not found. Unfortunately French monastic history of the seventeenth century is still very patchy, and quite overshadowed by the vast literature devoted to Jesuits and Jansenists, so that any reconsideration of the role of Rancé and la Trappe has to create its own context. It would be easy, but extremely tedious, to correct Dubois or refute Bremond, but the most urgent need is to make available a mass of original material which has been virtually neglected for close on three centuries.

The first biographers (including Dubois) tried to prove that Rancé was a saint, their critics (including Bremond) that he was a fanatic, and both parties made much play with his alleged pro- or anti-Jansenist sympathies. In more recent times a succession of excellent historians belonging to the Cistercian Common Observance have added enormously to knowledge of the order's

[1] Maupeou 1702, Marsollier 1703, le Nain 1715 and 1719, Dubois 1866 and 1869. See details in ch. 3 below.

troubled existence in the seventeenth century, and have clarified many hitherto obscure episodes in Rancé's career.[1] Without in any way impugning their scholarship or integrity one may fairly say that members of the Common Observance start with a bias against the Reform in general and Rancé in particular, and a certain imbalance in their work can hardly be denied. The common feature of all these approaches to Rancé is that they rely heavily on material either official (but hitherto unpublished) or selected and presented with a view to securing (or thwarting) Rancé's eventual canonization. The time is long overdue for a reconsideration of all the extant sources, in a spirit of inquiry, with as few prejudices as possible.

The main printed sources comprise the four principal biographies, Rancé's own published works, including one set of more than 200 letters published just after his death[2] and another of similar size, but more interesting, published in the nineteenth century,[3] the *Relations* of the life and death of many of the monks,[4] several descriptions by visitors, a substantial, but scattered, amount of information about friends and correspondents, and, in the last few years, some important documents published for the first time by Father Zakar and his fellow Cistercians. It should be said that many of these printed sources are exceedingly rare. In addition, and of decisive importance, are the manuscript sources, which include more than 2,000 letters written by Rancé (only about 500 of them originals), a very few written to him, and a large, but indeterminate, number of letters referring to him and la Trappe, as well as unpublished accounts by visitors, necrological and other registers, and some of the manuscript drafts of printed lives.[5] It is the consistent failure of biographers to reopen the manuscript sources which more than anything else explains the distortion of Rancé's picture and the excessive emphasis laid on his admittedly more spectacular sorties into the world of polemic.

It should be said at once that the policy of the first biographers does not facilitate a return to the manuscript sources. Many documents perished when the printer had finished with them, those

---

[1] Notably L. Lekai, P. Zakar, J. Leloczky, T. Nguyen-Dinh-Tuyen. See Bibliography.

[2] *Lettres de piété*, Muguet, 1701 and 1702.

[3] *Lettres de A.-J. le B. Rancé*, ed. B. Gonod, 1846.

[4] See below, p. 37, n. 1.   [5] Full details in Bibliography.

which survived were subjected to systematic censorship, so that proper names and even dates were obliterated in the supposed interests of security, and it requires much time and patience to decipher the vital information beneath the erasures. However, once the letters are grouped in chronological order, and by addressees, a remarkably full and coherent pattern emerges, and it becomes immediately apparent that Rancé's portrait has been diminished almost beyond recognition. It would be naïve to expect such long-standing misconceptions to yield before anything but hard facts, and the main part of this book is therefore devoted to presenting as large a sample as possible of this new evidence with chapter and verse. There is simply not room nowadays in a single volume for such a mass of original material together with the traditional life and works treatment, but if there is such a person as 'the real Rancé' it seems more likely that he will be revealed through private correspondence than public utterance, though both are obviously relevant.

This book aims to present an account of Rancé's influence in his own day, on men and women in the cloister and men and women in the world. It does not claim to be a new biography or portrait, though new facts about his life and new conclusions about his character are naturally included, but it does claim to introduce elements indispensable to any future conventional life of Rancé. The plan of the work is to start at the centre with Rancé himself and then work outwards to consider his influence on the cloister and then on the world beyond.

The first section tries to provide a chronological framework for what follows, by giving the sequence of the main events of Rancé's life and introducing the principal persons and problems which successively engaged his attention. It must always be remembered that for the last twenty-five years of his life his only contact with the world outside la Trappe came from letters or visits, thus what he did amounts to the same as what he wrote. An attempt to sketch his character and personality concludes this section on the man Rancé.

The second section poses special problems because it is concerned with unfamiliar persons and institutions, for which no accepted points of reference exist. Description of life at la Trappe and of vocations to that abbey is easy enough in itself, but constantly raises questions of the most fundamental importance about religious life in seventeenth-century France. The expectation of life, provenance of recruits, and regularity of observance are only three questions concerning which we know more about medieval England than seventeenth-century France. One cannot be sure how exceptional la Trappe was because there is almost no reliable basis of comparison. To go on from la Trappe, which is at least fully documented, to the Cistercian and other religious houses, and individual men and women, with whom Rancé was in contact is to sail almost wholly uncharted waters, but there is no other way of judging his real influence. The nebulous claims of supporters who invoke untold and unnamed scores and hundreds of monks and nuns gratefully mending their ways after reading Rancé's books, or the more specific assertions that he was acknowledged leader of reform within his order, are only as valid as the evidence that can be adduced to support them. It would seem preferable in every way to examine actual cases of influence for which documentary evidence survives, even when this involves obscure or anonymous people. The Celestine order, for instance, cannot be ignored just because it has disappeared from France and is unknown to any but the specialist historian. The anonymous prior of a now ruined house like Perseigne is of no less significance in a study of Rancé than the royal abbess of Maubuisson. It is confusing to find so many of his correspondents named Louise, but Carmelites, Visitandines, Cistercians, and Annonciades all favoured the name at the time, and one has no choice but to try and distinguish the apparently indistinguishable. To leave them out of account would be to omit a vital element in Rancé's activity.

While the second section deals on the whole with people who have virtually no identity apart from their involvement with Rancé, quite the contrary is true of the third section. Men and women as well known as Retz, Bossuet, James II, Mme de Guise, or Mme de La Fayette owe none of their celebrity to Rancé, but precisely because they are so well known the nature of their contacts with him helps to illuminate those which he had with less famous people. Besides, one of the chief purposes of this study is to demonstrate the immense range of Rancé's relationships with great and small alike, and the consistency of his approach to spiritual problems. His family connections constitute a special case and have been treated separately, but in many ways they represent a microcosm of all the rest.

Both the second and third sections deal only with a limited proportion of his known contacts, selected on the simple principle of disregarding all but discernible influence, and thus omitting all that is purely formal and routine, as well as much that is too fragmentary to be informative. If Rancé gave more time to some obscure monk or nun than to James II or Bossuet, or even if more evidence survives about the former than the latter, it is reasonable to reflect such facts in a global treatment of his influence. The vexed questions of his relations with Jansenists has been left to the end, and is complemented by a final summary of the positive lessons to be gleaned from his writings. Where possible the degree of intimacy or authority which he enjoyed with a given correspondent is estimated, but this study is neither exhaustive nor definitive and rather points the way to further detailed research that is needed.

Bremond chose for his own reasons to construct his book in terms of Rancé's successive offensives (against Cîteaux, Port-Royal, the Carthusians, and so on), thus depicting Rancé as an ecclesiastical pugilist always spoiling for a fight. He emphasizes Rancé's desire for publicity, and thus selects those aspects of his life which would make newspaper headlines today. It would be quite wrong to minimize this combative side of Rancé's character, and the main controversies in which he was involved are discussed as they come up. Some, like Quietism at the very end, barely touched him, and others, like the lengthy dispute with Mabillon,[1] have been treated at length by previous writers, so that only those aspects of his disputes which influenced other people, or which are centrally important, are described here. Similarly Chateaubriand and others were fascinated by the Romantic implications of Rancé's conversion, and devoted disproportionate space to the question of his relationship with Mme de Montbazon and the circumstances of her death. No new evidence has appeared since Rancé's death, nor is it likely to, and while it is fun to speculate about amorous abbés and headless corpses it is not very productive as history. In any case the whole question of conversion in the seventeenth century is extremely complex and some of the examples quoted in the course of this book (Mme de la Vallière, Pinette, Henri Barillon, Beaufort) are sufficiently varied to make one wary of simple explanations.

[1] H. Didio, *La Querelle de Mabillon et... Rancé*, 1892, is still the best book on the subject.

These departures from received myth are mentioned because they may disappoint those whose knowledge of Rancé derives from the two standard legends. There is one other major omission which is also deliberate, albeit reluctant. Rancé's spirituality deserves full-scale treatment by a specialist, and I have neither the space nor the competence to attempt it.[1] Also needed are detailed textual study of his rule compared to that of the Reformed and other Cistercians, and Benedictines, a full examination of his monastic sources, especially the Desert Fathers, and of his theology. The brief summary included here deals with specific issues, like penitence and sacramental discipline, on which his views are explicit and direct, but it should not be inferred from this that there is any lack of evidence on other topics, or that these are unimportant. In attempting the reassessment of any major figure one must make a beginning somewhere, but one must also know where to stop.

Although not technically a spiritual director, Rancé may worthily be set beside Bérulle, Saint-Cyran, or Monsieur Vincent in the religious history of his age. La Trappe acted as centre for a whole series of interlocking networks of spiritual affinity, some of them based on locality, some on *salons*, and as one studies the influence of Rancé one constantly comes up against the same links. More, for example, should be done on the connections between the former entourage of Gaston d'Orléans, the Oratory, Jansenism, and la Trappe. Port-Royal is not the only, nor perhaps the best, focus for studying a still obscure side of seventeenth-century religious life.

This study began as a voyage of discovery, with no particular thesis as its goal. First-hand acquaintance with Rancé and with the present community of la Trappe has, I hope, not impaired my judgement or impartiality, but has certainly filled me with respect, enthusiasm, and ultimately real affection for a man of uncommon gifts who still has much to offer.

---

[1] Important articles on Rancé's spirituality have been appearing in recent years, especially in *Collectanea*; the tercentenary number (1963) was particularly useful. Mlle Denise Pezzoli is still working on this subject. Important studies of aspects of Rancé's monastic teaching have also appeared in the *Analecta Cisterciensia* (of the Common Observance). See (with some reservations) the article by A. Mensaros, 'L'Abbé de Rancé et la règle bénédictine' in *Analecta*, xxii, 1966, pp. 161–217. Much still remains to be done and there can as yet be no question of a definitive bibliography.

PART I

THE MAN AND HIS LIFE

1. Life: 1626–1664

IT cannot be very plausibly maintained that Rancé's future career was predictable from an early age, nor even that, like a second Bernard, the road on which he initially embarked was bound to lead him to a single decisive conversion. It is still true that his family, education, and youthful companions provided a background which remained directly relevant throughout his life and, moreover, comparison with a number of other men and women from similar backgrounds shows that his life was by no means an isolated case. What makes him unique is the exact nature of the memorial he left behind him.

Armand-Jean was born on 26 January 1626 as the second son of Denis Bouthillier, or le Bouthillier,[1] who had taken the name Rancé to distinguish him from his elder brother Claude. Vagueness and contradictions abound in all accounts of Rancé's family, and neither dates nor even names are consistent or reliable, but some facts remain clear. The Bouthilliers were a legal family who had come to Paris from Angoulême at the end of the sixteenth century. Claude, the eldest (1581–1652), was a favourite of Marie de Medicis and he, and later his son Léon, comte de Chavigny (1608–52), rose rapidly to ministerial office. One of his brothers, Sébastien (1582–1625), became Bishop of Aire, and a close friend of Saint-Cyran, while another, Victor (1596–1670), after a few years at the Oratory also became a bishop, first of Boulogne, then, in 1649, Archbishop of Tours. Denis was not so fortunate as Claude, but by 1618 he was appointed Conseiller to the Parlement of Burgundy at Dijon, and on 3 February 1619 he

---

[1] Dubois is completely inconsistent. Denis himself always signed 'Bouthillier', but some time after his death his son, Henri, adopted the prefix 'le' and signed thus, in 1672, for example, Rancé did not use his family name in signatures after he became a monk but, presumably by analogy with Henri, is usually referred to by the same style. None of the standard biographies, nor works of reference like P. Anselme and La Chesnaye Desbois, give full or accurate facts about the family, and the disappearance in the Commune of the baptismal registers of Saint-Cosme makes it impossible even to explain Dubois's confident but manifestly incorrect statements. The best hope of establishing the facts lies in the still largely untapped resources of the Minutier Central. What follows is a summary of the biographical facts given by Dubois from various sources, corrected as appropriate and possible.

married Charlotte Joly, daughter of a prominent Dijon family of magistrates. In the course of the next ten years he was promoted to successive posts in Dijon, but throughout this period he served also as secretary to Marie de Medicis and spent the greater part of his time in Paris, where most of his children were born. In December 1630 he was made Conseiller d'État, and only then abandoned Dijon for permanent residence in Paris.

Armand-Jean was, as mentioned above, the second of three sons, and had two elder and two younger sisters, with a fifth whose age is unclear. His very name accurately reflects the fortunes of the family, for his godfather was Richelieu himself (and his godmother the marquise d'Effiat), a distinction that none of his brothers or sisters could equal. Unhappily for Denis he had put his trust too readily in princes, or at least in a princess, for the definitive disgrace and flight of Marie in 1631, only a year after his promotion to Conseiller, did him no good. At just this time (1630) Victor had moved to Tours as coadjutor, and in the course of the next few years Denis, encouraged by his brother, began to acquire property at Véretz, not far from the town, which he was finally able to buy in 1637,[1] by which time he had returned to favour with Anne of Austria. From an early age, therefore, Armand knew and loved this splendid estate which was to play such a critical role in his life, but as so often in later years everything began to happen at once.

His eldest sister, Claude-Charlotte, had been chosen by Anne as maid of honour, and in 1637 or soon after left home to marry the comte de Belin. Meanwhile the health of the eldest son, Denis-François, grew unmistakably worse, and in September 1637 he died. Even before his death urgent steps were taken to preserve within the family the valuable beneficies of which he had been nominal possessor, and Armand suddenly found his destiny changed from that of a Knight of Malta (now assigned to Henri, the third son) to that of a future *abbé de cour*. He was tonsured already at the end of 1635, in 1637 was installed as a boy canon of Notre-Dame de Paris, and by the time he was 12 was commendatory abbot[2] of Saint-Symphorien de Beauvais (Bene-

---

[1] See Bosseboeuf, *Le Château de Véretz*, pp. 143–201 and 501–5.

[2] The system whereby religious houses were placed *in commendam* had been enormously extended by the Concordat of 1516, and permitted the Crown to assign the revenues and titles of such houses to any nominee, who need not even be in orders

dictine), Notre-Dame du Val, near Bayeux (Augustinian Canons), and la Trappe (Cistercian), as well as prior of Boulogne, near Chambord (Grammontine) and of Saint-Clémentin in Poitou (Benedictine). It should at once be said that these benefices were for the young Rancé little more than, say, a mining company for an infant shareholder today. He was, it is true, destined for an ecclesiastical career after his brother's death, but by the standards of the time he could be a perfectly acceptable priest even if he never went near any of his five religious houses. At the same time it is obvious in retrospect that his acquisition of la Trappe at this early age was the first link in a long causal chain.

His sister's marriage, his brother's death, and his own precocious début as a Church dignitary were followed within a year by the death of his mother, on 14 October 1638. The pious paradigm of biographers is so inevitable, that it is hard to be sure how close relations were between Rancé and his mother, or whether he really was the favourite among her eight children. At all events the loss of elder brother and mother at such a critical stage in the boy's development is a major factor to be reckoned with. Another factor of perhaps equal importance is the influence of the two Auvergnat tutors, Jean Favier and Bellérophon,[1] especially the former, who had looked after the children's education from a very early age. The extraordinary chance which has preserved Rancé's correspondence with Favier reveals a stability of respect and affection—and, one might say, a tacit need for approval—extending unbroken for fifty years and more. As far as one can judge, they were effective teachers, though the famous Anacreon

---

and was frequently a minor. Plurality was frowned upon by rigorists but very common. It was the prevalence of this class of honorary abbots (or priors) which led to the use of the courtesy title 'abbé' for clergy in general. Though some commendatory abbots took an active part in supervising their monastery, and even resided, the effective superior of such houses was the prior, and the fact that in the Cistercian Order the overworked and underprivileged priors played little or no part in General Chapters, while the few regular abbots, often heading much smaller houses, made all the decisions caused much bad feeling. It should be noted that some houses were never granted the dignity of abbeys, in which case the sub-prior ran them for the commendatory prior, and that in some orders, notably the Celestines and Grammontines, the title of abbot was either not used at all or confined to the mother-house and one or two others.

[1] See Jaloustre, Un Précepteur auvergnat on both tutors. Gonod published the originals of Rancé's letters to Favier (now at Clermont-Ferrand), and an important series of copies survives at the Arsenal.

commentary presented to Richelieu in 1637, to which the lad gave his name, is a dubious piece of evidence.[1]

The next stage of Armand's education took him, from about 1642, to the Collège d'Harcourt, but he had not been there long before death struck his family once more. His brother-in-law, Belin, was murdered in cold blood by Bonnivet, his own sister's husband, leaving a young girl and a boy, who did not live long.[2] As Rancé was particularly fond of his sister, Claude-Charlotte, this odious deed shocked him profoundly, as we see from a letter to Favier, and yet again underlined, at this most impressionable age, the transitory nature of all earthly affections. On a different plane the death of Richelieu in the same week, followed by that of Louis XIII in May 1643, was a serious blow to the family's hopes, for Mazarin lost no time in dismissing Claude Bouthillier and his son Chavigny, and showed no sign of favour to Denis. The one bright spot was Victor, safely installed as Archbishop of Tours, and, of course, Armand's very real intellectual gifts, which gave some hope that a judicious mixture of talent and influence would yet take him to the top.

Having taken his Master of Arts in 1643 Armand did not pursue the next part of his studies, towards his doctorate in theology, in public classes but at home with tutors. This is not to say that he led a secluded life, just that he had less contact with other students than would normally have been the case. Whether in Paris or Véretz, or other country houses, he began about this time making the friends whom he remembered throughout his life—the brothers Paul and Henri Barillon, Étienne le Camus, François de Harlay, Lascaris d'Urfé, Honoré Courtin (who later in fact claimed to have known him from the age of 5).[3] As well as these young men must be mentioned his near neighbour in Touraine, the duchesse de Montbazon (1612–57) who lived with her aged husband (forty-four years older than she) at Couziers. He became very friendly with her, and she must have been one

[1] Published by Jacques Dugast, 1639 (two years after completion). See Dubois, i, p. 23. (N.B. This and all later references are to the edition of 1866.)

[2] Rancé's reaction in Gonod, p. 5. On the Belin family see article by M. Prevost in DBF s.v. Averton.

[3] Rapin in his Mémoires several times mentions Rancé and his friends (e.g. ii, p. 367). The source for Courtin's remark seems to be M. de Saint-Louis, AE 1442, p. 160, quoted also by le Nain, Vie.

of the first to introduce him into the *beau monde* of the *salons*.[1] This beautiful and worldly woman, married to such an unsuitable companion, could have filled a variety of roles for a headstrong and sensitive boy, early deprived of a mother and eager for recognition in every sphere. When one has said, however, that his affection and admiration for her are not in doubt, one has reached the limit of useful speculation about their relationship. Some degree of romantic attachment is obviously quite likely, but to speak of a liaison, actual or incipient, is merely to indulge one's fancy gratuitiously. In fact, one point which seems to have escaped the notice of biographers anxious to sensationalize Rancé's life is that he comes in one important respect much closer to Hippolyte than Mme de Montbazon does to Phèdre: he was a passionate, almost an obsessional, horseman. Everyone quotes his passion for hunting, the aristocratic sport *par excellence*, but a document attributed to him by Gervaise[2] unconsciously reflects Rancé's own emphasis on horses: of thirteen specific perils from which, he claimed, God, had preserved him, the first two are childhood illnesses, the next two shooting accidents, and then eight are concerned with riding (the last is a boating incident). Very many years later, when he was already old, he advised M. de Saint-Louis to retain two horses during his retirement at la Trappe as a useful means of relaxation and exercise.[3] One could not have a clearer example of the directly physical expression of his restless and impetuous temperament, or of what it meant to him to shut himself up for twenty-five years in his enclosure, never to ride a horse again.

For the ten years following the death of his mother Rancé grew to manhood very much like other young men of his class. His ecclesiastical cloth did not keep him from *salon* or saddle; his studies went ahead, so far as one can judge from the recorded results, brilliantly; and he made his début as a preacher when his sister, Louise-Isabelle, was received in 1647 at the Annonciades

---

[1] Portraits of Mme de Montbazon exist, and plenty of gossip about her in memoirs of the period, but not so many facts, and no verifiable facts at all concerning the circumstances of her death, let alone her relationship with Rancé. Those who could have spoken (her sisters or children) did not; those who did offered no proof and contradict each other.

[2] *Jugement critique*, p. 76, quoted Dubois, i, pp. 119–21.

[3] Saint-Louis, *AE* 1442, pp. 106–7.

being known thereafter as Marie-Louise.[1] Claude-Charlotte had married again, in 1644, the comte d'Albon, who was well favoured at Court as well as in his native Auvergne. Favier remained closely in touch (he apparently knew the Albon family before this second marriage), and Rancé's letters to him provide a sporadic commentary on all his activities. Just ten years after his mother's death, then, Rancé entered upon a decade, or more, of varied but major significance. This began in December 1648 when, after the customary retreat with Monsieur Vincent at Saint-Lazare, Rancé received privately, on three successive days, minor orders, subdiaconate, and diaconate. These were conferred by Paul de Gondi, 'Monsieur le Coadjuteur' and future Cardinal de Retz, who only the previous August had distinguished himself on the barricades with which the Fronde began. Rancé would have known Retz both through Notre-Dame and the *salons* (he was the friend and contemporary of Mme de Montbazon), but the pressures of the Fronde, and common hostility to Mazarin, no doubt brought them closer and sooner together than would otherwise have been the case.

By the time Rancé was ordained, on 22 January 1651 by his archiepiscopal uncle at the Annonciades, Retz had just instigated the second Fronde (des Princes), but in the meantime Rancé had suffered the cruel blow of losing his father, who died at Véretz in May 1650.[2] He did not allow this to hold up his career, and in 1652 proceeded to his *licence*, in which he was listed first (Bossuet

[1] Confusion about this sister is universal. Discovery of documents in the Minutier Central at last enables me to clear up some of the fog. Denis agreed on 27 Apr. 1648 to pay the community 18,000 *livres* in return for accepting his daughter as 'fondatrice' until her health permitted her to be fully professed (if ever). Rancé must have preached at her 'prise d'habit' in 1647, when she took the name Marie-Louise (and thus signs in 1648). Further research may well reveal more, but it can be finally stated that Louise-Isabelle and Marie-Louise are one and the same person. See *MC* LI. 516, 518, 621 (Jérome Cousinet).

[2] Le Nain gives the right date, but Dubois, to establish his independence, gives 1653, relying on an alleged inscription on the coffin. Denis made his will on 23 Oct. 1647, saying he had never felt in better health, adding various codicils later. One concerned a natural son, entrusted to the care of a surgeon at Tours, and though the dates suggest that the liaison followed the death of Mme de Rancé, it is worth considering what effect this information (hitherto unrecorded) had on Rancé, who inherited Véretz, while Henri had what was left. This will (proved on 17 May 1650) mentions that Rancé's sister Thérèse, already a nun in 1647, is to receive a pension 'sur les biens de sa mère', but says nothing of Louise-Isabelle (provided for as above) or the other sisters. Archbishop Victor inherited a relic of the true cross. See *MC* LI. 229 (Richer).

came third).[1] A few months later the battle of the faubourg Saint-Antoine destroyed the last hope of the Frondeurs, and nearly cost La Rochefoucauld his life. As if this were not enough to impress on him the instability of earthly affairs, he lost his uncle Claude and cousin Léon that same year (1652), and early in 1653 saw Mazarin return triumphantly to Paris on the ignominious collapse of the Fronde.

The death of so many hopes, the disgrace of so many formerly influential friends, like Retz, who had won his cardinal's hat in 1652 only to be imprisoned by a vengeful Mazarin next year, the loss of his surviving parent, constitute a disturbing counterpoint to the continuing theme of Rancé's academic success and ecclesiastical advancement. As head of the family, Rancé now found himself a wealthy man, though the problems of succession were tedious; as nephew of an archbishop and, from 1654, a doctor of the Sorbonne, he was well placed for a successful career in the Church and, with what convictions one can only surmise, this is the course on which he now embarked. His uncle appointed him to one of the archdeaconries of his diocese (d'Outre-Vienne) and the next year, in October 1655, employed all his influence to send him as a delegate to the Assembly of the Clergy, meeting in Paris. Rancé served on various commissions, apparently playing a quite active part in proceedings, and must have made a generally good impression because in June 1656 he was appointed chaplain to Gaston d'Orléans (as his uncle had been) and the Assembly duly recorded its gratification.[2] Early in 1657 there was an abortive attempt to have Rancé named coadjutor to his uncle; Mazarin's refusal should not be taken too tragically at such an early stage in the young abbé's career, though it is true that Rancé had already had more than one brush with the Cardinal, who could not be expected to show much favour to such a loyal supporter of Retz.

Just as the Fronde had provided counterpoint for the first stages of Rancé's studies and ordination, now the Jansenist crisis began to run parallel with his initiation into higher Church politics. Indeed the Assembly was seized, among other things, with this question, and in September 1656 Rancé, together with other

---

[1] This seems to have been a courtesy accorded to his noble rank rather than a sign of his intellectual superiority over Bossuet. Placed second was one G. Chamillart, 'prior' of the Sorbonne, that is a student appointed for a year to preside over certain exercises. The date of Rancé's doctorate is subject to caution.

[2] Villars, *Procez-verbal de l' Assemblée du Clergé 1655–6*, pp. 487 and 496.

members, subscribed the Formulaire. This did not inhibit him (and many colleagues) from attending gatherings where the *Lettres provinciales* were read and admired, and Rapin, a hostile witness it is true, depicts him as a quite active supporter of Arnauld,[1] no doubt 'jusques au feu exclusivement'. So, of course, were a lot of other perfectly orthodox Catholics, and Rancé was no more heretical in opposing the Jesuits than subversive for defending Retz against Mazarin, but at this stage in his worldly career, final and crucial as it was, his sympathies were distinct enough. No doubt agreeably stimulated by his first taste of intrigue, certainly found stimulating by the men and women of *salon* society, Rancé was showing every sign of becoming a fashionable *abbé de cour*, with a brilliant future once Mazarin was out of the way. None the less the facts so far related sufficiently indicate a dark side to his experience, a fundamental insecurity requiring ever more vigorous distractions to keep it at bay, and his contacts with Port-Royal prove at the very least that he well knew the remedy chosen by many of his friends who had once been as worldly as he. Consciously or unconsciously he needed a sign, a catalyst. There is general agreement that this came about with the sudden death, a few days after an attack of scarlet fever, of Mme de Montbazon on 28 April 1657.

The details of her death seem for ever shrouded in myth or plain mendacity, and leaving aside the more bizarre versions which involve headless corpses (to fit the allegedly too short coffin) and horrific visions (by moonlit pools),[2] the most one can say is that she died so suddenly, at the height of her social success and still quite young, that any intimate and impressionable friend was bound to feel shock. Rancé's pride had suffered at Mazarin's hands, and he had returned to Véretz rather than stay in Paris for the concluding weeks of the Assembly, so that the sudden loss of his main focus of worldly distraction could hardly have found him more defenceless. He did not attend Mme de Montbazon's funeral at Montargis (he had not in fact been with her at the end), but after his brief visit to Paris withdrew again to Véretz. From this moment on one may say he was converted, in the sense that he

---

[1] *Mémoires*, ii, p. 367 and 389.

[2] Larroque was the first to put this about, in 1685, but the story improved in the telling. Maupeou talks of weird nocturnal apparitions, but not of the headless corpse (*Vie*, i, p. 87). Thereafter most writers refer to one or other story, if only to refute it.

abruptly gave up a worldly life, repudiated ambition and luxury, and began to look for a new, spiritual, basis for his life. There is no question of a sudden, clear revelation of the path ahead, only rejection of that behind. Soon, perhaps at once, he sought help from another woman, and went to Tours to consult Mère Louise Rogier at the Visitation.[1] Family connections with the convent were close and numerous. The Archbishop had introduced the order to Tours; his sister-in-law, Mme Bouthillier, had accepted the charge of bringing up Claude-Charlotte's daughters, and since 1650 or so had sent first one, then a second (Louise-Henriette, who became a nun) to the Visitation to be educated. Rancé himself, as chaplain to Gaston, had every reason to know of Louise's brief career at Gaston's mistress years before, for his own cousin, Chavigny, had managed the whole affair. The ties between Rancé's aunt, whom he greatly respected, and Mère Louise are particularly significant in view of what happened next, for it looks as if their advice may have been very much the same.

In his spiritual crisis he was sent by Mère Louise to Séguenot, an Oratorian at Tours of pronounced Jansenist leanings. Séguenot sent him on to Paris, where Rancé went to the Institution recently founded by Nicholas Pinette (Gaston's former treasurer) and made a general confession to Père Bouchard, whose *confrère* Monchy became his director and intimate friend.[2] With their approval, and at his aunt's suggestion, he then went (in July) to yet another of Gaston's former friends, Arnauld d'Andilly, who had been allowed to return to Port-Royal as a solitary after the others had been expelled. He did not stay more than a week or two at Port-Royal, discussing his future course of action, and then went off to Auvergne to stay with the Albons before retiring to Véretz in October.

Thus in the six months following Mme de Montbazon's death he had gone to his aunt and to Mère Louise for advice, had entered the circle of the Oratory, with which he was henceforth always to be associated, and had put himself under the direction of a leading Jansenist. The initial phase of withdrawal went no further than a country retreat at Véretz, with a few chosen companions from time to time, a mildly austere diet, a course of

[1] On Louise Rogier see ch. 9, below. On Mme Bouthillier and nieces (and great-nieces) see *Vis, Lettres circulaires*, Tours, 1689.
[2] On the Oratory see ch. 11, below.

spiritual reading, and a determined effort to find a sense of direction. He was not yet committed to any specific way of life, and
certainly not to Jansenism in a partisan sense. He was, in Pas-
calian terms, seeking without having found. For the next three
years, to the beginning of 1661, nearly fifty extant letters to
Andilly and about thirty to Mère Louise enable us to build up a
very full picture of his evolution.[1]

An extensive study programme included Saint-Cyran's huge
Petrus Aurelius, the Church histories of Baronius and Eusebius,
and the apologetic works of Cardinal du Perron. Rancé also did
some translation (of Basil) and commented on Andilly's own
translations of early Fathers. In the course of his first year's retreat he mentions certain visitors with approval—Barillon,
Caumartin, the duc de Luynes—and refers to an unwelcome visit
from Mme de Saint-Loup, whose importunities he was to endure
for many years to come. For the first six months or so he seems
hardly to have left Véretz, and his uncle became alarmed and
annoyed, now offering him a post as director of all the women
religious in the diocese, now complaining that he had refused a
request to go to Paris.

By the spring of 1658 one can begin to see a plan gradually take
shape. First he went to Beauvais to look at his abbey, and took
the opportunity of calling in briefly at Port-Royal. Then in June
he visited his aunt, at Ponts-sur-Seine, did his two days' duty with
Gaston at Blois and, for the record, announced his intention of
going, apparently for the first time, to la Trappe, which he visited
in early July. In September he reports a visit to Saint-Clémentin,
and by October had come back to Véretz. Thus his decision to
reduce the number of his benefices was translated into a systematic
tour of inspection to see what was required in each before deciding which to retain. A letter of 1659 expresses his regret at
having to leave Boulogne, and there is some evidence that Gaston
toyed with the idea of retiring there, so Rancé's choice may already have been made by then. For a few weeks at the end of 1658
the subsequently famous abbé Têtu, a *bel esprit* and later

---

[1] Letters to Andilly at the Arsenal (MSS. 6035 etc.) and a few in private hands, to
Mère Rogier in Mazarine (MS. 1214) with duplicate at Sainte-Geneviève (MS. Df 49)
and defective copy at Arsenal (MS. 2106). Most of the following details come from
these two sources. A very partial (in every sense) treatment of the Andilly correspondence is in Varin, *Vérité sur les Arnauld*.

academician, tried sharing Rancé's retreat, but the experiment was not a success and allegedly undermined Têtu's health.[1]

Most of the winter Rancé spent alone, but by the spring was ready to travel again. By July 1659 he had been back to Saint-Clémentin, Beauvais, and, briefly, Port-Royal, had visited his aunt again, and had then gone to stay for some weeks at Châlons with the bishop, Vialart de Hersé. This prelate was a good friend of Port-Royal, and of the Oratory, but above all a man of moderation and good sense who always exercised a restraining influence on Rancé. Also in 1659 Rancé had a visit from Gilbert de Choiseul, Bishop of Comminges (later of Tournai), who suggested a journey to see his saintly neighbour, Nicolas Pavillon, Bishop of Alet. The decisive influences were now all converging on Rancé and the fruit of his two and a half years' pondering seemed to be ripe.

In September he was back at Véretz, this time with Guillaume Le Roy as his companion. Like Rancé a boy canon of Notre-Dame, a commendatory abbot (of the Cistercian Hautefontaine) and a disciple of Andilly, Le Roy was an intransigent Jansenist, as Rancé never was, and later used his abbey as an asylum and retreat for his friends.[2] Dubois, and others, never fail to see sinister attempts at conversion behind every one of Rancé's numerous Jansenist contacts, but, in the case of Le Roy, long-standing friendship and similar temperament would fully explain the visit, to which sudden acute eye trouble put an abrupt end just after Christmas. Rancé spent the rest of the winter alone.

Quite suddenly, at the end of January 1660 Gaston fell ill, and Rancé, who had only recently been on duty at Blois, returned there. He was at Gaston's deathbed, on 2 February 1660, together with Monchy, remained for the funeral, and then went to stay with M. de la Rivière near Laval before going to Paris in May. Freed now of his largely nominal duties to Gaston, Rancé saw no further obstacles to his plan for complete withdrawal from the world, though he met with little support from his friends and only unconcealed disapproval from his uncle. His reactions to the imperative need for decision took a strangely physical form; we learn from a letter to Favier[3] that he had planned a journey to the

---

[1] On Têtu, see article in Moréri. Rancé and Têtu himself both wrote to Andilly about the visit.

[2] Namer, *L'Abbé Le Roy* is quite informative, but rather unsatisfactory.

[3] *A* 2106 of 10 May 1660.

Grande Chartreuse, though there is no evidence that at that moment he contemplated a Carthusian vocation, but when this was abandoned he decided instead to go to the Pyrenees. It is oddly symbolic, and consistent with his passion for riding, that he should feel drawn to the highest and most remote mountains, perhaps in the same way that St. Francis and St. Ignatius had felt drawn to the Holy Land. The actual human links in this chain of decision were the Bishops of Châlons and Comminges, whom he already knew, and Alet, whose advice he was specifically going to ask.[1]

He left Paris in June for Châlons, and then by stages went on to Comminges, where he had to wait a week or two for Alet to return from his pastoral visitation. At last, early in August, he arrived at Alet, where he spent the whole month. Pavillon had long been an associate of Monsieur Vincent in Paris, but his reputation for sanctity and austerity grew still more during the nearly forty years he devoted to his poor and remote diocese. He was a man of inflexible principle, a staunch ally of Port-Royal, but much more of a pastor than a polemist. In his tiny episcopal town with his cathedral in ruins (as it still is) after being sacked by the Huguenots in the Wars of Religion, and his 'palace' a great deal more modest than Véretz,[2] the bishop represented all the simplicity and wisdom Rancé needed. By his age and remoteness he fulfilled the oracular role which closer friends could not.

In a way it is obvious that Rancé already knew the answer to most of the questions he put to Alet; he knew that apostolic poverty, like that of the bishop rather than that of a Mendicant, could not long be delayed; he knew that his plurality of benefices was consistent only with the letter of the law; he knew too that solitude, withdrawal from worldly affairs, was to be the basis of his new life, and that continued gentlemanly retreat at Véretz was not enough. All this Alet confirmed, but the outstanding problem was still that of responsibility. Alet, whose own experience was a concrete example, saw Rancé as a future bishop instructing his flock. Étienne Caulet, bishop of the neighbouring see of Pamiers, when consulted similarly thought in terms of an active apostolate, and interestingly enough it was Comminges,

---

[1] On these bishops see below, pp. 219-22.
[2] In 1969 part of the 'palace' had been made into a reasonably comfortable but hardly palatial hotel.

who had started off the chain of consultation, who was inspired to challenge Rancé to become regular abbot of one of his houses, so combining all the requirements of canonical exactitude, poverty, solitude, and, above all, specific responsibility for others. We have the bishop's own word for it when, writing many years later, he describes Rancé's appalled reaction to the proposal that he might become a monk, instead of clinging to the compromise status of commendatory abbot. Rancé returned to Véretz in October 1660 to wrestle with the final and hardest problem since his initial conversion.[1]

'Forsake all and follow me' was not an easy call to obey literally in the seventeenth century for someone in Rancé's position. He could not give away his material possessions, because he had obligations to other members of his family, the sale of Véretz in particular demanded lengthy negotiations, and royal policy regarding disposal of benefices in commend did not facilitate his task there. His uncle seems at last to have become reconciled to his nephew's behaviour—he is described in December as 'de bonne humeur'—but there were still so many obstacles to overcome before he could give himself up to the life of penitence and retreat he had chosen. In the course of 1661 and the first part of 1662 he gradually solved the material problems, though spiritual ones remained. Véretz was finally bought by the abbé d'Effiat (son of Rancé's godmother)[2] and his nephew, duc de Mazarin (who later acquired it wholly for himself). Saint-Symphorien went to Favier. Val, after several false starts, went to one Nicholas Druel, recommended by friends in the Oratory; Saint-Clémentin to his old friend Pierre Félibien of Chartres. Only la Trappe and Boulogne remained, after an abortive attempt to transfer the latter to the Tours Oratory for a seminary.

In August 1662 an end was in sight, but still not the right one. He arranged with the authorities of the Reformed Cistercians to have half a dozen monks sent from Perseigne nearby to introduce

---

[1] The details of these consultations are related in all the biographies and seem to have been widely known at the time, especially in Jansenist circles. Cf Batterel, *Mémoires*, i, pp. 394–6 (on Victor le Bouthillier). Comminges's part is attested by copies of letters written in 1688 to a mutual friend of Rancé and the bishop, by then translated to Tournai (*T* 1689).

[2] When the Visitation at Tours celebrated the second anniversary of the canonization of St. François de Sales in 1667, Effiat lent from Véretz 'tapisseries, chandeliers, lustres et cristaux'; Rancé's niece was of course there (*Vis, Relation de... la Canonisation*, p. 14).

the reform into a house as dilapidated materially as it was spiritually. This happened on 17 August, and a few days later (29 August) he wrote to Mère Louise Rogier from Boulogne a letter which clearly marks a turning-point, in fact the turning-point in the whole of this arduous process of conversion. He refers to the reform just introduced at la Trappe, and comments that he has had to change his plan for spending the winter at Boulogne: 'cet œuvre-là [la Trappe] me paroit de telle importance pour la gloire de Dieu qu'il ne m'est pas possible de l'abandonner plus long-temps dans ses commencements... Ne vous imaginez pas que cela m'éloigne de Boulogne', where, he goes on to say, he still intends to retire.[1] In September he was back at la Trappe, lodging for the winter with the agent and his numerous family. A letter written to Alet the following year (confirmed by others) dates from this period (August–October 1662) the time when 'je commence à voir clair'. Ever on the lookout for a sign, he may have found it in an accident from which he narrowly escaped with his life in the course of building operations, and which he reported on 1 November 1662 as having occurred the day before.

At the turn of the year he went to Paris, and in the course of his stay at the Institution met Comminges (in February 1663) who reminded him of their conversation more than two years ago in the Pyrenees. Not long after Easter, in April, he had at last not only made up his mind but taken the irrevocable step of accepting a monastic vocation in the Cistercian Order.

Several elements concurred in ending this long period of uncertainty. The site must have had a lot to do with it. Boulogne was in a remote part of the forest of Chambord, but still comparatively accessible, while la Trappe was far away from fashionable hunting lodges. Then the ruins of the buildings were at once a challenge and a goad to his conscience, because from childhood he had enjoyed revenues which could, and should, have been applied to their repair. The violent hostility of the unreformed monks, from whom he was actually in some danger, averted by the timely intervention of the hitherto unknown M. de Saint-Louis, was a further factor; and in general Rancé could feel, and see, that at la Trappe as nowhere else his presence was needed and beneficial. A will drawn up in December in favour of the monks to some extent salved his conscience on the material plane; a close

[1] M 1214, 48 seq.

(and for him) protracted contact with true monastic life clearly stirred it further; and it is very likely that the final impetus came from Comminges's reminder in Paris of the earlier conversation about taking the habit, for which a real context had now been provided.[1] The fact that his niece, Louise-Henriette d'Albon, was professed at the Visitation at Tours early in 1663 is interesting but hardly relevant; she had gone back at the latest in December 1661 and her profession can hardly be compared with Rancé's own decision.

The formalities did not last very long: in April he saw Jouaud, Abbot of Prières and Vicar-General of the Cistercian Reform (or Abstinents) in Paris, and secured his at first sceptical and reluctant approval; in May he obtained the necessary royal permission to transform a commendatory into a regular title (but in the first instance as a purely personal favour), and transferred his remaining benefice, Boulogne, to Henri Barillon (who had himself just come back from a visit to Alet). His last ties with the external world were now loosed, and by an extraordinary trick of cosmic accountancy he began a completely new life just half-way through what was to be his total life span. Writing on 30 April 1663 either to Mère Louise or his aunt (different copies give different addresses) he says: 'Dieu m'a conduit par des voies qui m'estoient fort inconnues pendant plusieurs années, mais enfin depuis 8 ou 10 mois [Oct. 1662]... j'ai commencé à voir plus clair..'[2] The successive stages of his conversion must be seen as the logical elimination of one choice after another, until only the hardest, and least expected, remained.

He was at la Trappe at the end of May to tell the monks officially of his decision, and then set off for Perseigne on 30 May 1663, where he was to serve the minimum one year's novitiate before being professed. He formally took the Cistercian habit on 13 June as a simple monk in the company of his personal servant,[3] and from that moment on regarded himself as dead to the world he had left.

The year of novitiate must have been a rude shock to him in every way. For the first time in his independent and wilful existence he found himself surrendering his will to that of others in

[1] T 1689.
[2] M 1214, 53.
[3] Antoine Noël Gelanne (*Archives de la Sarthe*, vol. iii, H, p. 412).

obedience. Perseigne was the novitiate for the Western province of the Abstinents, but it was not a very big or important house and, being under a commendatory abbot, was ruled effectively by the prior, dom Michel Guitton. By no means young, accustomed so far to having his own way, Rancé had to change his entire way of life for every hour of the day, with no choice but to obey or fail. The physical rigours of diet, broken sleep, and manual labour went far beyond anything he had so far experienced, but even more the need to go at the pace of the slowest recruit must have been a sore trial for one as intelligent and eager as Rancé. Not surprisingly all this proved too much for him, and at the end of October he was so ill that he had to go back to la Trappe to be looked after. By the New Year he was back at Perseigne to resume his interrupted exercises, but had not been there long before he was sent off for a week or so to restore order in the abbey of Champagne not far away, where reform was being violently resisted. He had hardly returned from successfully accomplishing this mission before he was bidden to go on another, and had to go to Vaux-de-Cernay (near Paris) for an interview with Jouaud, who eventually supported his refusal. Presumably on the way back he passed by la Trappe and told the monks the details of his final will (on profession a religious ceased to have any legal existence in respect of property). It is foolish to pretend in the light of these facts that he had anything like a normal novitiate, but in the light of what followed it seems abundantly clear that it was his superiors who brought this about, not Rancé himself. Perhaps if he had known what was in store for him he might have acted differently.

The concluding stages of this strange novitiate were rapid. His bulls (authorizing him to become regular abbot) arrived from Rome on 19 June 1664, on [Thursday] 26 June 1664 he was solemnly professed, and on 3 July 1664 Félibien took possession of la Trappe in his name. He was blessed as abbot at Séez (in which diocese la Trappe lay) by Patrick Plunket, exiled Bishop of Ardagh, on 19 July, and next day the whole process was completed when he arrived to take over his new charge in person. His comment on this to Mère Louise Rogier is typical (30 July 1664):[1] 'je me suis consacré à Dieu pour le reste de mes jours dans une

----

[1] M 1214, 60.

condition qui m'a paru très vile et très méprisable, et par con-
séquent très propre pour faire pénitence de mes péchés... Je me
suis vu comme un homme condamné à l'Enfer par le nombre et
la grandeur de ses péchés, et j'ai cru en même temps que l'unique
moyen pour apaiser la colère de Dieu était celui de m'engager
dans une pénitence qui ne finit qu'avec ma vie.' The emphasis on
his desire for personal penitence and the complete absence of any
reference to plans for la Trappe, let alone the order as a whole,
certainly reflect his priorities at that time and are quite consistent
with the whole course of his spiritual development since 1657.

Twenty years later, when he was embroiled in bitter polemic,
his critics were not slow to advertise his inexperience of religious
life on a humble level and his fundamental ignorance of the
monastic tradition represented by Benedictine and Cistercian
usage. These charges are fair, and relevant: in 1664 when he took
up his abbatial staff he knew far more about the Eastern solitaries,
especially his favourite St. John Climachus, than Western monasticism. This knowledge he had moreover acquired under the
guidance of Andilly, and largely through his editions, at a time
when he was not himself contemplating community life. However,
when this criticism has been duly acknowledged, it is essential to
set it in its historical context: Rancé made many mistakes in his
early years, but the amount he learned from experience, and put
into practice, is far more remarkable.

2. Life: 1664–1675

THE next ten or eleven years should have enabled Rancé to enjoy
and consolidate the peace he had so arduously won, but yet
again all his own desires were countermanded by the peremptory
demands made upon him by his fellow superiors, and what at
first he took to be God's will for him (he was less sure later). As
soon as he took up residence at la Trappe he found himself
loaded with administrative business, and he had been there little
more than a month before he had to go to Paris for an assembly
of the main superiors of the Abstinents at the Collège des Bernardins.

When in 1662 Rancé introduced the reform to his abbey it was
no doubt because he felt that any less drastic measures would fall
short of what was needed to arrest the hopeless decay of the
community. He must have taken advice about this, as about his
other benefices, but there is no reason to suppose that he was
particularly well informed about the disputes and divisions within
the Cistercian Order. His year at Perseigne, including the foray
to Champagne, must have given him a much clearer idea of what
was at stake, and when he took over as abbot he was inevitably
committed to the Abstinent cause, but very much as a willing
though inexpert recruit. The Assembly in September thought
otherwise, and within a few weeks of his installation at la Trappe
Rancé was nominated against his most vehement protests as one
of the two delegates to plead the cause of reform in Rome.[1] It
must be remembered that he was at this time not only junior to
almost every other monk, let alone superior, in the order, he stood
at the head of a very recently reformed community of only nine in
all, with no very assured future. It is all the more strange that his
fellow envoy should be Dominique Georges, Abbot of Val-
Richer[2] (1613–93), who had also become a monk late in life after a

---

[1] The fullest treatment of the negotiations in Rome is in T. Nguyen-Dinh-Tuyen,
'Histoire des controverses à Rome... 1662–66' in *Analecta*, xxvi, 1970; a briefer
account in Lekai, *Rise of the Cistercian Strict Observance*, who corrects Gervaise and
Dubois on numerous points.
[2] See Buffier, *Vie de M. l'abbé de Val-Richer*.

distinguished career as a secular and took over from the former
commendatory abbot, his friend J.-B. de la Place, in 1651. Abbot
Georges was on good terms with the Jesuits, Rancé with the
Oratorians and Port-Royal; both men knew a much wider world
than that of the order, and their personal distinction was an
obvious asset. The choice is nevertheless odd.

Rancé paid a hurried visit back to la Trappe, left instructions
with the prior, dom Gautier, for the future conduct of the community and on 9 September had to leave behind the task he had
hardly commenced. It was two years before he could return to
the cloister, and in the meantime he was more involved in intrigue, public and private, than at any time since he walked out of
the Assembly of Clergy in 1657. The points at issue had become
so distorted in the course of litigation that it seems no longer possible to judge the case on its merits. The situation has been greatly
clarified by the brilliant researches of a team of modern Cistercians
of the Common Observance,[1] and facts are now available which
permit a fairly complete chronology, but it is only fair to say that
the real significance of the dispute, at least in so far as Rancé and
his closest friends were involved, does not emerge too clearly
from the bare facts. In plain terms, if the Common Observance is
to justify its continued existence it can only be, as its members see
it, at the expense of the Strict Observance, and, of course, vice
versa. To an outsider the situation appears very different, and it
certainly looks as though by the time Rancé came on the scene a
disagreement about particular detailed practices had become one
about principles and finally one, quite simply, about power and
personalities. Talk of right and wrong, winning and losing, is not
very helpful when it is now abundantly clear that there was always
room for two (or more) Cistercian traditions, but their accommodation within a single administrative framework could only
lead to friction under seventeenth-century conditions. There is no
room here to retrace the whole course of the dispute, from the
first modest attempts at reform at Clairvaux and elsewhere,
through the unfortunate intervention of Cardinal de La Rochefoucauld and the still more unfortunate action of Richelieu, who
appointed himself abbot of Cîteaux, to the increasingly en-
venomed rivalry between Abbot Vaussin of Cîteaux and Abbot

[1] As well as Nguyen and Lekai, see P. Zakar, *Histoire de la Stricte Observance* and
J. D. Leloczky, *Constitutiones et Acta S.O. Cist.*

Jouaud of Prières,[1] reflected in the not infrequent physical clashes between their respective adherents (as at Champagne). As in all disputes which extend into a second generation and beyond, each side had taken up entrenched positions. Two separate elements may be discerned: the sort of life Cistercians of each observance wished to lead and the way to safeguard the interests of both parties. The latter was negotiable, and in fact the subject of the negotiations; the former in practice was not.

Ever since its foundation and later expansion under St. Bernard, the Cistercian Order had been systematically centralized. The mother-house at Cîteaux provided in its abbot the legal head of the many hundreds of houses throughout Europe. The four first daughters of Cîteaux, above all Clairvaux, provided in their superiors (proto-abbots) leaders for their respective filiations, who in turn retained control through Visitors. The General Chapter was always held at Cîteaux, and the Order's principal house of study was the Collège des Bernardins in Paris. Thus, by its history and organization, the Cistercian Order was an international body with a headquarters based in France and with its senior officers always French. Had the reformers therefore effectively gained control of Cîteaux (or even of Clairvaux), the repercussions would have been felt far beyond the frontiers of France. Ideally they would have liked their way of life to be adopted by the whole order, but, as this was manifestly impossible, they sought instead virtual autonomy under the titular leadership of Cîteaux, and authority to expand their numbers to the maximum inside France. Clearly the central authority of the Common Observance could not survive a decisive shift in the balance of numbers (of houses rather than religious; it was superiors who counted) in favour of the Reform; equally clearly the Reform had come to stay, and the best hope of its opponents was to contain it. Royal policy in France had for some time prevented new monastic foundations (for financial reasons), so that what had been at stake throughout fifty years or so had been a fixed number of buildings, enjoying a notionally fixed revenue from land or dependent benefices, but inhabited by monks whose number and quality fluctuated widely, especially in war-ravaged areas. In a place like the Collège des Bernardins, which was financed by a levy from all

[1] Lekai, *Rise of Cist. S.O.*, chs. VI–XI, gives the most accessible account of Vaussin and Jouaud and their duel.

French houses, the situation was acutely uneasy, with two mutually incompatible factions under the same roof.

The main points to be decided were, in this domain, severely
practical ones of organization, jurisdiction, and property. The
Abstinents wanted to keep as their head a Vicar-General
(currently Jouaud), hold separate General Chapters, compulsorily
transfer or pension off all those monks who would not accept
reformed rules in newly reformed houses, maintain separate
identity at the Collège, and, if they could, see that further novices
would be trained in reformed houses, so that they would before
long outvote the Common Observance in France (they controlled
so far about 50 out of 200 houses).

These claims and counter-claims are objective enough, and are,
on the face of it, what Rancé was sent to Rome to press. The
fundamental issue, however, to this day remains in dispute.
According to the seventeenth-century Common Observance and
their modern successors, the only real difference concerned the
eating of meat, and all the other points raised by the Abstinents
(who in fact resented this name given them by their opponents
whom, in return, they dubbed 'Mitigés') were secondary, ir-
relevant or just false. It is very hard to see how this view can be
maintained in the light of the evidence.

Whatever the actual state of affairs may have been in some or
all houses of the two Observances, it is hardly controvertible that
the Abstinents had laid down, professed to practise, and can
sometimes be shown to have practised rules which they were
quite convinced were not respected by their opponents. It is true
that they went on from there to use emotive and intemperate
language about laxity, but regarding the specific practices they
seem to have been factually correct in their criticism. They were,
of course, using statements of fact as a basis for value judgements,
and their constant contention was that the *true* Cistercian rule
consisted of St. Benedict's Rule as modified and adapted by the
primitive usages of Cîteaux, the Carta Caritatis, and so on. Moreover they insisted (to quote one of their documents submitted to
the Pontifical Commission in 1664) 'Monastica vita poenitentia
est.'[1] Thus, like reformers all down the ages, they were appealing
to the sources and refusing to accept later accretions which they
judged to be mitigations of the original rule and incompatible with

---

[1] Quoted by Nguyen, op. cit., p. 102.

the spirit of voluntary penitence. On the issue of meat eating, for example, it was undeniable that papal approval came only in the fifteenth century, though it was then probably no more than belated recognition and regularization of a long-standing practice.

The members of the Common Observance, now and then, maintain very reasonably that new circumstances require new measures, and that a fossilized and stagnant rule is less healthy than one evolving by constitutional means. They argue moreover, which is less reasonable, that their way of life, then and now, comes closer to the true spirit of the first Cîteaux, which excessive zeal and obsession with penitence had distorted into something no doubt valuable, but decidedly different, in the rule of the reformers. In the seventeenth-century monastic context, in the aftermath of late medieval decay, Reformation, Wars of Religion, Fronde, a more perfect life meant, for those who wanted it, a more austere life. The Cistercian Order was only one among many which underwent reform from within, and was then subjected to external judges for legislation, because the identification of perfection with austerity once accepted made it hard to preserve the *status quo*.

The Cistercian reformers, anticipating Rancé, had always stressed penitence as the basis for their spirituality, thus inevitably condemning concessions to human frailty granted at the request of men with different priorities. The life of prayer, they claimed, must be set in a context of maximum physical self-denial, not because external mortifications had any value in themselves, but because they were at once the sign and spur of a contrite heart. A document of about 1657[1] puts the flesh question in perspective, and remains to be properly answered by the modern scholars of the Common Observance, who tend to play it down. In this, eleven points in dispute are enumerated: fasting (not just abstinence from meat), clothing, bedding, sleeping fully dressed, rising at 2 a.m., manual labour, total silence except during the permitted hour of creation, daily spiritual reading, private prayer, solitude within the enclosure, total poverty. The same document goes on to admit that life at Cîteaux and Clairvaux is edifying, and no doubt in other houses too, but even if the points listed are not all of equal importance and even if some (like the private prayer) depend on a largely subjective assessment, it is disingenuous to

[1] *Response aux dernières objections des Premiers Abbez...* pp. 6–7.

pretend that fasting, silence, and manual labour are minor points of litigation compared to abstinence from meat. Making every allowance for exaggeration and for exceptions, one can see that the Reformers had a coherent programme which, they were convinced, the Common Observance rejected. Whether it made better monks or not is another question, but it is well to underline the range of disputed points, and essential to do so if one is to understand the subsequent conduct of Rancé at la Trappe.

Either the reforms already practised by the Abstinents could be imposed on the whole order from outside, which is what La Rochefoucauld had tried to do, or voluntarily adopted by agreed stages, or restricted to existing reformed houses, perhaps with provision for controlled extension, or prohibited altogether as being inimical to the authority of Cîteaux and the unity of the order, especially outside France. The last possibility could by no means be ruled out, the first one probably could, otherwise variations on these lines were to be the subject of negotiations in Rome. On one point no one could be in any doubt: Rancé had not come the long hard road he had only to settle for compromise on his own or his observance's behalf. He had been fully briefed; his task was to conclude successfully litigation which was diverting monks from their proper exercises.

The identity of those who wrote to Rome in support of Rancé largely explains his nomination: Anne of Austria, the widow and the daughter of Gaston, Mme de Longueville, Retz, all knew him personally, and it was no doubt felt by Jouaud (a much respected friend of Anne) that influence in such high places would turn out to be the most cogent argument. Rancé set off early in October, called on Retz at Commercy for support and advice about the Curia, and then joined Val-Richer and Félibien at Chalon-sur-Saône.[1] On 12 November they arrived in Rome, and on 2 December had their first interview with the Pope, Alexander VII. The subsequent course of negotiations is now largely charted, thanks to the work of P. Zakar and his colleagues. Abbot Vaussin, who had come in person to lend the weight of his authority, was ably supported by Jean Malgoirez, for some thirty years past

---

[1] Félibien kept an account, now lost, of the journey, referred to by the standard biographers, and Rancé himself must have kept some account, because le Nain, for example, quotes very circumstantial details of the Lyons episode which can hardly have come from anyone else.

Cistercian Procurator in Rome, and could represent, as Rancé could not, the likely repercussions outside France of any given course. The Swiss and German abbots, for example, had strong views, and the secession of the Feuillants, and of the Spanish and Italian Bernardines, in the previous century illustrated the danger of exacerbating national feelings in a federation always vulnerable to political pressure.

Impatient and frustrated, Rancé felt (quite rightly) that his cause was getting nowhere, and quite suddenly he left Rome, at the beginning of February 1665. He had found active and worthy friends, above all the Feuillant Bona,[1] but against the leisurely habits of the Curia he found it impossible to force a decision. In a letter to Mère Louise he claims: ' Je ne le fis ni par humeur ni par passion, je déférai au sentiment des autres ',[2] and he seems to have believed that his departure precipitated that of Vaussin, who did in fact leave Rome shortly afterwards, but more probably because he was confident of victory than worried about what Rancé might do in France behind his back. Whatever may have been Rancé's motives for leaving, he got no further than Lyons, and returned to Rome by 1 April 1665 in reluctant obedience to his superiors.

In his absence Val-Richer had been patiently pursuing a rather more moderate line than his colleague, and all was not yet lost. The arrival in Rome of Retz, on 13 June, raised new hopes in Rancé, but a tiresome incident in April had not helped the Abstinents. No Pope could be expected to show much sympathy for Gallican views, and any suspicion that the Reformers inclined that way could only be damaging. Jouaud had presided over the thesis of a Perseigne monk called Monthulé, who attacked the doctrine of papal infallibility and duly received his degree. The affair caused a mild scandal, reported to Rome by the Nuncio, but the irritation does not seem to have been as crucial as some historians have made out.[3] However, the Gallican stigma was always a lurking suspicion, and Rancé himself was such a passionate royalist that he was not the best person to allay it. By this time it is doubtful whether Retz, or Rancé, or anyone could fight more than a delaying action.

[1] On Bona see review article by L. Ceyssens 'Le Cardinal Bona et le Jansénisme'. The contemporary Latin *Vie*, translated by du Suel, is uninformative. See also below, pp. 216–17.

[2] *M* 1214, 71 of 8 July 1665 (wrongly dated 7 Dec. 1664).

[3] See Nguyen, op. cit., pp. 41–2.

The long hot summer dragged drearily on, Rancé hated every moment of it. The Roman Oratorians, at whose church he said mass, proved false friends. Cistercian houses in and around Rome disgusted him, pious pilgrimages to the tombs of early Christian martyrs and even to Subiaco afforded meagre consolation. Endless family squabbles over his father's succession were further embittered by the premature death in October of his sister Marie, comtesse de Vernassal. He sadly wrote: 'nos affaires se rendent immortelles; Rome [m'est] aussi insupportable que la Cour autrefois.'[1] Yet again one blow seemed to follow another: Anne of Austria died on 20 January 1666, thus depriving Jouaud of his most powerful supporter, and Rancé saw little hope left for his mission. Biographers claim that in his despair at the future of the Reform Rancé secured through Retz a papal brief authorizing him to withdraw to the Grande Chartreuse.[2] No trace of this brief (allegedly preserved at la Trappe until the Revolution) survives, but the story is possible, and in any case represents his state of mind. All he wanted was to return to la Trappe and solitude, and in February his long ordeal came to an end. He took leave of the Pope on 21 February 1666 and began his journey back to France via Florence, whither he had the misfortune to be accompanied by Nicaise, who re-entered his life years later.[3] A detour to Clairvaux allowed him to visit St. Bernard's tomb, and he arrived in Paris to report to his assembled fellow abbots at the end of April. His message brought little joy, for on 19 April 1666 the deliberations of the commission seized of the Cistercian dispute were at last published in the form of the brief *In Suprema*.[4]

This document made a few minor changes to the rule of the Common Observance, but deprived the Abstinents of almost all they had so far won. They lost their right of electing their own Vicar-General, of having separate Chapters and gained only that of having their own Visitors (appointed by the General Chapter at Cîteaux) and of having in that Chapter the same number of definitors (ten) as the Common Observance. The brief generally consolidated the legal position of the Abstinents, safeguarding them from eviction, for example, and confirming their professions,

[1] M 1214, 77, of 15 Oct. 1665.   [2] Dubois, i, p. 317.
[3] On Nicaise see below, pp. 49–50.
[4] For text and valuable notes on the brief see Nguyen, op. cit., pp. 223–41.

but it not only fell far short of what they had sought, it almost certainly fell short of what they could have obtained with different tactics. They came to see, however, that it was their only effective defence against further erosion of their position, and all in all the brief may now be seen as a reasonable compromise.

For just a year Rancé was left in relative peace to set his monastery in order. He arrived there on 5 June, and took the road a year later for the General Chapter at Cîteaux. Depressing as it had been, his long stay in Rome had clarified things as a more leisurely initiation at la Trappe would not. He knew with absolute certainty what it meant to conduct top-level negotiations, and would never again be lured into that position; he knew Rome and the Curia, and learned in later years how to win them over; he knew above all every detail of the reformed programme, every charge and counter-charge, and had had to argue constantly about where this or that prescription stood with relation to Cistercian origins. As far as the theory of Cistercian monachism is concerned, he had had the unique opportunity of studying it for nearly a year as a humble novice and then for half as long again as the accredited spokesman for his whole Observance. This fact is very relevant when it comes to assessing the charge of inexperience so frequently levelled at him by his critics. During his time away he had kept in touch with la Trappe, and records of some of his letters survive. It seems from odd facts that even in his absence he had encouraged his monks to take the usual Abstinent rule as a minimum rather than a maximum of austerity, and that already at this early stage his personal reputation was beginning to attract recruits of high quality, of whom dom Rigobert Levesque and dom Jean-François Cornuty are the two best known. By the time he came back from Rome there was no longer the slightest chance that he would settle for any monastic compromise at la Trappe short of total sacrifice.[1]

As had been the case in his first conversion, so in his first years as abbot one can see the process of elimination inexorably pushing him into the position which he finally took up. A year in his own monastery, with a small but dedicated body of like-minded men, the chance to build, literally and figuratively, from foundations painfully laid, the day-to-day problems, both spiritual and temporal, of his office—all this was so much more congenial to him

[1] See Dubois, i, pp. 305–7, quoting le Nain.

than the weary hours spent arguing and intriguing in Rome, that his sense of personal vocation became daily stronger and more specific. In May 1667 he attended his first and last General Chapter at Cîteaux, and once again took a decisive step along his chosen road. The purpose of the Chapter, well attended by superiors from France and abroad, was to receive and approve *In Suprema*, but Rancé claimed the right, as definitor for the Abstinents, to challenge the official account of what had happened in Rome, and to protest against the terms of the brief which had so disappointed his colleagues. His protest, even in the impersonal Latin paraphrase of the minutes, was so vigorous that none of those present can have been left in any doubt as to the quality of their new colleague.[1] Vaussin later tried to conciliate him by offering him, in vain, the post of Visitor; and it is probably true to say that the reluctant delegate of 1664 had become the still more reluctant leader of 1667. The publicity value of his conduct at the Chapter was immense, but the point needs yet again to be made that it was not the still largely unknown quality of life at la Trappe that was being publicized, but the character of its extraordinary abbot. Later the balance would shift, but in 1667 Rancé's appeal was almost entirely to a future vision, not to a solid achievement. This visit to Cîteaux removed any hope the Common Observance may have had of stifling opposition, and cast him in the role of active leader in the continuing fight against the brief, especially in forthcoming appeals to King and Parlement. Besides those who were more interested in struggle than a quiet monastic life, there were scores of monks, including some superiors, who shared Rancé's priorities, and his early appearance on the public scene was an important factor in promoting recruitment to la Trappe.

One of the first consequences of this spread of Rancé's reputation was the visit of the abbot of Sept-Fons, Eustache de Beaufort, who had, at about the same time as Rancé, undergone a similar conversion and was now trying to reform his abbey.[2] Rancé would not allow him to retire to la Trappe, but lent him two or three monks and agreed to accept a few from Sept-Fons for training. The next few years are dominated by the question of recruitment and consolidation at la Trappe, which very soon became as

[1] See Canivez, *Statuta Cap. Gen. Ord. Cist*, vol. vii, p. 449 for Rancé's protest in minutes for Chapter of 1667.

[2] On Beaufort and Sept-Fons see below, pp. 127–29.

famous as its abbot. Two phenomena, not wholly separable, can now be observed: one concerning postulants from other orders, the other relations with Jansenist sympathizers.

Already in 1668 Rancé was involved in major conflicts with other orders, first with the Celestines, over dom Jacques Puiperrou, then with Saint-Victor over dom Pierre le Nain.[1] The whole pattern of vocations will be discussed in a later chapter, but these two cases may be mentioned now as being typical. We do not know nearly enough about the over-all pattern of religious vocation and migration in the period, but it is very likely that la Trappe is unique not only in the survival of very detailed records but also in the degree of attraction it exercised over the whole field of possible candidates. The prospectus was explicit from the start: Rancé had given up everything to follow the path of absolute penitence, and from that path he and his growing community never swerved. At La Trappe more than anywhere else men knew what to expect. The Celestines were going through an uneasy period of dilatory reform, the great house of Saint-Victor had been reformed by Cardinal de La Rochefoucauld but was far from united. The life that Jacques and Pierre wanted was not quite impossible where they were, but would inevitably put them at odds with their companions, so it was entirely reasonable that their quest for religious perfection should lead them to a community where factions were unknown. Once they had shown the way, and reported back to their former comrades, the effect was cumulative. Other Celestines came, and so threatened the cohesion of the order that Rancé eventually made an agreement with the Provincial; Gourdan and others followed dom Pierre, but did not stay; Benedictines of Saint-Maur and Saint-Vanne secured a brief to prevent further defections, although only one of the numerous postulants from them stayed; and so on. La Trappe very quickly established such drawing power that in quantity and quality of recruits it became and remained quite exceptional, but this could only be achieved at the expense of other houses and orders, however much Rancé might protest that they had only to reform themselves in order to keep their own subjects.

The second phenomenon will also be examined in detail in

---

[1] See ch. 6 on vocations in general and ch. 8 on Celestines and Victorines in particular.

another chapter,[1] but as a constant factor should be mentioned
here in its place. It so happens that all three choir monks admitted
in 1667 had known links with Port-Royal: Jacques through a
group of Celestines of known Jansenist sympathies, Benoît
Deschamps and Pierre le Nain through their respective brothers.
Moreover in 1668 Rancé renewed contact with Andilly, after
seven years, and was in close touch with Pontchâteau and his old
friend Le Roy, whose prior at Hautefontaine had been Rigobert.
Leaving aside for the moment the question of Rancé's doctrinal
sympathies, two things are clear: he had always had friends of all
shades of Jansenist opinion, and retained most of them after his
conversion; la Trappe exercised from the first a strong attraction
for those temperamentally inclined to rigorism, whether expressed
in the specifically partisan context of Port-Royal or not. There
existed a vast unsatisfied demand for a more simple and severe
form of Christianity of which la Trappe seemed an unusually
authentic expression. That said, one must add that Rancé's
absolute prohibition of theological study or debate at la Trappe,
his personal refusal to engage in it in conversation or correspondence, and the exclusive concentration on a life of work, prayer, and
penitence meant that only those interested in practising ideals,
not just talking about them, would find fulfilment at la Trappe.

The Peace of the Church in 1669 gave point to both these facts.
Jansenists were more free to come and go, and monks who had
perhaps found in Augustinian theology a focus for their dissatisfaction with mitigated observances were tempted during the
temporary lull in the dispute to try migrating to la Trappe. At
the same time the desultory agitation of the reformers within the
Cistercian Order led some bolder spirits to use their own initiative in trying to emulate Rancé's measures at la Trappe. In this
way Charles Benzeradt at Orval, following Beaufort, agreed with
Rancé to send one or two monks to la Trappe for training, and
Châtillon and Hautefontaine were associated with this move towards independent local action within the Reform.[2] Le Roy, who
actually obtained royal permission to give up his abbey in favour
of Rigobert, was very upset at the latter's refusal, which he suspected was due to Rancé's veto, but the episode illustrates the

---

[1] Ch. 15. Le Roy and Andilly have already been mentioned, and more details can
be found in B. Neveu, *Pontchâteau*, especially pp. 44–71.

[2] Details on these abbeys in ch. 7.

growing influence of la Trappe.[1] At the same time the influx of Jansenist visitors, like dom Pierre's brother, le Nain de Tillemont, and Quesnel, meant that a large and closely knit circle soon came to have first-hand experience of the monastery, whose fame consequently spread among candidates inclined to strict standards. Under such circumstances Rancé could not avoid contacts with Jansenists, even if he wanted to, and however often or loudly he affirmed his neutrality he could not avoid being drawn into a controversy which recognized no neutrals.

From 1671 a new element has to be reckoned with in the history of la Trappe: the first printed accounts of the monastery appeared in the shape of Félibien's *Description* and an unauthorized version of the *Règlements*.[2] Thenceforth publicity continued to grow, and with it controversy. It must be remembered that in the seventeenth century any dispute was liable to erupt into a pamphlet war, and the output in the Cistercian quarrel, for instance, is prodigious.[3] But it looks as though no other French Cistercian house was the subject of any purely descriptive literature in this period (a little book about Sept-Fons came much later),[4] and it is certain that no other house inspired so much. This meant that long before Rancé himself was persuaded to publish, a considerable public knew about la Trappe and its abbot.

The death of Vaussin in 1670 and the election in his stead of Jean Petit[5] gave momentary hope of an improvement in relations between the two branches of the order, but such hope did not survive convocation of the delayed General Chapter in 1672. What happened next is a little obscure; Rancé set off for Cîteaux at the beginning of May, but had gone (he said) only seven leagues when a feverish cold prevented him from continuing his journey, and he went back to la Trappe. There his health recovered sufficiently for him to write (5 May 1672) a long and extremely powerful letter to the Abbot of Cîteaux deploring the state of the order, but also sending formal apologies for absence. All the

[1] See Dubois, i, pp. 364–6.
[2] André Félibien (brother of Pierre), *Description de l'abbaye de la Trappe* (sometimes, probably incorrectly, attributed to the Oratorian T. Desmares); *Constitutions de l'Abbaye de la Trappe*, in later versions called *Règlements*.
[3] An excellent list is given in a bibliographical appendix to Lekai, *Rise of Cist. S.O.*, pp. 241–8 (183 of them).
[4] Drouet de Maupertuy, *Histoire de la réforme de Sept Fons*, 1702.
[5] On Petit see Lekai, *Rise of Cist. S.O.*, ch. XI.

circumstances suggest a diplomatic illness, but it is significant that Rancé went through the motions of complying with his canonical duty to attend. Like his predecessor, Petit tried to conciliate Rancé by offering him the charge of Visitor, but once again Rancé refused, at length.[1] It is unnecessary to invoke the dubious legality of the Chapter as constituted to explain his refusal; from 1667 it had been clear that he would never accept any charge other than that of his own abbey. 1672 thus marks the end of his actual relations with Cîteaux and Petit, though he never ceased formally to acknowledge their authority. On his side, Petit, and his supporters, and perhaps some Abstinents as well, began to show disapproval of the way Rancé was conducting himself and his monastery, but neither then nor later did this make the least difference.

It so happened at just this time, in fact early in July, that Rancé found himself yet again at the centre of a quarrel which finally assumed vast proportions: the so-called affair of the fictions.[2] Always worse served by his friends than his enemies, Rancé had gladly welcomed Le Roy to la Trappe for a week or two in June 1671. While there, Le Roy heard of a recent incident in which the mature and much respected M. Hardy had, as the novice dom Paul, been taken to task by Rigobert, as novice master, for inadvertent use of his previously habitual rhetorical delivery (he had been canon and théologal of Alet). Paul had meekly accepted his penance, and everyone was edified except Le Roy. Rancé explained his point of view, stressing the paramount need of inculcating humility, especially into novices, even at the cost of magnifying disapproval for what might be an insignificant and involuntary lapse. Le Roy was so dissatisfied with this view that, like so many others of the time, he was determined to prove that he was right, and spent the best part of a year taking advice and composing a dissertation to refute Rancé's doctrine of penitence, which in fact derived directly from St. John Climachus. It should be said that not only was Le Roy an old friend of Rancé, he was also a competent theologian with a practical interest in the pastoral

---

[1] Text of letter in Dubois, i, pp. 430–2. Chapter minutes in Canivez, *Statuta Cap. Gen. Ord. Cist.*, vii, pp. 475 seq.

[2] Dubois, i, pp. 413–18. Bibliography in Namer, *Le Roy* and a useful note in Bossuet, *Correspondance*, ii, pp. 36 seq. The crucial document is *M* 1241, giving Le Roy's *Dissertation* and Rancé's *Response*. See also dossier of letters to Le Roy in *U* 738–74.

direction of men and women in religion, though, of course, it was none of his business what went on at la Trappe.

The main bone of contention lies in Le Roy's use of the words 'mensonges ou fictions' referring to his misunderstanding of Rancé's position. Rancé distinguished between reproof administered for some minimal fault which, in the judgement of a superior, might lead to worse and the deliberate invention of faults where there had been none. Naturally if the superior were mistaken and reproved an innocent man, it was generally admitted that the rebuke was to be humbly accepted with no defence offered, more or less on the grounds that no one is innocent all the time, but this is very different from systematic humiliation for false reasons. At all events the collision occurred in July 1672. Rancé had sent Le Roy a reasoned reply[1] to the criticisms which by now were widely circulating against the use of fictions, but Le Roy's dissertation crossed on the way—carried, curiously enough, by some Heisterbach monks coming to see the truth about la Trappe for themselves. This particular quarrel went on rumbling subterraneously until 1677, by which time it had become confused with so many others that when it finally burst into the open it caused much unnecessary pain and bitterness, but that must be discussed later. The dispute is significant at this stage as representing hostile reaction from a previously favourable quarter.

Meanwhile the rearguard action of the Abstinents was entering its final phase. In June 1673 Jouaud died, three years after his rival Vaussin, and Claude le Maître, of Châtillon,[2] became effective leader of the Abstinents. Early in August Rancé answered the pressing invitation of his colleagues and joined the assembly of Abstinent abbots in Paris. His own experience in Rome, and his innate reverence for the Crown, made him recommend an approach to the King in their appeal against the allegedly improper proceedings of the last Chapter at Cîteaux. The abbots drew up a collective document, and for some reason Rancé composed another *Requête au Roi*[3] in his own name. The two humble appeals were presented to Louis at Nancy by Châtillon (22 August 1673). Rancé's came as near an overt declaration of Gallicanism as Louis could have wished (it even compared St. Teresa's appeal to

---

[1] In *U* 767 of 6 July 1672.   [2] On Châtillon see below, pp. 130–35.
[3] Printed in 1673 (two editions).

her own monarch in Spain with the present state of the Cistercian Order) and it was effective. Louis, who was heartily sick of the endless wrangle, appointed a committee to look into it, and it looked as though he, the Grand Conseil, and the new commissioners might between them win a reprieve from the harsh judgement of Rome.

The pamphlet war went on, and one (*Éclaircissement sur l'état présent de l'ordre de Cisteaux*)[1] is due to Rancé. Three of the commissioners, Fieubet, Caumartin, and Harlay, Archbishop of Paris,[2] knew Rancé. Retz's help was enlisted to win over others, and the lobbying which had been so fruitless in Rome promised to be more effective in Paris. Even the support of Arnauld, who visited la Trappe in September 1673,[3] might be helpful, for his nephew, Pomponne (son of Andilly), was once more in favour at Court.

All this activity interrupted Rancé's quest for solitude and at the same time he suffered severe ill health, with what he described as 'une chaleur continuelle'. He had to go to Paris for two weeks in November 1674, but refused to stay with the others at the Collège, preferring his quieter friends at the Institution de l'Oratoire, some distance away.[4] He found time to visit the Carmelites in the rue Saint-Jacques, meeting among others the recently converted Mme de la Vallière.[5] In January 1675 he had to spend more time in Paris, and in April, just before Easter, had to make one more flying visit there, being obliged to leave Bellefonds (who had come on a retreat) and Paul Hardy, who was on his death-bed. All was in vain, and on 19 April 1675 the Conseil d'État pronounced in favour of the Common Observance. One of the strengths of the Abstinents turned out to be a weakness: against their Gallican loyalties the Abbot of Cîteaux had been able to whip up international support from abbots in countries like Germany which Louis could not afford to antagonize. The genealogy of the two Observances to the present day reflects the events of three centuries ago, with the ironical twist that the Common Observance almost disappeared from France although it survived in Central Europe. Perhaps the bitterest blow for the

---

[1] This, a pamphlet of 24 pages, was published in 1674.
[2] On Fieubet and Caumartin see below pp. 272–74, on Harlay p. 6.
[3] Arnauld to Le Roy 30 Sept. 1673, in *U* 739, published in Arnauld, *Lettres*, ix, p. xx.
[4] Rancé to Favier, Gonod, p. 54.
[5] La Vallière to Bellefonds, 7 Nov. 1674, in J. Lair, *Louise de la Vallière*, letter 18.

Reformers was the decision that they might meet whenever they wished, but under the presidency of the Abbot of Cîteaux.[1]

For Rancé this was the end. He had loyally, if reluctantly, taken part in the concluding phases of the dispute ever since he had become regular abbot. He had allowed his reputation and talents to be used for the benefit of his Observance, and the only result that he could see was victory for the unrighteous and vain dissipation of time and energy for him. The numerous friends to whom he told his resolution never again to leave his monastery may have been sceptical, but Rancé was a man of his word and he literally never left the enclosure for the twenty-five years up to his death except for his four brief visits to les Clairets. Rather optimistically he looked forward to peace and oblivion; the next quarter-century brought him neither.

[1] Laid down in *In Suprema*, Nguyen, op. cit., p. 227, sect. 11.

3. Life: 1675–1700

THE period that now began was full of the most bitter disappointments and misunderstandings, but in one vital respect it justified all that had gone before and determined all that was to follow. Free at last of litigation and assemblies, Rancé could concentrate solely on his own community, and it was from the ever closer union of abbot and monks that flowed the influence increasingly exercised by Rancé on the world outside. The first of the blows really to hurt him was the heavy incidence of mortality between 1674 and 1676, when he lost twelve monks, including some of the best. The loss was bad enough in itself, but it inevitably aroused criticism, even from close friends, who saw it as the direct consequence of excessive austerities. They were not slow to point out that, should his own indifferent health give way, the whole work of la Trappe might collapse. Sustained by his monks, who had come to meet, not escape, death Rancé resisted the temptation to relax his rule. Whether this was wise or not is a matter of one's ultimate criteria, but pragmatically it did no harm either to recruitment or the quality of spiritual life. Above all, it identified Rancé and his community to an ever wider public, and was the immediate cause of the *Relations* which began to circulate in manuscript in 1675 and in print from 1677. Deaths so edifying could be turned to good account, and henceforth, for better or worse, the *Relations* played a typical and conspicuous role in advertising la Trappe throughout the world.[1]

In this connection, an important event took place in February 1676 which made it hard for Rancé's increasingly numerous critics

---

[1] The first *relations* concern the first two religious to die, namely Joseph Bernier and an oblate from Champagne (in Félibien, *Description de la Trappe*, pp. 108–24). Brief as they are, these announced the pattern of the many that followed. Biographical and other details can only have come from Rancé, and some of the pieces contain his exhortations, but the genre is clearly literary rather than oral. The 1677 edition of *Relations de la vie et de la mort de quelques religieux de la Trappe* dealt with 3 or 4 religious, the last to appear in Rancé's lifetime with 14. Although Rancé composed the original, some of the pieces were no doubt edited before publication, and the most complete series (in 5 vols. in 1755) is obviously by several hands; it deals with nearly 60 monks, including Rancé and dom le Nain. References are to this edition throughout.

to pursue their campaign in quite the same way as before. His independent attitude, and notoriously original application of the rule, did not please some of his colleagues in the Reform any more than the Abbot of Cîteaux and his followers, and ever since the Chapter of 1672 there had been murmurs about possible irregularities. Jouaud had been succeeded at Prières by Hervé du Tertre, and it was he who had assumed the charge of Visitor refused by Rancé. In this capacity he came in 1676 to la Trappe, conducted a canonical visit in due form, and left a report (his *Carte de visite*, frequently published from that time on) completely vindicating Rancé, praising his community, and depriving his enemies of a major weapon. A second visit in 1678 confirmed the first; subsequent regular visits repeated what Prières had said and thereafter Rancé was left alone.[1]

The implications of these official visits are considerable; it must have been fairly obvious to his colleagues that Rancé would attend no further Assemblies, let alone General Chapters; and though his invariable plea of poor health was always accepted as a valid excuse for absence, no one can have believed that it was the sole or main reason.[2] Going his own way at la Trappe, staying away from all official gatherings, Rancé's connections with his order were not entirely normal, and he was sometimes accused of trying to found a new one. Thus his formal (and real) submission to an official appointed by his colleagues, and the evidently searching character of the visit, preserved all the constitutional proprieties, left him with his virtual autonomy, accepted and retained within the order its most outstanding member, with all the benefits that might entail for all concerned. He therefore remained largely alone, but exonerated from any suspicion of defiance or irregularity. It is probably fair to trace the Trappist revival in the nineteenth century to Rancé's scrupulous regard for form in accepting these visits from 1676 and so maintaining his abbey as an integral, though unique, part of the Cistercian Order.

From now on, that is after his return from his final visit to Paris, one of the chief problems of Rancé's life was that of communication. If he had religiously kept silent, very little harm

[1] Dubois gives the substance of these (e.g. i, p. 536) and they were also published separately as well as being included in some editions of the *Règlements* (e.g. 1718).

[2] See Canivez, *Statuta Cap. Gen. Ord. Cist.* vii, p. 558, where the Chapter of 1683 investigated various absentees but accepted without question Rancé's apologies 'ob gravem infirmitatem'.

would have been done; if he had been able to meet people reasonably often and talk to them, most misunderstandings would have
been cleared up; but the written word allied to oral rumour
created a situation from which he never fully extricated himself.
The wearisome point–counterpoint of his quarrels and recon-
ciliations is an item almost wholly on the debit side, but it cannot
be ignored. Three quite separate entries for the year 1676 all refer
to this element in his life. The first cannot be dated exactly, but
had already occurred by 1676: the arrival of M. Maisne.[1] This
former lawyer's clerk came in the first instance to try his vocation,
but for reasons of health could not embrace a fully monastic life
and stayed on in the monastery as a secular, like other *donnés* who
often conducted the community's business outside. When Maisne
arrived, probably about 1674, Rancé employed a monk as secretary to write all his letters (apart from the time saved, his own
handwriting was atrocious), sometimes dom le Nain, most often
Rigobert. The latter's health was not good, and before he died in
1679 Maisne had already taken over some of his work, and very
soon became full-time secretary, especially when Rancé saw the
advantage of freeing monks from the increasingly onerous task
of coping with the huge volume of mail. In the early years of his
residence Maisne probably did little more than observe, but it was
not long before the great majority of Rancé's contacts went
through him. There is no need to doubt his devotion to Rancé, or
to impute to him any specifically sinister motive, but he did great,
perhaps irreparable, harm in the long run. His advent simply
nullified any benefit to be gained from Rancé's withdrawal because,
being only a secular and not under discipline, he was free to
talk or write to anyone and grossly abused his master's confidence.

[1] Dubois (ii, p. 5) gives a portrait of Maisne; Saint-Simon gives another in
Mémoires, i, p. 564, and had so much to do with him in Rancé's later years that a good
impression of his activities can be gained simply by checking references to la Trappe
in the *Mémoires*. Original letters survive from Maisne to Favier (ingratiating but
fruitless), to Nicaise (mock modest), to Bellefonds (deferential and informative),
and to others (see Tournoüer, *Bibliographie*, pp. 136–7 and 190–4). James II, Bossuet,
M. de Saint-Louis all knew him well, and there is no question but that he was a
highly efficient, energetic personal assistant to Rancé. What is more problematic is
how far he exceeded his brief in interpreting Rancé's instructions, in taking the
initiative himself without telling Rancé, or in misrepresenting people and situations
to his master. If Maisne would have been nothing without Rancé, it is not so easy
to say what Rancé would have been without Maisne.

The second item also involves a breach of confidence.[1] Beaufort, who had been one of the first to support and emulate Rancé, enjoyed his intimacy more than most. An aristocrat himself, he may have been jealous of Rancé's success at la Trappe compared to his own relative failure at Sept–Fons. He certainly resented Rancé's criticisms, rather freely given, and no doubt wanted to attract favourable attention. Some time in July or August 1676 he divulged a copy of Rancé's answer to Le Roy, lent to him in confidence, and directly or indirectly stirred up suspicions of Jansenism against Rancé. It was two years before the two men were reconciled, but the campaign of gossip and recrimination among monks, nuns, and others was unedifying and did no one any good.

The third incident again concerned a friend, albeit a new one, and indiscretion, but did not have repercussions at once, though when they came they were very serious. Recommended by several friends, including his kinsman Bellefonds, the comte de Brancas paid a visit to la Trappe in August, and at his request Rancé wrote him a long letter explaining why he had signed the Formulary against Jansenism, and why he had never ceased to regard as friends and good Christians those Jansenists whom he had known in earlier days. The subsequent circulation of this, and later, similar letters, coinciding with Beaufort's campaign of rumour did great harm.[2] It must be remembered that the Peace of the Church was still in force, and Rancé was in regular contact with men like Arnauld, Nicole, and Quesnel. While this was perfectly legitimate, it did not endear him to the Jesuits or their allies, and from 1675 he writes more in anger than sorrow about their whispering campaign against him.

As if all this were not enough, the following year the long smouldering quarrel with Le Roy burst into flame again. Yet again, one is tempted to say, as always, a friend, in this case André Félibien, was responsible; and it may well be said of Rancé that with such friends he had no need of enemies. For some reason, perhaps to put an end to rumours, but without permission, Félibien published Rancé's *Response* to Le Roy's *Dissertation*, already, it is true, leaked by Beaufort. Rancé was very annoyed, and wrote in April and again in June to apologize to Le Roy for a publication in which he had no part, but the

[1] For details see below, pp. 128–29.　　　[2] See below, pp. 259–61.

damage was done. Le Roy broke into a paroxysm of self-justifica-
tion and got his secretary Germain Vuillart (later Racine's) to
circulate dozens of men and women, religious and secular,
throughout France in a sort of opinion poll on the relative merits
of his case and that of Rancé.[1] Even if it had not been published,
Rancé's tone in his answer had not been conciliatory, and many
of those who wrote back in support of Le Roy show less concern
for the question of fictions than for Rancé's treatment of a person
generally liked and respected, especially, but not only, in Jansenist
circles. Among those who answered were Pascal's sister, Marguerite Périer, and Rancé's niece, Louise-Henriette, who was
much distressed by the quarrel. Personalities dominated the
majority of replies, but it is noteworthy that those who knew
Rancé well (Bishop of Châlons, Abbots of Châtillon and l'Étoile)
thought that he was basically right, but that he had reacted
excessively to Le Roy's misguided criticism. In the end a rather
reluctant silence was imposed on both contestants, largely thanks
to Bossuet, but the episode gave much satisfaction to those who
sought every opportunity to brand Rancé as an authoritarian fanatic who suffered no views contrary to his own.

   Not very long after silence, if not peace, had been restored in
this affair, another very different incident occurred which, on any
showing, is most extraordinary. The Abbot of Tamié, in Savoy,
the young Jean-Antoine de la Forêt de Somont (1645–1701), had
harboured a grudge against la Trappe ever since his close friend
and fellow student, Cornuty, had suddenly left Paris for la Trappe
in 1665.[2] Like other noble young abbots (he was only 20 when he
succeeded), he made up in vigour what he lacked in experience,
and had played a prominent part in the defeat of the Abstinents in
1673, through his personal friendship with Condé. For reasons
no clearer than those which inspired Cornuty, Somont decided
in September 1677 to go to la Trappe to see for himself. If he
went there in the hope of better understanding Cornuty's behaviour of a dozen years before he was not disappointed. A
highly emotional scene, or series of scenes, culminated in this
eloquent enemy of the Reform handing Rancé a signed promise to
introduce the Reform into Tamié forthwith. This, with the aid of

[1] See above, p. 33, n. 2. Vuillart (or Willart) is the subject of Ruth Clark, *Lettres
de G. Vuillart*, referring to a later period in his life.
[2]. On Cornuty see below, p. 108, on Tamié, pp. 137–38.

Cornuty, released from Foucarmont, and three monks from la Trappe, he did.

Coming so soon after the Le Roy affair, this strange episode illustrates very well the unique personal charm of Rancé, irresistible face to face, almost intolerable in written controversy. Exactly the same thing happened in 1679 when Beaufort next met Rancé and was fully reconciled. This characteristic must be stressed, otherwise one cannot hope to understand how Rancé achieved what he did—for good or bad.

With his unhappy genius for incurring hostility unnecessarily, Rancé was persuaded at the end of the following year (30 November 1678) to send Bellefonds a letter for general release (it was in fact later printed) stating his position on Jansenism.[1] Essentially this never varied: his friends remained his friends; he never regretted obeying his lawful superiors over the Signature; theological speculation was not his business. The immediate effect was mixed; in January 1679, for example, Quesnel received the honour of an Act of Association[2] and Arnauld sent a postulant,[3] a Vannist whom Rancé did not take, but others were displeased at his strict orthodoxy. The death of Mme de Longueville on 15 April 1679 precipitated a crisis: the precarious Peace of the Church came to an end, in May Port-Royal was evacuated. In June Arnauld fled into lifelong exile; in July Choart de Buzenval, Bishop of Beauvais, died, depriving Jansenists of a long-assured refuge in his diocese; in August Retz, always tolerant, died. The strain of the past few years almost removed Rancé too. He was so ill at the end of September that he received the viaticum and was widely reported, not for the first time, to have died. Happily in August 1677 he had secured a brief[4] guaranteeing the continuance of the reform at la Trappe after his eventual death, and allowing the religious to elect their own prior (a rare privilege) if the abbey returned, as it normally would, into commend, so that his illness was not quite the catastrophe it would have been a little earlier.

The death of Rigobert in 1679 left Maisne in a very strong position. Not only did he take over as secretary, but after Rancé's

[1] Original in *BN* n.a. 12959, f. 73, copy in Gonod, p. 360 and often elsewhere.

[2] Original in *U* 1168, published in Tans, 'Un Dialogue monologué', letter 39. Such an Act formally associates the recipient with the prayers of the Community issuing it and was quite often exchanged between communities.

[3] Copy in *U* 913.

[4] 2 Aug. 1677. Text in Dubois, i, p. 579.

narrow escape from death Maisne could set himself up as the indispensable guardian of the abbot's health. By April 1682 it became clear that he had even more lofty ambitions. On 30 April 1682 and again on 15 June he wrote two ingratiating letters to Favier (and almost certainly to others as well) in which he pressed him to send whatever he might possess of letters from Rancé or documents about him.[1] 'Vous vous croyez engagé de l'avertir qu'on le peut canoniser après sa mort, et l'on vous presse de fournir des mémoires pour cela... Tous ses amis ramassent dans le secret, et ne laissent rien perdre.' Among others, the brothers Félibien are mentioned as being involved in the pious enterprise. Maisne (who did not know Favier) reinforced his request with a reference to Favier's advanced age (in fact he outlived Rancé) and pressed him to act before it was too late—all this to be kept strictly secret from Rancé. In June Maisne had received nothing and tried again. This time he spoke of 'un jeune religieux' who after eight or ten months had been obliged to leave la Trappe for health reasons, and was now preparing not exactly a life of Rancé but a collection of all his letters with a view to such a life. Favier, whose devotion to Rancé was total, never co-operated with Maisne or the aspirant biographer, who can be identified as Pierre Maupeou.[2] Instead he kept his letters until six years later when he sent them to Riom, to Louise–Henriette, Rancé's niece, for copying, though she died so soon afterwards that she had no time to start the task.[3] The history and provenance of other series of letters show that Maisne was not entirely successful in extracting documents from interested parties.

The implications of Maisne's *démarche* are serious. On a practical plane he and his associates undoubtedly saved from loss or destruction a great mass of letters, but by forming this somewhat premature canonization committee they implicitly introduced a principle of selection which, in view of Maisne's character, may not have fallen far short of censorship, or even suppression. Maisne had so many opportunities from 1682 onwards for talking and writing to anyone he chose, he enjoyed such control of Rancé's correspondence and contacts, that one must constantly bear in mind his self-appointed role of impresario for a future saint.

[1] Originals in *CF* 344 D, published in Jaloustre, *Précepteur auvergnat*, pp. 16 and 20.
[2] On Maupeou see Gervaise, *Jugement critique, passim*.
[3] Jaloustre, *Précepteur auvergnat*, p. 27.

It is in this context that one should see the next critical decision
of Rancé's life. After several abortive attempts to visit la Trappe,
Bossuet finally managed to come in October 1682, that is just as
Maisne's campaign was in full flood.[1] In the course of his years
as abbot, Rancé had given numerous talks to his monks on the
duties of their calling. From notes these had developed into something more like a continuous draft. According to Maupeou, and
Dubois,[2] Abbot le Maître of Châtillon was the first to urge him to
publish them, then Favier is said to have seen the mansucript, and
there is an imaginative parenthesis concerning a Protestant brewer
from Caen who was entranced at what he managed to read of the
manuscript left open by Favier in the guest-house. Rancé allegedly flung the copy into the fire, whence part of it was saved by
an indignant Favier. All this would no doubt have sounded well
at the preliminary hearings of the cause for Rancé's beatification,
but the relevant facts are more prosaic. On Rigobert's death, or
perhaps before, Rancé dictated to Maisne a complete draft of
what was by now a book, *De la sainteté et des devoirs de la vie
monastique*. He apparently authorized several copies for domestic
consumption but, of course, had no control or even knowledge of
what Maisne did with them. One found its way into Bossuet's
hands by about 1681, supposedly without Rancé's knowledge,
though this particular ploy was very common in the seventeenth
century; and when Bossuet at last arrived at la Trappe he insisted
that Rancé should allow him to undertake its publication.[3]
Le Camus and Barillon would collaborate in reviewing the text,
and the approval of the Archbishops of Reims and Paris would
be enlisted. Barillon paid a visit in November and was thus also
able to discuss the book with Rancé.

The chronology of the affair leaves little doubt that Maisne
was the prime mover, aided, no doubt, by others. André Félibien,
for instance, read the proofs and must have been privy to the
scheme for forcing Rancé into print. Interesting corroboration
that this book belongs to the same general plan as the collection
of Rancé's letters comes from an admission of Maupeou that he
already in 1682, or thereabouts, possessed 'un corps de *Maximes*'
of which he lent a manuscript copy some ten years later, and

---

[1] See M. L. Serrent, *Rancé et Bossuet*, p. 188.   [2] Dubois, ii, pp. 1–4.
[3] Rancé to Bossuet, 27 June 1682, copy in *TB* 1684, published in Bossuet, *Correspondance*, ii, p. 306.

obviously clandestine collections of all that Rancé wrote were being gathered together.[1] In 1683 also a third edition of the *Relations* came out, expanded from six to thirteen entries. It seems only too clear that Rancé's serious illness of 1679 and Maisne's accession to power together removed any hope that he could ever again avoid publicity.

The book went very rapidly through the press and came out in March 1683.[2] The significance of this publication was immense. Everyone who knew about Rancé and la Trappe realized that he held and practised a highly personal monastic ideal. His view of Cistercian decadence, and the relative laxity of the Reform, was no secret, and so long as he was content to form an élite at la Trappe on these principles, giving what assistance and advice other superiors might request (and on occasion gratuitously), most people were ready enough to let well alone. The publication of *Sainteté*, with or without his original approval, changed all that. In this book he justifies what unquestionably worked well at la Trappe by laying down a whole set of principles which he considered binding on all true religious, or at least monks. Though the form of the book arises from the conferences he gave his own monks, no reader can escape the incessant comparison between the standards demanded at la Trappe and those tolerated elsewhere.

The work is divided into twenty-three chapters of very unequal length, and, from internal evidence, probably composed at different times. The brief introductory chapters on the basis of monastic life are couched in question-and-answer form, others vary from ten pages to sixty, and in one case over a hundred. A lot of the book consists in a compilation of monastic precedents, especially from the Desert Fathers, but also dealing extensively with the great medieval legislators, and even St. Ignatius and St. Teresa. The aim is patently apologetic as well as hortatory. Much the longest chapter is XVI, a complete essay on 'Retraite' of some 120 pages. The other long ones are about sixty pages each: V on 'Essence et perfection de la vie cénobitique', XII on 'Pénitence' (more or less a paraphrase of Rancé's earlier essay on humiliations addressed to Le Roy), XIX on 'Travail des mains' (an attack on monastic study), and XXII on 'Patience dans les

---

[1] Maupeou, *Vie*, ii, p. 142.

[2] Later editions made minor modifications, but the first shows Rancé's essential thought. References are to the first edition (reprinted 1972).

infirmités et les maladies' (Rancé constantly stressed that relaxations permitted in the infirmary are the usual source of mitigation subsequently accepted everywhere).

Le Roy, who died in 1684, and his friends were hardly likely to welcome another salvo on humiliations, toned down as it was, and the Common Observance were not disposed to view very kindly a fresh instalment of Rancé's long-familiar diatribes against their decadence (the Abstinents did not emerge unscathed either), but these were old enemies. New hostility was aroused not wholly unexpectedly from Benedictines and Carthusians.[1] It is true that Rancé had told Bossuet that other orders would be annoyed, but the specific offence given was rather different in the two cases. Several times Rancé goes out of his way to praise the Carthusians 'qui forment dans l'ordre monastique une des plus saintes et des plus célèbres observances',[2] but various remarks contrasting their primitive observance with that of the present day were judged amiss by dom le Masson, their General, who had other reasons for disliking Rancé. The ensuing dispute (discussed in a later chapter) ended in uneasy silence in 1689.

The issue with the Benedictines was different and quite fundamental. In his chapter on manual work Rancé dwelt at great length, adducing numerous authorities, on the question of study: 'Il est certain que les Moines n'ont point été destinés pour l'étude, mais pour la pénitence.'[3] Perhaps spontaneously, perhaps at the suggestion of his sponsors, he used temperate language and even allowed points to his opponents: 'Soyez persuadés que l'application aux sciences est ennemie de l'esprit qui doit animer toute la conduite des solitaires, et que, quoiqu'il y ait eu de saints Moines, et qu'il y en puisse encore avoir d'une érudition éminente, ce serait directement s'opposer à l'esprit d'une profession si sainte que de faire une règle générale de ces exemples.'[4] This was too much for the Maurists, who took special pride in their outstanding scholars; and in 1684 dom Jean Mabillon replied with his habitual courtesy, but firmly, in a letter of *Réflexions*, pointing out the perfect consistency of study with the Rule of St. Benedict. The dispute with Le Roy had been bad enough, but most of it was at least not conducted in print: that with Mabillon soon became international, though, one must add, remained polite. Rancé's letters

[1] See below, pp. 164–67. [2] *Sainteté*, XXII. vi, p. 480.
[3] Ibid., XIX, iv, p. 292. [4] *Ibid.* XIX, v., p. 298.

for the next ten years or so are full of the latest moves in the debate, and it is best to comment on them as they come.[1]

It is a relief to record at least one dispute which gave way to comparatively normal behaviour. In May 1683 there had been a General Chapter at Cîteaux, attended by most of the leading Abstinents, in which Petit fell out with the proto-abbots. The next year, knowing that about fifteen Abstinent superiors were meeting at the Collège des Bernardins, Petit for the first time exercised his prerogative and presided. Rancé excused himself from the meeting 'ob gravem infirmitatem', this time more real than diplomatic, but the appointment of his friends of Orval, Sept–Fons, and Val–Richer as Visitors showed that the highest office went to men of like mind. In Paris a complaint was lodged against Rancé for admitting two senior Premonstratensians, contrary to a concordat going back to the days of SS. Bernard and Norbert.[2] The assembly remitted inquiry into the affair to Orval; Rancé's action was upheld in Rome; and there seems to have been no further criticism of him—all this is significant of his status by then. Moreover the fact that such an assembly met at all, let alone amicably, under the Abbot of Cîteaux marks a great step forward towards common sense.

In August 1684 a second edition of *Sainteté* came out (and in 1685 a third) with quite a number of corrections; the book was a success, even among Protestants, in whom the frequent appeals to the Desert Fathers struck a sympathetic note. It also had a marked effect on vocations, and to the compendious list of orders offended by his admission of their subjects Rancé had to add the Feuillants in 1685.[3] The guerilla war with Mabillon continued, and in June 1685 Rancé published his *Éclaircissement*[4]—his method being the usual one of the age, to take point by point made by his opponent and laboriously refute him on detail, terminology, and so on. It is probable that some clarification resulted in the course of such debate, but agreement was hardly likely.

By now Rancé's reputation was universal, and his public image varied from that of saint to charlatan. A powerful contribu-

---

[1] See Didio, *La Querelle de Mabillon et... Rancé*. Mabillon's MS. *Réflexions* are given in full p. 440–56 (original in *BN* 23497, Corbie, no. 44).

[2] See Leloczky, *Constitutiones et Acta*, pp. 219–20. The religious in question were Éloi le Môle and Bruno Ferrand (see below, pp. 109 and 167).

[3] Details on Feuillants p. 113, below.

[4] *Éclaircissement de quelques difficultez quel'on a formées sur le livre de la sainteté...*

tion to the myth (on the 'no smoke without fire' principle) appeared in 1685 in the form of an anonymous book (actually by the Protestant Larroque) entitled *Les Véritables Motifs de la conversion de l'abbé de la Trappe... ou Entretiens de Timocrate et de Philandre sur un livre qui a pour titre les Saints Devoirs de la vie monastique*.[1] The aim was quite simply to discredit Rancé by attacking his personal life and his book, but the title shows that the attack was prompted by objections to the latter. The whole of the second part of this substantial pamphlet criticizes Rancé's declared belief that a professed religious has no further duty to his parents, though his community may well help them in need. This section of *Sainteté*, which occupies a good part of the longest chapter (XVI: 'Retraite'), had some years earlier been the subject of a quite friendly debate with the Jansenist Floriot,[2] and hardly invalidated the rest of Rancé's arguments, so that Larroque's choice of attack is a little strange. He came, however, much nearer his target of effective malice when, for the first time, he purveyed the gruesome tale of Mme de Montbazon's headless corpse, with suitable innuendo about Rancé's relations with her, and with slightly more verisimilitude attributed Rancé's conversion to the combined effect of this shock and that of being snubbed by Mazarin.[3] Jesuits, Jansenists, Benedictines have all at different times been linked with this libel, but there is not a shred of evidence beyond Larroque; his main importance lies in the extraordinary persistence of the myth he created.

As if to balance this calumny, la Trappe received in 1685 a canonical visit from Val-Richer, and as usual was the subject of a eulogistic report. Though the two men were again on good terms after a bad patch some years before, they moved in circles sufficiently different for this report to be accepted as fair and impartial. It showed once more how absurd was the claim that Rancé was trying to set up an independent order. Maupeou published anonymously a rather unimpressive refutation of Larroque called *Conduite et sentiments de M. l'abbé de la Trappe* (1685), but it probably did less real good than Val-Richer's *Carte de visite*, and it was foolish to throw into public debate,

---

[1] See Dubois, ii, pp. 62–8.
[2] See Floriot, *Recueil de pièces concernant la morale chrétienne... du Pater*, Bruxelles, 1745, vi, pp. i–xxi (following p. 74).
[3] See above, pp. 9–10.

thirty years after the event, the question of Rancé's relationship
with Mme de Montbazon. It is relevant in this connection to note
that Rancé replied in 1686 to the direct question of Mme de La
Fayette that his conversion was due to disillusionment with the
world and that he had never before told anyone this.[1] Such a
statement amounts to a tacit denial of the Larroque story and
suggests that the whole affair had, at any rate for a time, become a
talking-point in Paris society.

Perhaps as a relief from polemic, perhaps as an implied rebuke
to critics of his asceticism, Rancé published in 1686 a little book
containing a translation of St. Dorotheus's *Instructions*[2] and notes
on his life, which he offered as a gift to many friends at the time.
Nearer home, however, than the Desert Fathers were those of
Saint-Maur. One of them, dom Mège, joined the running battle
against Rancé with his *Commentaires* on the Rule of St. Benedict
(1687), which went so far in its attack on Rancé that the Maurist
authorities condemned him two years later.[3] Also in 1687 Rancé
finished his own *Explication* of the same Rule, published in 1689.[4]
With the exception of Mège and, later, Sainte-Marthe, it is fair to
say that the dispute with the Benedictines was on the whole
conducted with dignity, and it is even possible that both parties
gained something from it, time-consuming though it was.

Another event of 1687 deserves record, even though it amounted to nothing. On his way back from Rome in 1666 Rancé had
travelled as far as Florence with the abbé Nicaise. Though they
had friends in common, they made no direct contact again until
1680, when Nicaise began a correspondence with Rancé which
lasted until his death (Nicaise died in 1701).[5] It seems more than a
coincidence that Maisne had already taken over as secretary when
this correspondence began, and a number of letters exchanged
personally between him and Nicaise show that the two became

[1] Copy in *BN* 24123, published in Dubois, i, p. 112.
[2] *Les Instructions de saint Dorothée.*
[3] Bossuet told Rancé that he would secure his condemnation (*Correspondance*, iii,
pp. 426, of 4 Oct. 1687, and 444, of 11 Nov. 1687), on which Pontchâteau wryly
commented, 'Ce n'est pas l'inquisition de Goa, mais en vérité cela n'est guère
raisonnable' (ibid.).
[4] *La Règle de saint Benoist, traduite et expliquée…*
[5] Gonod published nearly all Rancé's letters to Nicaise (originals in *BN* 9363)
and gives some biographical details. See also Moréri and E. Caillemer, *Lettres… à
Nicaise*. On his visit see letters of Rancé and Maisne of June–July 1687, in Gonod,
pp. 129–34.

very friendly. As a man of some erudition and monumental in-discretion, Nicaise was well placed to publicize Rancé and la Trappe in the world of learning. He numbered among his friends Sluse, in Rome, Leibniz, Huet, and many other scholars of inter-national repute, and was epigrammatically dubbed the postman of Parnassus. He was always on the point of retiring to a life of retreat, and about to come to la Trappe (he lived in Dijon), per-haps to stay, but so many good intentions came to nothing. His insatiable curiosity and talent for learned gossip did not make him an obvious candidate for the silent life. However, in 1687 he finally organized himself to make the journey to la Trappe, but managed to stay only twenty-four hours, supposedly because his companion was in a hurry to get back. The best result of this visit was the non-publication of his account of it, on Maisne's advice, so one can only suppose that it exceeded the bounds of fulsome hagiography tolerable even to Maisne. The personal contact renewed face to face after twenty years conferred a certain authority on Nicaise, which was to cause much trouble later. In his favour it must be said that a very large number of original letters from Rancé and others at la Trappe have survived only because of his care.

In the same year, 1687, began a new episode of which the conse-quences became fully apparent only ten years later. Not very far from la Trappe was the convent of les Clairets,[1] where Rancé's sister Thérèse had spent some forty years. The abbey had originally been directed from la Trappe, but by now had become subject to a Visitor appointed directly by Clairvaux, currently Val-Richer. The election in 1687 of a new abbess, Angélique d'Étampes de Valençay, brought Rancé into touch with les Clairets again, and despite his very real infirmities he finally yielded to the abbess's pleading and in September 1688 consented to take over direction from Val-Richer. This obligation forced him, as nothing else could have done, to leave his enclosure, twice in 1690, and again in 1691 and 1692 to visit the abbey and bless the abbess. A fuller account of the affair is given later, but it should be mentioned now that this innocent excursion caused trouble. The publication of his *Carte de visite* in 1690 revealed that he strictly imposed the prescriptions of *Sainteté* on the nuns (who petitioned to join the

---

[1] On les Clairets see below, pp. 177–81. The *Carte de visite* was reprinted and in-cluded in the *Règlements* of 1718. See also Dubois, ii, pp. 207–9.

Reform) and in particular laid down that their reading should not include most of the Old Testament. Rancé's enemies were tireless in their attempts to compromise him, and this instruction raised a storm of protest, from Nicole, among others, who had been previously on good terms with Rance.[1] Much later it was the abbess's implacable hostility to Gervaise that stirred up the final crisis against Rancé's luckless successor.

With every year that passed Rancé's health now grew worse, and new attacks came from the most unexpected quarters. In August 1690 a young Franciscan Recollect, ironically named Candide Chalype, came for four days to la Trappe, very clearly as an *agent provocateur*. He vanished as suddenly as he had come, and with the apparent connivance of his superiors published a scurrilous pamphlet alleging with great wealth of detail that Rancé and his friends, including members of the Oratory, and even Bossuet, were crypto-Jansenists or worse, and implicating a whole network of noble men and women in a grand conspiracy to advance the cause of la Trappe. It was not so much his wickedness as his clumsiness that betrayed him, and a year or two later, after his superiors had been forced to discipline him, he made a full confession.[2] Such incidents may seem trivial now, but in the atmosphere of intrigue and rumour prevalent at Court they could and did do harm at the time.

Even the great honour of a visit paid by James II, after the Boyne, on 24 November 1690, brought criticism. Rancé was deeply touched by this mark of the King's esteem, and recounted his feelings to Bellefonds (who had had to leave hurriedly) in a letter which his enemies found politically unsound, because Rancé praised James's Christian resignation in the face of adversity when the official line supported strong retaliatory action to regain his throne.[3] This connection, however, brought lasting satisfaction to abbot and monarch, in their declining years (they died within a year of each other) and certainly did la Trappe a lot of good at Court just when it was most needed. Rancé spent more and more time in the infirmary; it was evident that even if he lived he would soon have to resign, and the future of la Trappe

[1] See *BN* 9363, f. 243, in Gonod, p. 184.
[2] There is an account of this strange affair in *A*, 3824, and also in le Nain, from whom Dubois copies.
[3] Letter of 29 Nov. 1690, original in *BN* n.a. 12959, f. 142, copy in Gonod, p. 385.

depended on Louis's approval of his eventual successor. It is in this light that one must judge Rancé's extreme sensitivity to anything that might provoke royal disfavour, as in the Maupas affair.[1]

This unfortunate cleric, of Jansenist convictions, had supported his diocesan, the late Bishop of Pamiers, in the dispute with the King over the Régale, and had spent four years in prison (accompanied, he was at pains to specify, by scorpions, of which he killed eleven). He was eventually released, and permitted to go into exile at la Trappe, where he duly arrived in June 1692. At first he was reasonably well received, then word came, rightly or wrongly, that he was of questionable loyalty, and after three weeks he was summarily ejected, and sent on his way to Paris, penniless and desperate. Next month he wrote a long account of his treatment, which circulated widely in manuscript to the satisfaction of some Jansenists glad of a chance to unmask Rancé. The real moral of the story is that Rancé (perhaps prompted by Maisne) was not prepared to take the slightest risk of becoming involved with anyone suspected of heresy or subversion. A later incident, in 1696, involving a harmless old Jansenist from Beauvais, Wallon de Beaupuis, shows exactly the same obsessive desire to avoid trouble at all costs; trouble, that is, with authority, for controversy was inescapable, and the treatment of Beaupuis brought him into painful conflict with dom Pierre's brother, le Nain de Tillemont.[2]

Meanwhile Mabillon had not said his last word about monastic study, and in 1691 he published his *Traité des études monastiques*, offering a solid and reasoned defence of the Maurist position, and relating it to ancient rule and tradition. References to Rancé's thesis were invariably courteous, but Mabillon totally rejected it as a general rule for all monks. The book remains the classic statement of the Benedictine attitude to scholarship, and shows Mabillon as a humane and holy man who found it perfectly proper to offer to God the labour of the mind no less than that of the body, which, incidentally, he by no means depreciated. Rancé felt

[1] A manuscript dossier on the Maupas affair exists both in *T* 2183 and *U* 863 and 3069. See also Dubois, ii, pp. 369 seq.

[2] Details in le Nain de Tillemont, *Lettre à feu M. l'abbé de la Trappe*, 1704, and in MSS. *T* 2183 and *U* 3069. Bremond makes the most of the incident, pp. 141 seq. For a more balanced account see B. Neveu, *Un Historien à l'École de Port-Royal*, pp. 111–21.

by now that too much was at stake for him to keep silent and, after taking the advice of friends, published in March 1692 his *Response*[1] to Mabillon's book. Opinions had by now polarized, and even those who did not feel very strongly about study took sides for or against Rancé for other reasons. The good faith of leading Jansenists like Arnauld, Nicole, and Quesnel need not be questioned, their own contribution to learning was conspicuous, but they and others like them were not sorry to see Rancé harried by the Benedictines, whose champion, Mabillon, was above reproach as a Christian and a scholar.[2]

The controversy promised to be sterile at best, counter-productive, if it went on, and some of Rancé's closest friends, like du Charmel and Marcel, curé of Saint-Jacques, tried to effect a reconciliation. Soon Mme de Guise decided that things had gone far enough, but the most she could achieve by all her efforts was to bring about an interview between Rancé and dom Lamy, one of Mabillon's close colleagues, at which she presided. As invariably happened, Rancé showed himself much more conciliatory in speech than in writing, and the meeting gave some hope of a solution. It did not, however, prevent Mabillon sending off a second broadside in the shape of his *Réflexions* (September 1692),[3] but Mme de Guise was not so easily discouraged and was determined to end the dispute once and for all by bringing the two adversaries face to face. A settlement was overdue, for the debate was now assuming the proportions of a sporting event in which more and more participated.

A Benedictine of Tours, dom Denis de Sainte-Marthe, published anonymously in June 1692 *Quatre lettres...* violently and satirically attacking Rancé's *Response*, then the vehement J.-B. Thiers[4] replied with an equally inflammatory attack on Sainte-Marthe (addressed by name). At last in May 1693 Mme de Guise had her way. Mabillon had to attend a Chapter of his Congregation at Marmoutiers, near Tours, and she persuaded him to call at

---

[1] *Response au traité des études monastiques.*

[2] For the full correspondence and details see Mabillon, *Ouvrages posthumes*, i, pp. 365 seq.

[3] *Réflexions sur la response... au traité...*

[4] Thiers (1636-1703) had been curé of Champrond (diocese of Chartres) and then moved to Vibraye, where the marquise had to be persuaded by Rancé to accept such a notorious firebrand. At one time a fierce critic of Rancé, he then became a somewhat dangerous friend. He comes up frequently in Rancé's letters to Nicaise. See also Dubois, ii, p. 361.

la Trappe on his way back. On 27 May 1693 the two men met at last, and it restores faith in human nature to read with what respect and affection they greeted each other and made their peace. Neither changed his opinion, but misunderstandings were dissipated, and letters written by each of them to third parties leave no doubt as to the sincerity of their personal reconciliation.[1] Time after time one is forced to wonder whether the course of Rancé's life would not have been eased, and disputes less protracted, if he had not confined himself so rigorously to his cloister.

The next unpleasantness was no more than an epilogue to much of what had preceded. In August 1694 Arnauld died in exile, venerated almost as a saint by his followers. In the course of a letter to Nicaise (2 September 1694) on a number of other subjects Rancé casually commented on this recent event: 'Enfin, voilà M. Arnauld mort... Quoi qu'on en dise, voilà bien des questions finies: son érudition et son autorité étaient d'un grand poids pour le parti. Heureux qui n'en a point d'autre que celui de Jésus-Christ...'[2] These words seem harmless enough, perhaps a little dismissive, but divulged by Nicaise they infuriated the Jansenists, who saw in them gross disrespect for their hero. After Rancé's death Quesnel reflected (quite accurately, as it happens) that these were almost the last words Rancé could sign, for by October he had lost the use of his right hand permanently,[3] Quesnel saw in this a clear sign of God's judgement, but by Rancé's standards his remark was barely imprudent, even if it was not precisely a glowing testimonial. It must be realized that from this moment Maisne wrote and signed everything that emanated from Rancé, and as Rancé's state of health severely limited the number of interviews he could grant, the events of his last years must be treated with great caution.

The end of which he had been thinking and speaking for thirty years was finally in sight. A combination of ailments, probably tubercular and rheumatic in origin, drove him to the infirmary at the end of 1694 and he no longer had any choice but to tender the resignation of which he had so often spoken, and thus had the advantage of proposing to the King his own successor, dom Zozime Foisil, on 30 May 1695. Louis granted the request without

---

[1] See Mabillon, *Ouvrages posthumes*, loc. cit.
[2] Original *BN* 9363, f. 200; in Gonod, p. 245.
[3] To Vuillart 5 Jan. 1701, in *Correspondance*, ii, p. 125.

trouble, and at last Rancé laid down the burden of office, Zozime taking possession officially on 28 December 1695.[1] It is worthy of record that Petit's successor at Cîteaux, Nicolas Larcher (elected 1692), sent Rancé a particularly kind letter on his resignation, full of goodwill for la Trappe, which no one any longer regarded as a threat to the unity of the order.[2]

A malign stroke of fate allowed Zozime only a few weeks in office: after a brief but sudden illness he died on 3 March 1696 and Rancé had to approach the King again. Under the circumstances there was no reason to refuse a request so recently granted. This time the name proposed by Rancé was that of dom Armand-François Gervaise, for many years a Carmelite in the diocese of Meaux, and the last choir monk professed by Rancé (September 1695) and thus given the name Armand as a mark of respect.[3] As he had been a superior in his previous order and was already in his forties, Zozime had made him prior, so the choice of such a newcomer was not so strange as it might seem. Gervaise took possession on 18 October 1696, and once more it looked as though Rancé could enjoy peace of mind. It is true that Bossuet persuaded him to write two letters[4] in 1697 condemning Quietism, and therefore Fénelon, whose supporters were upset, but serious controversy was over. Trouble lay nearer home.

Gervaise lacked the wisdom of Zozime and the authority of Rancé, and had not long been in office before he became involved in two affairs which soon brought him to disaster.[5] He had the idea of taking over an abandoned monastery, l'Estrées, near Dreux, the property of the Missions Étrangères, as a sort of

[1] Zozime is the subject of a *relation* published in 1702 and subsequently.

[2] See Dubois, ii, pp. 467–8.

[3] Gervaise (1662–1715) remains a fascinating but perplexing figure. He joined the Carmelites about 1678, and by 1683, as P. Agathange, was teaching philosophy and theology; he was clearly a learned man. He became prior of Grégy (Meaux) and despite later charges seems to have been a respected member of his order. A brother became Bishop of Horren (Louisiana), an uncle, Aubereau, was at Sainte-Geneviève. He wrote voluminously (bibliography in Tournoüer) and, with all their errors and prejudices, his *Jugement critique* and *Histoire de la réforme... de Cîteaux* are perhaps the best evidence of the sort of man he was. He fell foul of Maisne and Saint-Simon, but le Nain treats him fairly enough. Perhaps if he had been accepted earlier he would have prospered under Rancé's guidance, but, as it was, every man's hand was against him and he can be accounted neither happy nor fortunate, dying more or less under arrest at le Reclus in Champagne.

[4] In Gonod, pp. 397–9.

[5] Dubois gives a full chronicle of events, but useful corroborative evidence can be found in the letters sent to Noailles mentioned below.

convalescent home for sick members of la Trappe, rather than as a colony, though he was clearly bent on expanding numbers considerably. To stake his claim, pending agreement with the owners, he sent a few monks to occupy the house, thereby technically infringing the royal ban on new foundations. This seriously harmed his reputation at Court. Then he fell foul of the Abbess of les Clairets, probably for showing her less deference than she deemed proper; and she and her equally haughty prioress (niece of Cardinal de Bouillon) behaved quite outrageously in spreading tales about a man whose worst crime was imprudence.

A more serious element is harder to define; for reasons which can only be guessed at, Maisne disliked Gervaise intensely and before long was conducting private intrigues to do him the maximum harm. So long as Rancé was alive he *was* la Trappe for everyone outside, and Maisne was his spokesman, but in day-to-day administration the lawful head of the house was Gervaise. Even if Rancé had been capable of giving constant and detailed instructions, it would have been intolerable for a properly appointed abbot to abdicate all responsibility to his ailing predecessor. It seems that Maisne, no doubt in league with other malcontents inside and outside the community, put it about that Gervaise was showing insufficient respect for Rancé and even undoing some of his work. Letters from the Visitandine sister of the late Archbishop of Paris, François de Harlay, fell into Gervaise's hands, and were so compromising that Gervaise ordered Maisne to leave. Next day, on Rancé's intercession, the order was rescinded, but the damage had been done. Gervaise tried to win peace by resigning direction of les Clairets and by renouncing the l'Estrées project, but it was all in vain. In July he sent his resignation to Louis, but it was not at once accepted.

The next few months were confused and painful. Rancé was too sick, Gervaise too bewildered to control events; serious, though limited, dissension had arisen in the community; and Saint-Simon, latest and perhaps most harmful of Rancé's friends, was intriguing outside, with the active complicity of Maisne inside. Dubois reduces the dispute to one between Jesuits (Gervaise had been their pupil) and Jansenists, but it is more probable that it arose from basic conflicts of human nature. In September the monks addressed a joint letter to the King, begging him to leave Gervaise in charge, and individual religious, as well as Maupeou, now curé

of Nonancourt nearby and brother of dom Grégoire, let alone
Maisne's ally since 1682, wrote to the Archbishop of Paris,
Noailles, variously attacking and defending Gervaise or dom
Malachie Garneyrin, Rancé's first choice for a successor, if it
should come to that.[1] In October Gervaise had a long interview
at Fontainebleau with Père de la Chaise, and proposed dom
Jacques de la Cour for the succession. Some of the letters just
mentioned confirm that the question of Jansenism came up, but
Saint-Simon's highly coloured account of Gervaise scaring Père
de la Chaise with talk of a takeover bid at la Trappe by a Jansenist
cabal is no more credible than the odious anecdote in which he
proudly asserts that proof of Gervaise's unnatural vice fell into
his hands.[2] The circumstances of the latter are so grotesque as to
cast grave doubt on all Saint-Simon says about la Trappe. Rancé
at any rate was in no state to intervene at all usefully, though there
survives a pathetic document written by a trusted monk, signed
(or rather initialled) by Rancé's impotent hand guided by this
secretary, telling Noailles that these words at least were authentic,
that is, not dictated by Maisne.[3]

   In the end, early in December 1698, Gervaise went, and dom
Jacques de la Cour became the third abbot to receive obedience
from Rancé.[4] Jacques took possession on 5 April 1699; in July
Gervaise withdrew to Clairvaux, apparently with some kind of
nervous breakdown, but did not stay there long, and with him
went two of his most loyal supporters, the prior, dom Jean-
Baptiste de la Tour, and the procurator. He died in 1751, more
or less under protective custody, at le Reclus in Champagne, and
remains a controversial and tumultuous figure.

   This was the end of conflict, and the last year of Rancé's life
was as peaceful as his illness allowed. He kept in touch with a few
friends, especially Bossuet and James II, but the end for which he
had longed was no longer a mirage. On 26 October 1700 he fell
into his final agony, and at noon next day he died, attended by
Mgr d'Aquin, the new bishop of Séez, who left an account of the
last hours.[5] The death of Richelieu's godson at a time when men

[1] Some originals in *SG* Suppl. ZZ f 316, f. 112, and Suppl. Z f. 829, copies at
Reims, Pinchart, VII, 1145, pp. 108–25. There is also a copy of a particularly veno-
mous letter to Rancé from the abbess of les Clairets about Gervaise in *U* 863, of 3
Apr. 1699.
[2] Saint-Simon, *Mémoires*, i, pp. 564 and 572.   [3] *SG* Suppl. ZZ f 316.
[4] On Jacques see below, p. 109.   [5] *Imago R.P.... de Rancé.*

looked forward to Louis XIV's successor was seen as the end of a man indisputably great but of another era. Tributes came from all the great names in Church and State, from James II and his Queen, from the Grand Duke of Tuscany, from innumerable prelates. One of the memorial services was held at Saint-Jacques-du-Haut-Pas, the Jansenist parish, to Quesnel's intense annoyance, though even he did not withhold a sincere if frank tribute.[1]

Rancé was hardly laid to rest before tales of miracles began to flourish, and Bossuet sent strict instructions to his Vicar-General, M. de Saint-André, to ensure the safe keeping of Rancé's papers.[2] For many of his friends canonization now seemed a foregone conclusion. There can be no doubt that this thought was a major factor in determining Maisne's equivocal conduct in the last years; he was not going to relinquish his prize so easily, and quite obviously saw himself basking in the reflected halo of his master for years to come, granting interviews and dispensing odds and ends of pious relics to the curious faithful. What one might call the Saint-Simon party—including M. de Saint-Louis, Godet des Marets, Bishop of Chartres, abbé Berryer, and others—were ready to use Maisne, but the complications of Jansenist policy and personal rivalry, the divisions within the monastery, and the accident of chronology which made Rancé outlive some of his closest friends (Barillon, le Camus, Félibien, Louise-Henriette) while others much older survived him (Favier, Mère Louise Rogier) did not facilitate a concerted approach. The same accident of chronology removed some of the key figures within a year or two: James II (1701), Nicaise (1701), Bossuet (1704), though Rancé's sister, Marie-Louise, and his brother, Henri, lived on a little longer, and this affected availability and disposal of papers.

The patient Maupeou had not waited twenty years only to allow himself to be beaten to the post, and his *Vie* came out in 1702. It seems clear that he had, through Maisne, had access to a number of original documents, but that at some stage the supply had dried up. Apart from some errors and patent untruths, Maupeou's work is chiefly remarkable for a substantial number of letters from Rancé to Val-Richer (who had died in 1693) which had somehow found their way into his hands and are unknown elsewhere. If Maupeou's was the first biography, another

---

[1] Quesnel to du Vaucel, 4 Dec. 1700, in *Correspondance*, ii, p. 115.
[2] *Correspondence*, xii, pp. 369–71, of 14 and 26 Nov. 1700.

work of more value can challenge his priority: in 1701 appeared a
volume of *Lettres de piété*, followed by a second in 1702.[1] Each
contained 111 letters, but such was the haste of the editor that one
letter was printed twice in the first volume, and the dating of the
sixty or so which are dated is erratic; while the others in both
volumes (hardly any are to named addressees and none in Vol. II
is dated) are in chaotic disorder, as was acknowledged indeed by
the editor and smugly noted by Maupeou, who quotes extensively
from them. The inclusion of a large number of letters from Rancé
to Mme de Guise (d. 1696) strongly suggests that someone at
least as important as Bossuet had a hand in this first serious
posthumous tribute.

Next on the scene came Marsollier, to whom Maisne seems to
have transferred his allegiance. He had been for a while at Sainte-
Geneviève, had not known Rancé, but had published other biographies. His *Vie* appeared in 1703, and includes a few documents
not available elsewhere but is incomplete and uncritical. What
happened next is obscure; Bossuet and his friends had from the
start wanted a simple, authentic life of Rancé, and had picked on
dom Pierre le Nain as the most suitable person to write it with
help from outside. The details are confused and obscure, and
some will be discussed in a later chapter on Jansenists, but the
basic facts seem to be as follows:[2] by 1706 dom le Nain had
finished his task, modifications were imposed on him for reasons
to do with Jansenism, then there were delays owing to official
objections to yet a third life of Rancé, then, in 1713, dom le Nain
died. An edition of his work appeared in 1715, and another, considerably modified, in 1719. The enormous merit of dom le Nain's
work is due first to his long and intimate acquaintance with
Rancé (whom he had served as secretary and to whom he was
even distantly related) and second to his familiarity with a vast
mass of correspondence which he concentrated at la Trappe
and farmed out to a team of copyists there and outside. His

[1] Like most of Rancé's works these were published by Muguet, but the identity of
the editor, or editors, is still uncertain.
[2] Some of the facts are to be found in a long statement signed on each page by
dom le Nain (original in *T* 2183, copy in *U* 3069). An important MS. copy of the
original *Vie*, containing details of names and dates not reproduced in published
versions, is at Carpentras, MSS. 625 and 626. It is uniquely helpful in correcting
Dubois, who slavishly copied everything that was before him though he claimed to
have known this MS.

approach is naïvely hagiographic, but his sincerity is unmistakable.

Meanwhile a fourth *Vie* was under way, and it is this, and the raw material collected for it, which is the origin of the standard life by Dubois.[1] Whether in concert with dom le Nain or independently, the former prior, dom de la Tour, had collected a mass of documentation from which he had drawn a draft life when he died in 1708. He had gone with Gervaise, and, as he died at Cîteaux, the fate of his papers is unknown. In one form or another Gervaise, also of course out of contact (officially at least) with the monastery, had access to them, and in particular to the vital collection of letters addressed to Mère Louise Rogier (d. 1709) and probably to Favier and Louise-Henriette d'Albon as well, all of which went to the Paris Oratory.[2] He proceeded to complete the work of dom de la Tour, and if his own credit had allowed (and if a fourth life could have been justified) would have published what is essentially Dubois's *Vie* not long after Rancé's death. As it was, all he could do was to correct Maupeou and Marsollier with some asperity (and dom le Nain more gently) in a work published in 1742, *Jugement critique mais équitable des vies de feu M. l'abbé de Rancé*.[3]

All these details arise from consideration of the events from 1682 when Maisne first announced his project to Favier, and go far to explain not only the divergent character of the four extant lives, but also the regrettable dispersal and even destruction of so much original source materials—once a document had been printed it was not usually retained—and Dubois also has a lot to answer for. Gervaise and dom de la Tour were anathema to Maisne and Saint-Simon; Maupeou was not up to his ambitious

[1] See Lekai's important article 'The Problem of the Authorship of Rancé's "Standard" Biography'.

[2] Batterel, writing after 1723, confirms that the letters to Mère Rogier were there, *Mémoires*, i, p. 396, note. The MSS. at the Arsenal (2106) and Mazarine (1214), containing letters to Favier and Mères Rogier, de la Roche, and d'Albon (all from the Visitation at Tours), apparently once belonged to P. Jean Galipaud (d. 1742), who is known to have been at Riom in 1688 (when Rancé's niece was superior of the Visitation there) and 1693, when Favier was still at Thiers nearby. (See Ingold, *Le R.P. Galipaud et le Jansénisme*.)

[3] The full title speaks for itself and is worth quoting: *Jugement critique mais équitable des vies de feu M. l'abbé de Rancé, réformateur de l'abbaye de la Trappe, écrites par les sieurs Marsollier et Maupeou, divisé en deux parties où l'on voit toutes les fautes qu'ils ont commises contre la vérité de l'histoire, contre le bon sens, contre la vraisemblance, contre l'honneur même de M. de Rancé et de la maison de la Trappe.*

task; Marsollier was no better. Poor dom le Nain was not left alone for a moment by his external patrons, but would have made an excellent collaborator with Gervaise. If Rancé had died sooner, before the Gervaise scandal, if his friends had lived longer, if Gervaise had not had to resign—the possibilities are endless; but from so much confusion one fact stands out with reassuring clarity: the definitive life was never written, Rancé was never canonized, but his community lived on, contrary to the almost unanimous predictions of both friends and enemies. In the continuing spiritual life of la Trappe and the modern Cistercians who owe so much to that one house is the only memorial he would have wanted or recognized. Rancé and la Trappe were, and are, one.

4. Character and Personality

THE one point on which all Rancé's contemporaries, friend or foe, agreed was that la Trappe was the creation of its abbot, and that he and he alone was the magnet that drew pilgrims or postulants, the devout and the merely curious. How far the Reformed Cistercians of our own day represent Rancé's spirit, or how far partisan biographies have made of Rancé something he never was, are difficult problems, but it is clear that any study of his personal influence must begin with some attempt to describe his character and personality. Later chapters will go into the detail of his activity within and beyond the walls of la Trappe, and it is obvious that his conversation produced an effect, at which we can only guess, different from that of his correspondence, but some idea of the man he was can be reconstructed from the available evidence.

His outstanding characteristic seems to have been great personal charm combined with relentless energy in pursuing what he considered to be God's purpose, for so he would always regard his own aims. His early life had given him the ease of manner which contemporary society demanded of all *honnêtes gens*. Socially he had every reason to feel secure, for his family was not, like that of La Rochefoucauld, for example, so exalted that he would feel resentment at seeing others preferred, while the solidity of his family's position in royal favour both reflected and encouraged their loyalty to the Crown. As a youth of gentle birth he had not had to struggle up the educational ladder, but it seems clear that his intellectual ability would have taken him to the top if he had had to rely on that alone. One must be wary of the somewhat stereotyped praises of physical beauty inevitably lavished on the subjects of seventeenth-century biography, and his only authentic likeness was drawn so late that it is not a wholly reliable guide,[1] but he seems to have taken considerable pride in his appearance when in the world, and after he had become a monk even those who opposed him bear witness to his commanding

---

[1] See L. Aubry, 'A la recherche du vrai portrait de Rancé'.

presence. An anonymous Benedictine describes him in 1667 as
'fort bien fait, d'une haute taille... parle avec agrément et facilité',[1]
while in 1693 the abbé Louail found him 'un vénérable vieillard...
air majestueux'.[2]

The formal courtesy of his class was displayed to all alike,
high or low, though it must be admitted that it is more of a
positive asset when gratuitously directed at a social inferior
than when deployed in the full amplitude of ceremonial for the
reception of some royal person or in fulsome compliments to
some distinguished correspondent. At the same time this un-
failing courtesy could be accompanied by a disconcerting directness. All through his life his letters contain quite devastating
comments on persons and conduct of which he disapproved,
often addressed to the victim, and it seems very probable that in
direct speech he was even more forceful. His biographers usually
ascribe to him all the theological virtues, including humility, but
he was certainly no respecter of persons. His regard and friendship for Retz, and indeed for most of the leading Frondeurs, can
have done him no good in Mazarin's eyes, and all his biographers
stress how vigorously, considering his age and rank, he stood up
to the Cardinal during the Assembly of 1657, while seven years
later in Rome he did not allow his respect even for the Pope to
restrain his advocacy of the Abstinents' cause. Once he became
regular abbot he was absolute master in his own house, subject
only to canonical visitation, and it is noteworthy that during the
thirty or so years of his rule the only complaints about arrogant
or high-handed treatment concern controversial visitors, like
Maupas or Wallon de Beaupuis,[3] when it would have been only
too easy for him to become dictatorial, and even perverse, as
some contemporary brother-abbots seem to have been.

The reason why these two principal qualities of charm and
single-mindedness did not degenerate during Rancé's long
enjoyment of absolute power can be expressed in ordinary human
terms as well as the theological ones preferred by hagiographers:
he cared passionately about the people entrusted to his care, and
though he may sometimes have erred in his judgement, he always
put their interests above his own. This applies particularly to his

---

[1] F.F.P.A., *Description de l'abbaye.. de la Trappe..*, p. 2.
[2] Louail, *Relation d'un voyage à Mayenne... et... la Trappe*, in U 1797.
[3] See above, p. 52.

religious community, whether professed monks or those seculars who were attached in one way or another to the monastery. The death of each one of them was a drama which seized the imagination of outsiders who read about it in the *Relations* periodically published, but for Rancé and his brethren it was in the most literal sense the moment of truth. Each of them, from the abbot to the newest novice, had given up everything the world esteems and had often forsaken a moderately hard life in some other order or monastery to seek salvation at la Trappe. For it cannot be said too often that the total self-denial and rule of penitence was only a means to this eternal end. Rancé saw no great merit in austerity as such, and indeed banned the more spectacular practices in favour of regular deprivation of comfort, food, sleep, and relaxation, but he incessantly reminds his monks that this life, in which the pains are endured, is but a flash compared to the terrifying extent of eternity. Thus the moment which brought each of the dying monks to his goal was a lesson for those he left behind; a lesson of the frightening pains the human body can endure and of the radiant joy with which the faithful soul greets its release to higher things. The *Relations* were criticized at the time, and modern critics tend to dismiss them as literary or pious exercises, but whether factually accurate or not they show, as do letters written by Rancé on the various occasions of his monk's deaths, that he considered it his sacred duty and privilege to attend those whose spiritual father he was.

These were by no means the only people, nor death the only occasion, that aroused his compassion and, to use a more homely word, kindness. Numerous letters to men and women whom he had never seen, and never would see, offer consolation and encouragement in every sort of adversity, sickness, bereavement, disappointment, or simply the psychological stress of religious life, with its inevitable doubts, fears, and scruples. Some of the most appealing letters are to religious who were either prevented for some reason from fulfilling their desire to end their days at la Trappe or, having tried the life there, had been obliged to leave, usually for lack of stamina. The mere fact that these countless appeals for help never went unanswered is in itself a measure of Rancé's abiding concern for others.

As in speech, so in writing he could be outspoken, and when some particularly silly or obstinate correspondent goes too far he is not slow to say so, but never in a purely negative way, rather with brisk instructions for amendment. More serious is his reaction to criticism of his methods or views, especially when expressed by churchmen who, in his opinion, should be following his example. This side of his character has been brilliantly, and maliciously, represented by Bremond, and it is doing Rancé no service to pretend that the caricature—for such it is—has no basis in fact. In worldly terms many of Rancé's polemical writings give an impression of pride and anger, and if Bremond had had access to unpublished material he could have made out an even more convincing case. For an observer from outside the cloister it is easy enough to see how Rancé gave way to sentiments which it would be absurd to defend, but less easy to see how his peculiar qualities of mind and spirit could have resisted temptation in the quite abnormal circumstances of his life.

From 1675 until his death, he left la Trappe only to make his canonical visits to les Clairets, and then only for a day or two altogether, but from the first moment of his installation as abbot he was the subject of comment and criticism, much of it uninformed, just as he found himself drawn into constant disputes over issues for which proper first-hand evidence was seldom available to him. He recognized one aspect of his own weakness when he wrote[1] (on at least two occasions) 'je suis aisé à tromper', which was certainly true, but he showed surprising insensitivity when he went on to explain that as in the world he had always tended to distrust men's motives (a very Retzian echo), so in religion he tended to trust them too easily. It is true that he was gullible, but unfortunately he was just as ready to condemn a superior or an order on the basis of clearly interested criticism from disgruntled informants as he was to be deceived by confidence tricksters like frère Chalype or Beauchâteau.[2] It must be remembered that at the time of his conversion Rancé was a coming young man, almost certainly destined to succeed his uncle in the see of Tours, well placed at Court following his appointment as Gaston's chaplain, and eminently acceptable in the cultured *salons* of Paris as a more than usually personable *abbé de cour*. This is what he gave up, not failure or frustration, and what he sought instead was, as he constantly writes, to be forgotten by men, to

[1] To Mme de Guise.
[2] See respectively p. 51, above, and p. 121, below.

pass the rest of his days in silence, penitence, and retreat. Un-happily his previous reputation and the clear evidence of his personal talents prevented him from enjoying the unbroken peace he had craved. Until his final visit to Paris in 1675, he was for some ten years forced into a position of prominence in the affairs of the Reform, and since the continuance of la Trappe in its reformed state depended to some extent (or seemed at the time to depend) on the future of the wider reform, one can see how he felt obliged to continue a fight from which he would gladly have withdrawn. Disputes with enemies inside the order, from the abbot of Cîteaux down, disputes with superiors angry at the defection of their religious to la Trappe, constant gossip and intrigue, all led to a most unwelcome publicity and exacerbated those very weaknesses within himself which he had sought to cure in the cloister. He never in fact achieved the clean break with his past reputation for which he had hoped, and on top of the activity into which he was driven in legitimate defence of la Trappe, he was increasingly solicited by those who were only too anxious to enlist him as a spokesman for their personal or partisan interests.

Up to a point this is what his fellow abbots had done when they sent him to Rome only weeks after his abbatial consecration, but there his mission was directly relevant to the life he had embraced, though it came as a cruel interruption. The same cannot be said for the activists of Port-Royal, who ceaselessly tried to embroil him in their affairs, nor for Bossuet, and other friends, who persuaded him, almost certainly against his own inclination, to publish *Sainteté* and thus involved him for the rest of his life in acrimonious and sterile polemic. In these two cases, as also in that of Quietism, the issues were clear enough, and of major importance, but Rancé's too-ready acceptance of unconfirmed reports comes out in numerous affairs. To name only a few instances, he writes in the most scathing terms of the whole Celestine Order, of neighbouring monasteries, like Champagne and Tironneau, of others far away, like Orval, Tamié, or Sept-Fons, of fellow abbots, like Dominique Georges of Val-Richer, in terms that ordinary prudence, let alone charity, should have kept from his pen. As the years go on, more and more remarks are addressed to his correspondents 'sous le secret'. Regrettably these show that he was as quick to believe the worst in others as he acknowledged he was to believe the best. On the other hand, Retz and James II[1] are historical figures concerning whom there is abundance of contemporary evidence, but if nothing else had survived but Rancé's remarks to and about them our picture of them would be vastly different. This is not to say that they lacked the admirable qualities he found in them, but simply that his contacts were too brief and one sided for him to form a balanced judgement.

In this connection two men, not otherwise of any great distinction, played a decisive role, already mentioned.[2] The calculated indiscretions of the abbé Nicaise, a professional busybody, did great harm while Maisne, the other, exercised influence of a much closer but less easily detectable kind. We do not, and in the nature of things cannot, know how much harm he did, but in the Gervaise affair his conduct, especially his association with Saint-Simon, can be fairly well assessed from surviving records and gives cause for considerable disquiet. One can never be quite sure to what extent Maisne put ideas into Rancé's head, but it is well to remember that by far the best-documented period of Rancé's life coincides with that of Maisne's ascendancy, and in the sombre final years after 1694 Maisne invariably signed for his incapacitated master.

Turning from personal qualities to spirituality, one finds that from first to last Rancé's emphasis is on penitence: on the sin and vanity to be expiated, on the specific features of the penitential life to be followed, and on the eternity for which that life was to be a preparation. It has been frequently pointed out by Rancé's critics that he came to monastic life very late, and that his year of novitiate at Perseigne (and that was abridged by illness) was the only direct experience or training he had received by the time he came to rule over his own community. This is both true and relevant, explaining as it does the highly personal and unusual interpretation of the Rule as practised at la Trappe, but it should not be regarded as a primarily negative criticism. Rancé's conversion, as we have seen, was as sudden and dramatic as that of his many contemporaries who underwent profound spiritual experiences, but his precise vocation became clear to him only after a long period of self-examination, trial, and error. From Mme de Montbazon's death in 1657 until his decision to withdraw to la Trappe in 1662, and then his decision to become a Cistercian and regular abbot, took fully seven years. If his conception of monastic

---

[1] See respectively pp. 213–16 and 265–71, below.   [2] See above, pp. 39–50.

life was not based on direct acquaintance with the cloister it was, perhaps more importantly, the final product of a long search for a way of life which would satisfy his own needs. At some point, and apparently very late in the process of elimination, he seems to have realized that an integral part of his vocation was to share this life with others and, above all, assume responsibility for their salvation. He repeatedly emphasized the role played in his spiritual development by his reading of the Desert Fathers, especially St. John Climachus, for whom his admiration was unbounded and whom he had come to know through Arnauld d'Andilly in the early years of his quest. As regards documentary sources for his ideas, especially in his published work, there is no room for doubt that this influence preceded, and deeply affected, that of SS. Benedict and Bernard, whom he studied seriously only later. The point needs to be made that Rancé selected the Desert Fathers out of a substantial programme of reading recommended by Andilly, and no doubt others too, and he did so because they seemed more relevant than other writers to his own situation.

Larroque's highly coloured tale about Mme de Montbazon[1] inevitably attracted the Romantic imagination of Chateaubriand, and ever since then the sinful life for which Rancé subsequently tried to atone has usually been equated with sexual delinquency of greater or lesser degree. It is pointless to speculate on his experience in this field, but it is abundantly clear that neither the course of his conversion nor his subsequent views on penance can be explained by the hypothesis that some act (or thought) of impurity inspired in him a revulsion strong enough to dominate his thinking. The key to his views on sin and penitence is renunciation of self, the temptations he fears are those for which obedience and humility are the remedies. Corporal mortification is an essential element of the penitential life, and naturally that which is reflected in signs most immediately visible to the outside observer. The hard work, meagre diet, and so on certainly punish the body, and because this issue was the ostensible reason for the dispute between the Abstinents and the other Cistercians it has assumed undue prominence. Rancé was indeed inflexible in his refusal to make any concessions to bodily infirmity, but only because he saw such concessions as the prelude to further self-indulgence which must inevitably put self-love in the place of love

[1] See above, p. 48.

of God. The bitter controversy over humiliations and then the one over monastic study, show what Rancé really cared about. On the positive side he always warns intending postulants of the severity of the climate and arduous labour at la Trappe because he could not properly run a community in which too many members were sick, but silence and solitude, as he says, are much harder to bear. It is the will, not the body, that is the real enemy. Like Pascal, Rancé had recoiled from the vanity, the uselessness of a worldly life, which instead of lasting satisfaction could offer only a succession of equally illusory diversions. Thus the Desert Fathers, with their totally uncompromising insistence on self-denial, represented the opposite extreme to that which he had abandoned.

It is no accident that a phrase which recurs several times in his letters (and in *Sainteté*) should represent the total and definitive nature of the monk's sacrifice in terms of the grave: speaking sometimes of himself, sometimes of others, he opposes any absence from the monastery, let alone translation for personal convenience, on the grounds that the place of profession is to be regarded as the tomb. He says too that the monk 'livre son corps à une mort volontaire'.[1] From a very early date in his correspondence he speaks of his own physical death as imminent, and it is certain that he suffered constant ill health throughout his monastic career, but the preoccupation with death is invariably accompanied by assertions of his submission to God's will, of the insignificance of this life, and of the last judgement to be encountered for all eternity. The penitence, in fact, is both a renunciation of self and a renunciation of all earthly (and not just worldly) things which might deflect attention from God.

It may seem paradoxical, or even inconsistent, but in the advice he gave to men and women outside la Trappe, and from what we know of his policy inside, he lays some stress on the importance of moderation in external penitence, and on the primacy of interior dispositions. He fully recognized the value of an active ministry, and frequently dissuaded those engaged in such work from forsaking it for the solitude and silence of la Trappe. He recognized too the importance of family and social obligations, and quite often curbed the excessive ardour of those (usually women) who proposed to abandon everything but manifestly lacked any true vocation. One must not make oneself conspicuous,

[1] *Sainteté*, ii, xvi. vi, p. 32.

whether within or without the cloister; one must obey one's superior or director and acknowledge one's own insignificance. The monk's goal must be absolute sacrifice, but Rancé never thought this attainable by all, and never suggested that the only path to salvation lies in life such as it was led at la Trappe. For true religious, however, there can be no half measures, and those who count the cost or set a limit on their sacrifice are simply betraying their vocation. The opening words of *Sainteté* leave no room for doubt: 'Qu'est-ce qu'un véritable religieux?—C'est un homme qui, ayant renoncé, par un vœu solennel, au monde et à tout ce qu'il y a de sensible et de périssable, ne vit plus que pour Dieu et n'est plus occupé que des choses éternelles.'[1]

One of the main reasons for the general failure to appreciate Rancé's personality properly is that the published evidence is so one-sided. His most famous book, *Sainteté*, grew out of talks delivered over the years to his own monks, who needed no persuasion to follow the life at la Trappe, but who found in chapter and verse precedent and authority. The publication of the work in its present form was widely seen as implicit criticism of monastic practice outside la Trappe, and Rancé was driven from one polemical position to another, so that the impression of irascible, dogmatic rigidity is hard to refute. To see things in a truer perspective one must realize that the book was not a theoretical work, or an *ex cathedra* instruction for strangers, but a record, with historical justification, of what had been achieved at la Trappe over a period of some twenty years. It was also an attempt to set before the countless religious men and women whose aspirations could not be satisfied by translation to la Trappe a reasoned statement of what they could do, and why they should try. Some of the earlier mistakes committed at la Trappe, for instance, the excessively long fasts in Lent, were initially proposed not by the abbot but by his monks, but in the course of time, as familiarity welded the community together, a corporate life based on solid experience proved its worth day after day, year after year. To separate Rancé and his published work from the source of his confidence is a cardinal error of many of his critics.

It is certain that other rules, and other superiors, were just as efficacious in attracting recruits and providing spiritual satis-

[1] *Sainteté*, i, I, p. 1.

faction, but this is a positive, not a comparative question. Rancé only admitted those whom he judged capable of profiting from life at la Trappe, but, once they had been professed, often after many years' vain application, the failure rate was small of those who could not persevere. It is this long record of success with specific individuals, each one of whom he knew intimately, that lies behind Rancé's apparent intransigence. It is also relevant that in the course of discussing orally or by letter the vocations of those who wished for one reason or another to transfer to la Trappe, Rancé came to know the spiritual needs and dissatisfactions of a great number of religious, who may well have misrepresented the true state of affairs in their own houses, but are much less likely to have misrepresented what they found particularly attractive at la Trappe. This is another way of saying that, for all his rigidity in print, Rancé was a pragmatist, and recommended only what he saw to be working. It is only right to add the argument *a posteriori*: since the rule at la Trappe remained substantially the same until the Revolution, it would seem to have promoted rather than discouraged vocations even after Rancé's death, for only Cîteaux and Clairvaux came near la Trappe in numbers in 1789.[1] For the small spiritual élite involved, figures are not statistically very significant compared to the population at large, but in the specifically monastic context they cannot be disregarded.

These considerations of practical experience are directly relevant to another of the controversies in which Rancé became involved, though less bitterly than on other occasions. About ten years before publication of *Sainteté* Rancé had been asked by Floriot, a friend of Nicole, to give his views on the *Morale du Pater*.[2] One of the points raised concerned the duties of religious to their parents, whether, for example, they should be released permanently or temporarily from their monastery to help parents in sickness or indigence. Rancé had forcefully expressed the opinion that final vows are final, and that other means must be found for satisfying the law of charity and relieving such parents.

[1] See tables in Lekai, *The White Monks*, pp. 277–82, giving numbers and income for all Cistercian houses in France in 1768 according to the Commission of Regulars. The exact basis of the figures is unclear, but la Trappe comes first with 67 religious, then Cîteaux with 60 and Clairvaux 54. The respective incomes are very revealing: 17,000 *livres* (very modest), 70,000 and 78,711 (the two highest).

[2] See above, p. 48, n. 2.

In *Sainteté* he devotes a whole chapter to this evidently very real problem, and reaffirms the principle that a religious ceases to exist for the world outside once he has bound himself by vows. His views are stated in quite uncompromising terms, with reasoned argument, it is true, but without the slightest concession to human affections. On a purely practical plane, even before modern ideas of welfare states, some material relief could often be organized locally by the parish or some charitable body, and Rancé explicitly mentions that the monastery itself may well treat such dependants as first charge on their permanent obligation to dispense alms, but he goes out of his way to exclude the religious concerned from any participation in, or knowledge of, such relief. It would be idle to deny that this was indeed the principle he followed, but to take the abstract formulation out of its context of particular cases is again to falsify the picture of Rancé. There is documentary evidence that dom le Nain wrote annually to his father,[1] and at least sometimes to his Carmelite sister, throughout the many years of his professed life, and Rancé himself sent consoling messages when M. le Nain lost his sight. He always took great pains in composing letters of condolence to the parents of religious who had died, as he did to others who were bereaved and shows a fully human compassion at their loss. It is probable, though there is no evidence one way or another, that he withheld systematically from his monks news of their families (though there may have been other exceptions besides dom le Nain), but it is perfectly clear that this was, as he thought, in their best interests, to avoid disturbing the peace they had come to seek.

A much more positive aspect of this same question is Rancé's affective relationship with his monks. His personal involvement in their life and death is obvious and intense, and it is quite clear that nothing contributed more to the spiritual prosperity of the monastery. We know that he was normally confessor to all his monks (though they were free to choose others) and that he was not merely available at any time to give advice and encouragement, but spent many hours each week doing so as a matter of course.[2] It is self-evident that a normally affectionate son, especially in early manhood, cannot suddenly abandon his earthly family for a monastery, where all human affection is transferred to single-minded love of God, without serious problems of emotional

---

[1] Bibliography in Tournoüer, s.v. *le Nain*.　　[2] See Félibien, *Description*, p. 68.

adjustment. Rancé's genius seems to have been to fill what might be called the role of father figure and to transform a community of adult men into a family, rather than a regiment. Heroic as their endurance was, moral as well as physical, his monks remained human, helping each other and receiving constant help from their abbot.

The seventeenth century was an age preoccupied with violent passions and the means of controlling them, but whereas the outside world sought moderation through reason as a matter of prudence and expediency, Rancé's monks were exhorted to turn self-love, root of all the passions, into self-denial so that charity, loving God and one's neighbour as oneself, could fill the gap. Everyone, Christian or not, is familiar enough with this sort of exhortation, and if it so often falls on deaf ears it is because example is better than precept. To love is not to spoil, affection is not sentimentality, and the abbot could be harsh in day-to-day dealings with his monks, but it was precisely because he was more concerned with their spiritual health than his own popularity that he made no concessions to weakness, in them or in himself. However harsh he was, and it is hard to believe that the systematic use of humiliations was always necessary, they knew that he would never abandon them. The emotional needs of monks, three centuries ago, is not a fit subject for amateur speculation from a layman, but it is simply incredible that visitors should have reported the atmosphere of joy and serenity unless these needs had been satisfied, sublimated we might say, so as to preserve humanity in men who would otherwise have become insensitive, or fanatical, or completely self-absorbed. In this connection it is interesting to note that Rancé recognized that a very few men have a genuinely eremitical vocation, and over the years he allowed at least two solitaries to live in the woods near la Trappe, but without becoming professed members of the community.[1] Here, as is so often the case, he showed remarkable freedom from any doctrinaire notions of what ought to be good for people.

It is very commonly asserted by the critics of monastic life, and these include deeply religious persons, that an element of escapism is a strong, or main, component of such retreat, that monks and

[1] M. Nocey, the former Oratorian (see below, p. 99), and the former Paris grocer, M. Lyon (see p. 120, below).

nuns are people who cannot or will not face up to reality. The same reproach is also quite often levelled at scholars in their so-called ivory towers, perhaps with more justification, but, however that may be, it is well enough known that study, and especially the patient accumulation of facts, can be wholly absorbing for its own sake. Rancé forbade his monks to study (though again exceptions, like dom le Nain, are known) and provoked violent opposition by categorically excluding study from the proper pursuits of the true monk, first in *Sainteté*, then in the series of polemic works directed at his critics. Among his reasons for the ban was the pride that might result from such an occupation, but his fundamental objection was that study encouraged escape from the sole duty of religious life, that is meditation, prayer and penitence. He himself was a man of wide culture and, as his opponents were not slow to observe, considerable erudition, displayed in his published works, but the dangers of distraction from total commitment to work and prayer in his eyes outweighed any benefit to be derived from study. As for theology, he was adamant in forbidding discussion of theological questions at la Trappe. In the controversial context of the age, when all theologians had to take a view for or against Jansenism, this ban is understandable, but even without the fear that partisan loyalties would cause argument and even hostility within the community, Rancé was consistent in preventing his monks from engaging in any activity not directly necessary to their elected way of life. Intellectual abstinence represents at least as much of a sacrifice to some people as bodily abstinence.

It was partly for this reason, partly for reasons of a practical kind, partly because of his lofty conception of the priesthood, that Rancé almost never sent his monks for ordination.[1] Very many of them, of course, had come as priests, secular or regular, to la Trappe and there were more than enough for the liturgical needs of the community, so much so that some ceased to exercise priestly functions on profession. Anonymity, humility, total surrender of self constituted necessary, not optional, features of religious life for Rancé, and anything likely to relieve the monotony was suspect in his eyes. At the same time he left the monk very

[1] See letter of about 1675 to a fellow abbot (? of Sept-Fons) in Muguet, ii, p. 402. He did in fact send to Séez a good deal later Bazile Marteau and, on his death, Bazile Anzoux to be ordained priest and sub-deacon respectively.

little time to himself. As the details of the timetable clearly demonstrate, Rancé's conception of piety is not what would generally be considered contemplative. His own energy must have been prodigious; for on top of the hours spent at Divine Office or manual labour (which he normally shared with his monks) he bore the burden of administration, deciding on admissions, on economic policy, conducting chapter and conferences, interviewing visitors, and, an enormous burden, dealing with his correspondence or composing his books. Such a routine of intense activity left little time for quiet prayer and meditation, but in theory as in practice Rancé seems to have taken literally the motto 'laborare est orare'. Once again his attitude was essentially pragmatic: an hour with a spade or hoe, an hour spent in choir, may not bring the soul to ecstasy but, within broad limits, some results are guaranteed; while an hour of solitary contemplation, even by one versed in techniques of prayer, may often appear to be quite fruitless. Besides, all the emphasis at la Trappe, and in the Cistercian tradition generally, was on corporate as opposed to private life, and in this Rancé was by no means imposing on his monks a personal view of spirituality.

A further aspect of his spirituality needs to be approached with some caution: in his works and in his letters his references to the Virgin and saints are very sparse, perhaps surprisingly so. Setting aside quotations from or mentions of saints concerned with monastic life, from the Desert Fathers to St. Teresa, or with matters of discipline and doctrine, from St. Augustine to St. Charles, one finds almost nothing. What is particularly striking is his reticence about the Virgin. Even when writing to nuns, or on one of her feasts, Rancé almost never mentions her. One of his biographers goes out of his way to stress Rancé's deep reverence for Mary and his insistence that his monks should always mention her name with special respect, but this is in the context of an allegation that worship of the Virgin and saints was neglected at la Trappe (a familiar charge against supposed Jansenist sympathizers).[1] It is significant that an unpublished manuscript of some 700 pages consisting of an alphabetical anthology of Rancé's writings on every conceivable subject from *Abstinence* to *Zèle*

---

[1] Marsollier, *Vie*, ii, p. 125. Even Bremond *L'Abbé Tempête*, p. 112, quotes dom le Nain without argument, 'il ne prononçait jamais le nom de Marie sans incliner la tête.'

has only a single entry under *Vierge*.[1] At least one piece of evidence proves that this is reticence rather than indifference. When Rancé enlarged and altered the abbey church he replaced the usual tabernacle with a pyx, in which the Sacrament was reserved, suspended from the arm of a statue of the Virgin placed above the altar.[2] This unusual (but not unique) arrangement is as eloquent in its symbolism as any number of pious references in writing. In any case Cistercians have always, following St. Bernard's example, had a special devotion to the Virgin (they include her Little Office in their canonical hours), and no one who has attended the *Salve Regina* which concludes the Cistercian day will forget how deeply moving it is. In this la Trappe was no exception.

All this seems to be another instance of Rancé's general dislike for expressing emotion which he none the less felt deeply and of his reluctance to introduce variety into a single-minded concentration on God and penitence. He often included lives of saints in his lists of recommended reading, and their example must have helped him as it has helped others, but he treats the relationship between God and sinner as something essentially direct in which analogies and examples might prove distracting.

Apart from bereavements, no situation evoked from Rancé a more positive and humane response than illness, especially when chronic and incurable. He invariably made light of his own considerable ill health, though some of his distinguished friends, like Bellefonds or Mme de Guise, obliged him to report on it and even on occasion to try their remedies. There can be no doubt that he was drawing on his own spiritual reactions to sickness and the prospect of imminent death when he wrote to encourage and console invalids like Mlle de Vertus or Mme de la Sablière, or the several nuns whose constant infirmities come as a saddening refrain throughout many years of correspondence.[3] Like Pascal, himself a martyr to severe ill health for most of his life, Rancé saw such afflictions as a means sent by God both to aid in our self-mortification and to bring us to prepare adequately for death and judgement. Though this sounds grim, the actual letters are far from being so, and in the one case where his correspondent's letters survive rather than his (Mme de la Sablière) it is quite clear that he helped a great deal.

---

[1] *BN* 19324.   [2] Marsollier, *Vie*, ii, p. 84.
[3] See below, pp. 286–90.

His correspondence with women, especially society ladies, shows that they sought, and enjoyed, his advice in no spirit of masochism, but because he was understanding, if stern, and gave them the support they needed. This is perhaps another way of saying that the most effective sympathy may well be unemotional and, as has already been noted, people realized how much Rancé cared for them despite his reticence. Equally relevant is his sensitive handling of the very varied problems presented to him. It has been suggested somewhere that Molière may have had Rancé in mind when he composed Orgon's paraphrase of Tartuffe's counsel to despise the world, including his family, in favour of his blind dependence on the false man of God.[1] Such a view cannot survive acquaintance with Rancé's letters, where we find, to take only a few examples, advice to a husband estranged from his wife, to a daughter at odds with her mother, to a widow wondering how to cope with penniless daughters. Yet again it results from misapplying his remarks about religious, who by their vows effectively forsake all family ties, to people living in the world.

His good sense and humanity come out very clearly in a number of letters written to people like Mme de Guise, or Bellefonds, or the Bishop of Luçon, about the time of the Revocation of the Edict of Nantes. Such friends were in a position to direct events, and thus his observations on the treatment of Huguenots are more in the nature of advice to be followed than mere comment on current affairs. He comes out very strongly against compelling them to attend Catholic services, and equally against driving them into exile. For him the vital question is their salvation, not statistics of conversion or administrative convenience; and, since he believes the Catholic faith to be manifestly true, he is convinced that more will be converted, and more effectively, by gentle instruction than by coercion. He approves in the same spirit as Bossuet of Louis' suppression of heresy and never concedes that there is any room in God's kingdom, let alone in France, for active supporters of error, but he is not vindictive. In his own preference for austerity and simplicity in liturgy and architecture, and in his uncompromising moral austerity, he was temperamen-

---

[1] *Tartuffe*, Act II, sc. v, 'Qui suit bien ses leçons goûte une paix profonde/ Et comme du fumier regarde tout le monde.' The analogy is developed in Varin, *Vérité sur les Arnauld.*

tally a true disciple of St. Bernard, and totally opposed to the
Jesuit spirit, but in obedience and doctrine he never wavered for
a moment from strict orthodoxy of a pre-Tridentine flavour.

To the question of his Gallicanism it is hard to give a definite
answer. He always took care to maintain close relations with
Rome, and there is no reason to doubt his sincerity when he
speaks of his fidelity to the Pope or his deference for cardinals.
When he writes about the King or his family, however, it is with a
fervour far exceeding conventional compliment, and towards the
end of his life, when William of Orange threatened French
security and expelled James II, Rancé's patriotism knows no
bounds. *Te Deums* are sung for French victories, for Louis's
recovery from illness, prayers are offered for James and his family,
and for once Rancé obviously broke his rule of keeping the monks
in ignorance of outside affairs. His family record, and his own
attachment to Gaston, predisposed him to be more than usually
enthusiastic about the King; then the powerful support of Anne
of Austria, and later of Louis himself, in the struggle to establish
the Reform, and specifically to safeguard the future of la Trappe,
put him directly in debt to the Crown; but perhaps the influence
of Bossuet, accredited spokesman of Gallicanism, was the decisive factor in forming Rancé's attitude. At all events he went to
great lengths to win and maintain royal favour, and on his side
Louis seems to have held Rancé and la Trappe in real esteem, not
least because no party had managed to enlist them and their
independence commanded respect.

The nickname that Bremond has made famous, 'l'abbé Tempête', is not altogether inappropriate, but it is incomplete. Rancé
is very fond of images like the storm, rough seas, and so on, but
always in the context of the peace and haven awaiting the bat-
tered traveller. The English title 'The Thundering Abbot' is
particularly inept, and can only be justified if Rancé's life is identified with the succession of disputes in which he was indeed engaged, but only as part of his many-sided activity. It is true that
he saw the world as a bad place, that he had no time for laughter
or frivolity, that he was obsessed with the pointlessness and
mutability of this life compared to eternity. His style is never
comfortable, though it can be comforting, and a kind of apocalyptic gloom, with prophecies of divine wrath and universal dis-
solution, is very characteristic. A puff of smoke, a bird on the

branch, the dizzy speed with which life rushes by are images as typical as that of the storm, but to stop there is to mistake the means for the end. Peace, certainty, joy are what Rancé believes in. They have to be earned (and can never be deserved), but even in this life they are not out of reach. A set of commemorative essays published a few years ago included one by dom Jean Leclercq simply entitled 'La Joie dans Rancé',[1] and, as one would expect from such an authority, it is a wholly convincing demonstration, without special pleading, that joy is at the heart of Rancé's spirituality. He hated Paris (variously described as Babylon and Nineveh); he pitied his friends who had to live at Court, or assume high office in Church or State; he saw cultivated society as a threat to spiritual health; but simple life in a rural retreat, edifying family and domestics with pious instruction, he accepted as being perfectly compatible with giving oneself to God, with lasting joy and satisfaction.

There is a lot of the Old Testament prophet about Rancé, as there had been with the Desert Fathers, and it would be absurd to picture him as a smiling, gentle figure of universal appeal, a Francis of Assisi or of Sales, but it was not a smiling, gentle world he had abandoned. Pascal, La Rochefoucauld, Racine are far from reassuring in their depiction of man, and, if their testimony is suspect because tinged with the influence of Port-Royal, do Boileau, La Bruyère, even Molière show a world of peace and joy? The hollowness of daily life, the discrepancy between reality and appearance are constant themes in the *grand siècle*, and Rancé followed them to their logical conclusion. Objectively it is debatable whether life for most people (or most thinking people) was as frustrating and tedious as so many writers of the age seem to suggest, but subjectively it is quite certain that many men and women who shared these views found in private retreat, or the cloister, the serenity and fulfilment that eluded them in the world. To the extent that Rancé tried to communicate to others that he had once felt as they did but had then found the remedy, it is not too far-fetched to speak of him as a healer of the sick, a bringer of lasting joy if not of instant happiness.

[1] In the tercentenary number of *Collectanea*, xxv, 1963.

PART II

RANCÉ'S INFLUENCE IN THE CLOISTER

5. La Trappe

JUST why Rancé gave up his original plan of retiring to his Grammontine priory of Boulogne, near Chambord, in favour of la Trappe remains a mystery, but with hindsight one can see that he chose the only one of his five benefices which offered full scope for his talents and satisfaction of his needs. He so often speaks of the situation and climate of his 'desert' that it is very probable that these are what first appealed to him, and what invariably excited the comments of visitors. There was briefly some question of founding a community in the Pyrenees, in the diocese of Pamiers, and in a letter to the bishop, Caulet (1672), Rancé speaks approvingly of the remoteness of the region and the basic needs (e.g. water supply) of a monastic site.[1] Similarly his friend le Camus also offered him a site in the Alps in his diocese of Grenoble,[2] and though neither of these proposals came to anything, they both help to explain the qualities Rancé sought in the place which, as he so often says, is to be as it were his tomb. An even more circumstantial statement is contained in a letter to a Carthusian friend of his (20 January 1672)[3] where, quoting St. Bernard, he recalls that monks go into monasteries to destroy, not to preserve, their lives: 'nos maisons n'ont été bâties dans les vallées humides et malsaines qu'afin que nos santés n'y étant point assurées, et y étant souvent malades, nous eussions incessamment devant les yeux l'image de la mort.' The unhealthiness of the site is a point to which he returns time after time in his letters. To a nun who comments on the recent deaths of rather many of his monks, he attributes this less to their self-imposed austerities than to the site (24 June 1685):[4] 'entre 9 ou 10 étangs, environné de forêts' and often foggy, and he goes on with splendid understatement: 'les vents qui nous viennent le long des bois et des étangs nous apportent des froideurs et des humidités malignes et pénétrantes qui font sur les corps des impressions fâcheuses.' Anyone who knew the present monastery before the installation of central heating will appreciate the rigours endured by Rancé

---

[1] *TB* 92 of 23 July 1672. [2] Le Camus, *Lettres*, 51, to Arnauld, 28 Oct. 1673.
[3] *TB* 31, dom Simon Guérin. [4] *TC* I/98.

and his contemporaries. Summer was no better, with continuing humidity, and fever seems to have been a permanent hazard. The earliest extant full-length description of la Trappe (André Félibien, 1671) mentions these facts, and adds the detail that Rancé had had the main road from Mortagne to Paris re-routed so that it no longer disturbed the silence by passing, as it originally did, some 500 yards from the enclosure.[1] In letters Rancé sometimes refers to heavy rains making roads impassable, and in seventeenth-century conditions it is obvious that la Trappe was not easy of access to the hundreds of visitors who annually made their way there.

These points are of some importance both for understanding Rancé's intentions and the quality of life at la Trappe, and also for the impression they made on the public, for whom the monastery eventually acquired its own mythology. Rancé was, of course, quite right to cite the authority of St. Bernard in connection with monastic sites, and the medieval founders of la Trappe were following Cistercian practice (actually that of Savigny, soon to be taken over by Clairvaux) in choosing such a spot; but over the centuries the monks and their dependants, and the crowds of pilgrims, had so often made the desert bloom that monasteries were no longer automatically associated with wildness. An interesting example of the force of this Trappist mythology is the rather tart comment made in a manuscript review (24 March 1703) of Maupeou's recently published *Vie*.[2] The anonymous author (a Jansenist) is only a qualified admirer of Rancé, and has no use for Maupeou at all, but one of the numerous points on which he takes issue with the latter is the common belief that la Trappe is set in a peculiarly wild and remote place. If the reader really wants to see a monastery, he says, that is wild and remote, he should go a few miles from la Trappe to the small Carthusian priory of Val-Dieu (the author's brother was a Carthusian), but such an insignificant little house can of course not compete with Rancé's famous abbey. Thus, on so apparently objective a fact as the topography of la Trappe, mythology had provoked partisan sentiments.

If the location of la Trappe contributed both to Rancé's penitential intentions and to the abbey's reputation in the world outside, the same is true of the diet prescribed at the monastery.

[1] *Description*, p. 6.   [2] In U 812x.

Though perfectly well authenticated, the story of the duc d'Or-léans's (the future Regent) visit in 1693 belongs, with Mme de Montbazon's skull, to the folklore of la Trappe: duly edified by what he saw, the Prince took back with him to Versailles a sample of the bread served at the monastery, and the sleek, well-fed courtiers passed it round with appropriate exclamations.[1] It is fair to ask how they would have reacted to a similar exhibition of a peasant's daily fare at that time of rural penury, but, of course, one represented the voluntary choice of a noble abbot, the other the inevitable consequence of the inequality and extravagance on which life at Court depended. However that may be, the external signs of penitence are easily understood by outsiders, and in any case had long symbolized the split within the Cistercians (and indeed many monastic orders) between reformed and mitigated observance. It is quite absurd to pretend, as so many critics of the time and down to the present day have done, that the issue of flesh eating was the only, or even the main, source of contention, but, as with such other distinctions as Calced and Discalced (for Carmelites), it has become useful shorthand for two radically opposed points of view.

Since the history of ideas, or spirituality, is as much concerned with misunderstandings as with facts, it is useful to start with the sources of the Trappist legend, rather than with a strictly chrono-logical account of the facts. After his journey to Rome, Rancé had been back at la Trappe less than five years when two books appeared which spread his fame with more enthusiasm than discretion, and to which can be traced many of the beliefs commonly held about life at la Trappe. One of these is the so-called *Constitutions de la Trappe* of January 1671, with a brief historical and laudatory preface, which much later was expanded and published as *Règlements de la Trappe* and accompanied by a letter over the signature of an otherwise unknown abbé de Lignage (possibly the abbé de Villars, Bellefonds's nephew), also dated 1671. The other is the most famous of all the *Descriptions de la Trappe*, often (despite his explicit denial) attributed to the Oratorian Toussaint Desmares, then living at Liancourt, near Beauvais, but now generally acknowledged to be the work of André Félibien des Avaux (1619–95), the distinguished historian and architect, whose brother Pierre, canon of Chartres, was one of Rancé's most

[1] Dubois, ii, p. 389.

intimate friends and frequent visitors.[1] The book was printed on
9 February 1671 and describes the most recent of several visits,
which, from internal evidence, had taken place between September and Christmas 1670. Written in the form of a letter to Mme de
Liancourt (wife of Arnauld's celebrated 'duc et pair'), it is short
and very readable, accompanied by a neatly drawn plan of the
abbey, and it met with understandable success, going into numerous editions. It is incidentally this little book, translated into
English apparently by James Drummond[2] (later Duke of Perth),
which may first have aroused the interest of James II in la Trappe.
Apart from a very detailed topographical description, it contains a
summary of the daily life, with precise details of the timetable
and various austerities practised, a historical account of Rancé and
his reform, and some interesting personal touches from one who
clearly knew and loved him well.

Publication of these two books caused Rancé considerable
embarrassment for, as has been shown, the protracted dispute
with the Common Observance was moving into its most critical
and final phase, and the position of la Trappe and its abbot was
already sufficiently anomalous for wide publicity to constitute a
real threat. It should, therefore, be seen as something more than
the ritual disavowal of authorship so common in the age, when
Rancé writes to an unknown correspondent (perhaps du Suel):
'ces deux Ecritures... nous n'y avions nulle part... ils paroissent
sans notre participation... Pour ce qui est des *Constitutions*, vous
savez que nous avons quelques petits règlements... mais ils sont
si peu de chose, que l'on ne peut pas les nommer des constitutions.
Ils sont fort différents de ceux que vous nous avez envoyés,
quoiqu'ils conviennent en quelques articles.'[3] Answering a query
from dom Robert Couturier, a monk of Barbeaux appointed prior
of Preuilly in 1664, he writes (12 December 1671) of the 'pré-
tendues constitutions de la Trappe' that 'ce sont quelques petits
règlements pour le dedans de la maison auxquels on a voulu
donner le nom de constitutions dont ils ne sont pas dignes... nous
avons pris des *Us* [de Cîteaux] tout ce que nous avons pu...'[4] A
little later he tells dom François Weber, monk of Heisterbach,

---

[1] For a discussion of the authorship see Tournoüer, *Bibliographie*, s.v. *Desmares*.
[2] See A. Joly, *James Drummond, duc de Perth*. I have been unable to authenticate the
story of his alleged translation.
[3] Du Suel, *Entretiens de l'abbé Jean*, p. 735.   [4] Original in *SS*.

that la Trappe follows as faithfully as possible the *Us* and statutes of Cîteaux (14 May 1672).[1] Much later (26 May 1690), in a very important letter addressed to abbé Têtu, the companion of his original retreat at Véretz, he is formal and consistent: 'Pour ce qui est des *Règlements*... les novices en ont même souvent emporté les originaux avec eux, ce sont les mêmes qui furent imprimés il y a vingt ans' (sc. 1671).[2]

Thus what Rancé is denying is not so much the facts disclosed in these documents as their official status. Leloczky examines in great detail the manuscript Constitutions of the Abstinents (probably composed 1660–6 but never authorized for publication)[3] and compares their text with that of Rancé's own version (preserved in a Latin manuscript with facing French translation) of *Declarationes* on the Rule of St. Benedict, which diverges in a number of places.[4] The historical significance of the Trappist rules (under whatever name) has already been discussed, but it is worth recalling that just before the final settlement of 1675 a pamphlet put out by the aggrieved claustral priors of the Abstinents[5] praises Rancé and approvingly describes the regime at la Trappe as 'une réforme particulière'. Caught up in the ceaseless flood of polemic, with charges and countercharges, allegations and denials, the real situation at la Trappe, let alone its canonical status, is not completely clear, but, for all Rancé's denials, the *Constitutions* and *Description* come as near to being reliable documentary evidence as one can now hope to get. It must, however, be realized that, short of joining the community at least temporarily (like Maupeou), chroniclers of la Trappe were much more likely to rely on such written sources, cross-checked wherever possible by questioning the very few monks encountered by guests, than to find out for themselves. It is not altogether fanciful under such circumstances to say 'in the beginning was the legend'.

As regards the diet, legend could hardly improve on fact. In line with the Abstinents' eponymous rule, Rancé forbade the use of flesh at all times, with the sole exception of serious and protracted illness in the infirmary. Similarly, following the general rule of the Abstinents, he prohibited the use of poultry at all times, and of any meat products in cooking. Discussion in

---

[1] *TB* 44. [2] *TC* I/70. [3] In *Constitutiones et Acta.* [4] *BN* lat. 17134.
[5] *Éclaircissement sur les différends...* Dom A. Presse, 'Rancé a-t-il voulu fonder une observance particulière?' makes a strong case, but is ultimately unconvincing.

Chapter of this rule (whose widespread relaxation had set off the seventeenth-century move to reform) was absolutely forbidden (*Const.* 39). This was not enough for Rancé, and he added further abstinence of a kind unknown in other houses of the Observance. Despite the productive fisheries literally at the bottom of the garden, he forbade the use of fish and reproved the prior for permitting it while he was away in Rome. Details of fish eating in other houses are not easily available, but in a letter (probably to the commendatory abbot of Perseigne)[1] Rancé refers to the fish enjoyed, presumably by the monks, at the big Breton abbey of Prières. Eggs too were forbidden, except in the infirmary; the use of milk, cheese, and butter was strictly regulated, and even in cooking only a very small amount was used during the brief season when it was permitted at all. White bread was served only in the infirmary, and the coarseness of the black bread was exceptional enough to pass into legend. Even as vegetarians they were allowed nothing that might please the palate, and a little oil or salt was the only concession in a diet hardly better than that of the cattle. Roots, beans, lentils, rice, and cereals, apples, pears, or nuts, potherbs and bread were all they had to live on, year in, year out. Strong flavours, like thyme or garlic, were excluded, and only because the Benedictine Rule expressly provides for a reasonable amount of the local drink was cider (usually diluted with water) permitted, though many of them took only water. Rancé forbade wine, and an attempt to brew their own beer was a failure, but from such accounts as we have the thin and acid cider cannot have been much of a solace to palate or stomach.

It is hardly necessary to add that the quantity of food in no way made up for the quality. Every fast was rigorously observed, and milk, for instance, was not served at all in Advent and Lent, while the size of the unconsumed portion retained from midday dinner for the evening collation was reduced on the many occasions of fast days or penitential seasons. The fact that Rancé reluctantly allowed butter, eggs, and, in extreme cases, meat to the sick shows that he was fully aware that the normal diet came near to the barest minimum of what was needed for subsistence.

The men thus undernourished were not leading a sedentary life. The Abstinents had always reproached the Common Observance for abolishing manual labour, and Rancé was undoubtedly

[1] *TB* 1159 of 1680.

returning to an older tradition when he insisted that all, himself
included, should earn their bread not merely with the tears of
penitence but also with the sweat of their brow.[1] It is not clear
how long the average daily stint of manual labour was for monks
in other reformed houses, but at la Trappe it was clearly stated
that they should spend about three hours a day, usually on work
in the fields, but in bad weather on various maintenance jobs
about the monastery. In this connection one of the details given
in the *Description* at once passed into legend, but was subsequently
challenged by an authoritative critic, and shows once more how
hard it is to establish the real facts. Speaking of Rancé's participation in the manual labour, Félibien writes: 'Va-t-on au travail... il
s'épargne si peu que dans l'Eté il en sort de même que ses Religieux,
tout trempé de sueur pour aller à l'église, où alors il fait très-
froid: Ainsi ils demeurent tous avec une eau sur le corps qui se
conserve de telle sorte dans leurs habits de serge que souvent
ils retournent le lendemain au travail encore mouillez de celluy
du jour précédent.'[2]

This picturesque and realistic detail graphically illustrated the
rigorous labour and equally rigorous self-denial of Rancé and his
monks, and is repeated by Maupeou, perhaps copying Félibien,
perhaps drawing on a source of his own. However, when Gervaise came to publish his *Jugement critique* in 1742 this was one of
the alleged inaccuracies on which he seized, and he refutes the
tale with chapter and verse:[3] 'il est ordonné aux religieux lorsqu'ils sortent du travail trempés de sueurs d'aller dans leur cellule
changer de tunique, ou sergette', of which they have three or four,
and they are reproved if they fail to do so, 'la propreté n'étant
point contraire à l'esprit de mortification, ainsi que le dit St
Bernard. D'ailleurs la charité fraternelle exige qu'on n'incom-
mode point ses voisins au chœur, par la mauvaise odeur qui sort
d'un corps ainsi trempé de sueurs, et des vêtements qui en sont
imbibes.' The *Règlements* in fact order (13/V): 'on ne doit laisser
dans sa cellule rien qui soit sale' and (71/X) 'Lorsqu'aprés le
travail on sera bien échauffé, on n'ira point à l'Eglise... mais on se
retirera dans sa cellule jusqu'à ce que la grande chaleur soit
passée';[4] and Gervaise's commonsense explanation sounds
reasonable.

[1] See Félibien, *Description*, pp. 54 seq.
[2] Ibid., p. 82.   [3] op. cit., pp. 308–9.   [4] *Règlements* of 1718.

In itself the point is trivial, but it is details like this (of which Gervaise gives very many) which have gone into making the legend, and they should always be treated with great caution. Apart from the manual work, the monk's chief occupation was the *opus Dei*, the corporate acts of worship performed in church and the private prayer offered there or elsewhere. On working days this accounted for about eight hours, on Sundays and festivals a good deal more, and the distribution of time also varied in respect of priests who had their private masses to celebrate. Recreation as understood in other orders[1] (e.g. the *spatiamentum*, or conversation permitted while walking, or in the calefactory) did not exist at all, but conferences (discussion of sacred subjects, but never of theology) lasting about an hour were held on Sundays, always under the abbot's presidency, and perhaps four or five times a year the monks were allowed into the surrounding woods, there to pray or meditate for a while individually before being assembled for the conference in the open air.

As for sleep, Rancé drove himself and his monks to the limit. They retired (as they still do) at 8 p.m., after Compline and *Salve*, and were up again on working days at 2 a.m. for Matins, or on Sundays and festivals at 1 a.m. or midnight respectively. Only when they had risen earlier than usual were they allowed up to an hour and a half's rest after Matins; otherwise the long monastic day wore on with no break, except for an hour at midday conceded in summer when the work in the fields was particularly arduous. Even this repose was made as austere as possible, for the monks had to sleep fully dressed, on a straw mattress laid on boards, with no bed linen. The concessions granted to the sick emphasize the austerity prescribed for the healthy, for the use of slightly more comfortable palliasses and bed linen was permitted exceptionally in the infirmary. In all these prescriptions Rancé was again carrying the Abstinents' programme to its logical conclusion: already in 1656, in the *Défense des règlements... pour la réformation de l'ordre*,[2] before Rancé's conversion. the reform programme

---

[1] The Rule of St. Benedict lays down very general lines on the questions of silence, conferences, and so on, and implicitly on recreation. All houses, however, had a calefactory, but at la Trappe talking there was forbidden. Even the Carthusians have always insisted on a period of conversation once a week. Rancé's views on the subject were very firm, and he left no latitude in the conduct of conferences. On the calefactory ('chauffoir') see *Règlements* ch. 4, on conferences ch. 8, on 'spaciment' ch. 9.   [2] BN Ld[17]. 43.

specified 'lits de paille, simplicité des habits, chemises de serge, travail des mains, silence exact, veilles...' and accused the Common Observance of ignoring all these points. As Félibien puts it:[1] 'Mais sur tout cette uniformité de vie où la nature ne trouve aucun relasche ny aucun soulagement par la diversité même ou le changement des austeritez et des travaux' is the real burden.

The spiritual fruits of this way of life are plain enough in the light of history, but its physical effects are more controversial. At first all seemed to be well, and in 1671 Félibien could comment that eight years after the introduction of the Reform only two monks had died, the second in fact just before he finished his book; but a few years later mortality struck hard, and between 1674 and 1682 some thirty monks in all died, and Rancé himself was seriously ill. The only evidence on which even tentative medical conclusions can be based is that supplied in the *Relations de la mort de quelques religieux...*, which began to appear at this time.[2] The principal symptoms include flesh ulcers, abscesses, and even gangrene, necessitating lancing and rough surgery, together with fevers, continual coughs, and every sort of gout, rheumatism, and the like. The sudden onset of deaths in 1674, after twelve years of generally good health, suggests an epidemic —evidently exacerbated by living constantly at such close quarters—no doubt of tubercular origin and accompanied by familiar symptoms of vitamin deficiency. The rheumatic ailments, as one would expect from the damp, unheated conditions in which the monks lived, seem to have been chronic. Rancé himself, as already noted, always attributed the mortality to the site and climate, rather than to any austerity, but of course even people who ate their fill in the seventeenth century understood so little about dietetics that they too were prone to gout and kindred disorders.

The other relevant evidence concerns the incidence of death at various ages, and the length of time spent at la Trappe.[3] Such findings do not take account of those who died elsewhere, either for reasons of health or otherwise; nor are the figures for age at profession always reliable; and finally it is not too clear which comparable statistics for the population at large would be rele-

---

[1] *Description*, p. 79.   [2] See above, p. 37, n. 1.

[3] There are several statistical tables in L. Dubois (*not* the biographer), *Histoire civile... de la Trappe*, but more reliable figures can be compiled from the *Registre mortuaire* kept at la Trappe (MS. 308.1).

vant, in view of the very wide social spectrum represented from
lay brothers through to choir monks. However, it is worth
noting that of 426 monks who died from the beginning of the
reform up to 1739, 100 were under 30, 129 between 30 and 40,
138 between 40 and 60, and 70 over 60. More significant is the
fact that 106 died within two years of admission, a further 110 in
the next three years, and a total of 296 in the first ten years; while
67 lasted more than ten years, 37 more than twenty, and 27 more
than thirty. It is a sobering thought that one in four entrants had
only two years to prepare for death, and more than half did not
survive five years.

It may well be that these figures would turn out to be typical of
other, less austere, houses, but one thing is certain: men came to
la Trappe, as they did not come to other monasteries, with the
firm intention of sacrificing their lives there, and preferably soon.
This was by no means the only motivation, and a later chapter
will examine the whole question of vocation and recruitment, but
it was the motivation by far the best known to the world at large.
In this connection a major instrument of publicity has already
been mentioned, namely the *Relations*. External publicity in the
form of accounts, whether printed or circulated in manuscript by
visitors, was very important, but the image, as the modern phrase
goes, projected by Rancé himself is as revealing in its defects as in
its positive qualities, and was immensely influential in adding to
the legend.

The origin of these obituaries was the address given by Rancé
when the monk died, and it is not quite clear when, or why, he
decided to make this pious tribute into something more literary
and permanent. Writing to Bellefonds on 10 April 1675,[1] he
sends the *relations* of fr. Benoît Deschamps (d. 20 August 1674)
and dom Jacques Puiperrou (d. December 1674), and describes
the death of dom Paul Hardy just a week earlier (5 April 1675),
but particularly asks Bellefonds to treat the accounts as confidential. Paul Hardy, formerly théologal of Alet, had caused a stir by
entering la Trappe in 1671 and, like Benoît who had a brother at
Port-Royal, was of special interest to Jansenists from his association with Pavillon, Bishop of Alet, to whom in fact Rancé sent
the first full account of his death (in a letter of 15 April 1675).[2]
No doubt edified by these accounts, and eager for more, various

---

[1] Original in *BN* n.a. 12959, f. 24.   [2] *TC* I/19.

admirers of Rancé must have persuaded him to publish to a
wider public what they had found so impressive. Thus the
former Mme de la Vallière, then sœur Louise de la Miséricorde, writes to Bellefonds that Tréville has just been to the
Carmelites (1 September 1675) and has there read out in the
parlour the *relation* of Charles Denis[1] (d. 20 July 1675). Her comment is worth quoting: 'dans tout ce que j'entendis hier il me
semble qu'il y a une certaine onction... Car tout est dans ce saint
une austérité rigoureuse avec une faiblesse extrême.' She herself
had taken the habit little more than a year before. We know from
several letters of the time, especially 1675–6, that Rancé was
deeply despondent about the affairs of the order and sad at losing
so many of his best religious in so short a time, and it may well
be that he found some consolation in displaying to the world at
large the triumph, *sub specie aeternitatis*, of his much criticized
monastery. By 1683, when the mortality rate had settled down,
the *Relations* were into their third edition and concerned altogether thirteen monks out of thirty or so who had died. Félibien
had already given in 1671 *relations* of the two who had died by
then,[2] which are obviously edited versions of what Rancé told him,
not subsequently repeated in Rancé's own *Relations*. By 1755, when
the *Relations* had been through many editions, they comprised
five volumes, of which the first two describe the deaths of 41
monks out of 119 (with notes on three others) who died before
Rancé; while Volume III begins with a long account of Rancé's
own death and continues with details of other monks, mostly of
noble birth.[3] Much the most famous of these essays of very varying length is that devoted to dom Muce (d. 13 May 1689) and
published separately as *La Mort du Grenadier*. It provoked a
storm of criticism, several parodies, and a vigorous defence by
Rancé and his friends. As publicity it was undeniably effective and
on balance probably did la Trappe more good than harm.

It is worth examining some of the earlier *Relations*, since it was
presumably the favourable reception accorded to them that
guided Rancé in composing the rest. Frère Benoît was professed
five and a half years before dying aged about 37 (ages are often
inconsistently and ambiguously recorded). He had been ill for four
years with pulmonary congestion ('fluxion'). Dom Jacques, a

[1] Lair, *Louise de la Vallière*, p. 369.   [2] A *donné* and Joseph Bernier.
[3] For full bibliographical details on the *Relations* see Tournoüer, s.v. *Rancé*.

former Celestine, had been professed rather more than six years, and ill for more than a year with hernia, fluxion, fever, mouth ulcers, and haemorrhoids. Frère Bernard Molac, who had begun in the Paris Oratory, was professed at 34 and died four and a half years later. Shortly after profession he fell ill with a fever, but recovered, to his great disappointment. His final illness was 'oppression de poitrine' for more than a year. Dom Paul Hardy came from Alet aged 46 or so, and died four years later, having undergone surgery for a gangrened finger while still a novice. Dom Benoît Pisseau, another former Celestine, died at 33, four years after entering la Trappe, after four months 'fluxion de poitrine'. These first five entries[1] in the necrology, all relating to deaths occurring in a period of nine months in 1674–5, are enough to prove the frequency of pulmonary complaints.

Others illustrate the state of mind prevalent among the monks. Of the sub-prior, dom Augustin Chappon (yet another ex-Celestine), Rancé writes: 'la plus grande de ses joies aurait été de mourir martyr de la pénitence, et de succomber dans quelque entreprise qui eût surpassé ses forces.'[2] After a year of fluxion, fever, and rheumatism he had his wish. A note on his last moments is characteristic: 'Sur les 8 heures du soir, le Père Abbé qui étoit malade, accablé de lassitude, et qui ne pouvoit être davantage avec lui, pour lui rendre les dernières assistances, lui dit: Mon Frère, je m'en vais vous dire un grand adieu: mon impuissance me contraint de vous quitter: je vous laisse avec Jésus-Christ.'

Frère Théodore Faverolles was 23 when professed, and already very sick with a fluxion. At his insistence he went ahead with his profession, and died just three weeks later. Frère Euthyme l'Épinoy had originally postulated as a lay brother, but Rancé sent him away to learn Latin and ten months later he came back as a choir monk. Throughout his two years in the monastery he was sick with cough and fever, and with something cryptically described as temptations against purity, and in his final illness refused the addition of wine to his tisane, saying: 'Il vaut mieux que je meure, si je ne puis vivre qu'en violant un Règlement de la Maison.'[3]

---

[1] These five occur in varying order according to the editions, and are the first listed in Vol. I of the 1755 ed. quoted here and throughout.

[2] Ibid., p. 102.

[3] The fullest account of Théodore comes in some letters written to the Oratorian Bruscoly, examined below, pp. 118–19. He and Euthyme both come in Vol. I.

Then there is the celebrated dom Muce Faure, the ex-grenadier.[1] He started out as a Benedictine, took orders, and was then so appalled at his sacrilege that he fled abroad as a soldier of fortune, to England, Germany, Hungary, even Turkey, where he joined up as a mercenary and, sacrilege on sacrilege, wore a turban on his once tonsured head. Suddenly stricken with remorse he decided to come to la Trappe to expiate his crimes, walking all the way (from Burgundy, it seems) in foul weather. He caught pneumonia, but was exceptionally received into the community after a few weeks as a novice and died three months later. The highly coloured and somewhat improbable details of his career aroused so much scepticism in Rancé's enemies that the abbot, who had presumably taken it all on trust, was obliged to seek a certificate from the judicial authorities in Burgundy authenticating Muce's bad character. When the certificate eventually arrived, Rancé published it with some satisfaction.

Another *relation* which circulated separately and became famous was that of frère Palémon, former comte de Santéna.[2] He had been a soldier, but regular rather than irregular like Muce. When his father, Governor of Turin, died, the young officer became converted to piety. He happened to visit la Trappe just as an earlier frère Palémon (des Arcis), a former captain of infantry, lay dying, and was so impressed by the change of heart of a soldier like himself that he at once asked to be admitted, and was duly given the name Palémon, held by two soldiers and a sailor before him. The noble rank of this recruit made him one of the sights of la Trappe, and numerous distinguished visitors, such as Bellefonds, James II, and Cardinal de Bouillon, were taken to meet him. He contracted ulcers in his arms and legs, which turned gangrenous, and died two years after profession, aged 42.

Finally frère Zénon de Montbel, a former captain in the Régiment du Roi, and a Musketeer for six years, died two years after profession and spent his time in charge of the stove, cutting and carrying logs. His *relation* is specially interesting because it tells us that he quite exceptionally obtained permission to use the discipline on himself and wear a penitential belt.[3]

[1] See above.   [2] The three Palémons and Zénon come in Vol. II.
[3] Use of the discipline, or penitential scourge, was a regular feature of monastic penance, normally practised by Cistercians once a week or ordered by the abbot as punishment for some particular fault. Rancé seems to have been quite exceptional in his own day in making no provision for it (and incidentally, not for retreats either).

These examples show quite well which details Rancé found significant, apart from the somewhat monotonous account of the piety, fortitude, and so on displayed by the monks in life as in death. He always emphasizes, to the point of exaggeration, the sinfulness of the life from which monks were converted, in the many cases where this is appropriate, then the gruesome course of their sufferings, and always the peace and eagerness of their departure. As elements in the legend of la Trappe, these accounts can be said to have attracted one kind of man rather than another; and as the number of *relations* grew, the consistency of the picture became ever more apparent.

An obvious question in the face of such documents concerns the medical attention available or permitted. Here the *Constitutions* had already publicized the policy from which Rancé never deviated: monks come to expiate their sins and, far from seeking to prolong their unworthy lives, have no dearer wish than to offer them as a final sacrifice. To this end the attentions of outside doctors, or remedies other than simple herbal ones, were allowed only in cases of extreme urgency. On at least one occasion Rancé brusquely refused to see a doctor (in fact the saintly M. Hamon sent from Port-Royal by the well-meaning Mme de Saint-Loup), explaining (4 July 1677) that this was his rule.[1] A good deal later he began to accept remedies for himself and others at the insistence of Bellefonds, and Maisne reported on their effects.[2] One letter describes in an unintentionally comic way how one of the bottles of medicine burst, sending a spout right up to the ceiling, but leaving just enough to be retrieved for the patient (who got better). Bleeding, too, was practised, as the *Règlements* show, and it should be said that if the sick were certainly not pampered, and would not have wanted to be, they were treated with charity and consideration. None the less it is perfectly clear that most of the monks, sick or not, positively looked forward to the day when they would be laid out on straw and ashes to breathe their last, with their abbot by their side. Incidentally one of the more mysterious features of the Trappist legend is that which has them digging a bit more of their own graves each day. Graves are, and were, dug by religious assigned to that duty, and it evidently could happen that a gravedigger could die suddenly enough to be

---

[1] *TB* 843.   [2] See *BN* n.a. 12959, ff. 123, 125, 127, all of July 1689.

buried in his own work, but despite its wide currency the story seems to be a pure invention.[1]

To speak in this context of the death wish at la Trappe is not unreasonable, provided that the description is not interpreted in merely negative terms. Félibien has an arresting phrase which puts in perspective both Rancé's role and his community's spirit: 'ce ne sont point des Esclaves timides et lasches, conduits par un vaillant Capitaine, ce sont des personnes libres, et généreuses, qui marchent sur les pas de leur Chef, qui luy obéissent avec un amour extrême...' Another comment is also revealing: 'Car s'il ne descouvre pas dans ses Religieux la moindre imperfection sans les en corriger aussitost, il a aussi une discrétion admirable à ne les pas surcharger de pénitences, croyant qu'il seroit également coupable davant Dieu de leur estre trop rude ou trop indulgent.'[2] Some of the *relations* unmistakably describe abnormal personalities, what would appear to be obsessive neuroses or masochistic tendencies, and it is not altogether reassuring to read such un-critical eulogies as that, for example, of frère Basile Anzoux, who, afflicted with an abscess on his chest, 'appréhendoit mille fois plus que les plus vives douleurs' to uncover it, 'une chose où il croyoit intéresser sa pudeur'.[3] At the same time the norms of seventeenth-century psychology were so different from our own, and casual experience of death and extreme pain so common, that one must be careful to avoid over-simplification. With so much physical ill health, mental morbidity could hardly be excluded infallibly. What is remarkable is the sanity and vigour of Rancé and his monks as illustrated in descriptions by visitors or correspondence.

The publicity effect of the *Relations* was considerable, and very varied. They undoubtedly encouraged some vocations; there is evidence that some readers were deeply affected, even to the point of conversion; others were openly annoyed, but probably the main result was to stimulate curiosity. In reading the accounts by seventeenth-century visitors of what they saw and what impressed them, the modern reader is seriously hampered by lack of a reliable context. Today the relationship between society and

---

[1] The nearest I can come to an explanation is in some words from a letter of the Oratorian Bourrée after a visit in 1684: 'il y a une fosse qu'on laisse toujours ouverte pour celui qui mourra le premier afin qu'elle serve de sujet de méditation et d'avis aux autres pour se préparer à la mort.' *BN* Coll. Moreau 793, t. IV.

[2] *Description*, pp. 81 and 84.   [3] *Relations*, i, p. 260.

monks is so utterly different, even in Catholic countries, from what it was 300 years ago that comparisons are bound to be misleading. In particular, Cistercian monasteries are so similar one to another (at any rate in the same country) and so totally divorced from the world outside that any visitor is at once aware of observing an exceptional situation. In Rancé's day visitors evidently found la Trappe notably different from the innumerable other monasteries (there were in France more than 300 Cistercian houses alone)[1] with which no one could fail to be acquainted in town or country, but some of the points on which they remarked are so unexpected that one is bound to wonder about the others they do not mention. The site, the slow and dignified chanting of the Office, the communal labour, the austerity, the visibly flourishing community are always commented on, and it is only when one reads of so-called abbeys with only two or three monks living in ruins, or of others where the abbot holds court like a secular noble, that one realizes that the seventeenth-century legend of la Trappe arose as much as anything for want of a recognized monastic norm.

A small point helps to emphasize the strangeness experienced by so many visitors when confronted with something we should today probably take for granted. All over the monastery Rancé had put up inscriptions, usually from the Bible or Fathers, occasionally of his own composition, to catch the eye and guide the thoughts. Félibien is the first to record these, but they had the most extraordinary vogue. On entering the guest-house the visitor would see the words of Jeremiah: 'Sedebit solitarius et tacebit', and in the vestibule the verse from the Psalm: 'Melius est dies una in atriis tuis super millia'. James II was so impressed when he came twenty years later that he asked for a copy of the inscriptions he had seen in the guests' refectory,[2] and about the same time, Mlle de Théméricourt, the tireless copyist of Port-Royal, wrote out no fewer than forty-three pages of *Sentences de la Trappe*.[3] In an age of maxim, epigram, couplet, *pensée*, the Renaissance craze for quotable aphorism and *sententia* had passed into the

---

[1] Lekai, *Rise of Cist. S.O.*, gives copious details concerning the state of the whole order in the seventeenth century. The complaint of abbots living like *grands seigneurs* comes from an Abstinent pamphlet of *c.* 1657 *Response aux dernières objections...* (BN Ld¹⁷. 85).

[2] James to Rancé 17 Jan. 1691, copy in (Alençon) Tournoüer MS. 13, letter 2.

[3] In *U* 3201.

salons, where brevity enhanced both wit and wisdom, and before Rancé died, extracts from his letters and books were already in print as *Maximes chrétiennes* (1698). The attention paid to these modest inscriptions does, however, seem rather excessive.

Different visitors naturally acquired different impressions. M. de Saint-Louis, a distinguished ex-officer, had taken up residence in the former commendatory abbot's lodging, abandoned by Rancé, and though remaining a secular, followed the religious exercises of the community.[1] The aristocratic M. de Nocey, after trying his vocation at the Oratory, settled down as a hermit a little way from the monastery (1679), and until his death in 1692 also joined the monks at prayer without taking the habit.[2] These two aroused a good deal of interest from visitors, though Nocey went to some lengths to avoid them. They, like Maisne and others, seculars or so-called 'donnés' (a sort of oblate class), passed on much more of the community's gossip than could any of the monks. The latter were of course a prime attraction, and those assigned to the guest-house the immediate target of curiosity. Apart from Rancé himself, guests might expect to meet the Prior or Sub-Prior (for many years dom le Nain), but such senior religious would be more discreet than those who actually waited upon the guests. One monk who caused a lot of trouble was frère Armand-Climaque de l'Orme, a young converted Huguenot from Nîmes, to whom Rancé gave his own name as a sign of trust and affection.[3] He was professed in 1689, and quite soon was put in charge of the guest-house. The erudite abbé Louail speaks of meeting him in 1693,[4] and he had played a leading (and somewhat equivocal) role in the Maupas affair the previous year. He evidently talked too much, and the instability of his character is demonstrated by his sudden departure from la Trappe to resume his former religion abroad. In general it seems that it was rather the illustrious convert, like the soldiers Santéna or Albergotti, than the humble 'good monk' with whom visitors made contact, and then only very fleetingly. One of frère Armand's predecessors in the guest-house had been the Fleming from Cambrai, Robert Ghoissez (professed 1676, d. 1699), whose accent was so thick that one

---

[1] Dubois quotes extensively from his memoirs. Original in *AE* 1440–44. See below, p. 276.

[2] See Rancé's letters to Mme de Guise on his death, 24 Feb. and 3 Mar. 1692, in Gonod, pp. 174–5.

[3] See Dubois, ii, p. 413.   [4] In *U* 1797. On Maupas see above, p. 52.

visitor reports that he could barely understand him.[1] Guest masters must have varied a good deal in conversational ability and inclination, but it was primarily with these monks, and others like porters and cellarer, that outsiders came into contact. It follows that, for all their curiosity, visitors had to depend on what they saw almost entirely, and what they heard from the few sources available to them was not necessarily representative or very informative.

This all amounts to saying that the main source of information about la Trappe was always Rancé himself, supplemented by such other sources as he himself selected. Anyone familiar with the domestic disputes of other monasteries in the seventeenth century, and with the intrigues so frequent in ecclesiastical circles generally, will appreciate how unusual the reticence and harmony of la Trappe appeared to contemporary visitors. Rancé felt very strongly indeed about this, and condemned 'murmure' within a monastery as being almost as bad as murder (to Leyme, 7 March 1678) or blasphemy (to Perseigne, 20 November 1681).[2] It is extraordinary proof of the success of his policy that la Trappe was able to survive the really vicious intrigues directed against Gervaise. In this respect the unity and loyalty of the community went even beyond the legend.

There is one other point of relevance here. Though the monks came from many different monasteries and orders, and from all over France, and even beyond the frontiers, once they had been admitted to la Trappe they completely adopted the ways of that house. Some, as will be seen in the next chapter, moved permanently to another house, but there was very little interchange of a temporary kind. For one thing, la Trappe was unique among Cistercian houses of comparable size in never, under any circumstances, sending any of its monks to study in Paris at the Cistercian Collège des Bernardins, and Rancé was unique among abbots in absenting himself from every chapter held after 1675. La Trappe quite often received monks from other houses for training (e.g. Orval, Sept-Fons, Tamié) and sometimes lent one or two of its own, but such exchanges were strictly limited. Thus the

---

[1] U 3061, p. 4: 'il est wallon et presque flamand... ne dit rien que le nécessaire et par les manières il ôte aux étrangers la tentation de trop parler; nous sûmes que c'est la raison pourquoi l'abbé lui a donné l'emploi de recevoir les hôtes.' The author, probably an Oratorian, visited la Trappe in 1686.

[2] TB 939 and 1444.

community always remained much more closely knit and stable than was usually the case even among reformed houses. The only important exception to this rule was the supply of confessors to Cistercian nuns, notably Maubuisson and les Clairets, but it is interesting that dom Alain Morony[1] in the former case and dom Jacques Lanchal[2] in the latter were both Perseigne monks who had spent some time at la Trappe. Similarly, dom François Cornuty, who had been professed at Tamié and eventually returned there, was chosen by Rancé to go for several years to Foucarmont as novice master.[3] It looks as though he regarded monks from other houses as his mobile reserve, and however highly he thought of them (and all the three just mentioned enjoyed his esteem) preferred to send them on missions rather than any of his own religious. This policy both spread first-hand knowledge of la Trappe to other communities of men and women and also maintained the cohesion and, it is fair to say, isolation of Rancé's monks.

[1] Mentioned in correspondence with the abbess of Maubuisson in 1682, *TB* 1697.
[2] Letter to les Clairets of 9 June 1688, *TC* I/108.   [3] See below, p. 108.

6. Vocations

It is exceedingly difficult to give precise answers to most of the questions concerning the composition of the community at la Trappe during Rancé's lifetime, and impossible to relate even the known facts to a broader historical context. Fortunately the surviving documents allow much of the picture to emerge, even though it would be most unwise to rely too much on purely statistical conclusions. The basic published evidence is the necrological table, compiled by the chevalier d'Espoisse, of which, regrettably, several mutually inconsistent versions exist, but on the whole the inconsistencies affect spelling and dates rather than more substantial matters.[1] As a basis of comparison it may be noted that records for the neighbouring abbey of Perseigne are so defective that it is not even possible to reconstruct the chronological order of the claustral priors, let alone their tenure, for the same period.

When Rancé first visited la Trappe as commendatory abbot in 1660 he found six monks living in material and spiritual squalor. Two years later when, still a secular, he introduced the reform, three of the original six stayed on and were joined by a colony of six sent from Perseigne. By 1671 the community numbered more than forty; in 1676 there were 27 choir monks, 6 novices, and 12 lay brothers; in 1684 27 choir monks, 11 novices and 13 lay brothers; in 1686 34 choir monks, 10 novices, and 18 lay brothers; and by 1700, at Rancé's death, the total was about 90, at which figure it remained until the Revolution drove the monks into exile in 1790.[2] By any computation the expansion was re-

---

[1] Much the most reliable source is the *Registre mortuaire, 1667–1792*, kept at la Trappe (MS. 308.1), which includes all *convers* (lay brothers) and even several *donnés* (oblates) who died at la Trappe. Cross-references in the document show that it was compiled directly from the now lost register of professions. Further details, sometimes unknown elsewhere, are in the *Necrologium* (Rouen, MS. Montbret y 29) which goes up to 1733 (and has been transposed on to *fiches* kept at la Trappe). These MS. sources are far more accurate than the lists published by the chevalier d'Espoisse, which omit *convers*, but no list covers those who died away from the monastery, or who did die there but were stabilized elsewhere.

[2] 1671, according to Félibien, *Description*; 1676 from the *Carte de visite* of Hervé du Tertre, Abbot of Prières, in Dubois, i, p. 536; 1684 BN Coll. Moreau 793, t.IV;

markable, indeed astonishing, but these figures conceal problems of definition. In 1691, for example, an Act of Association was sent at his request to James II.[1] This very formal document was signed by Rancé and 34 choir monks. Allowing for temporary absence, sickness, and so on, this still falls short of the 44 recorded six years earlier, and it seems as though the status of novices, of monks from other houses living, but not stabilized,[2] at la Trappe, and similarly variable factors account for discrepancies.

Other factors which lead to discrepancy include inconsistent methods of defining membership of the community, confusion between age at entry and age at death, and failure to mention previous ecclesiastical status. For example, membership is normally reckoned from date of profession, but sometimes the taking of the habit or, in the case of Cistercians, simply arrival at la la Trappe is the starting-point. More seriously, the published registers are incomplete in respect of monks still living when they were compiled (1713) or who died away from la Trappe.

With all these qualifications certain trends are marked enough to be statistically significant. Of the first 100 choir monks professed between 1662 and 1690 at least 25 came from other religious orders. 7 Celestines head the list, with 5 Canons Regular of various kinds, 4 Benedictines, and 3 Oratorians. Each of the Mendicant Orders, Dominicans, Franciscans, and Carmelites, supply one apiece, but it is most striking that in the five years immediately following Rancé's resignation no fewer than 12 Franciscans were admitted. In the same period, up to 1690, 15 or 16 Cistercians from other houses were professed at la Trappe, but some of them subsequently went elsewhere. The great majority, perhaps nearly all, of these religious were already in orders when they arrived, and to their number must be added a constant stream of secular clergy, often quite senior, who must have

1686 U 3061; in 1697 the anonymous author (?Masson or Treuvé) of the *Deux discours sur la vie... de la Trappe* reported 50 professed monks, 35 or 40 novices, and an unstated number of lay brothers.

[1] *SP*, p. 65, of 12 Nov. 1691.

[2] *Stabilitas* in the Benedictine Rule binds a monk to the monastery of his profession, even though he may physically live elsewhere. Change of stability is possible, but rare and only permitted for good reason shown. In the seventeenth-century context it was a normal consequence of passing from the Common to the Strict Observance of Cîteaux, and there are cases at la Trappe of Cistercians being professed a second time even though they came from an Abstinent house (e.g. Jacques Minguet, former abbot of Châtillon).

brought the total of priests to something like half of all those admitted. Rancé's aversion to theology has already been noted, and also his reluctance to send any of his monks for ordination, but it should be stressed that these figures, rough as they may be, represent an exceptional, if not unique, situation by seventeenth-century monastic standards. A community comprising so many monks already versed in theology, as well as monastic life, before they even entered the novitiate enjoyed considerable advantages over the normal house which had to devote a far higher pro-portion of its time to forming monks and priests from scratch.

If canon law had permitted unrestricted entry to la Trappe, the composition of the community would undoubtedly have been very different, but after the bitter quarrels of Rancé's early years as abbot he took great care to avoid giving offence to other orders unless compelled to do so by circumstances. Seculars were, of course, canonically free to enter the monastery of their choice, but even so the admission of a Paul Hardy or a Jean-Baptiste Vitry, canons respectively of Alet and Meaux, was not a precedent likely to find favour with many diocesans. The absence of Jesuits from the list calls for no comment; some, Rapin,[1] for instance, must occasionally have visited la Trappe, but none ever sought to enter. Carthusians, on the other hand, might have been ex-pected, and at least two cases (dom Braquiti in 1680 and a dom D in 1686) are known where Rancé categorically rejected their application,[2] rightly supposing that their superiors would object and would be supported in the highest quarters.

With regard to Mendicants the situation is rather odd. A Minor, Eustache Picot, was professed in 1672, and evidently gave every satisfaction, for he was prior when he died in 1687, but in 1676 Rancé wrote (probably to Arnauld)[3] that he will in future accept no further Mendicants as they cause so much trouble, and in 1680 he politely informs a Capuchin of Béthune that he cannot accept him;[4] it may be this same friar who came in 1699 but went away again soon afterwards. A Carmelite, Bernard Soyrot of Dijon, was admitted in May 1680, perhaps encouraging the application

[1] Rapin apparently went there about 1669–70 with another Jesuit and gave a cri-tical account of his visit as he passed through Perseigne (Benoît Luce to Pont-château, 9 Nov. 1675, PR 47, f. 415).

[2] Braquiti in TB 1264 of 8 Feb. 1680; dom D to Nicaise, 12 May 1685 in Gonod, p. 110.

[3] T 2183, f. 28.   [4] TB 1223 of 24 Jan. 1680.

of the sub-prior of the Carmelites of Besançon to whom Rancé
wrote in June,[1] but in a letter of 1694 is described, with good
cause, as 'instable'.[2] Another Carmelite, after years of pleading,
was in fact the last monk professed by Rancé as abbot, took his
name (Armand), and within three years had succeeded him as
abbot Gervaise; it would not be unreasonable to describe him
too as unstable. With him was admitted a Dominican, Jean-
Baptiste de la Tour, who became prior, but who left with Gervaise.
Another Dominican was Antoine Lafarge (1693); he supported
Rancé during the great dispute of 1698 and wrote to Noailles[3]
(whom he had known at Châlons) on his behalf. The only other
admitted by Rancé (in 1686) was the brother of Maupeou,[4] his
trouble-making biographer, who in the course of this same crisis
refused a summons to return to la Trappe from his post as confessor at les Clairets and in fact died at Prières. It is extraordinary
that these six (one other Franciscan admitted in 1693 died two
years later) should have provided la Trappe with an abbot and two
priors, while in other ways justifying his reluctance to accept
Mendicants. One would like to know what prompted the reversal
of this policy after Rancé's resignation, and whether the change
was justified by results. In general it is hardly surprising that men
who had originally been attracted to an active and itinerant
ministry should have found it hard to settle down at la Trappe,
but it would be interesting to know how many of the Mendicants
refused by Rancé entered other Cistercian houses, and with what
success.

Again as a matter of policy Rancé was opposed to the admission
of what he called 'ecclésiastiques', that is secular clergy or members of such orders as the Oratorians, and in an outspoken letter to
Pasquier Quesnel (29 July 1673),[5] whose brother had unsuccessfully tried his vocation at la Trappe a year or so before, he says
that such men are rarely meant for la Trappe and need 'une
double vocation' to succeed there. The exceptions to this rule
are even more striking than is the case with the Mendicants.
Charles Denis and Isidore Simon from the Oratory, Pierre le

[1] *TD*, series D, 82, of 13 June 1680.
[2] To Nicaise, 6 June 1694 in *BN* 9363, f. 194.
[3] *SG* Suppl. Z f in 40 829, 3.
[4] Frère Grégoire. As cellarer he wrote to Gerbais a letter still extant (*A* 5172, f. 58).
Gervaise, *Jugement critique*, speaks of him without enthusiasm.
[5] In *U* 1168, published by Tans, letter, 24.

Nain from Saint-Victor, Paul Ferrand from the Premonstratensians all became exemplary monks, but the Oratorian Malebranche and the Victorine Simon Gourdan both failed to find the
vocation at la Trappe which they had tried to persuade Rancé was
genuine.[1]

Of all religious, those belonging to the Benedictine family,
whether from the Congregations of Saint-Maur or Saint-Vanne,
or from separate orders like Celestines, Feuillants,[2] or Cistercians,
were most obviously suited for life at la Trappe, but again
canonical difficulties limited recruitment. Maurists and Vannists
were engaged on their own successful reform and were not
anxious to see their best men go off to la Trappe; the Celestines
were going through a period of internal crisis, and the mass
defection of seven of their number (two subsequently returned)
at one time forced them to take defensive measures; the Feuillants represented a thriving Cistercian reform, and only two were
professed at la Trappe under Rancé, while a third was the subject
of acrimonious correspondence and seems to have obeyed his
General's order to return.

There remained the most natural pool of recruitment: the
Cistercian Order itself, Abstinents or otherwise. Here the question of poaching was most delicate and, since the traffic was in
both directions, it is not easy to assess with accuracy. After the
final settlement of 1675 superiors of the Common Observance
showed no enthusiasm for releasing their subjects. Thus we find
Rancé writing in 1676–7 to a lady (perhaps Mlle de Vertus)[3] who
had passed on the application of a R. P. Montmouton for transfer
to la Trappe, that he must first get the permission of his superior
(the abbot of la Ferté, newly appointed), which will be difficult.
In fact we hear no more of him. Another case caused protracted
correspondence and appeals to Caumartin, Conseiller d'État and
Intendant of Champagne, an old friend of Rancé.[4] One Joseph
Garreau, doctor of the Sorbonne, former prior of Buzey and a
monk of some consequence, had for some reason been disgraced
and sent to Fonfroide, though he wanted to come to la Trappe.[5]
Rancé wrote to him in 1680–1, telling him to delay no longer, and

---

[1] On Malebranche see below, pp. 251–52, on Gourdan, pp. 169–73.

[2] Affair of the Feuillants discussed below, p. 113.   [3] *U* 863.

[4] The correspondence with Caumartin is to be found scattered through the *BN Fichiers Charavay* and the *Autographes de Troussures*, ed. Denis, pp. 418–19.

[5] See *Relations*, i, on dom Joseph.

to Caumartin, from 1680 to 1684, trying, in the end successfully, to get the Abbot of Clairvaux (in the jurisdiction of Champagne) to revoke the *lettre de cachet* against Garreau, who finally came to la Trappe, was professed in 1684 and died an edifying death in 1690.

Such cases as these show that the amount of perseverance required even for Cistercians to come to la Trappe meant that a considerable degree of pre-selection took place before they ever arrived. Things were naturally easier with other houses of the Reform, and there was a good deal of interchange in any case as the Reform spread and became organized. It is very striking how many of those who came to la Trappe had held positions of authority in the secular clergy or in other orders, and this is equally true of recruits from other Cistercian houses. Dom Garreau has just been mentioned, then there was dom Rigobert Levesque, professed at Clairvaux, where he became novice master, before going on to Hautefontaine as prior. He came to la Trappe in 1665, became Rancé's secretary (with a beautifully clear hand), was re-professed in 1670, with a change of stability from Clairvaux to la Trappe, just after refusing an official and pressing invitation to become regular abbot of Hautefontaine in succession to Rancé's friend Le Roy, the commendatory abbot. He died in 1679 after being ill for seven years.[1] With the abbey of Perseigne, where he himself had been professed when it was the novitiate for the whole province, Rancé always maintained the closest relations. Two priors of Perseigne came to la Trappe within a few years: the Irishman Alain Morony in about 1666 (he seems not to have been re-professed at la Trappe, and eventually went on to Tamié and then went as confessor to the nuns at Maubuisson)[2] and Urbain le Pannetier, who shortly after arriving in 1671 found himself made prior of la Trappe.[3] The most unusual case of translation was that of Jacques Minguet.[4] Born in 1597, he had played an active part in the reform movement as abbot of Châtillon from 1657 to 1669, and on retirement from that office finally prevailed upon Rancé to admit him as a simple monk of la Trappe in 1674. Even this was not enough for him, and three years later,

[1] Ibid. i.
[2] His profession in *Archives de la Sarthe*, iii, H, p. 412; prior according to G. Fleury, 'L'Abbaye cist. de Perseigne', p. 41; to Tamié 20 Sept. 1681, *TB* 1536; to Maubuisson 6 July 1682, *TB* 1697.
[3] See *Archives de la Sarthe*, loc. cit., and *Relations*, i.   [4] *Relations*, i.

at the age of 80, he insisted on being professed a second time. He died in 1681, blind and infirm, a genuine example of the true monk so often portrayed by imaginative chroniclers.

The story of dom Jean-François Cornuty is strange in a different way, and exceptionally well documented.[1] Born in 1641 of a Savoyard legal family, he entered the abbey of Tamié, where his elder brother was prior, about 1660. In 1662 he went to Paris with his abbot, Jean Antoine de la Forêt de Somont, to study at the Collège des Bernardins. For reasons which are obscure he suddenly decided to go to la Trappe without telling anyone, and made his way on foot in December 1665. Rancé himself was away in Rome, but he wrote at once to welcome the young recruit, who was then re-professed with the unusual proviso that his vow of stability would bind him to Tamié in the then highly unlikely event that his abbot embraced the Reform. Against his reiterated pleas to be allowed to remain at la Trappe he was sent to Foucarmont, where he was ordained in 1672 and acted as novice master for six years or so. Then in 1677, again for reasons that remain obscure, his abbot, an outspoken critic of Rancé and the Reform, came from Paris on a visit to la Trappe and in a very emotional reconciliation with Rancé gave him a written promise to introduce the Reform as soon as he got back to Tamié. Cornuty was recalled from Foucarmont, reunited in Paris with his abbot, and returned to keep his vow at Tamié, where he at once became prior and effective head of the community during the abbot's protracted absences on business of the order. In 1682 he was still begging Rancé to allow him back to la Trappe, but to no avail, although Somont himself paid another visit there in 1683. On Somont's death he became abbot of Tamié in 1702 and died in 1707.

These examples are enough to show to what extent Rancé both attracted and formed a monastic élite, men whose qualities could not fail to be recognized, but who, in many cases, cheerfully laid down their authority for the privilege of joining the community of la Trappe. Others would have liked to do the same, but were given no encouragement by Rancé. Dom Eustache de Beaufort,[2] Abbot of Sept-Fons, was almost certainly sincere in his request to be admitted to la Trappe as an ordinary monk, for his attempts to reform his own house met at first with little success, but one

---

[1] The full story in J. Garin, *Histoire de l'abbaye de Tamié*, pp. 164 seq.
[2] Dubois, i, pp. 354-5.

must be cautious in taking too literally such statements. Rancé himself had, after all, secured papal permission to retire to the Chartreuse should the Reform fail, and frequently in his letters expressed his desire to lay down his burden long before ill health compelled him to do so. It is logical enough that men whose integrity and positive example had elicited the respect of their brethren should feel the pull of la Trappe, where the best was only just good enough.

Some of the cases recorded show a pattern too marked to be coincidental. As already noted, quite a number of the postulants had great trouble in securing authorization to leave their orders and their perseverance was often tried for years on end, but others who were perfectly free to come were kept waiting by Rancé himself. Honoré Simon tried for more than ten years to gain admission, but Rancé would not let him come, saying that he was too valuable as a spiritual director in the Paris Oratory. He was eventually professed in 1682, dying six years later as dom Isidore. Dorothée Colas[1] was rather different. He took the habit in 1675, but after a few months went off to a seminary and only came back in 1686, to die four years later. At the same time as dom Dorothée, Jacques de la Cour[2] came to la Trappe as a boy of 17, but his health was not equal to the rigours of the novitiate, and in 1675 he transferred to le Pin, where he was professed and later ordained. He still cherished the hope of coming to la Trappe, however, and in 1686 was readmitted. After acting as novice master and subprior, he was sent on a reforming mission to Perrecy, in Burgundy, whence he was recalled to succeed Gervaise as abbot in 1698. Oddly enough, Gervaise's story is similar.[3] As a young man he made a career for himself as a theologian with the Carmelites, becoming prior of Grégy, near Meaux, where Bossuet knew him. It is not clear whether, or how often, he visited la Trappe, but he is said to have been kept waiting for fourteen years before Rancé finally relented and admitted him in 1695.

A very strange case is that of Bernard (Éloi) le Môle. He had been a Premonstratensian for forty-five years and then, for some unexplained reason, took a vow that he would come to la Trappe if cured of an illness. He was apparently a friend of M. Pinette, one of Rancé's oldest and closest friends, for we find Rancé writing

---

[1] Both in *Relations*, i.   [2] Some details in *BN* 24123, f. 51.
[3] See above, p. 55, n. 3.

to Pinette (6 December 1683/4) that the undertaking must be honoured. At all events he was professed in 1685, aged 64, and the *Relation* of his death quotes a letter he wrote to Pinette saying how happy he was in his new home. He died in 1690.[1]

The strangest case of all unfortunately lacks date or name, but deserves mention. This concerns a 'R.P. de Flandre' who had already made two unsuccessful attempts to settle down at la Trappe, and whom Rancé agreed to accept for a third time.[2] Without a date the subject cannot be identified, but it seems unlikely that he did stay, for in that case the incident would surely have been more fully recorded.

A point of some interest concerns what might be called plural entry. The most considerable example is that of the Celestines,[3] seven in number, who came after Jacques Puiperrou had, so to speak, established a bridgehead. They were not all, or even most, from the same house (Celestine houses were in any case quite small), and it is fascinating to speculate on how the members of the little group first met, laid their plans, and then executed them, though it is now possible to be reasonably certain why they came just when they did. In a decision of such gravity, men naturally seek moral support from each other, and whether in forsaking their original order or in undergoing the novitiate at la Trappe, the presence of familiar faces must always have been reassuring. Such mass exodus was rare, and on the whole undesirable, but a lot of postulants seem to have come in pairs, or at least soon to have joined friends already at la Trappe. When Bernard Molac came from the Paris Oratory he found Quesnel's formerly Oratorian brother already there, though Bernard stayed and Quesnel did not.[4] Pierre le Nain similarly was followed from Saint-Victor by Simon Gourdan[5] some four years after his flight, but it took Gourdan, who much admired him, only a few days to discover that his true vocation was not by his friend's side, though he later made a serious application to try again. Oddly enough, relatives figure very rarely in the lists. Very little is known of the *donnés*, but one pair of brothers, gentlemen from Champagne, is

---

[1] See below, *Relations*, i; letter to Pinette *TC* I/150; it was his translation that caused the Premonstratensians to protest to the Chapter of 1684.
[2] *TC* II/108.   [3] On Celestines see below, pp. 158–61.
[4] See his original letters to P. Quesnel, in *U* 970.
[5] On Gourdan see below, pp. 169–73.

recorded by Félibien. Besides these two we know that Pierre Maupeou briefly tried his vocation and that his brother persevered to become dom Grégoire. A pair of cousins, Bazile Anzoux (1689) and Bernard Michel (1691), are recorded as such in the *Relations*, and there may well have been others not mentioned (dom le Nain was in fact distantly related to Rancé). In the seventeenth century, it was very common for brothers (or sisters) to join the same house: Rancé had two sisters at the Annonciades, and Cornuty had an elder brother with him at Tamié; and on such evidence as is available la Trappe seems to have been exceptional in this, as in so many other other respects, whether by accident or by Rancé's design.

This inevitably reintroduces the difficult question of statistics. Practically all the records preserved concern choir monks and lay brothers actually professed and dying at la Trappe. Occasionally, for special reasons, we hear of *donnés*, like the two brothers just mentioned or frère Chanvier, the trusted courier and man of affairs of Rancé's later years, but no estimate of numbers or identity is possible. Even for professed monks one is driven back to generalities, like 'many are called but few are chosen', which is not very helpful for constructing an accurate picture of the community. Odd scraps of information suggest certain limits: thus in 1674 (23 October 1674) Rancé writes that he cannot for the moment accept any more lay brothers as there is no more room in the dormitory.[1] At that time there were six or seven lay brothers, and it was not until 1678 that any more were admitted. In 1680 he once more writes, to the Carmelites at Besançon,[2] that he has no room for lay brothers, and again in 1695 (18 October 1695) he tells Gerbais[3] that there is no room for a proposed lay brother, but that while waiting the man should learn to weave stockings on a loom so that he can be useful when he can be admitted. The life of lay brothers was extremely rigorous, but it looks as though many postulants, however suitable, were excluded over the years simply from lack of space. Overall one lay brother was admitted for every four choir monks during Rancé's abbacy, but this does not of course necessarily mean that the proportion within the community at any given time was so low, and

[1] To Arnauld, copy in *T* 2183, f. 28.
[2] *TD*, series D, 82, of 13 June 1680.   [3] *A* 5172, f. 148.

in 1676 and 1685 (two years for which figures exist) it was more like one to three.[1]

As for choir monks, it is even harder to calculate how many may have applied for every one that was admitted. Up to Rancé's resignation in 1695 the greatest intake for any one year was 9 in 1672, only exceeded in 1692 with 10, but in the next six years up to his death a marked increase is apparent (11, 6, 19, 13, 10, 11). Unfortunately the only firm figures available refer precisely to this period: Gervaise states[2] that in his three years as abbot (1696–8) he admitted 40 out of 400 postulants. As the 40 is a roughly correct figure, the other may well be so. Similarly the novice master, dom Paulin, in 1696, his first year in office, reports sending away 50 postulants while 46 novices remained, of whom only a small number was later professed.[3] Limitations of space must at all times have determined the rate of expansion, but if it is really true that about 130 men postulated each year from 1696 to 1698, of whom only one in ten was accepted, similar proportions are perfectly possible for the smaller intake of earlier years. It follows from this that it is quite impossible to assess the numbers from various categories of those rejected, and wholly unreasonable with such a ratio to extrapolate any detailed information from the small number of those accepted. Thus it may well be that various orders supplied postulants in numbers quite unrelated to those professed, or that close relatives came together much more often than records suggest: it is impossible to establish such facts with certainty and pointless to speculate. Despite all this, something is known of the reasons for rejection and of Rancé's relations both with those who sent him postulants and with the rejected candidates.

For those already in monastic houses the principal motive for seeking entry to la Trappe is summed up in the words 'une observance plus exacte'. That is to say, their original aspirations to live as monks under the Benedictine, or some other, rule remained the same, but had not found satisfaction in the house or order to which they went. For these men, a large number over the years, la Trappe represented the purest expression of the monastic ideal which all reforms claimed to have revived, and

---

[1] These figures calculated from the mortuary lists are reasonably reliable.
[2] *Jugement critique*, p. 407.
[3] Abbé Lambert, *L'Idée d'un vrai religieux*; dom Paulin's letters are all in Part 1.

their motive was, in human terms, the quest for perfection, for the absolute, as against the compromise, however good in itself. Whether such candidates were correct or not in their assessment is another question, it was what Rancé himself believed, and constantly wrote, thereby involving himself in ceaseless polemic and publicity. One case in which he seems to have erred in judgement is also very characteristic of his general attitude, and is unusual, if not unique, in being documented on both sides.[1] In October 1685 a young Feuillant, Jacques de Saint-Gabriel Mauclerc, aged about 18, just entering his second year in the novitiate, arrived at la Trappe, without the permission, but equally not against any express order, of his superiors at Notre-Dame du Val, near Paris. Rancé thereupon wrote direct to the General of the Feuillants, J.B. Pradillon, requesting him most politely to release the young man on the grounds that after a few days' reflection Rancé did not doubt: 'qu'il n'eut besoin d'une vie plus retirée et d'une discipline plus exacte que celle qui s'observe dans votre Congrégation.' The young man wrote as well, but his letter is not recorded.

The General replied in firm and measured tones that he knew of Jacques's request, had promised to discuss it orally when he was next in Paris, and, while not surprised that such an immature boy should run away, was surprised that Rancé should receive him. Above all, the General regrets that Rancé should judge the state of the Feuillants from the word of a mere boy, adding that the Feuillants 'ont une observance suffisante pour contenter les forts, et ne pas accabler les faibles'. He goes on to say that the perfection of la Trappe (which he does not contest) seems to depend solely on Rancé himself and with devastating irony concludes: 'il n'a pas plu à la divine Providence pour des secrets que nous devons adorer de donner à votre réforme la grâce de la multiplication.' He ends by formally asking Rancé to send back Jacques, and encloses a stern and peremptory summons to the boy to return. This *démarche* failed, and the General was driven to obtain a papal bull in August 1686 peremptorily ordering Jacques to go back, which there is every reason to suppose he did, and formally prohibiting Feuillants to pass to any other order, even the Carthusians, but especially la Trappe.

---

[1] The complete dossier, with copies of MS letters, printed papal and royal orders, at Grenoble, C 3553–4, ff. 258–64.

Not all postulants were as young and impatient as Jacques, not all superiors as wise and temperate as the Feuillant General, but in its broad outlines the case is typical of many attempted transfers. It should be noted that the General defends his own observance, which was in fact sound and flourishing, without denying the greater austerity, or perfection, of la Trappe, and indeed without excluding the possibility of eventual transfer after mature reflection. One wonders how many idealistic but impetuous young monks came in this way to la Trappe out of defiance, or curiosity, and then fell by the wayside, despite initial encouragement from Rancé.

A partial answer to this question is given in a letter to dom Paulin de l'Isle, then for twenty-five years a Benedictine of Saint-Vanne in the diocese of Châlons, who was finally professed, after long years of waiting and determined opposition from his order, in 1687, aged 45 (he died in 1698). Rancé writes (26 September 1686);[1] 'si je m'arrêtais au peu de succès qu'a eu le dessein de ceux de votre observance qui s'étoient retirés dans notre monastère... j'aurois peine à me resoudre de faire ce que vous désirez de moi.' Up to that date only one Benedictine (dom Maur, in 1671) had persevered, but one must presume that many others had tried, only to find, in the words of the Feuillant, that the perfection of la Trappe 'accabloit les faibles'. It is incidentally interesting that when dom Paulin became novice master in 1696 he took the initiative of inviting a former colleague, then novice master at Mouzon, to send two good novices to la Trappe, so that Vannists could be represented as well as Maurists who were regularly sending postulants.

The quest for the absolute was undoubtedly also the prime motive of those who came from the secular life to the monastery, and a recurrent theme in Rancé's correspondence is that of sacrifice. 'Forsake all' meant just that for those who entered la Trappe. Another theme of a more positive kind is that of peace and joy. Dom Paulin, for example, once professed 'a joui d'une paix et d'une tranquillité... profonde' (29 June 1687)[2] and the image of the haven reached after the tempest is often used in this

---

[1] Lambert, *L'Idée*, pp. 60 seq.; this very rare book is a mine of useful information, apparently not recorded elsewhere, on the Vannists and also on the relations between la Trappe and other orders towards the end of Rancé's life.
[2] Ibid., p. 83.

connection. The sheer pressure of worldly affairs, of pastoral activity even, may deny a man the peace he craves, and in the more extreme cases, such as soldiers, the motivation is obvious. There is no need to pursue the point further, since it is not specific either to la Trappe or the seventeenth century, being rather a constant factor of the monastic, as opposed to active, vocation.

One very specifically seventeenth-century motive should, however, be mentioned. Not the least of the tempests from which both men and women sought refuge in Rancé's day was the Jansenist controversy. Many, of course, sought and found houses like Hautefontaine, Orval, or (it seems) Châtillon[1] where the superiors were known Jansenist sympathizers and where Jansenist ways were tolerated or encouraged, but the case of la Trappe was in this, as in so much else, quite unusual. A later chapter will discuss the whole question of Rancé's position with regard to Jansenism, but one or two case histories may now illustrate how relevant the question is to that of vocations.

We know that Benoît Deschamps,[2] who had a brother at Port-Royal and was a friend of the Jansenist Pontchâteau, found the peace he wanted at la Trappe. Similarly Arsène Cordon, who had been deeply involved in polemic while curé of the very Jansenist parish of Saint-Maurice, near Sens, became an exemplary monk; Cordon's predecessor, the saintly M. Du Hamel,[3] who had suffered much persecution for his Jansenist loyalties, made several retreats, some prolonged, at la Trappe and would have stayed there if Rancé had been willing. Paul Hardy, former théologal of Alet, was another leading figure closely associated with the cause who became an exceptionally good monk.[4] In all these cases we know that no discussion of their views, for or against, was ever permitted in the monastery, and thus they completely abandoned controversy on profession. The peace they found was in silence, not in tacit complicity, and once they became monks they put their past behind them.

A contrary case further emphasizes this point. Late in 1678 a Benedictine of the Congregation of Saint-Vanne, long since infiltrated by Jansenist sympathizers, one dom Henri de Fouchières, came to la Trappe on Arnauld's recommendation, but

[1] Some references in Neveu, *Pontchâteau*, p. 44.
[2] *Relations*, i.   [3] See below, pp. 236–38.
[4] *Relations*, i and letter from Rancé to Alet, of 15 Apr. 1675, *TC* I/19.

after discussion with Rancé was rejected as unsuitable. In January 1679 Rancé wrote to both Fouchieres and Arnauld,[1] saying in effect that they disagreed so much, and Fouchières showed so little confidence in Rancé, that he would do better to stay where he was. This incident caused a storm in Jansenist circles, and a letter from Pontchâteau to Le Roy makes it clear that Fouchières had not been found acceptable because he was 'fort Augustinien', that is, Jansenist. It is relevant that about the same time another monk of the same Congregation, dom Paulin de l'Isle, with known Jansenist interests, first thought of coming to la Trappe, and, as we have seen, was finally accepted many years later. The point is obvious: Rancé was perfectly prepared to accept convinced and prominent Jansenists on condition that they obeyed his orders forbidding discussion, but not such as saw in la Trappe a sanctuary from which they could safely serve their cause or even conceal their private refusal to submit to the Church's authority.

One more motive should be added: that of atonement for an evil life. Dom Muce is the most famous example of this, but others include Abraham Beugnet,[2] a parish priest from Saint-Pol, who came in 1696, aged 58, after a scandal involving a woman followed by years of disgrace and perhaps infamy (rather an overdone word in conversion literature). Such men are extreme examples of the thirst for the absolute and can hardly be regarded as typical.

Personal recommendation played a major part in producing candidates for la Trappe, and not surprisingly the quality of the referees is a valuable clue to that of the recruits. Rancé's correspondence with them also reveals a much more complex concern than might be expected both for those who try and for those who, having tried, fail. Some time in 1672 Favier, then living in Auvergne, sent along a pious young man, frère Edmond, apparently for domestic service at la Trappe.[3] Rancé did his best to oblige his old tutor, but in 1673 writes to say that he cannot keep Edmond, who is unable to stand the solitude. He is 'un bon garçon, très pieux... Cependant... depuis que les domestiques vont à un certain degré de piété, on ne peut plus s'en servir.' A month or two later the young man has still failed to gain acceptance in any house in Auvergne, and by the end of the year is

---

[1] Copies to Arnauld in *U* 913, to Fouchières *TD*, series C, 69.
[2] *Relations*, ii.   [3] Gonod, pp. 46 seq.

pleading to be allowed back to la Trappe, but he has not changed, life at la Trappe has not changed, and the two are simply incompatible. A full year after Edmond had been sent home, Rancé is still sorry for him, and would do anything to help, but it is just not possible to have him back. He is still writing of Edmond in 1676, and perhaps as late as 1677 (the reference is not explicit). This tale speaks for itself of Rancé's care for others, as well as his kindly firmness. It is very likely that Favier was instrumental in sending other postulants to his former pupil, but details have not survived.

The Paris Oratory had played a major part in Rancé's life from the earliest days of his conversion.[1] M. Pinette, the secular founder of the Institution (near the present Observatoire), where Rancé always stayed when in Paris, remained his lifelong friend, so did Père de Monchy, and so, until the Jansenist quarrel split them, did Pasquier Quesnel. In the nature of their ministry the Fathers of the Faubourg Saint-Honoré, of Saint-Magloire, and of the Institution were uniquely well placed as intermediaries between la Trappe, where many of them were frequent visitors, and the world. Thus it is almost certainly more than an accident of documentary survival that makes it seem as though the Oratory was the most important single channel through which recruits came, or applied to come, to la Trappe. Already in 1670 Quesnel's brother Guillaume was trying his vocation, but did not stay. That same year Bernard Molac came and did stay, sending back to Quesnel a number of letters of some interest, of which five are preserved. Quesnel sends him books, a Saint Bernard, the Desert Fathers, and is asked to look after Molac's copy of *L'Astrée* 'et les autres livres que vous jugerez préjudiciables au salut de mes sœurs', whom he particularly exhorts (through Quesnel) to obey their apparently widowed mother. His first letter shows an enthusiasm which was to last until his death five years later: 'La Trappe est un paradis pour ceux qui savent goûter les délices de la solitude, de la retraite, et spécialement du silence..' In 1673 Quesnel's *confrère*, Payen, tried his vocation, only to be told that solitude does not suit him, and that same summer Rancé sent Quesnel an answer to the Oratorian Hubert, saying 'il est rare que les ecclésiastiques soient destinés pour la Trappe', quoting St.

[1] On the Oratory see below, pp. 246–255; on Quesnel and the others see also Tans, 'Dialogue monologué'.

Bernard 'Clericum delicatum et laboris inexpertem recipere formidamus'. In 1677 he writes that a young Oratorian from Aix is doing well as a lay brother (it does not look as though he stayed) and that he is ready to accept a lad recommended by Père de Chevigny: 'la première de toutes les qualités que nous demandons à nos religieux.. est une souveraine docilité.' About the same time Quesnel himself came on a visit, and Rancé says how glad he was to see him: 'mais pour toujours c'est une autre affaire, et je ferais grand scruple de vous retirer d'une Congrégation qui a besoin d'hommes et d'ouvriers..' Quesnel's subsequent career makes it easy to be wise after the event, but it is fair to say that right up to the end he kept his admiration for la Trappe, despite estrangement from Rancé, and felt at home at Orval, which he visited from exile. By 1679 it is the turn of Père de Nocey, who had left the Oratory to become a hermit in the woods near la Trappe, where he died in 1692. Charles Denis in 1672, Isidore (Honoré) Simon in 1682, Bruno Servet in 1692, Placide Boquillon in 1694, all came and stayed, and we have no means of knowing how many other Oratorians tried unsuccessfully, nor how many other postulants came through their good offices.

A rather pathetic case is that of frère Théodore Faverolles. This young man was apparently sent by Quesnel, but his full story is related in six letters sent by Rancé to Quesnel's friend, Père François Bruscoly,[1] who died on 9 December 1678. We first hear of the young man in February 1677 in a letter to Quesnel. Next month we learn that the mother of this young man of 23 (she was presumably a widow, since no father is mentioned) approves his desire to join la Trappe. A year later frère Théodore has fallen ill, but is giving every satisfaction. At his insistence he was professed next month (March), but less than four weeks later he was dead. Rancé asks Bruscoly to break the news to Mme Faverolles, and later refuses her offer of a gift to la Trappe in memory of her son. The same letter reports to Bruscoly that a Feuillant (Jean-François Fournier) is showing promise (actually fulfilled) of staying at la Trappe, and asks that his mother be informed that they will take

---

[1] Originals in U 483. Batterel does not mention Bruscoly, and I am most grateful to P. Auvray, archivist of the Oratorian house at Montsoult, for information about him. He joined the Oratory at Lyons in 1655, was ordained priest in 1657, and returned to Paris in 1659. He seems to have stayed there until 9 Dec. 1678, when he died at Saint-Honoré, where he was buried. Apart from his contacts with Quesnel and Rancé, no more is known of him.

every care of him. It is incidentally interesting to note that in the
three cases of Molac, Faverolles, and Fournier the mother seems
to be alone, presumably widowed and thus more reliant on
priestly advice.

Bruscoly must have been a very active recruiting agent, for in
the year or so covered by these six letters we hear not only of the
two young men who did stay, but of an unnamed 'Monsieur'
who had to leave for reasons of health and a canon of Séez who is
advised to remain where he is.

Yet another link with the Oratory is François du Suel,[1] who
after training at the Oratory became curé of Châtres (now Arpajon)
and then, in 1676, canon-penitentiary at Arras. In 1673 he came on
a visit of three weeks, as a result of which he published early in
1674 the *Entretiens de l'abbé Jean...*, which had some success in
spreading a highly favourable but scarcely lifelike impression of
Rancé. He toyed with the idea (or so it seems) of retiring to la
Trappe himself, and on at least two occasions sent postulants
there, one, in 1678, Siméon Lambert, who stayed on as a lay
brother, and the other (15 January 1682) 'un jeune homme d'une
grossièreté naturelle, mais simple et docile', who cannot be
identified.[2] The six monks from the diocese of Arras professed
between 1696 and 1699 probably owed nothing directly to du
Suel, who died in 1686, but rather to the impossible conditions
in that war-ravaged area.

If the Oratory and its associates were of major importance,
there were many other channels open. Arnauld, as we have seen,
sent Fouchières in 1679, and others unknown; Quéras, of Sens
and then Troyes, Nicaise, from Dijon, Gerbais, from Paris, are
three others to whom Rancé writes at different times about candidates. His episcopal friends, particularly of Luçon, Grenoble,
Limoges, and Meaux, may well have sent him recruits, but on the
evidence of the correspondence it was rather Rancé who sent
deserving subjects to them, often after failure at la Trappe. It is
clear that in the course of time more and more priests and others
(like Tréville or du Charmel) visited la Trappe and came to know
enough about life there, and the qualities needed for admission,
to be able to advise those who came to consult them about a
vocation. It is certain that the largely misleading legend of la

---

[1] See the excellent article by I. Noye in *Dict. de spiritualité*.
[2] *TB* 948 and 1598.

Trappe continued—and perhaps continues—to exercise a strong attraction, but the steady dissemination of reliable facts by responsible people must have helped. One interesting case concerns Simon Gourdan, of Saint-Victor. His own attempt to embrace the life there with his friend, dom le Nain, had not succeeded, but he continued in close and sympathetic contact with la Trappe to the end of his long life (1729). He acquired a great reputation for sanctity, fully discussed in his life by Gervaise, and was a natural Parisian focus for those seeking spiritual guidance. We do not know how many of his *confrères* owed their contact with Rancé to him, but many of them, including the only intermittently pious Santeuil, were among Rancé's correspondents. In 1688 a young Victorine, frère Gueston, came to la Trappe against his prior's orders, and the authorities demanded his return. Gourdan was enlisted in the prior's support, and wrote a letter defending Saint-Victor, to which Rancé replied with a very long and detailed refutation. Gueston in the end proved unsuitable, and was duly sent back, but the incident did nothing to harm relations between Rancé and Gourdan, for in 1695 he sent a somewhat unusual recruit to la Trappe. A rich grocer of les Halles, one Étienne Lyon, on becoming widowed, suddenly decided to follow the religious life. He consulted Gourdan among others, and improbably enough was recommended to go to la Trappe. Here he took up a semi-eremitical life as frère Théonas (he was never professed, and never took orders) and seems to have found what he was looking for, in a hut a few hundred yards from the monastery, where he attended mass every day. His children were provided for and, as Rancé says in a letter to an interested Benedictine, Lyon has simply followed the Evangelical precept to forsake father, mother, and all the rest for God's service.[1]

Rancé's attitude to those who failed to stand the rigours of la Trappe has already been discussed in connection with particular cases, such as Edmond or Gourdan, but the issue is important enough to merit closer study. An early example of one side of this question occurs in a letter to Le Roy,[2] where Rancé speaks of a certain frère Martelot who 'commence à changer de maniéres et de maximes, ce ne sera jamais un grand personnage'. Six months

---

[1] *Vie du vén. P. Gourdan*; on Gueston, pp. 76 seq.; on Lyon, pp. 103 seq.; see also Rancé's letter to dom A. Jounel, of 3 Dec. 1695, original in U 6094.

[2] Originals in U 767 of 6 July and 2 Dec. 1672 published by Tans.

later Martelot has left, for la Trappe demands 'un esprit solide et un cœur humilié: comme ces dispositions sont fort rares, il nous vient beaucoup de gens, mais nous en retenons peu'. A little later he tells Le Roy how difficult it is to be sure: 'les hommes, et particulièrement ceux qui sont sans lumière comme moi, ont besoin de temps et de longues épreuves pour pouvour s'assurer [des vocations] et encore avec incertitude des dispositions secrètes des personnes.' Addressed to the companion of his own early struggle to find a vocation, these words should not be taken as mere conventional self-depreciation.

His poor opinion of Martelot is mild compared to what he has to say (also probably to Le Roy) of 'un misérable' who had taken the habit at la Trappe early in 1675, having come with a recommendation from the Bishop of Autun, but left after a fort-night.[1] This was the egregious confidence trickster Hippolyte-Châtelet Beauchâteau who, after some years as a Prêtre de la Doctrine Chrétienne in the diocese of Autun, left his congrega-tion in 1672 to go to Le Roy at Hautefontaine. From la Trappe he must have gone almost at once to London, for in July 1675 he abjured there, pretending to be Arnauld's brother, Luzancy, and professing disgust at the Jansenist heresy. He later claimed to have been offered money by a Jesuit to return to Rome, became a deacon (Anglican) and M.A. at Oxford, and twenty years later was notorious enough to be mentioned by James II in a letter to Rancé about his gross impostures in London (12 December 1695).[2] 'Misérable' he may have been, but he undeniably had panache.

Neither of these two seems to have done la Trappe much harm, but there were others who did. The converted Huguenot, frère Armand-Climaque, has already been mentioned, and must have been a particularly sad disappointment to Rancé. He was involved, at the very least imprudently, in the case of frère Chalype,[3] a young Recollect (Franciscan) who came in 1690, the year after frère Armand's profession, apparently with the specific intention of collecting evidence harmful to Rancé. He left to spread calumnies so extreme that he was severely disciplined by his own superiors and obliged publicly to exonerate Rancé. A less vicious, but still

---

[1] Copy in U 3069; see also Moréri, s.v. *Beauchâteau*, and Feydeau, *Mémoires*, pp. 304 seq.

[2] (Alençon) MS. Tournoüer 13, letter 17.

[3] On both see above, pp. 51 and 99.

highly embarrassing, affair was that of dom Muguet, nephew of Rancé's publisher, who in 1684 secured reluctant admission from Rancé against the strong opposition of his Maurist superiors, and then had to be sent away as unsuitable. The Maurists refused to have him back, and the whole business was most unfortunate.[1]

Such casualties are not very surprising, and Rancé reacted rather in sorrow than in anger, but they are not the most interesting. To an unnamed brother he writes[2] that he has asked another abbot to give him a place, since the austerity of la Trappe is beyond him, but: 'je ressens plus de peine que je ne puis vous exprimer de notre séparation', and will pray for him 'comme pour le reste de nos frères, au nombre desquels vous serez toujours dans le sentiment de mon cœur'. To Père André, of the Theatines, he regrets that a M. Rousseau, despite the firmness of his resolve, has neither the physical nor the spiritual qualities required at la Trappe, but hopes Père André will help to 'adoucir l'ennui que ma réponse pourra lui causer'.[3] A year later he writes (13 June 1682) to frère Théodore, at l'Étoile,[4] that having unsuccessfully tried his vocation at la Trappe, he can now at l'Étoile build on those foundations. Rancé is glad that Théodore obeyed his injunction to go, and will always feel responsible for his well-being. Several very interesting documents written by Théodore survive, and show him to be a worthy and serious person. Similarly Rancé writes to an anonymous Maurist (13 February 1681); 'vous ne m'êtes pas moins cher que si la divine Providence avait permis que vous eussiez achevé parmi nous ce que vous y aviez commencé.'[5]

Over the years one finds time and time again inquiries about the welfare of some member of another community who had originally tried la Trappe, invitations to try again if the urge persisted despite disappointment, consolations to those like his former valet, Antoine, at Tamié, prevented from return for physical reasons or, like Cornuty, for canonical ones. It may well be said that such a concern is no more than Christian charity, but for a man as busy as Rancé it is a form of charity rare enough to be noteworthy.

[1] Bossuet, *Correspondance*, iii, p. 47, of 8 Dec. 1684 and p. 55 of 6 Jan. 1685.
[2] Muguet, i, p. 330.   [3] *TB* 1435 of 1681.
[4] *TB* 1676; this was the former fr. Maxime sent with the blessing of Arnauld and M. le Nain.
[5] *TD* series B, 44.

7. Religious of the Cistercian Order

IT was natural that Rancé's influence should be most directly felt among his fellow monks, especially Cistercians, and to a somewhat lesser extent other religious, notably Canons Regular, since these had the best reasons for contact with him and shared many of the same problems. Here, as always, the decisive influence must have been exerted in personal encounters, but his correspondence was no less important, often leading eventually to a meeting or to continuing discussions which had begun face to face. It is particularly tantalizing to have just enough evidence to prove how numerous and intimate his contacts were without having enough positive identification in many cases to permit reconstruction of the whole story, but the patterns are clear. As well as interviews and correspondence, his published works made an immense impact, and inevitably generated still more correspondence, both favourable and unfavourable, especially from those whose way of life was examined. By a particularly malign trick of fate, the year from which most letters survive is 1682, the year before *Sainteté* appeared, so that the quantitative effect of that work and the ensuing polemic is hard to assess. Thus, by a pure accident of survival, most of the evidence to be discussed here dates from the earlier part of Rancé's career, but fortunately the later period is by no means barren.

The chronological sequence of events in Rancé's life has already been sketched, and though it may seem a little artificial to separate his public and formal utterances from those more private and familiar to be found in his letters, the difference is really of kind rather than degree. At the very beginning Rancé was himself much influenced by members of the order he had just joined, and whatever may have been his original plans for la Trappe, he soon discovered that they could only be implemented with the active help or at least implicit approval of such authorities as the Visitor, superiors whose monks he needed as a nucleus for reform, and the Abstinent leaders, especially Jouaud. Through his contacts at Court, Jouaud must have had some knowledge of Rancé, and had perhaps even met him, before his conversion and profession, but the rest of the monastic world can have been scarcely familiar to this young priest whose ecclesiastical friends were either *abbés de cour* and careerists, as he had been, or connected with Port-Royal, through Andilly, or the Oratory, through Bouchard, Monchy, and, ultimately, Mère Louise. What lifelong monks can have made of their newest recruit is not clear, but they certainly recognized in him the qualities most needed for the advancement of their cause in a world of high-level intrigue for which they were not themselves suited.[1]

The consequences of Rancé's almost immediate involvement in the increasingly bitter struggle between Abstinents and Common Observance were twofold: he became known in France and Rome in a role very similar (though now much more prominent) to that which he had begun to play in the Assembly of Clergy just before his conversion, and his personality as a spiritual leader, animated by reforming zeal but with almost no practical experience, was that which a very wide public came to know. By his Abstinent colleagues he was judged on his conduct of their cause; by the Abbot of Cîteaux and his supporters he was seen as the latest in a long line of malcontents, no doubt sincere, certainly troublesome; by the rank and file it seems that he was already credited with highly original and attractive ideas on monastic life. An early pointer to his reputation and influence is the migration of Cornuty to la Trappe while Rancé was still in Rome, whence he wrote to welcome the new recruit.[2] In this, and no doubt other cases, the centre of information about la Trappe was apparently the Collège des Bernardins, which served the whole order, and with which Perseigne, as novitiate for the Western province, had close and continuous ties. The behaviour of this aristocratic novice, delicate but determined, the fact that he entered with the dignity of commendatory abbot and left a year later to be consecrated as regular abbot, must have inspired discussions wherever monks gathered together on the business of the order.

Rancé himself would have repudiated any distinction between his role as spokesman for the Abstinents and his vocation as abbot of la Trappe, because for him the endless negotiations into which he had been most reluctantly drawn made no sense

---

[1] Suited no doubt by temperament, but hardly suited by talent or justified by results.

[2] See above, p. 108.

outside the context of the life he and his monks wished to live at la Trappe. In the nature of things, however, the distinction was made, and to some extent remained a permanent source of misunderstanding throughout his life. Obviously there is no point in fighting unless you intend to win, whatever the odds against you, but equally there is not much point in fighting for a cause which the mere fact of fighting prevents you from serving properly. Jouaud at Prières, others at la Charmoie and elsewhere left their abbeys in the hands of coadjutors for years on end in order to conduct the endless litigation and lobbying in Paris.[1] This was one of the specific charges laid against the Abstinents, or at least their abbots, by critics within and without the movement, and it was a point on which Rancé felt very keenly. It is therefore not surprising to find him insisting with increasing frequency and emphasis on a superior's paramount duty of residence, first as it regarded himself, and then in advice given to superiors, men and women, who consulted him. This in turn reflects his conviction that the cause of reform would best be served not by argument but by example. Always impatient over juridical questions, Rancé was concerned only with establishing a newly purified religious life in as many houses as possible and, if all else failed, among as many individual religious as possible, even against the general practice of their own house. For him appeals to king or pope, debates in General Chapter or special assemblies, were regrettably necessary in order to obtain the legal sanction without which the whole reform movement would be in jeopardy. Unlike his colleagues, however, Rancé only lent his considerable support to these various activities as a last resort. He believed, and in the long run proved, that the cause could only be won in the cloister, but something in him led him time after time to bludgeon his opponents with precedent, quotation, and authority. As a result there was constant tension between his desire for peace and silence in his abbey on the one hand and his almost obsessive need to prove the rightness of his case on the other.

All these considerations come out from his correspondence and contacts up to 1675, when there occurs a sharp break with the world outside la Trappe, but, as had been the case with his conversion, the change of heart was heralded long before it took place. The Chapter of 1667, in which he played a leading part,

[1] See Lekai, *Rise of Cist, S.O.*, *passim*.

was the only one he attended at Cîteaux, and though he actually
set out for that of 1672, he had to turn back. Sickness was the
official reason for his non-attendance, and was no doubt the immediate cause, but it was certainly not sickness that made him
reject the office of Visitor to which that Chapter nominated him.[1]
In his letter of refusal he makes it quite clear that he will not
lend his name and prestige to a compromise solution when only
root-and-branch reformation of the whole order will satisfy him.
His attitude to Abbot Vaussin might be described as one of
deferential insubordination; to Petit he combines nominal deference with exhortation and startling candour; to the Abbot of
Clairvaux (Pierre Henry until 1676, then Pierre Bouchu), his
immediate superior, he writes in exactly similar terms,[2] at once
protesting his respectful submission and leaving no room for
doubt that he is going to do what he wants to do with or without
permission. It is highly improbable that the Abbot of Cîteaux
and the other proto-abbots took the slightest notice of Rancé's
appeals, though they very likely respected him as a man of principles and true piety; they were more likely to be concerned with
his influence in high places. In the struggle in which both parties
were engaged, votes counted more obviously than sanctity (which
might of course win votes). To the end of his life Rancé continued to profess respect for his superiors, and after Petit's death
in 1692 relations with Cîteaux seem to have become notably more
cordial, but in fact the best that can be said is that Rancé and they
agreed to differ, going their separate ways except when some
dispute arose over jurisdiction. His influence on the authorities of
the Common Observance was therefore minimal, and amounted
to no more than goading them into action on particular issues from
time to time.

In his relations with other Abstinent leaders the picture is very
different. The first with whom he came into contact was Jouaud,
who was initially sceptical about the plans for la Trappe and
doubted whether Rancé would ever win a following. Then, in
the course of his long and frustrating mission in Rome, he got to
know Dominique Georges, Abbot of Val-Richer in Normandy,

---

[1] Rancé's letter of refusal was published in a long pamphlet giving full details of
the Abstinent cause and high praise of Rancé himself, *Examen du Chapitre... 1672*,
pp. 92–5.
[2] For samples of his letters to Henry see copy in *U* 863 of 4 Jan. 1673 and to
Bouchu *TB* 1068, also in Muguet, ii, p. 194.

very well.[1] Georges, with his long training as a secular priest in the community based on Saint-Nicolas-du-Chardonnet in Paris, was another latecomer to monastic life, but though he was clearly a man of great energy and integrity, he had very little in common with Rancé, a comparatively near neighbour of his. By 1675, indeed, Rancé is writing in most uncomplimentary terms about his colleague: 'un esprit plat et grossier'[2] and blaming him for harmful rumours concerning Bellefonds. Both Jouaud, for personal reasons (he had been active in securing Saint-Cyran's imprisonment), and Georges, who maintained close relations with Jesuits and whose biographer, Buffier, was himself a Jesuit, were strongly anti-Jansenist and, rightly or wrongly, suspected Rancé of Jansenist sympathies, viewing his austere regime at la Trappe with some unease. It is only fair to say that Rancé maintained outwardly cordial relations with Georges until his death in 1693, and the correspondence between them (from 1688) preserved by Maupeou[3] indicates a genuine mutual respect, while there seems to have been no awkwardness in Rancé's reluctant replacement of Georges as Visitor to les Clairets. In the same order of hierarchical relationships may be mentioned that which Rancé came to have with Hervé du Tertre, Jouaud's coadjutor and then successor at Prières and canonical Visitor in 1676 and 1678. His *cartes de visite* show that la Trappe was in flourishing condition and that the Visitor, whatever his private misgivings, was quite happy to put the stamp of his official approval on what he saw there.[4]

After the General Chapter of 1667 and subsequent Abstinent assemblies in Paris, other abbots and priors began to take more interest in substance than in tactics. The first close contact was with Eustache de Beaufort, Abbot of Sept-Fons.[5] This young nobleman had become abbot (regular, not commendatory) of his

---

[1] See Buffier, *Vie de M. l'abbé de Val-Richer.*
[2] Copies of letter to Mère Agnès de Bellefonds in U 3069 and T 2183.
[3] At the end of vol. ii of his *Vie*.   [4] See above, p. 38.
[5] Drouet de Maupertuy, *Histoire de la réforme de Sept-Fons,* contains most of the standard details, though Beaufort himself angrily disclaimed the book in a letter published the same year (14 June 1702). A much better and fuller account is in a MS. kept at la Trappe, *Mémoires sur la réforme de Sept-Fons,* dated 24 Nov. 1759 but stated to be a copy of a document originally compiled in *c.* 1709 by a monk who had lived thirty years with Beaufort. It is interesting that in forty-three years as abbot, Beaufort sent only 12 candidates for Holy Orders (p. 70). Cf. Rancé's policy mentioned above, p. 74. Even fuller is F. Lamy, *L'Ancien Sept-Fons* (based on a MS. kept at that abbey), especially pp. 125–70. He dismisses Drouet as quite unreliable.

very run-down community in 1654, at the age of 19. He underwent some kind of conversion (accounts differ as to the details),
and as early as 1666 he came to la Trappe, paying another visit
after the Chapter of 1667, this time asking to be accepted there as
an ordinary monk. Rancé, however, never approved of abdication
and instead sent Beaufort back to Sept-Fons but agreed to train
novices for him, and in fact took four in the two years 1666–8.
Things unfortunately went wrong from the start. Already in 1669
we find Rancé writing[1] to a monk of Sept-Fons, frère Alexandre
de Patras, to remind him of his duty to his abbot, expressing
satisfaction that he has returned to his monastery but admitting
that, compared to la Trappe, all is not well at Sept-Fons. The
main trouble seems to have been shortage of recruits, and re-
calcitrance of the unreformed monks whom Beaufort could not
dislodge. In 1670 Rancé can still describe Beaufort as 'ami intime'
in a letter to Quesnel,[2] and it is hard to know just how bad things
were, for le Camus writes[3] from Grenoble to Pontchâteau, another of Rancé's friends, that Sept-Fons under Beaufort is the
'copie de la Trappe'. This was on 17 March 1673, but only three
years later Rancé had a bitter quarrel with Beaufort in the course
of which mutual accusations were made to third parties.

It seems that the original cause of the quarrel was Beaufort's
betrayal of Rancé's confidence in the affair of the fictions, and
specifically that he had shown a copy of Rancé's answer to Le
Roy to some Parisian Carmelites (those of the rue du Bouloy, not
the rue Saint-Jacques) who had promptly passed it on to some
doctors of the Sorbonne as smacking of Jansenism. Rancé was
furious, especially at the suspicion of Jansenism to which he always reacted violently, and criticism of Beaufort occurs in several
letters of the period.[4] Mostly he is concerned to refute the charges
against himself, but more general criticism is to be found in a letter
to the Abbess of Leyme of January 1676. He tells her that the
reform at Sept-Fons never really got under way, that the monks

---

[1] *TD* series B, 54 of 17 July 1669. He was already 44 when he first went to Sept-
Fons, and his failure to get on with his young abbot is not surprising. See Lamy,
op. cit., p. 143.

[2] In Tans, letter 5 of 17 Aug. 1670.   [3] *Lettres*, no. 40.

[4] Original letters to Bellefonds of 6 Nov. 1676 in *BN* n.a. 12959, f. 49, to Brancas
of 21 Nov. 1676, in *SS* and copy to Leyme in *TB* 624. Reconciliation in copies to
Leyme, *TB* 1026 and Châtillon, *TB* 1119 of 17 Aug. 1679. Lamy says nothing of the
quarrel, but indicates the extent to which material problems preoccupied Beaufort
for years.

he sent to help Beaufort 'ne trouvaient régularité quelconque', that there were not enough to perform the office properly, though Beaufort insisted on singing High Mass with only four or five monks, and so on. Obviously Rancé regarded Beaufort's personal incapacity ('défaut de lumières... trop grande incrédulité') as the principal cause of this sorry state of affairs, and the history of Sept-Fons does suggest that it took Beaufort an unusually long time to find his feet. It looks too as if he allowed himself for a time to become involved in intrigue and absenteeism, perhaps as a relief from his failure at home. However, that may be, the story has a happy ending. In 1677 Rancé is still telling Mère Agnès of his distrust, but by 1679 a reconciliation has been affected, Beaufort has twice visited la Trappe, and a few months later Rancé is telling the Abbot of Châtillon that things at Sept-Fons are now much better. In fact recruits slowly began to come in, and by the end of the century the abbey was flourishing and contained about a hundred monks. Personal relations between Rancé and Beaufort remained good, and an unexpected visit is recorded as late as November 1698,[1] when Rancé was having serious trouble over Gervaise and seeking the support of Noailles, whose Vicar-General was Beaufort's brother.

The story of Beaufort and Sept-Fons is both typical and illuminating. Rancé's influence was invariably exercised as an individual on individuals, not on institutions or groups, and when he did influence a community it was always through the superior, or sometimes the leader of a reforming group within the community (as at Saint-Antoine or Saint-Victor). Consequently personal relations determined the degree to which individuals followed Rancé, and this in turn ultimately determined the future course of such relations. There was no direct causal connection between Beaufort's indiscretion in Paris and his failure at Sept-Fons, but in Rancé's eyes the same defects of character were responsible for both. It is also true that recruitment to one house rather than another depended, for all but local residents, on the superior's reputation, and Rancé's approval was a factor to be reckoned with.

A group of abbeys over which Rancé exercised lasting influence centred on Hautefontaine, whose commendatory abbot, Guillaume Le Roy, remained one of Rancé's closest friends until

[1] In *SG*, Suppl. ZZ f in fo. 316, f. 112 of 23 Nov. 1698.

the quarrel over fictions. By complete coincidence several independent contacts led Rancé to eastern France in the early days of his conversion. Vialart de Hersé, Bishop of Châlons-sur-Marne, was one of the first people he consulted, and visited, in 1661, and was also a friend of Le Roy's. Retz, living in exile at Commercy, had always been friendly with Rancé, and in 1664, on the way to Rome, Rancé called at both Châlons and Commercy, paying another visit in 1669. A little further away, the abbey of Châtillon had close ties with la Trappe; the venerable abbot, Jacques Minguet, resigned his charge in 1669, after a lifetime of active service in the Reform, and retired to la Trappe as an ordinary monk, to be succeeded by Claude le Maître[1] (until 1693), former prior of Hautefontaine, a close friend of Le Roy and, through him, of Nicole. If dom Rigobert, another former prior, had accepted Le Roy's pressing invitation to return to Hautefontaine as regular abbot the ties would have been still stronger, but in fact Bernard Soyrot later went there from la Trappe to maintain the connection.[2]

Châtillon's nearest neighbour was Orval, today literally astride the Franco-Belgian frontier, but then in the province of Luxembourg under the Empire. In 1669 Rancé profited from his visit to Commercy by going on to Châtillon, where he met Abbot Charles Benzeradt of Orval, another young aristocrat who had succeded in 1668 after two years as coadjutor. He too was anxious to introduce the Reform, later paid a visit to la Trappe, and sent one monk (and perhaps more) to be trained there as a nucleus for his reformed community. Three years later, in 1672, these contacts produced yet another, this time with some monks from Heisterbach, whose way from Germany to France led quite naturally through Orval and Hautefontaine, and though Rancé seems to have had no influence at all on Heisterbach as a community, he wrote to at least three monks from there,[3] and it was in fact their visit to la Trappe that marks the beginning of the long quarrel over fictions. As late as 1679 Rancé is still discussing with the prior of Perseigne the unhappy situation of a Heisterbach monk (unnamed, but presumably one of the three) who has still

[1] Seven original letters from him to Le Roy and one to Cappé in U 745.
[2] According to the *Necrologium* (*fiche* from Rouen, Montbret y 29).
[3] For the first time to dom Fr. Weber on 14 May 1672 (*TB* 44) and also to Lapp and Bourlez (*TB* 67), whose Latin reply is also preserved in a copy, Also letter to Perseigne of 5 Dec. 1679 in Denis, *Autographes de Troussures*.

not succeeded in finding a house of the Common Observance in
which to lead the kind of religious life he seeks. It may be added
that it was in this same region of eastern France that the Benedictine Congregation of Saint-Vanne flourished, and contact
between black and white monks, as well as Retz's close association
with the important Benedictine abbey of Saint-Mihiel, are further
elements to be considered in tracing Rancé's influence on local
monks.

At first, naturally enough, it was with his old friend Le Roy
that Rancé had the closest contact, but their estrangement after
1672, and more positive causes as well, led him into unusually
close contact with Abbot Claude of Châtillon, to whom at least a
dozen letters survive (1673–83) and from whom, quite exceptionally, are preserved seven letters written to Le Roy (1673–9).[1]
Thanks to this correspondence, much of the pattern of relationships involved can be reconstructed, for, apart from the dispute
between Rancé and Le Roy on which Châtillon throws light, it is
to Châtillon that Rancé sends detailed advice on how to conduct
his own reform, together with valuable comments on the situation
at Orval, Sept-Fons, and elsewhere. An additional point of
interest is that, with the death of Jouaud in 1673, Châtillon suddenly found himself one of the leaders of the Abstinents in the
concluding stages of their litigation, and indeed it is in this connection that Rancé's earliest surviving letter is addressed to him.
Châtillon tells Le Roy (22 June 1673) of the disarray caused to
'notre misérable réforme' by Jouaud's death, of Rancé's despondency, and of his own wish that his brethren would show
'moins de timidité et plus de zèle et de ferveur accompagnée d'une
grande oraison'. A week later (30 June), still in Paris, he learns
with regret of the strained relations between Rancé and Le Roy
and would like to mediate. In an unusually revealing passage he
goes on: 'Je voudrais voler à la Trappe pour y témoigner mes
pensées à ce saint abbé... Croyez-vous que je suis capable de
ramener à la paix un homme de cette force? Je sais qu'il m'aime
beaucoup mais s'il aime plus son propre sentiment je ne gagnerais
rien sur son esprit.' The same letter incidentally discloses his
intention of going with Nicole to Maubuisson, whose abbess, a
friend of Port-Royal, soon became one of Rancé's devoted
followers. Another three weeks pass, with Châtillon seeking

---

[1] All references to letters from Châtillon are to *U* 745.

support and preparing for his mission to Rome. He has still not been able to see Rancé, but hopes that the latter will soon return to a more charitable frame of mind. Meanwhile he fears the worst, while determined to fight to the end: 'Quoi qu'il arrive nous aimons mieux périr par Rome que par nous-mêmes.' and if the worst comes to the worst, 'nous nous retirerons chacun dans nos maisons, pour y déplorer l'abomination de la désolation.' One can see why Rancé and Châtillon got on so well; they spoke the same language and shared the same standards.

A few days later (23 July 1673) Rancé writes[1] in cordial terms ('mon très-cher Père', a relatively rare form of address in his letters) to wish his friend godspeed to Rome, but 'souvenez-vous qu'il faut que vous le fassiez [le voyage] en esprit de pénitence'. Rancé himself would dearly like to repair the faults (presumably against charity and humility) he had committed during his own visit there. Contact was undoubtedly maintained, and some as yet unidentified letters may turn out to belong to this correspondence, but the next certain addition is in 1677. Châtillon, from Paris again (in fact from the Institution de l'Oratoire where Rancé had always stayed), feels obliged to warn Le Roy that Rancé's very hostile *Dissertation* on fictions has appeared in print. He blames Beaufort's imprudence, says that Rancé will be very upset when he learns what has happened and had done all he could to prevent it. Later in the year Châtillon is detained by sickness (the same affliction of the right arm suffered by Rancé) at the abbey of la Piété in Champagne, and is still in touch with Rancé. In August a very informative letter from Paris shows Châtillon to be on close terms with both Simon Treuvé, later biographer of M. Du Hamel,[2] and the Bishop of Châlons, who had also tried to mediate between Rancé and Le Roy. According to Châlons, Rancé was not really wrong, but the divulgation of his *Dissertation* had done la Trappe a lot of harm and had even deterred some potential recruits who had thought to go to la Trappe. At the end of September Châtillon fears that he will be unable after all to accompany abbé Fléchier[3] to la Trappe and would in any case not be hopeful of effecting a reconciliation.

It must always be remembered that after 1675 Rancé depended

---

[1] Muguet, i, p. 296.   [2] On Treuvé and Du Hamel see below, pp. 236–240.
[3] This Fléchier was a friend of Feydeau and Le Roy, but not necessarily the future Bishop of Nîmes (1632–1710), the friend of Caumartin.

entirely for news of the outside world on letters and the reports of visitors, and it is therefore all the more impressive that Châtillon, clearly a much respected monk with a mind of his own, never wavered in his loyal support for both his friends, Rancé and Le Roy, though he could very easily have criticized either behind his back. We are particularly fortunate in possessing this correspondence, fragmentary as it is, because it permits a much more reliable assessment of that which ensued, and of which only Rancé's letters survive.

In 1679 (10 June),[1] evidently in answer to a specific inquiry, Rancé tells Châtillon that he must not demand money (i.e. endowments) from novices and that he should exclude a particular novice who showed 'légèreté et peu de dévotion; pour ce qui est du silence, nous l'avons fait aimer à nos frères avant que de l'établir aussi exact qu'il est parmi nous'. A month later[2] he is worried about Orval ('peu de retraite et de silence'), with whose abbot he maintains a quite separate correspondence. Next month[3] (17 August), after writing direct to Orval, he again reports to Châtillon that he is worried about the situation there. He goes on to discuss Tamié (a smaller community than Châtillon had supposed) and Sept-Fons, at last growing and establishing 'l'observance... exacte et régulière, mais il y a douze ans qu'il y travaille'. He adds that all is now forgiven between Beaufort and himself and goes on to reflect: 'il est très difficile de se séparer des hommes [in enmity]... sans se séparer de Dieu.'

Most of the letters to Châtillon contain news of the community at la Trappe, which Châtillon evidently knew very well, especially his aged predecessor: 'je pense qu'il aura dès cette vie le don de l'immortalité, le bonhomme a honte de tant vivre'.[4] Recruits were still too few at Châtillon, but by the last day of January 1680 Rancé sees the beginning of progress and sends his friend the rules on novices observed at la Trappe, with the rest to follow. By June Rancé would be glad if Châtillon had 'des personnes à qui les [règlements] faire pratiquer.'[5] In September two postulants have arrived, and Rancé adds, a little harshly, that things are at last moving at Orval, though the abbot has been there fourteen years without accomplishing much.[6] The next identifiable letter comes a year later. Rancé is delighted to see that postulants are

[1] *TB* 1076. [2] *TB* 1086. [3] *TB* 1119.
[4] *TB* 1251. [5] *TB* 1302. [6] *TB* 1345.

staying at Châtillon, and even has a word of qualified praise for Orval, 'une grande chose par rapport aux dispositions du pais et de la nation [sc. Germany]', despite continuing laxity. He finally states his view: 'aller peu à peu [est] une maxime dangereuse, surtout dans l'observation du silence et les entretiens avec les religieux.'[1]

Again a long gap occurs in the correspondence, broken by a particularly detailed letter the following summer (27 June 1682).[2] Rancé tells Châtillon to pay no attention to what people say about his attempts at reform; of those who come few will stay (one in ten at la Trappe), but this is no reason to feel discouraged. In fact the numbers were only sixteen in 1660 and cannot have improved much in wartime conditions. He advises his friend to allow a sick monk meat if a vegetarian diet is no longer sufficient for his health, and gives details of the refreshment (water) permitted in case of need during work and of the siesta (counted against the total hours of rest) sometimes allowed at midday. Surprisingly perhaps he says: 'il ne faut point condescendre aux relâchements, il ne faut pas aussi tenir trop ferme quand les nécessités sont réelles.'

The last known letter to Châtillon comes early next year (11 January 1683).[3] Rancé tells him that he must go to the General Chapter but must combine firmness with respect. He criticizes the Abbot of Vauclair for so easily forsaking the reform, saying that in some monasteries they talk of regularity but 'tout y est digne de compassion'. Orval he praises, with the same qualifications as before, but he thinks the abbot has 'beaucoup de piété et de vertus' and that his work will last. As for la Trappe and its finances, 'notre pauvreté est notre richesse, c'est notre gloire'. Châtillon too, ravaged by wars, fires, and other calamities was desperately poor, and was exempted from contributions to central funds of the order.[4]

This correspondence is remarkable in many respects, not least because the relationship between Rancé and Châtillon follows a course quite contrary to what one would normally expect. Châtillon, after all, first appears as one of the most highly respected men in the order, entrusted with a mission to Rome and appointed spokesman for the Abstinents before the King, the

---

[1] TB 1527.   [2] TB 1680.   [3] TB 1828.
[4] Quoted in Lekai, Rise of Cist. S.O., p. 194.

friend and familiar of bishops, magistrates, scholars, and leading clergy, and it is in this capacity that Rancé first addresses him. His unswerving friendship and integrity enabled him to retain the confidence of both Rancé and Le Roy during their painful quarrel, and in everything we know of him he seems to have been an admirable and energetic person, despite the usual rheumatic troubles of his age and profession. Yet in the later stages of the extant correspondence Châtillon can be seen referring matters of detail, even of day-to-day policy, for Rancé's decision. It is of course true that high-sounding programmes of reform, religious or otherwise, can only be realized through specific application to individuals and situations. This was the lesson Rancé himself had learnt in Rome, and it would seem that Châtillon, though a much more experienced monk, had belatedly come to the same conclusion for similar reasons. It is also very relevant that the Rule of St. Benedict goes into precise detail about diet, clothing, and the like, and though the prescriptions gave rise to much debate in the seventeenth century, no one queried the value of exact measures and regulations. It is none the less striking to see how practical and how humble an attitude Châtillon adopted in consulting his colleague.

The situation at Orval always seems to have worried Rancé, but on the evidence it is not certain how clearly he foresaw just what was to happen there. The first contact seems to have been in 1669, when Rancé agreed to make the considerable journey to Châtillon (24 March) in order to meet Benzeradt and advise him about his projects for reform.[1] Four years later (25 January 1673)[2] things have not progressed very far, for the usual reasons: the 'anciens' jealously preserve their vested interests, and reform cannot make headway against their resistance. Despite the distance, however, Rancé offers to accept Orval's postulants for training, and one had apparently come in 1672. By 1679 things are improving: the 'anciens' are dwindling, 'véritables religieux' are coming along in good numbers, and, despite the increasing austerity of life, health remains good. Rancé sounds a note of caution in finding that conferences are too frequent, and that outside contacts are too easy, but his tone is encouraging.[3] In August he returns to the same points, adding the special consideration that usage varies in France and Germany (he speaks

[1] Muguet, i, p. 96.   [2] Ibid., p. 269.   [3] Ibid. ii, p. 265.

of two French monks at Orval), and advising the abbot against attending the States General (of the Empire) for which his rank qualified him.[1] By 12 May 1684 reform is fully under way:[2] there is no more organ music; manual labour is yet to be introduced (1688) as at la Trappe, but the Visitor and the Abbot of Clairvaux have approved of what they found; twelve priests and four lay brothers continue in the Common Observance, with fifty-three others reformed; and all seems to be well. An undated letter[3] emphasizes the need for still stricter silence and abstinence, and advises the abbot not to undertake the unpromising task of reforming an unnamed monastery in the Netherlands.

What the correspondence does not reveal is that contacts with Jansenists were becoming more and more frequent towards the end of the period, and it seems very likely that Rancé's references to outsiders and conferences may have something to do with this fact. Nicole, a friend of Châtillon as we have already seen, spent some time at Orval in 1679–80; in 1683 the prior was sent with some monks to Le Roy at Hautefontaine, the regional centre for Jansenists, and on Le Roy's death in 1684 they came back to Orval, soon to be followed by Pontchâteau, who stayed there several years. Quesnel was another visitor, and by the turn of the century Orval had become a leading centre and refuge of Jansenism. A very hostile modern Benedictine scholar[4] blamed the spread of Jansenism at Orval on 'le manque de perspicacité et de science' of Benzeradt, who 'avait négligé pour lui-même et pour ses religieux la culture intellectuelle, philosophique et théologique'.

Whether or not the undeniable effect is here attributed to the right cause, Benzeradt himself gives valuable evidence concerning the origins of his anti-intellectual policy. Writing to Mabillon on 7 August 1691 (they may have met in Paris when Benzeradt played a major part in the Abstinents' Chapter of 1684) in the context of the dispute over monastic studies, he says plainly that he had formerly consulted 'un célèbre abbé de notre ordre [sc. Rancé] qui me dit que si j'établissois l'étude, je gasterois tout le bien que Dieu avoit commencé chez nous. J'ai eu d'abord de la

---

[1] *TB* 1108.   [2] *TC* I/23.   [3] *TC* II/3.

[4] See the long critical articles of dom Thierry Réjalot, 'Le Jansénisme à l'abbaye d'Orval, 1674–1764', pp. 59–82 on Benzeradt, and 'Correspondance de… Benzeradt … avec Mabillon', pp. 133–49.

peine d'entrer dans son sentiment, mais l'expérience m'a fait
connaître ensuite que son avis avoit été très bon et très salutaire...'
In 1694 (13 November) he tells Mabillon that studies have been
resumed 'par une petite philosophie que j'ai fait composer exprès...
elle sera suivie d'une théologie qui tiendra plus de la positive que
de la scolastique...' Jansenist or not, accounts of life at Orval
agree on the edifying and regular observance, and, in the light
of the evidence just presented, the nature of Rancé's direct influence is quite clear, though there is room for disagreement as to
its consequences. What we do not know is how far Le Roy, and
then Pontchâteau, Nicole, and Quesnel were themselves influenced
by what they had seen at la Trappe, of which they always spoke
with warm approval even after relations with Rancé himself had
become strained, and how far they, and even more their friend
Châtillon, influenced life at Orval independently of Rancé.[1]

The case of Tamié has already been discussed in connection
with Cornuty, but it is worth recalling because it is rather different from those just mentioned.[2] The total submission of Abbot
Somont after prolonged and bitter hostility to Rancé is quite a
different phenomenon from the consistently favourable response
of Châtillon, Orval, Sept-Fons, and Hautefontaine. It also serves
to emphasize once more the essentially personal character of
Rancé's influence. His original dispute with Somont had been as
much due to the defection of Cornuty as to any wider motive, and,
once reconciliation had been effected, the first consequence was
the return of Cornuty to Tamié, together with the dispatch of
Alain, Antoine, and Anselme from la Trappe. Under such circumstances, with four experienced monks to set the example
they had learnt at la Trappe, there was no need for such detailed
prescriptions as were sent to Châtillon or Orval. All the same,
Rancé stresses from the outset the importance of admitting only
suitably qualified recruits, even at the cost of low numbers (the
community never went much above a dozen), and above all of
banning the study of philosophy: 'vous leur dessécherez le cœur,
vous leur ôterez par l'étude l'esprit de prières, vous les dégoûterez
du travail des mains.'[3] A few months later[4] he expresses the same

[1] For further details on Orval see also Neveu, *Pontchâteau*, pp. 279 seq. Unlike
Rancé, Pontchâteau thought that the reform would last at Orval but not at Châtillon.

[2] General details and text of several of Rancé's letters in Garin, *Histoire... de
Tamié*. On Cornuty see above, p. 108.

[3] *TB* 923, of 6 Feb. 1678.   [4] *TB* 977, of 5 Nov. 1678.

confidence as he was to show to Orval regarding official approval
for the way of life practised at la Trappe and Tamié, and was proved
right by events. Two years later (20 September 1681)[1] there is an
exchange of views over the best employment for the three monks
sent to Tamié: Antoine, Rancé's former servant, must stay there,
because the solitude and silence at la Trappe had proved too
much for him; Anselme wants to come back, but is also unable to
face the rigours of la Trappe; while Alain is destined for Maubuisson. Rancé himself says he has little direct contact with
Somont, largely because le Camus, a frequent and regular correspondent, keeps him informed from Grenoble. In any case
during Somont's protracted absences in Rome and elsewhere on
the business of the order. Cornuty, as prior, acted as effective head
of the community and remained in contact with Rancé, whom he
always longed to rejoin. More than anything else, Cornuty's close
personal attachment to Rancé ensured that Tamié followed as
faithfully as possible the model of la Trappe, though the comments just quoted on the respective rigours of the two houses
speak for themselves. It was incidentally another monk of la
Trappe, the Savoyard Malachie Garneyrin, who was at first proposed as Somont's successor before the final choice fell on Cornuty in 1701.

All these abbeys may be said to have followed Rancé's example
in principle, and often in detail, but for geographical reasons
none of the superiors in question had opportunity for very frequent contact. In the case of Perseigne, a strenuous day's journey
on foot, contact was constant and intimate. By some extraordinary
fluke seventeen letters, nearly all original, survive from Rancé
to the prior for the thirty months from June 1679 to December
1681,[2] and almost certainly represent a regular monthly, or
even more frequent, correspondence. Perseigne[3] was never a very
large house (about seventeen in 1660) and being in commend

---

[1] *TB* 1536.

[2] The text (or part of it) of many of them is only available in the *Fichiers Charavay*
at the BN, or in the *Autographes de Troussures* (of which the present whereabouts is a
mystery), and while some were acquired by Tournoüer and are known to survive, it
is unfortunately possible that the others have perished in private hands.

[3] Information about Perseigne is scattered and scanty. Most of the hard facts are
in *Archives de la Sarthe*, iii, H; there are a few facts in G. Fleury, 'L'Abbaye cist. de
Perseigne' (very vague on sources) and even fewer in J. Wehrle, 'Malebranche et
l'abbaye de Perseigne'. Rancé's surviving letters add considerably to knowledge of
the abbey.

had limited resources, but it was the provincial novitiate. Many of its monks went on to the Collège des Bernardins in Paris; it had a reputation for learning (Malebranche chose it for his periodic retreats) and supplied several other houses with priors. Alain Morony and Urbain le Pannetier had both left Perseigne, where they had in turn succeeded Michel Guitton as prior, to go to la Trappe (Urbain as prior there), and interchange of personnel went on all the time. The neighbouring abbeys of Champagne and Tironneau, both in commend and not very flourishing, came under Perseigne's influence, so that this group of abbeys were very closely linked to each other and to la Trappe. Rancé had indeed sent three of his monks to Champagne very early on to improve morale there.[1]

At first Rancé depended on Perseigne, but the emigration of Alain and Urbain probably marks a final shift in the balance, and thereafter la Trappe grew steadily in numbers and importance, perhaps directly at the expense of Perseigne. Defective records make it exceedingly hard to be sure what happened after the departure from Perseigne in about 1664 of prior Michel Guitton, who had guided Rancé's first steps in monastic life. In 1664 the Irishman, Alain Morony, was named prior (he had been professed in 1657), but by 1666 he was at la Trappe. He seems to have been followed as prior by Urbain, who, in his turn went to la Trappe in 1672. After him, and perhaps directly, came the very odd appointment of dom Jean le Comte. He had been professed at Perseigne as long ago as 1625, and as prior introduced the reform there in 1637 with six monks from Prières. About 1645 he became abbot of la Charité-sur-Lezinne, but this seems to have been a sinecure, for the so-called abbey numbered only two or three monks, of whom some were detached for other duties. Dom Jean appears in 1660 as 'commissaire' for Perseigne, and in 1664 for Ourscamp, but by 1670 he is apparently back at Perseigne, having resigned his abbey, for which a successor had been appointed by 1675.[2] He is recorded as giving up his superiority in 1678, and did not die until December 1682 'dans une heureuse vieillesse',[3] so that it looks as though he acted as prior after an interval of

---

[1] Rancé to Clairvaux, *TB* 1462 of 2 Feb. 1681.
[2] References in Leloczky, *Constitutiones et Acta*, pp. 184 and 198, and in *GC* xiv, 517–24.
[3] *Archives de la Sarthe*, loc. cit.

some twenty-five or thirty years, at least until 1678. In the same period, in 1673, a new commendatory abbot was appointed, Philippe-Jean Guestre de Préval, who was then barely 21,[1] and under such circumstances one can see that the situation at Perseigne must have been rather critical by 1679 when Rancé's extant correspondence begins.[2]

The prior may well have been Alberic de Vienne (professed at Perseigne in 1652), sent as prior to Champagne in 1664, or just possibly Benoît Luce, sent to succeed Rigobert at Hautefontaine in 1664, but all that is certain is that he did not enjoy good health and found his task very onerous. In June Rancé is giving advice about novices and silence, in July about a monk of irregular behaviour. Another letter in September refers to a reply given earlier, but, from the fact that Rancé discusses the right address to use and regrets postal delays, it looks very much as though he had previously relied for contact on monks or others passing directly between la Trappe and Perseigne. The prior had evidently consulted Rancé on the subject of study and manual work, for Rancé repeats his view that study could only be restricted if the religious agree, especially if the superior is only a prior and can thus be overruled by appeals over his head to major superiors. He then speaks of a Benedictine whom he has been unwilling to accept, but who may fare better at Perseigne, and of M. de Nocey, the ex-Oratorian whose first retreat was at Perseigne (with Jacques de Lanchal who remained to be professed there) before he came back to live in the woods near la Trappe. The abbot of Cîteaux has written in strong terms to Perseigne, ordering the prior to take charge of an unruly monk who, with another, should never have been allowed out 'de si mauvaise édification qu'on ne peut pas en conscience souffrir qu'ils aillent par le monde'. Rancé ends with his judgement on a certain dom Julien (?Davoust) and a warm invitation to the prior to pay a visit when he can. The very next day he is writing again, sending back by dom Paul some documents the prior has been translating and editing. In December Rancé thanks the prior for having come over to inquire after him in his illness, though he was too sick to see him, and mentions the unfortunate monk of Heisterbach who

---

[1] GC loc. cit.

[2] The series of letters here analysed is to be found in Denis, *Autographes de Troussures*, pp. 533–48.

is still seeking his monastic salvation. Only a week later a very brief note confirms that Rancé preferred to transact really confidential business by word of mouth.

The prior seems to have made very heavy weather of his task. In August 1680 Rancé is advising him about matters of discipline, and in November things have come to a head. The prior's health does not allow him to realize all his projects, and he cannot resign, or move, without incurring general censure, though 'l'indocilité et l'incorrigibilité du troupeau donne aux pasteurs une raison légitime pour en abandonner la conduite'. One of the Perseigne monks, a frère Étienne, seems to have found the situation intolerable, and has asked to come to la Trappe; Rancé leaves it to the prior to decide on the application, though the man in question is exposed to 'mauvais exemples et méchants discours'. Unfortunately Rancé fears that the Visitor, Hervé du Tertre of Prières, will not support the prior in his attempts to impose reform on an unwilling community, and conflict between the prior and his monks will lead to growing discontent. In fact the abbot of Prières died only a fortnight after this letter was written (8 December 1680) so that Rancé's forecast was never put to the test.

On Christmas Eve Rancé writes again, complaining of the difficulties of postal communication and saying that one of his letters must have been lost. The prior was apparently worried about the rules concerning religious profession, for Rancé repeats his advice that the brief of Alexander VII (1666) has not changed the fundamental Benedictine rule, but he goes on to say that until the prior told him about it he knew nothing of the new order requiring that a register of professions, duly witnessed, should be kept. He adds the information that parents and friends never attend the ceremony of profession at la Trappe (the only exceptions recorded occur after his resignation) and cannot therefore sign as witnesses, though this is clearly expected to be the general rule elsewhere. Even on so domestic a matter as the cemetery the prior has asked Rancé's advice. It is incidentally interesting that Rancé did not learn of the abbot of Prières's death until the end of the month, three full weeks after the event, though his canonical visitation had long been awaited. If it was so difficult to exchange letters over the short distance between la Trappe and Prières, more remote correspondents must clearly have been kept waiting for much longer.

By February 1681 the prior feels that without the backing of a Visitor he cannot proceed, and has written to Cîteaux to ask for one. Meanwhile the commendatory abbot is not making things easier, and Rancé promises to speak to him if an opportunity presents itself during an intended visit. In an earlier letter[1] (perhaps at the turn of the year 1680/1) Rancé had discussed with Préval the possibility of asking for Barbéry (returned to commend in 1678) or Prières (recently vacated by death, but not in fact returned to commend), but had strongly opposed any such move, saying that it was up to Préval to introduce a regular observance at Perseigne whenever he so decided, and that in any case as commendatory abbot (he was also a canon of le Mans) he should seriously consider becoming a regular. Since the finances of Perseigne were considerably affected by the abbot's attitude, the ultimately determining factor in any material expansion, Rancé's intervention was a direct contribution to the prior's schemes for reform. Préval never did become regular abbot, but he gave important assistance to the abbey, bequeathing to it his large library; and the lengthy tenure of Étienne Gruel, prior for fourteen years, must have been due partly to his influence.

Letters in March and May deal with routine matters, with frère Étienne again (quite possibly Étienne Gruel just mentioned) and with a novice, but in September more serious problems have arisen and it seems that at one time the monks even thought of letting the prior go elsewhere. Fortunately the new Visitor, Abbot Georges of Val-Richer, has now made the deferred inspection and has given the prior his approval, but all is not well and the prior's health is causing grave concern. Like so many of his contemporaries, he believes that taking the waters (probably at Vichy) is his only hope of a cure, and has asked Rancé his opinion. Predictably Rancé replies with a categorical veto, as he had already done in the case of his sister Thérèse in 1679, and as he was to do several times again. The prior must not avail himself of facilities denied to his monks, and since life at watering places is wholly incompatible with religious retreat it must be forbidden to all. 'Je vous parle contre l'usage et la coutume mais selon la vérité qui seule doit être la règle de notre conduite', but even so prominent a reformer as Benzeradt of Orval did not scruple to spend a month (in 1687) at Aachen recovering from a broken leg.[2]

---

[1] In *TB* 1159.   [2] See Réjalot, 'Le Jansenisme à l'abbaye d'Orval'.

Though sympathetic, all Rancé can suggest is a purge two or three times a week to relieve the worst of the pain. By mid-October the prior is so much worse that he has had to dictate his letter, but Rancé does not relent of his prohibition to visit a spa: 'je vous ai simplement dit le conseil que j'aurois pris pour moi-même.' The same month Rancé reports that he has now had a discussion with Préval, to whom he has given clear and detailed advice. It is his duty to see that the community leads an edifying religious life, free from temporal cares, and to apply any surplus revenue for the relief of the poor. Rancé denies that he has spoken ill of the present state of Perseigne, presumably in answer to a pained inquiry from the prior, and adds a little disingenuously that Préval is in any case better acquainted with the situation than he. Apparently the idea of becoming a regular has not been dropped, for Rancé has talked to him about it. After this important business, Rancé gives his opinion that dom 'A.' (almost certainly Alain Morony, back from Tamié and on the way to Maubuisson) should abstain from celebrating mass for a time, because a monk whom he had struck in anger had died three days afterwards. He ends by promising to refer to Perseigne more discreetly in future, which seems like a tacit admission of over-candid criticism in the recent past.

In November it is once more with individual problems that the prior is concerned. Rancé approves his decision to send away the troublesome dom Julien, who had evidently been fomenting discontent: 'Dieu jugera le murmure avec autant de sévérité que le blasphème.' The question of frère Étienne is still unresolved and a frère Ernoul is mentioned, whose destiny is also uncertain. Only a day or two later Rancé has to report that dom Alain had already gone by the time the prior's inquiry arrived, but that he seems disposed to maintain regularity of discipline (presumably at Maubuisson). The prior's health is no better, and all Rancé can suggest is massage in front of a fire with spirits of wine, which sounds as if the trouble is the inevitable rheumatism provoked by winter.

The last letter in this series continues the same rather gloomy tone (8 December 1681). The Procurator-General, Malgoirez, had died in Rome on 31 October, and, in an obvious attempt to conciliate the Abstinents, Abbot Petit of Cîteaux nominated Somont of Tamié, now Rancé's staunch ally, to succeed him. The appointment was announced in January 1682, and at the same time preparations began for the General Chapter, delayed by war and finally announced in August 1682 for the following May. Rancé must have known a good deal of what was proposed, for he begins his letter to the prior with the hope that the new remedies will work for the good of the order: 'l'infirmité est si générale qu'il faut une espèce de résurrection pour rétablir presque partout le principe de la vie; car il n'y a guère de différence entre la mort et la langueur dans laquelle notre observance se trouve.' It would seem that the prior had begun to become too involved in the politics of the order, for Rancé goes on to express the fear that while he is busy 'à éteindre le feu dans la maison des autres la vôtre ne brûle'. His sole duty and responsibility is the conduct of the souls entrusted to him as superior. The prior will be very welcome at la Trappe whenever he is free to come, but Rancé regrets that he cannot accept a visitor proposed by the prior (perhaps from Tironneau; the reading is doubtful) because of deceptions in the past.

For some reason no more letters from this correspondence survive, identifiably at least, but four years later (3 October 1685) a single letter, almost certainly to the same prior, shows that nothing much has changed.[1] The prior's health is still poor, but Rancé tells him that it is perfectly permissible to give up cider for wine, not usually served in houses of the province. A monk from Fontaine-Daniel must be kept pending further instructions; dom 'P.' (no doubt the Paul of an earlier letter) should take care of himself; the prior of la Trappe (Eustache Picot) cannot be sent to Perseigne, where his presence would only cause trouble. Once more Rancé reminds the prior of his duty to his own monastery, and disapproves of his proposed transfer to Barbeaux. And there the story ends. The connection with Barbeaux may have been through a monk of that house, one dom Paul, whom Rancé had had to refuse on grounds of poor health, and who may well be the same one referred to above.[2] The prior of Perseigne may have moved to Barbeaux, to whose prior Rancé writes in 1688–90,[3] and was certainly replaced by 1687, when the Abstinent Chapter appointed Jacques Jarniguen of Savigny to the post. The only

---

[1] In (Alençon) MS Tournoüer.
[2] Letters of 6 Sept. 1682 (TB 1756) and 7 Feb. 1683 (TB 1845).
[3] See BN, Fichiers Charavay and Denis, Autographes de Troussures.

other entry under the heading Perseigne is an extract from an undated letter[1] to the sub-prior of Perseigne supporting 'le bon
père' for not wishing to hear his confession, because Rancé himself had always refused to hear the confession of a superior of any
kind; this may well be a reference to the retired abbot and prior
Jean le Comte.

The importance of this correspondence is exceptional. The
survival of so many original letters over such a short period is
almost without parallel in the rest of Rancé's voluminous correspondence. Only to Arnauld d'Andilly, in the first years of his
conversion, to Mme de Guise, who expected rapid answers, to
Gerbais, on specific points of business, and to his intimate friends
Bellefonds and Barillon can anything like a comparable number of
letters be found for a similar period. This anonymous monk
(even if he were Alberic de Vienne we know next to nothing about
him) must be typical of many others whose correspondence has
perished, and even if Rancé did not write before June 1679 or
after December 1681 (or perhaps October 1685) the preceding
analysis shows what infinite care he took to answer questions and
problems so specific as to appear almost trivial. Exactly as with
Sept-Fons, Orval, Châtillon, or Tamié, Rancé sees the reform
desired at Perseigne as involving very precise decisions, about
discipline, diet, study, health, finance, which in practice demand
immediate action on individual monks and day-to-day problems of
tactics, not strategy. Far too much is made by Rancé's biographers,
hostile or friendly, of his sweeping claims to interpret the monastic
life correctly in theory and practice, and far too little is said of
the intimate relationship he enjoyed with those who sought his
advice. The prior of Perseigne, who though a neighbour was in
no sense under Rancé's jurisdiction or authority, is the best
example available of the nature of Rancé's influence, as well as
affording a unique guide to the frequency and content of a
correspondence intended solely for personal perusal (only four of
the letters exist in copies even at la Trappe).

The scattered fragments of correspondence to other houses
cannot be analysed statistically or chronologically, but they do
make up a jigsaw puzzle from which much can be inferred. A long
letter of 30 October 1668 to an unnamed prior is early evidence
of the role Rancé had already begun to play.[2] He had waited

[1] Extract in *BN* 19324, p. 157.   [2] Denis, *Autographes de Troussures*, p. 533.

some time before answering all the detailed questions 'et puis on ne prend point plaisir à confier au papier des choses qui doivent être très secrètes'. The prior, like so many other superiors, including Rancé himself, feels oppressed by the burden of his office and resents the 'dissipation continuelle' which interferes with his own spiritual life. Rancé is reluctant to assume the responsibility of advising the prior to resign; no one else can make the decision but himself, or weigh the good of the house against the damage to the individual. In the end only personal discussion can enable Rancé to judge, and letters are not reliable enough. After some consideration of devotional questions, Rancé advises the prior successively about study, for which he will hardly find time, about the relief of necessitous relatives, 'on les doit préférer dans les aumônes aux autres pauvres.. on pourroit même les consoler par lettres..', and about the wisdom of avoiding as much as possible contact with the unreformed members of his community. He ends by asking the prior not to pay too much attention to his advice, and apologizes for the haste and untidiness of the letter. Such advice, and such problems, are a recurrent feature of Rancé's correspondence to the end of his life, and it hardly matters who this particular prior was—the principles governing Rancé's reply are always the same.

A house with which Rancé certainly had continuous contact over the years was Barbeaux, but only a few letters survive and no continuity can be established. The letter just mentioned may well (because of the provenance of others in the same collection) have been addressed to Barbeaux; another of 1671 is addressed to dom Robert Couturier,[1] a monk of Barbeaux who in 1667 was sent as prior to the daughter-house of Preuilly for an unknown period. In 1678 Rancé writes to the prior of Barbeaux explaining his willingness to stretch a point in favour of a Barbeaux monk who, with the approval of the abbot of Prières (as Visitor), wants to come to la Trappe for a limited period, preferably after Easter when the regime will be less severe.[2] It is highly probable that this was the same dom Paul who carried a message to Perseigne next year, and to whom Rancé wrote at Barbeaux in 1682 and 1683, regretting that his poor health made it impossible to accept him at la Trappe and emphatically ruling that a monk must not leave his monastery to help his parents even in need. In 1688 (22 Septem-

[1] Original in SS.   [2] Denis, *Autographes de Troussures*, pp. 537–8.

ber) he is still in correspondence with the prior of Barbeaux, mentioning dom Paul, and as dom Paul Eudeline, monk of Barbeaux,[1] became in 1683 proviseur of the Collège des Bernardins, where at least three of the letters for Barbeaux are addressed, it may well be he who became prior later. On Christmas Eve 1690 Rancé writes in very cordial terms to the prior, at the college,[2] who has asked for two religious to help reform Barbeaux. Rancé refuses to let them go, although they are in indifferent health, because of their personal attachment to him and his general disapproval of such transfers.

Scattered as the pieces are, the pattern of relationships extending over twelve years, or more, is clear enough: the prior warmly approves dom Paul's pressing request to try life at la Trappe, despite his health dom Paul persists, vainly, in his pleas, and continues to seek Rancé's advice even when firmly refused transfer. Successive priors (one of whom may have been dom Paul himself) and another monk, dom Robert (again possibly prior of Barbeaux after Preuilly), maintain contact, and even in 1690 beg Rancé to send two of his monks to set an example. Whether in belated answer to this request or not, he did in 1694 send to Barbeaux dom Arsène de la Croix (brother of the abbot of Cîteaux's secretary) who had been professed in 1687.[3] Under the circumstances it seems idle to deny that in the spirit, if not in the letter, successive superiors, and some monks, at Barbeaux consciously sought to follow Rancé, as always on the basis of direct personal contact.[4]

Another personal contact of considerable importance was that established perhaps as early as 1671 with Bernard de Cerisey du Teillé.[5] Professed at Perseigne in 1657, he may still have been there during Rancé's novitiate; in 1664 he was named prior of Tironneau nearby, so that it is highly probable that Rancé knew him already then. A brief letter to the prior of Tironneau in January 1670[6] thanks him for sending on some mail which has

[1] In (Alençon) MS. Tournoüer.   [2] Denis, *Autographes de Troussures*, p. 547.
[3] See Dubois, ii, p. 407, and list of professions; he seems to have been something of a malcontent.
[4] There is even less information about Barbeaux in the period than Perseigne, and apart from the brief entry in *GC* xii, 236, and scattered references in Canivez and Leloczky, these few letters are virtually all. It may be relevant that like Perseigne Barbeaux was in commend.
[5] See *Archives de la Sarthe*, loc. cit., Leloczky, *Constitutiones et Acta*, p. 199, and *GC* ii, 1352 (s.v. *B. Maria de Stella*).   [6] Copy in *TD*, series A, 79.

gone astray, but, in view of what follows, Rancé's reference to the 'mauvaise édification' afforded by the prior can hardly be addressed to dom Bernard, who on 27 January 1671 (the date is not quite certain) is addressed as sub-prior at the Collège des Bernardins.[1] As this was the headquarters and assembly place for meetings of the Abstinents throughout the period, any official of the college would be at the centre of things and could not fail to make the acquaintance of visiting superiors. In this letter Rancé speaks of the indiscipline of the students, some fifty in number, and the difficulty of regulating leave, and is clearly already on close terms with his correspondent. In 1672 Bernard was appointed to the important position of *proviseur* (normally held for three years) and next year, on the death of Jouaud, was nominated as Visitor by the Abbot of Cîteaux, and therefore rejected on principle by the Abstinents, who recognized only Abbot Gaultier of le Pin. There is probably an allusion to this incident in an undated letter (? September 1673), but by 1675 Bernard has completed his visit, for Rancé writes to sympathize (18 October 1675):[2] 'Je ne suis point surpris que vous ayez rencontré de grandes misères dans le cours de votre visite, et que ceux qui devaient vous donner la main... s'y soient opposés... dans peu l'on aura le déplaisir de voir dans tous les monastères de l'une et l'autre observance une uniformité parfaite.' He respects the Abbot of Cîteaux for his rank and as a person, but wants nothing more to do with the affairs of the order. On 25 September 1676 Abbot Claude Petit of l'Étoile (third abbot of his name) died and Bernard was appointed to succeed him, again becoming Visitor, this time with Abstinent approval. L'Étoile was not a very big house (six or seven monks it seems), but it had a good reputation and Bernard stayed there until his death in 1702.

By November 1678 Bernard in Paris has forwarded to Rancé a letter from Le Roy,[3] and is using his good offices to try to reconcile the two men. Four days later he is glad to send on Rancé's reply. In December he tells Le Roy that he is sorry Rancé's letter is so brief, but he, Bernard, had arrived at la Trappe late in the day and had been urged by Rancé to go on to Paris at dawn next day before he had had a chance to breach the subject of reconciliation. Meanwhile he is doing what he can with the Abbot of

---

[1] In Gonod, p. 346.   [2] Original in *T* 2240, no. 13.
[3] Originals of these four letters to Le Roy in *U* 749.

Clairvaux to have a new prior sent to Hautefontaine (perhaps to replace Rigobert's successor, Benoît Luce of Perseigne). Next March he is still (or again) in Paris, passing on correspondence from Le Roy to Rancé, and to Pomponne, a friend of both Rancé and Le Roy, and hoping to visit Hautefontaine after Easter to see what he can do to help. The new prior is unfortunately not behaving too well, and Bernard sadly observes: 'notre Observance est sur le point de sa ruine par le mélange de différents supérieurs que leur état différent et leurs différentes prétentions mettent dans quelque sorte de nécessité de vivre dans une continuelle défiance et donnent lieu aux supérieurs locaux d'être dans une continuelle balance et incertitude à qui ils s'attacheront davantage.' From his experience at the Collège, and as Visitor, Bernard must have been more intimately acquainted with the current problems of numerous houses, some ruled by commendatory abbots, some by absentee regulars, a few by resident regulars, than almost anyone else, and was in a position to exercise considerable influence.

A year or so later (20 January 1680)[1] Rancé writes to say how badly the cause of reform is going and how wise Bernard was to abandon his charge of *proviseur*, and in June 1683[2] he sends him a copy of *Sainteté* (acknowledged with thanks a month later), once again saying that he is glad that Bernard is at last free to attend to his own house after exercising the charge of Visitor. Rancé had in fact written to him in that capacity a few months earlier on behalf of M. de Montholon, whose son wanted a reliable prior for his abbey in Bernard's province.[3] A further link with l'Étoile was through frère Théodore, who had briefly tried his vocation at la Trappe before going on to l'Étoile, where Rancé is glad to think he can build on the foundations laid at la Trappe.[4] On the basis of this evidence it is not possible to assess at all accurately the nature and duration of the influence exercised by Rancé on Bernard personally and through him on his monastery, but it is reasonable to suppose that so long-standing a friendship bespeaks mutual respect and common ideals. In any case Bernard's career and status in the order are sufficient evidence of his gifts.

[1] *TB* 1225.   [2] Gonod, p. 348.
[3] Sold by Charavay, June, 1965, text in *Bulletin du Bibliophile*, 1872, p. 387.
[4] *TB* 1676.

Evidence about other superiors and monasteries is either too scanty to be much use or remains still concealed behind anonymity, but there are some links to be followed up. Through Cornuty, who held the vital post of novice master for seven years, Rancé was in close touch with the very influential abbot of Foucarmont, Julien Paris (1645–71), and his equally influential successor, Jacques Fleur de Montagne, former prior, who died while on a crucially important mission to Rome (1671–8), but no letters seem to have survived, although the correspondence with Cornuty specifically refers to such letters.[1] The abbot of la Colombe, Pierre de la Salle, a senior Abstinent, consulted Rancé at least three times between 1679 and 1682 on plurality of benefices and attendance at General Chapters, and in 1681 Rancé sent him 'un religieux serviable et docile'. Dom Guy, a monk of la Colombe, was in touch with Rancé at the same time and received general encouragement, but this hardly amounts to influence.[2]

The aged abbot of Cambron, in Belgium, wrote to support Rancé in 1672,[3] after hearing from his guests, monks of Heister-bach, how much they admired him; and it was almost certainly to one of these German monks that Rancé wrote in 1682 his long and famous letter on the religious life, copied so often afterwards.[4] The abbot of the ruined abbey of Pairis, near Épinal in the Vosges, wrote in 1681 inviting Rancé to take it over;[5] countless religious from houses all over France and beyond wrote asking to be allowed to come to la Trappe, and many came, only to return to their original houses fortified by Rancé's encouragement to persevere as best they could. There is no need to exaggerate the scope and importance of Rancé's role and influence: the facts speak for themselves, and far more evidence has been lost than will ever come to light.

The conclusion is inescapable: as a negotiator and leader of the Abstinents Rancé's influence was temporary and limited, but as an abbot, respected for himself and for the community he had created, he affected others, especially superiors, to a degree which no formal statement of adherence or obedience could ever represent. L'Étoile and Foucarmont, as well as Châtillon, Orval,

---

[1] See letters to Cornuty in Garin, *Histoire... de Tamié*.

[2] To Abbot de la Salle on 19 Sept. 1679 (*TB* 1137), 31 Aug. 1681 (*TB* 1514), 27 June 1682 (*TB* 1680); and to Guy 29 Jan. 1680 (*TB* 1249) and 31 Aug. 1681 (*TB* 1516).

[3] In Latin, 3 June 1672 (*TB* 69).

[4] Gonod, p. 225.   [5] *TB* 1458; Rancé politely refused.

Sept-Fons, Tamié, looked up to him, so did Barbeaux, Perseigne, and Champagne. He did not lead a movement in any organizational sense, but he certainly polarized a recognizable desire for a more perfect religious life than that currently offered even in the Cistercian Reform.

8. Religious of Other Orders

WHATEVER Rancé's personal standing in the world of religion he could naturally not influence those communities or individuals outside his own order to the same extent as those within. Unhappily the often bitter disputes with Cistercian opponents—and on occasion lukewarm allies—of reform can be paralleled in Rancé's frequently acrimonious exchanges with the superiors of other orders. None the less the balance is not an entirely negative one, and in some respects it is fairly even. As one might expect, the range of effects produced is much wider than that discussed in the previous chapter, but all can be traced to the single cause of Rancé's personality, however expressed.

Rancé's first task on his conversion was the rehabilitation of his five benefices, including la Trappe, and the transfer of all but the one he was to retain (originally Boulogne, then la Trappe) into the hands of responsible persons. In the case of Saint-Clémentin and Boulogne, assigned to Félibien and Barillon[1] (soon replaced by Picquet) respectively, he seems to have left things alone, but both le Val, near Bayeux, and Saint-Symphorien at Beauvais engaged his attention for some time. Le Val was not really a problem, once he had overcome the initially acute administrative difficulties of disposing of it. He eventually established a decently devout community of Canons Regular to perform the office in seemly fashion with Nicolas Druel, a gentleman of Rouen, as commendatory abbot. For fourteen years (1662–76) everything seems to have gone smoothly enough, but suddenly Druel decided to become a regular, and resigned his abbey in favour of his nephew. He wrote to Rancé about his impending novitiate, and received an encouraging reply,[2] accompanied by the Constitutions of Saint-Victor as a guide. No more is known of relations between Rancé and Druel, or indeed with le Val, but the episode is typical.

At Beauvais the situation was less straightforward. Rancé had visited this Benedictine abbey in 1659 to see things for himself,

---

[1] To Barillon, in *P* f. 601 of 17 Feb. 1672.   [2] *TB* 740 of 15 June 1676.

and by the time he had resolved to give up all his benefices save la Trappe had decided to give Beauvais to Favier. Rumour was not slow to associate Favier with Jansenist sympathies, but he duly took possession in 1661. For the next thirty years the problems of Beauvais continued to plague him, and he kept Rancé informed throughout and usually took his advice. The first troubles were, inevitably, material ones, and by 1671 religious life was so far from exemplary that Rancé tells Favier that the only hope is to get the Maurists to take over the abbey, by then containing five monks.[1] Two weeks later (23 July 1671) Rancé sent the monks, at their request, a letter couched in the most vigorous terms, reminding them of their duties and exhorting them to amend their lives worthily.[2] Nothing very much seems to have happened, however, because on his return from a visit to Paris for the affairs of his own order's reform (9 February 1673) Rancé writes despondently to Favier[3] to say that monastic reform is not in favour, and that the Maurists are unwilling to co-operate. A letter to Favier from one of the monks at Beauvais four years later[4] is a little more encouraging, and speaks warmly of him as a commendatory abbot who has done as much for Benedictine piety as many a regular. A few months later Rancé tells Favier (now nearly 70) that he quite understands that he would like to resign, and would support him in this if a worthy successor were likely to be found.[5] By the end of the same year (1678) Favier has received specific proposals from the diocesan authorities to permute the abbey for one, or more, priories in the same area. His age, and by now permanent residence in Auvergne, left Favier very little chance of improving the situation. In 1682 one of the four monks remaining[6] thanks him for a letter which has encouraged the fainthearted; two years later Rancé sadly writes of the reversal of the good order established at Beauvais;[7] by 1689 only three religious remain, giving little cause for edification, and the bishop has his eye on the abbey for a seminary.[8] The trouble dragged wearily on until 1692, when Favier received formal notice that no more entries would be permitted at Saint-Symphorien. By then he must have been too old to care very much, but for his part Rancé

[1] A 2106, f. 62.   [2] M 1214, 84 and Muguet, i, p. 156.
[3] A 2106, f. 71.   [4] Dom J. B. Boulenger, in CF 344 D of 9 Oct. 1677.
[5] Gonod, p. 61, of 5 Mar. 1678.
[6] Dom Bourdois, in CF 344 D of 4 Sept. 1682.
[7] A 2106, f. 130 of 15 Oct. 1684.   [8] Gonod, p. 70 of 14 Sept. 1689.

continued to comment on the protracted litigation and to offer what moral support he could. No doubt something useful could have been achieved if either Rancé or Favier had lived nearer to Beauvais, or been able to pay more frequent visits, or if the Maurists had incorporated the abbey into their flourishing reform. As it is, the lesson is all too clear: mere advice on general principles, however admirable, is no substitute for personal contact and guidance. Rancé and Favier wanted exactly the same thing for Saint-Symphorien, but under the circumstances it is hard to see how their failure could have been averted.

By some curious symmetry the failure at Beauvais coincided almost exactly with a very similar venture in which Rancé acted quite differently. In 1674 the young Louis Berryer (1655–1739) became a canon of Notre-Dame de Paris (as Rancé had been at an even more tender age) and shortly afterwards founded a house for nuns at Torcy in the diocese of Meaux.[1] Bossuet thought well of him, and he pursued a successful and lucrative career, becoming a *conseiller* at the Paris Parlement in 1687 and enjoying the revenues from several benefices. It is not clear when he first met Rancé, whose sister Marie-Louise he seems to have known as well, but in 1689 he came to la Trappe to present some relics, originally from Fleury-sur-Loire, which had been kept at his Benedictine priory of Perrecy in the diocese of Autun. The following year he underwent some kind of conversion and gave up all his benefices except Perrecy, where he retired to embrace the life of a regular and introduced reform. In 1694 Rancé writes to Gerbais[2] (a mutual friend) that two religious have gone from la Trappe to Perrecy to help in the work of reform, though it is odd, to say the least, that they should have been sent thus to a house of another order with no canonical links with la Trappe whatever. Coming so soon after the débâcle at Beauvais this episode may well have been a conscious attempt on Rancé's part to redress the balance. At all events, one of the monks he sent was his sub-prior and former novice master, dom Jacques de la Cour, who was actually still at Perrecy in 1698 when recalled to succeed Gervaise as abbot. How long he would otherwise have stayed there it is impossible to say, nor is it known when the lay brother who originally accompanied him returned to la Trappe, but Perrecy seems to have

---

[1] See useful note in Bossuet, *Correspondance*, viii, p. 109.
[2] See *A* 5172, f. 102 of 30 Aug. 1694 and subsequent letters.

prospered under Berryer's rule. Berryer himself played an important part in the negotiations concerning dom le Nain's life of Rancé.[1] Yet again the impossibility of effective influence without direct personal contact is demonstrated by the quite different course of events at Beauvais and Perrecy.

Rancé's relations with other members of the Benedictine family, reformed or unreformed, fall into no set pattern, although certain incidents tended to polarize disagreement, at least for a time. In the early days of la Trappe, considerable friction was generated by Rancé's open-door policy for religious of other orders. A good number, perhaps ten or a dozen, Benedictines tried their vocation, and beyond doubt many more made inquiries or even visits, though only one, dom Maur Aubert, was professed (in 1671) and actually stayed. Presumably in connection with Maur or one of his *confrères*, Rancé writes to the General's Assistant of the Congregation of Saint-Maur that he had had no idea that Père X was going to arrive, had no part in persuading him to leave his post, and 'il n'y a point de Congrégation que je considère tant que la vôtre'. A month later (19 February 1670) he writes back to the General[2] refusing to return the religious in question. It is not quite clear what happened next, though it looks as though the failure of so many Benedictine postulants to stay the course may have discouraged others. Since this was just the time that Rancé was trying to enlist Maurist support for Favier at Beauvais, the whole episode was most unfortunate. In 1673, as mentioned above, he recognized that for one reason or another the Maurists would not solve the Beauvais problem, but there is strong evidence for believing him to be sincere in his expressed admiration for their work. For instance, writing in 1675 to Mère Agnès[3] about Bellefonds's recent retreat at Val-Richer, Rancé criticizes the abbot for spreading rumours against him and, in the Jansenist–Molinist context, says that Bellefonds would be better off with the reformed Benedictines near Valognes.

The allied Congregation of Saint-Vanne meanwhile also began to feel the attraction of la Trappe, and in 1678 a monk of Luxueil (dom François Orival) was invited to come if he wanted to;[4] he was followed early in 1679 by dom Henri Fouchières,[5] though

---

[1] See account in *T* 2183 and *U* 3069.   [2] In *TC* II/35 and I/22.
[3] In *T* 2183 and *U* 3069, f. 108.   [4] *TB* 1008 of 8 Dec. 1678.
[5] *TD*, series C, 69 of Jan. 1679. He was from Saint-Vincent at Besançon.

neither of them stayed. There must have been others, before dom Paulin de l'Isle, who, as discussed earlier,[1] specifically invited Vannist postulants when he became novice master, and it is very likely that some of them may simply have been trying to escape renewed persecution of Jansenist sympathizers, always rather numerous in the Congregation. Rightly or wrongly the Benedictines became alarmed, and in 1681 Rancé writes to his legal friend, M. Dirois[2] in Rome, that they have obtained a brief against migrations to la Trappe, though he cannot think why: 'il est aisé de juger qu'un petit monastère qui ne peut au plus porter que 35 ou 40 religieux n'est point capable de causer l'ébranlement dont ils se plaignent.' Rancé thinks this is unfair, and asks Dirois to do what he can to have the ruling rescinded. Only four days later (29 August 1681) he is writing to the General of the Congregation of Cluny[3] (dom Pierre de Laurens) to say that the monk who had been sent as novice master to Saint-Martin-des-Champs had stopped at la Trappe on his way and asked to be admitted. Rancé is so convinced of the man's sincerity that he asks the General's permission to keep him. In fact the man did not stay, but it is easy to see how disturbing such defections could have been for the Benedictines, especially when they affected key posts like those of novice master, as was often the case.

Even so one must be careful not to generalize about Rancé's external relations. Less than a year after the letters to Dirois and Cluny, Rancé received a pressing request for advice from dom Robert Itar, Visitor of the Maurists, who wanted his views on the best man to choose as their new General. Rancé answered (April 1682)[4] rather unexpectedly that they should prefer a man of piety and virtue, acceptable at Court (in the context, that of Louis XIV rather than of Rome) in preference to another who might be more firm but 'désagréable, et soupçonné de favoriser ce qu'on appelle le parti des Jansénistes', and thus likely to plunge the Maurists into the same kind of crisis that the Oratorians had recently undergone. Even in 1687, when the polemic ensuing from publication of *Sainteté* was well under way, Rancé goes out of his way in a letter to Ranuzzi, the Nuncio, on the perennially vexed subject of translations from other orders, to praise the Maurists.[5]

---

[1] See above, p. 114.   [2] *TB* 1509 of 25 Aug. 1681.   [3] *TB* 1511.
[4] *TB* 1640.   [5] *TC* I/20 of 27 Oct. 1687.

If Rancé may be suspected of deploying merely tactical sincerity in such official exchanges, it is instructive to turn to an entirely private series of five letters written to a Maurist who had unsuccessfully tried his vocation at la Trappe.[1] His name and monastery cannot at present unfortunately be identified, but he is clearly on very cordial terms with Rancé. The letters extend over one year, and go into the same kind of detail as has already been discussed in previous chapters. It seems that his correspondent had defended Rancé against attacks, presumably, in view of the date, from Jansenists incensed at the letter to Bellefonds or perhaps supporters of Le Roy in the quarrel over fictions. Rancé briefly discussed texts of St. Anselm and St. John Climachus on this subject, and then gives his interpretation of St. Benedict's intentions with regard to conferences, 'pulmenta', and rules for sleeping. Later he thanks his friend for sending a book, and speaks highly of the Maurist edition of St. Augustine, but in the following letter takes a strong line on erudition: 'l'écueil de l'humilité, et souvent la vanité qui est la production la plus ordinaire de l'étude a fait mille blessures mortelles dans le cœur d'un homme savant.' The last of these letters advises his friend to accept ordination, although Rancé considers it unsuitable for men of their profession. He ends very personally: 'vous ne m'êtes pas moins cher que si la divine Providence avoit permis que vous eussiez achevé parmi nous ce que vous y aviez commencé.'

Another letter of September or October 1682 is also addressed to a Benedictine, dom André (? Ferrand),[2] perhaps a relative of the former Premonstratensian and old friend of Rancé, dom Paul Ferrand, who came to la Trappe in 1683. Rancé answers specific questions under five headings: dom André must avoid all worldly conversation; must accept, albeit reluctantly, remedies prescribed by the doctor summoned by his superiors; may refrain from celebrating mass 'par esprit de religion', but not otherwise; should avoid being conspicuous in individual practices not prescribed by his mitigated observance; and only in the last resort should seek advice from anyone other than his superior.

Such letters as these are very common in Rancé's correspondence, and if only the dates and addressees could be ascertained a great many loose ends could be tied up. As it is, all one can say

---

[1] TD, series B, 40–4, of 14 Feb. 1680–13 Feb. 1681.
[2] TC II/155. It is just possible he was a Celestine.

with confidence is that at all times Rancé had close friends among black monks, to whom he gave detailed advice on their religious life, and that, despite official opposition to translation, he enjoyed the respect of at least some Benedictine superiors, and held the reformed congregations in high esteem himself. There is no need to rehearse here the important, but tedious, dispute with Mabillon over monastic studies; and if excesses were committed by men like dom Denis de Saint-Marthe or dom Mège on the one hand and by Thiers, or Rancé himself, on the other, the reconciliation of 1693 was a genuine one. Individual animosities remained but against the malice of one or two one must set the courtesy of dom Claude le Vert, treasurer of Cluny, in publishing Rancé's translation of St. Benedict's Rule with a eulogistic preface (1689). Rancé certainly retained friends among Benedictines all his life, and it is interesting to note that after his resignation six came to la Trappe within four years and stayed, compared to four in the previous thirty. Even if dom Paulin were immediately responsible in his capacity as novice master, we know from him that his friend the novice master at Mouzon, a dom Léon, from whom he sought recruits, had been a correspondent of Rancé from about 1689 and needed no advocacy from dom Paulin to be persuaded of the spiritual eminence of la Trappe.[1]

Precisely the same pattern is repeated in Rancé's relations with another branch of the Benedictine family, the Celestines.[2] Founded in the thirteenth century by Pope Celestine V and introduced into France in 1300, the order had a mother-house at the abbey of Sulmona, in Italy, whose superior was General, and by the seventeenth century a score of houses, all priories, in France. There was a protracted dispute over jurisdiction between the General and the French Provincial, who had always enjoyed a considerable measure of autonomy, and this was in fact only settled in 1678 with a firm reassertion of the French position. In the general wave of monastic reform accelerated by Richelieu the order made some attempts at improving discipline, and the Chapters of 1661, 1664,

[1] See his letters, and references above, p. 114.

[2] Besides the standard reference books, the fullest details on the Celestine Order are to be found in A 5145, Histoire des Célestins en France, and in A 5098 which contains a large number of informative letters and other documents written by and to various members of the order 1661–79, including some known correspondents of Rancé like Ronat, Chapon, and Bauduy (one original letter from Rancé is in the same collection).

and 1667 hammered out new constitutions, which were printed in 1670. The fact that it took a decade to finalize reform (in any case not helped by the clash with the Italian Celestines) strongly suggests that impatience at such slow progress and dissatisfaction with existing conditions must have been fairly widespread. A very interesting correspondence between half a dozen members of the order, covering this period of reappraisal, shows that some at least of them, especially at Sens, turned to Jansenism in their search for a way of improving the quality of religious life. The chronology also suggests that the Celestines cannot have been indifferent to the exactly parallel debates going on among the Cistercians, and, meeting in Paris as they did every three years, they could hardly have failed to hear what was going on at the Collège des Bernardins and of the role played by Rancé. Their reformed constitutions sound strict enough; a midnight office, abstinence from flesh always, and from eggs and dairy produce in Advent and Lent, and so on. What is harder to assess is the degree of fidelity with which these rules were observed. In important respects their austerities corresponded to those of the Cistercian Abstinents, and it is reasonable to assume that the reformers among them, who, like all reformers, simply wanted to recover the original spirit of their founding fathers, were animated by ideals very similar to those of Rancé. Like the most fervent of the Abstinents, however, they must soon have realized that an order with no permanent major superiors, with triennial priors, limited finances, and small communities could not hope to achieve in seventeenth-century France the totality of the monastic revival they sought. It is in this context that one must set the defection of Jacques de Puiperrou in 1668 and of his seven confrères three years later.

The order of events enables a story to be pieced together. In August 1668 Rancé writes[1] to the Celestine General (or it may have been the Provincial, Louis Tertorin) that only after a year's wait had he admitted Puiperrou to visit la Trappe, but that once there he had decided he could not remain with the Celestines and applied for admission. The timing suggests that it was the Chapter of 1669, which finally adopted the new constitutions, that forced Puiperrou's decision, but it is also relevant that the *paix de l'église* came to an end at just this time and exposed Jansenist

---

[1] These letters are to be found in *TC* I/60–3 and Muguet, i, p. 135.

sympathizers to renewed persecution. A second letter from Rancé in October adds the bleak consolation that Puiperrou will always be grateful to the order in which he began the religious life. A year later (17 August 1669) we learn that Puiperrou has been writing to one of his former brethren criticizing the Celestines, no doubt for reforming too little and too late, as we see from another letter of the same year written by the Celestine Lardenois, at Sens, to a colleague. Rancé somewhat implausibly claims that he could not prevent the interchange of correspondence, although he took a firm enough line on other occasions. By 1670 others have come along, and Rancé once more protests that their visit was unsolicited. He justifies his position by saying that he would gladly do all he could to restore the Celestines to a healthier situation, but is less optimistic about their state than the General, who by this time had resorted to personal attacks on Rancé's religion and orthodoxy. In Rancé's view the present decadence of the Celestines simply nullified the Bull of their founder. To the Provincial he writes a good deal more cordially, regretting the disorders within the Celestines, and saying that it is immaterial to him in which place religious glorify Christ, whether at la Trappe or elsewhere, and but for the fear of offending Christ he would send back his Celestine recruits at once.

Alarmed at these wholesale defections, and obviously afraid that there would soon be no one left to execute the reforms so laboriously agreed, the Celestine authorities first secured a brief from the Pope (in about 1672), and then the new Provincial, André de l'Aage, elected in 1674, received written assurance from Rancé that he would henceforth accept no more Celestines without the permission of their superiors.[1] It will be seen that this accommodation coincides with the final rejection of Italian pretensions to run the French province and the adoption of new constitutions, so that Rancé may have been genuinely convinced that things were going to improve. He continued to correspond with members of the order, including P. Ronat, prior of Sens, the erudite Bonaventure Bauduy, and an unnamed religious (who may be the same as Ronat) whose brother wanted to come to la Trappe despite the handicap of deafness. Rancé agreed to take Ronat in June 1672,[2] but, whether because of the brief or because Ronat changed his mind, nothing came of it; however, in

[1] A 5145, p. 535.   [2] TB 148 of 4 Nov. 1672.

1675 a Celestine from the house at Sens, Bernard Vingtain, came and stayed, presumably with the approval of his superiors. By 1681 only one of the band of Celestine recruits, dom Joseph, was still alive, and, passing on the news to one of their former brethren, Rancé remains convinced that he did right: 'Je ne sais pas s'ils eussent vécu plus longtemps dans leur première observance, mais je sais bien qu'ils ont suivi l'ordre de Dieu en la quittant, et qu'il avoit attaché leur salut à leur translation.'[1]

Two out of the original group of nine returned to the Celestines (François and Jean), and one of these is probably the recipient of the letter just quoted, but Rancé must have maintained some contact with others who shrank from the decisive step of migration while continuing to share the aspirations of their bolder colleagues. Knowledge of life at la Trappe must have been very widespread among Celestines, and, especially after the defections, the superiors must have been on their mettle to refute in deeds as well as words Rancé's charges of decadence. Too little is known of Celestine history at this time for a balanced assessment of Rancé's influence to be possible, and indeed nearly all the details just given derive from manuscript sources hitherto apparently unknown or ignored, but in view of the chronology and other factors just mentioned it is very likely that Rancé's influence acted as a catalyst at this crucial moment in Celestine affairs. Besides, with an order so small in numbers his influence must have been felt more widely and deeply both by individuals and in general than would be the case with the much larger Benedictine congregations. It is worth adding that at the height of his dispute with the Celestine authorities Rancé was objective enough to write to the prior of Sens (4 November 1672): 'Dieu n'appelle pas toutes sortes de personnes à des vies également rigoureuses et pénitentes.'[2]

Another minor branch of the Benedictine family was the originally French order of Grandmont, founded in the eleventh century.[3] Had Rancé kept to his original plan of retiring to his priory of Boulogne, which belonged to the order, his influence might well have been decisive, but as it was he changed his mind and corresponded with the General of Grandmont only on the question of his replacement. However, it so happened that through

---

[1] *TB* 1502 of Aug. 1681.   [2] *TB* 148.
[3] See Hélyot, *Dict. des ordres religieux* (ed. 1847), cols. 422–8.

Favier he had occasion to hear of the small order's affairs. In 1642 Charles Frémont, who had been successively prior of the mother-house and then of the college in Paris, secured Richelieu's per-mission to return to the order's primitive observance, and began by reforming the monastery at Époisse, near Dijon. In 1650 Thiers followed, and then in 1668 Chavanon, also in Auvergne, and eventually four other houses. Thiers became the chief house of the reform, and Favier, who lived in the town, had several friends and correspondents among the religious both there and at Chavanon.[1] When, in 1673, frère Edmond had to be sent back from la Trappe to Auvergne, Favier naturally thought of the local order of Grandmont, but Rancé was not enthusiastic: ' Je ne pense pas que Grandmont soit son fait. Cette réforme, à ce que j'ai ouy dire, n'a rien d'assuré: l'établissement en est tellement entre les mains du général qu'il le peut renverser quand il lui plaira.'[2] By 1677 he had been proved right on the first count, for Edmond failed with the order, and, more interestingly, the death of Frémont at Thiers in 1689 proved him right on the second count too, for the reform made no further progress and the order just dwindled away in the next century, even before the Revolution. Favier remained in correspondence with monks of the order until his death, but none ever tried la Trappe, nor does Rancé seem to have been in contact with them. What is interesting is that Rancé should have been so sure that Frémont's work, thriving in 1673, would not survive, because this was exactly the forecast of both friends and enemies with regard to his own achievement at la Trappe.

The evolution of Rancé's relations with the Carthusians is not so simple. Already in his worldly phase he was one of the group which used to meet in the cell of dom Carrouges at the Paris Chartreuse, if we are to believe Rapin.[3] Carrouges was a sym-pathizer of Port-Royal, but Rancé presumably knew other less partisan members of the community and something about their life. By 1666, thoroughly disillusioned with his mission to Rome, he obtained through Retz a brief authorizing him to withdraw to the Grande Chartreuse in case the Cistercian reform collapsed, and we know from a much earlier letter to Favier (10 May 1660)[4] that he had intended to pay a visit to the Chartreuse but had post-poned the journey (apparently never made) because of Gaston's

---

[1] See Jaloustre, *Précepteur auvergnat*, p. 34.   [2] Gonod, p. 46, of 11 June 1673.
[3] Rapin, *Mémoires*, i, p. 439.   [4] *A* 2106, f. 12.

death. It seems unlikely that he ever did go there, but he evidently had the greatest respect for Carthusian life. He kept in touch with various Carthusians, at Val-Dieu,[1] near la Trappe, at Basseville (near Clamecy), where he wrote in the warmest terms to dom Guérin in 1672,[2] at Bonpas, Avignon, where he answers dom Braquiti in 1680,[3] and in 1684 he tells Bellefonds, just back from a visit to the Grande Chartreuse, that it is 'un des plus grands monuments de mortification et de pénitence qui nous reste en ce monde.'[4] As late as 1685 we hear of a dom D. applying for admission to la Trappe, only to be refused on canonical grounds.[5] This is enough to show that Rancé remained favourably disposed to an order he always admired. However, the Carthusians were among the first to protest at what they considered the derogatory references to their order in *Sainteté*. Rancé's picture of universal monastic decadence, however regretful, seemed to challenge their proud boast 'never reformed because never deformed' and their motto 'stat crux dum volvitur orbis'. Their General, dom Innocent le Masson, was not slow to take up the defence of his order.

The two men had so many traits in common that the clash between them seems inevitable. Dom Innocent (1628–1703)[6] became a Carthusian at Noyon, his birthplace, before he was 20 and rose to the office of prior within the next twenty years. Most unwillingly he accepted election as General in October 1675, pleading chronic ill health and insomnia, but became an outstanding leader at a very difficult time. As General he resided permanently within the enclosure of the Grande Chartreuse, and thus never had an opportunity to meet Rancé. He kept a firm rein on the order, then comprising some 170 houses, of which the French numbered 75 (with a population of 1,700), both by the highly efficient system of Visitors and by a voluminous correspondence, of which much survives. One biographer[7] claims that he wrote at least sixty letters every week, and sometimes twice

[1] Only one formal letter to Val-Dieu survives in a copy (*TD*, series A, 81 of 1670) but it is clear from dom le Masson's correspondence (discussed below) that contact between the two houses was regular and perhaps close.

[2] *TB* 31.   [3] *TB* 1624.   [4] *BN* n.a. 12959, f. 106.

[5] Gonod, p. 110 of 12 May 1685.

[6] See the most recent edition of *La Grande Chartreuse par un Chartreux* (10th ed. 1964), pp. 85–95, and the fuller MS. *Vie de dom le Masson*, by A. Charentin, in *G* 633, pp. 138–72.

[7] Charentin.

that number, and though many were brief administrative notes, such figures afford a useful point of comparison with Rancé. The same biographer stresses the essentially personal nature of his rule, saying that he never refused an interview and listened 'avec beaucoup de patience et y répondoit avec une douceur extrême'. In 1676, a few months after his arrival, a disastrous fire destroyed most of the buildings, and it took him twelve years to rebuild the monastery in the form in which it survives today. In this connection another biographer[1] comments on dom Innocent's preoccupation with external matters, like building and polemic, and admits that he says little in his numerous published works of contemplation: 'Mais ce sont souvent les circonstances qui lui ont mis la plume ou la truelle à la main. Il est aussi sans aucun doute un maître spirituel.' Rancé's situation was so similar that it is a little ironic that he should incur exactly the same criticism without earning the same excuse.

One of dom Innocent's main concerns was to preserve his order from the contagion of Jansenism, always a risk among those dedicated to austerity, and he personally supervised the burning of Jansenist works which he had had collected from all houses of the order (the Jansenists maliciously, but regardless of chronology, blamed the fire on this summary execution). A cryptic reference in a letter of 1678[2] suggests that he was already wary of Rancé (perhaps in the context of the letter to Bellefonds) and *Sainteté* brought things to a head. In 1689 (1690 is probably an error) he published a detailed refutation of Rancé's criticism in a substantial volume entitled *Explication de quelques endroits des anciens statuts de l'ordre des Chartreux*, which also contains a record of events going back to 1683 and some trenchant comments on Rancé.

In May 1683 a Carthusian, apparently of Paris, read *Sainteté* and decided that he had a vocation for la Trappe, his own order being too decadent. A M. Loisel, curé of Saint-Jean-en-Grève, since deceased, and an intimate friend of the Carthusian prior, helped to dissuade him. On 25 June a letter reporting developments suggests that the restless monk has probably been led into temptation, perhaps by some Jansenist sympathizers, but also perhaps provoked by Rancé (called 'N' throughout); 'Car si une fois cette porte étoit ouverte, des instables et des inobservants voudroient y passer, ne fussent que pour contenter leur fantaisie

---

[1] *Grande Chartreuse*, p. 92.   [2] G 948, V, f. 17, of 2 Feb. 1678.

pendant quelques mois.'[1] There follows a quotation from *Sainteté*
and this conclusion: 'C'est une décision surprenante et dont les
disciples de M. Jansenius s'accommoderoient fort bien.'

On his own account dom le Masson attacks the life at la Trappe
as having 'ni fond, ni rive, ni mesure, ni discrétion'.[2] This, he
says, is not surprising, for Rancé's book clearly reflects the fact
that he had been a superior before he had been a novice, and a
master before he was an apprentice. The next thing to happen was
that in 1684 the Carthusian Visitor for Brittany found a copy of the
now banned *Sainteté* in one of the houses and promptly confiscated
it. According to the General, Rancé protested against this act in a
clandestine pamphlet, and must therefore have had some inside
agent to reveal to him the secrets of a canonical visit. It seems that
the correspondent in question was 'un jeune indiscipliné, enfariné
de la nouvelle doctrine de M. Jansenius, qui croit n'être obligé
à rien faire que lors que la grace victorieuse l'entraîne par un
plaisir insurmontable'.[3] The repetition of this extremely damaging
charge of Jansenist support was no doubt sincere, but, true or not,
such an accusation was bound to be tactically effective. M. Tron-
son, of Saint-Sulpice, was a friend of dom le Masson, and is known
to have taken his part, as one would expect of such a fervent anti-
Jansenist, though in fact he was a friend too of Rancé's friend the
Bishop of Limoges.

As dom le Masson warms to his task, the suspicion grows
that any stick will do to beat Rancé with. Criticizing Rancé for
exaggerating the excellence of early monks, he says in solemn
admonition: 'Souvenez-vous, Monsieur, d'un Pélage qui étoit
un de ces anciens moines, si austère et si irréprochable dans sa
vie.'[4] Finally in examining Rancé's thesis of general monastic
decadence, the General adds to Jansenius and Pelagius a further
provocative piece of name-dropping: 'Mais je ne croy pas qu'on
puisse fournir aux Prédicans de Genève et de la Hollande des
lieux communs plus beaux, plus convenables, mieux préparés et
plus efficaces que ceux que l'auteur leur fournit par son livre pour
faire valoir les déclamations qu'ils font contre l'Etat Ecclésiastique.'[5] The charge-sheet could hardly be more comprehensive.

Rancé did not take this lying down; in a letter to le Camus,
friend and neighbour of dom le Masson, written 20 July 1689

---

[1] *Explication,* p. 12.   [2] Ibid., p. 52.   [3] Ibid., p. 56.
[4] Ibid., p. 94.   [5] Ibid., p. 159.

but not published until 1710,[1] he went into a lengthy and some-what tedious refutation of the General's objections. His principal point is that mitigations of the primitive rule are notoriously practised now, and he lists the white bread, fish, eggs, butter, white wine, and so on allegedly permitted. Even the magnificence of the Carthusians' new buildings contrasts with their former poverty. Despite all this Rancé has plenty of good to say for the Carthusians: 'assez dignes qu'on les considère.. qu'on les estime de s'être soutenus et de s'être distingués comme ils ont fait dans cette décadence presque universelle des observances monas-tiques; sans qu'il soit besoin d'avoir recours à une immutabilité prétendue, qui n'est point de ce monde.'[2]

In 1690 there was a brief lull in hostilities, when Rancé was instrumental in bringing about the capture of a fugitive Car-thusian malefactor,[3] for which he received a personal letter of thanks from dom le Masson, who also praised him in letters to several Carthusian superiors. This did not last, and early in 1692 dom le Masson tells the prior of Val-Dieu (who, being nearest, had most to do with Rancé) that he possesses Rancé's latest attack on their order and deplores it in a man 'qui passe pour quelque chose de grand et de spirituel.'[4] Later the same year he sent a copy of his own reply to the minister Le Peletier, but both he and Rancé obeyed the royal injunction to keep public silence. It is interesting and typical of dom le Masson's fair-mindedness that when Thiers composed a violent answer to the *Quatre lettres* of Sainte-Marthe, attacking the Maurists in general, le Masson, who knew him personally, took the trouble to inform Mabillon that Rancé had nothing to do with this work (seized and de-stroyed by the authorities), and in 1694 wrote in kindly terms to Thiers to dissuade him from doing further harm.[5]

Dom le Masson's last recorded word on the subject of la Trappe is revealing and almost comic. He writes to the prior of Bordeaux (21 November 1692)[6] with some asperity to condemn as absolute nonsense the story that Rancé has secured a bull allowing him to receive religious of any order without permission 'et même que pour attirer les gens il fait les frais du voyage'. If the young monk who is seeking thus to support his application for transfer persists

---

[1] In *Nouvelles de la République des Lettres*, mai–juin 1710, pp. 488–519 and 628–61.
[2] Ibid., p. 656.   [3] One dom Chéron, G 948, V, f. 137.
[4] Ibid., f. 158.   [5] See G 633.   [6] G 948, VI, f. 94.

in such insolence he is to be locked up. Absurd as it was, such a legend was clearly invented to attract religious whose motives were far from pure, and unfortunately by 1692 trouble-makers genuinely associated with Jansenism or indiscipline (like Braquiti, condemned for scurrilous pamphleteering in a letter of 1689)[1] did not scruple to drag Rancé's name in even when he knew nothing about them.

There is nothing good to be said of the steadily worsening relations between two men who should have made common cause. One can see how the clash arose, and though it was fortunate that its public repercussions were damped down, with more goodwill and better communications on each side a positive reconciliation should have been possible, especially through the good offices of le Camus, a respected friend of both men. The real trouble was that dom le Masson was actually head of an ancient and admirable international order, with a lifetime in the cloister behind him, and he thought, with some justification, that Rancé ,whose jurisdiction extended no further than the walls of la Trappe, had no right to set himself up as an authority over anyone else, let alone his seniors.

Rancé had quite a number of correspondents among the large but amorphous body of religious known generically as Canons Regular, but for the most part he was concerned with individuals rather than communities, and only on the usual question of translation is it relevant to speak of orders. The Premonstratensians, most centralized of the Canons, clashed with him over his reception of two of their number, and sent their Procurator-General to the Abstinent Chapter of 1684 to protest at this breach of a pact traditionally going back to St. Bernard's day, but a commission headed by the Abbot of Orval upheld Rancé's act. One of the two, Bruno Ferrand, was an old friend from before Rancé's conversion, the other, Éloi le Môle, a friend of Pinette, and there is no record of any other contacts Rancé may have had with Premonstratensians.[2]

Contacts with Canons living under the Augustinian rule, sometimes in the loose federation known as the Congrégation de France, show no definite pattern. Rancé does not seem to have had much to do with his former abbey of le Val after Druel resigned, but it was near enough for visits. In 1682 the prior of

---

[1] Ibid., f. 77.
[2] See above, pp. 47 and 109–110 and Leloczky, *Constitutiones et Acta*, pp. 219–20.

Provins inquires[1] about three of his canons interested in coming to la Trappe, and Rancé tells him that he will gladly accept them, but warns him of the austerities they will have to face. The abbot, François d'Aligre, was a Canon Regular who left his abbey from 1672 to 1677 to help his father, *garde des sceaux* and later chancellor, and had an excellent record of good works.[2] It may be of him ('M. l'abbé de Saint-Jacques') that Rancé writes[3] in 1699 to James II, saying that he wants to stay at la Trappe. With Sainte-Geneviève, headquarters of the Congrégation de France, Rancé does not seem to have had much contact. One Génovefain, Placide Morel, came in 1694 and died within the year; another, Dorothée de l'Épine lived till 1704. This may explain why Rancé, also in 1694, wrote a very friendly letter to P. Chartonnet,[4] who later became Visitor of the Congregation, to express his pleasure at the way harmony had been maintained at the recently concluded General Chapter. It is clear that translations constituted no problem with these Canons Regular.

A rather different case is that of Saint-Jean-des-Vignes, the important abbey of Canons Regular at Soissons. In about 1673 the young Jacques de la Cour[5] came to try his vocation at la Trappe, but his health was not sufficiently robust and he went on to le Pin, where he was eventually ordained. While he was still at le Pin his brother, Canon Regular at Soissons, became increasingly unhappy at the state of affairs in his abbey, and in about 1682, or a little before, began to seek Rancé's advice.[6] He had already paid a visit, it seems, and is worried by his impending nomination as novice master at Soissons. His picture of life there was so depressing that Rancé found it impossible to recommend him to stay, and by October invited him to try his vocation either at la Trappe or with his brother at le Pin. It is not possible to say with certainty which, if any, of the many letters addressed to unnamed Canons Regular went to Soissons, nor indeed what became of dom Jacques's brother, but in 1686 Jacques himself came back to la

---

[1] *TB* 1766 of 13 Sept. 1682.

[2] See article in *DBF* by M. Prevost on Fr. d'Aligre; it seems that his visits to la Trappe were well known to his contemporaries.

[3] *SP*, p. 142, of 10 Oct. 1699.

[4] In Reims, Tarbé XV, 139. Antoine-Fr. Chartonnet (d. 1729) wrote a number of books, including one about the Dijon philanthropist, Bénigne Joly, a friend of his known to Rancé (*Dict de spiritualité*).

[5] On dom Jacques see *BN* 24123, f. 51 (P. Léonard de Sainte-Catherine).

[6] Copies in *TB* 1624, of 6 Mar. 1682 and *TB* 1783, of 19 Oct. 1682.

Trappe, becoming abbot in 1698, so that it is reasonable to suppose that contact continued with his home town and the abbey. It is relevant that Rancé wrote to Bossuet[1] about the prieur-curé of la Ferté-Gaucher, a Canon of Soissons, at the end of 1683, and it may one day be possible to reconstruct a little more of the story. To this canon, Nicolas de Brie, or another he wrote that a proposed nomination as claustral prior at Soissons was not compatible with his continued tenure of a prieur-curé post in a small town (the usual employment for canons serving outside the mother-house) even if he does put in a vicar: 'Seriez-vous Pasteur en deux endroits? et conducteur tout à la fois de deux églises?'[2] One does not know, of course, whether such advice was heeded, nor whether Rancé was the only person whose opinion was sought but the precise nature of question and answer suggests something other than formal consultations.

Of all the houses of Canons Regular that with which Rancé had the longest and closest connection was Saint-Victor in Paris. As usual the initial contact was a personal one: the arrival of dom Pierre le Nain in 1668 and the visit of Simon Gourdan in 1673 led to a close association, of which Gervaise gives many details in his biography of Gourdan (1755).[3] The first exchange was unpromising and consisted of the usual attempt to secure the return of the unauthorized recruit, met by the usual refusal from Rancé, unshaken even by the personal intervention of the Archbishop of Paris. Dom le Nain himself sent a long letter to his former brethren, justifying his move and speaking enthusiastically of life at la Trappe. Eventually the *fait accompli* was accepted, but dom le Nain's initiative led Gourdan to follow in due course, although he only stayed a few days. According to Gervaise,[4] he left his cloister on only one other occasion until his death in 1729. On his return to Saint-Victor Gourdan apparently decided that if he could not serve God with his friend at la Trappe he could at least practise something like the Trappist way of life in his own monastery. The tradition of Canons Regular had never been one of great austerity, and it seems a little strange that Gourdan preferred to

---

[1] Bossuet, *Correspondance*, ii, p. 397, of 31 Dec. 1683.

[2] In *TC* I/114.

[3] Gervaise is in fact the main source for the chapters on the period in F. Bonnard, *Histoire de l'abbaye royale de Saint-Victor*, who does, however, give some useful tables and lists.

[4] *Vie de Gourdan*, p. 28.

remain at Saint-Victor, where he could never hope to win many
supporters, rather than transfer to another house or order where
austerity was more normal. Gervaise describes Gourdan's way of
life,[1] and the details are fully corroborated by Rancé's letters over
a period of years, advising Gourdan on the best course to follow.
He abstained completely from meat or fish, rarely took eggs,
never drank wine, fasted scrupulously, observed perpetual silence
(not in an absolute sense, but in the usual monastic sense of never
speaking except when told to), slept only three or four hours at a
time, never warmed himself at the fire (that is, in the room set
aside for recreation and warmth), renounced personal property,
and wore only the simplest habit. Not unnaturally, such a way of
life, and the spiritual assumptions behind it, caused dissension in
the community, and it was only on the intervention of Harlay,
Archbishop of Paris, advised by the Sorbonne, that Gourdan was
finally authorized to persist in his lonely demonstration. Despite
his reputation for sanctity, and the consequently large number of
people eager to seek his advice, he always refused to hear confessions, and in this too he was following Rancé's explicit counsel.[2]

There is little doubt that reports of dom le Nain's spiritual
fulfilment, and of Gourdan's own encounter with Rancé, were the
immediate cause of the attempt to introduce Trappist ways to
Saint-Victor, but there is evidence that in some ways the disciple
tried to outstrip the master. A letter written by Rancé in 1681[3]
is a model of common sense, and shows Rancé trying to restrain
the impetuosity which had brought Gourdan to la Trappe in vain.
Rancé doubts whether Gourdan is strong enough to do without
a fire, but since the Victorine rule does not forbid such concessions to frailty, Gourdan may warm himself without scruple.
Similarly he should adopt clothing (presumably underwear, warm
covering, and so on) suitable to his delicate temperament. In all
things Rancé tells him to do what he can without going to ex-
tremes, and above all not to distinguish himself in external observance from his brethren. Some months later, in March 1682,[4]
Gourdan is finding it hard to follow his own version of the reformed rule against the opposition of his prior, Claude de la
Lane. This time Rancé is a good deal more forthright: obedience
to a superior ceases to be a categorical imperative when the

---

[1] Ibid., p. 37.   [2] TB 1632.   [3] TD, series B, 60 of 15 Nov. 1681.
[4] TB 1632.

superior strays from God's ways. In a superbly characteristic for-
mula Rancé tells Gourdan 'il faut accompagner la résistance qu'on
est obligé de lui faire des marques extérieures de la considération
qu'on a pour sa qualité'—an exact description of his own conduct
towards his nominal superiors. If the prior thinks that Gourdan's
hair is too short, or his fasts too long, let the letter of the statute
decide. This time Rancé tells him not to be afraid of being singu-
lar (which is not the same thing as conspicuous) and tells him too
that he must accept the duty of preaching, though not that of
hearing confessions, 'un écueil pour la plupart de ceux qui s'en
mêlent', because at Saint-Victor men and women of the world
presented themselves in the confessional. In August Gourdan is
still worried, but has so far accepted Rancé's advice. This time he
wants a ruling on the entry of women into the cloister. Rancé
says[1] that ladies of royal blood, and their suite, cannot be excluded,
but that the religious would do well to stay out of the way until
they have gone, and that in any case relatives and friends of religious are entirely forbidden. Reverting to the question of observance, he firmly asserts that the prior has no power to abrogate
the statutes of the order.

It is only too easy to see how the scrupulosity of a Gourdan
could irk a prior of average piety who was doing his best during
his three-year tenure to run a large monastery near the centre of
Paris (on the site of the present Faculty of Science) with no help
from a commendatory abbot. If Gourdan wanted to shiver, or
shave his head, or starve, that was perhaps his business, but if he
started appealing to Rancé as an oracle on Canon Law (when the
Sorbonne was just round the corner) or on such questions of
general policy as the entry of women, he put the prior in a very
difficult position. Gervaise tells us a lot about Gourdan, but it is
only from Rancé's letters that we can piece together a partial
picture of the prior's position.

In 1677 Nicolas Taconnet[2] was elected prior, still quite young
and with a reputation for modest piety, an ardent Augustinian
but never suspected of heresy. Early the next year Rancé wrote
to him[3] to say that if he cannot bring his religious to a more proper

---

[1] *TB* 1745 of 27 Aug. 1682.
[2] Bonnard, *Hist de... Saint-Victor*, p. 191. The copyist sometimes misread his
name and renders it as Falconnet.
[3] *TB* 908.

sense of their duties he should resign: 'il n'est pas nécessaire...
qu'un religieux tombe dans des excès grossiers... pour être
ennemi de Dieu... puisqu'une vie commune suffit pour la con-
damnation de ceux qui sont obligés d'en mener une qui soit
parfaite.' By February Taconnet had written twice to Rancé, who
again advises him to resign,[1] since he lacks 'une force, une sagesse
et une vertu plus qu'humaine' necessary for the reformation of
his canons' misconduct: and very shortly afterwards Taconnet
did in fact resign, completing less than a year of his triennate. In
1679 they are still in contact, and Rancé reminds him that he
cannot go back on his obligation of retreat.[2] Next year in fact he
went as confessor to Port-Royal-des-Champs, where he died in
1684, with a great reputation for sanctity and much loved by
Gourdan, who wrote of him 'sa charité pour les âmes m'a toujours paru incomparable.'[3] He was succeeded by Jacques Trincart,
a less distinguished religious. Writing to Gourdan in 1680, Rancé
tells him that it would be better not to accept the new breviary,
but that if refusal would lead to trouble he should take the line of
least resistance. He should also, however reluctantly, accept the
charge of 'vestiaire'.[4]

One can see that such apparently straightforward matters of
obedience could not be queried in this way without putting the
prior in an impossible position. Some time after the letter quoted
above, in which Rancé tells Gourdan how far obedience should
go, the prior (by now Claude de la Lane) seems to have paid a
visit, not necessarily his first, to la Trappe. Rancé refers to this
visit in a letter giving his view about a pension paid to the prior
which Rancé now advises him to renounce as being inconsistent
with the spirit of poverty. Even if he uses the money for the relief
of the poor, says Rancé in another letter, he should not keep the
pension. It is not possible to identify the addressees of subsequent
letters with certainty, but from time to time Rancé alludes to successive priors in letters to Gourdan.[5]

At the end of 1682 Gourdan was still worried about his way of
life at Saint-Victor. Not for the first time Rancé tells him[6] that
there is no reason for him to abstain from celebrating mass (Gour-

---

[1] TB 926.   [2] TD, series C, 90.   [3] Bonnard, loc. cit.
[4] TB 1326, of 12 Sept. 1680. Apparently this was not a sinecure as it involved
oversight of the clothes and a fund for replenishing them, which brought in the
vexed question of personal property.
[5] TB 1703; TC II/278, I/38, II/38.   [6] TB 1806.

dan had been most unwilling to accept ordination on the grounds
of his own unfitness). Gourdan is worried too that silence is not
complete at Saint-Victor (it is hard to imagine how it could have
been in view of the abbey's tradition and location), but Rancé
tells him it is quite legitimate to talk from time to time as may be
required. Yet again the question of a pension comes up, and
Gourdan is told that a certain novice can quite well give up his
pension to the poor without keeping anything back for himself.
Rancé repeats his objection to study, and specifically bids Gourdan to become reconciled with his 'père et maître', presumably
the prior.

Just two years later[1] some old problems are still coming up, and
a new one appears. Silence, abstinence from meat in the common
refectory, and retreat are constant elements in the reformed life
that Gourdan, with Rancé's encouragement, is trying to lead, but
exeats have not previously been discussed. Rancé thinks that to
permit such excursions 'soit aux champs, soit à la ville pour aller
diner chez leurs amis et leurs parents, c'est favoriser la licence.'
Vainly trying year after year to stem the relentless tide of per-
missiveness, Gourdan quite often despairs. On one occasion in
1686[2] Rancé tells him to leave Saint-Victor before it is too late:
'ceux qui sont engagés dans des observances relachées sont
exposés à de grands inconvénients... vos Pères donnent le dernier coup à votre Congrégation.' If he feels like trying la Trappe
again, Rancé will be glad to see him, but without much hope. The
next trace we have is 1688,[3] when Gourdan rather unexpectedly
takes up the defence of Saint-Victor against Rancé's detailed
charge of decadence in connection with frère Gueston's abortive
attempt at transfer to la Trappe, but we know from Gervaise
that correspondence continued until Rancé's death.

The full effect of Rancé's influence on Saint-Victor is hard to
calculate, but on Gourdan himself it seems to have been decisive.
From the evidence just examined, which is no more than fragmentary, it is abundantly clear that Gourdan took no decision
regarding external observance or interior spirituality without
consulting Rancé, and that successive priors knew, and to some
extent accepted, the situation. It is clear too that in those areas
(e.g. novices) over which Gourdan had some measure of

[1] *TC* I/75 of 9 Dec. 1684.
[2] *TC* I/146 of 28 July 1686.   [3] Gervaise, *Vie de Gourdan*, pp. 76–85.

autonomous control, Rancé's advice must have been felt by other members of the community at Saint-Victor. It is known that other religious, of whom la Grange,[1] confessor at Port-Royal in 1683–8, is one, were in contact with Rancé, and Gueston was not the only one to try his vocation, or at least to think of trying it. It looks very much as though Rancé enjoyed a quite privileged status at Saint-Victor, even if his influence sometimes led to dissension, and it would otherwise be hard to explain the surprising correspondence with Santeuil of which four letters survive from 1689 to 1692.[2] It is not particularly odd that Santeuil, a singularly unascetic person, should have thought of la Trappe when he came to compose hymns in Latin about St. Bernard and solitaries, but the tone of the correspondence, and references by Rancé to Santeuil in letters to Nicaise and others, go far beyond mere formal acknowledgement. The playful and talented Santeuil seems to have been perfectly sincere in his change of heart, and after a severe illness in 1689 he became friendly with Têtu, who retired to Saint-Victor at about the same time;[3] he may even have been tempted by the the prospect of inner peace at la Trappe, where he spent several weeks in 1697; but what is certain is that, like others of his brethren at Saint-Victor, he regarded Rancé with more than ordinary respect.

It is important to note once more that the contact with Saint-Victor began and continued as a personal one, originally through dom le Nain, then through Gourdan, Taconnet, and others. By the time *Sainteté* appeared, Rancé's influence at Saint-Victor was so well established that publication could hardly have produced any notable new effects, though Gourdan for one wrote to support him in the ensuing polemic. The many letters addressed to unidentified Canons Regular must involve some destined for Soissons or Saint-Victor, but there can be little doubt that if other, as yet unnamed, houses were involved it was, as always, as the consequence of a specific contact with a specific individual. Perhaps the most important lesson to be drawn from all this is that the harsh, dogmatic, legislative tone so often adopted by Rancé in print is essentially different from the sensible modera-

[1] Bonnard, *Hist de... Saint-Victor*, p. 164, and Rancé's letter of 29 June 1688 in *TC* I/107.

[2] Published in *La Vie et les bons mots de J. B. Santeuil*, ii, pp. 70 and 80–3.

[3] Bonnard, *Hist de... Saint-Victor*, p. 170.

tion, tempered with firmness, to be found in his private dealings with individuals. Unhappily his official dealings with superiors, and orders, and congregations belong to that class of juridical contact which brings out the worst in him; he was never willing to concede that he might be wrong in judging a vocation and thus, by implication, the inadequacy of another observance. When faced with concrete problems, however, he sees things in a practical and humane way, relating each given question to the daily reality he sees around him, and in this he excels. There is no need to make extravagant claims for his influence on the religious life of his age; the foregoing examples are explicit enough.

9. Women in Religion

As might be expected, a very high proportion of Rancé's letters were addressed to religious women. Any man with a reputation for piety in the seventeenth century was liable to find himself the recipient of problems submitted by women, secular or religious, and in the case of a monk, and especially of Rancé, who neither left his enclosure nor granted interviews to women, letters were the only regular means of contact. Three of Rancé's sisters, and a niece, were nuns, and he also had close ties with other nuns whom he had known, or known of, before their entry into religion. As a result three particular nuns between them account for more of the surviving letters than all other religious women combined to whom Rancé wrote. It must be admitted that the numerous, but mercifully brief, letters written to usually anonymous reverend mothers and sisters do not now make very good reading. There is a sameness about the problems and the advice, an inevitability about the ill health and periodic despondency, a sense of claustrophobic uniformity about the endless struggle for perfection that palls with repetition. This is not to say that Rancé's advice is not good, or that many of his remarks are not worth quoting; it is in fact almost certain that, with problems of chronology and identification solved, some really interesting series of letters could be constructed. For influence to be perceptible, however, some degree of continuity and evolution must be established, and for this reason it is more helpful to select a few specific examples than to range more widely.

Three groups of letters may be quite reasonably distinguished: first there are those addressed to Cistercians who on one side or the other were directly involved in the question of the order's reform; then there are those addressed to houses of other orders, to one Benedictine and one Augustinian abbess in particular; and finally much the most numerous group consists of those sent to his sister Marie-Louise (and her prioress) at the Annonciades in Paris, to his close friend Mère Agnès de Bellefonds and others at the great Carmelite house in the rue Saint-Jacques, and, above all, to his lifelong friend, Mère Louise Rogier at the Visitation in Tours, and her fellow nuns, his niece Louise-Henriette d'Albon and her niece Mère de la Roche, and possibly others. This grouping corresponds closely to that of his male religious contacts, except that his only close male relative, the Chevalier de Rancé, was not a religious and received rather few letters, while intimate friends among the higher clergy or in the Oratory make up a group comparable in quantity and quality of letters to the third one just mentioned. Even within these groups there is much more variety than one might expect, and the pattern that emerges does not encourage generalization.

The first group comprises les Clairets, in two quite distinct phases, Saint-Antoine in Paris, Maubuisson and Leyme, each very different from the others. His contact with les Clairets[1] comes first in time, and was with his elder sister, Thérèse. None of Rancé's biographers has so far ventured to fix any of the details of her life and death, and archive material from les Clairets is too scanty to raise many hopes, but some facts none the less emerge. She was born between 1620 and 1625, and by 1647 was already a nun, quite probably from an early age. In the last stages of his conversion Rancé writes to say (4 November 1662)[2] that he had hoped to see her on his way back from Boulogne (Chambord) but for some reason had gone straight on to la Trappe, where he was to spend the winter. The tone is cordial and affectionate, and suggests that brother and sister have maintained regular contact. Soon after Easter 1663 he writes,[3] from la Trappe, to regret the long gaps in correspondence, but assures her that his silence does not mean that he is unmindful of her. In 1671 her abbess, Louise de Thou, died after a reign of thirty years, leaving a reputation for great humility and piety. Rancé offers Thérèse his condolences[4] on what sounds like a real personal loss rather than a formal bereavement.

Thereafter relations seem to have changed somewhat. The new abbess, Charlotte-Elisabeth de Fiennes, cousin of her predecessor, had some pretensions to learning—she read the Fathers in Latin and cultivated *belles lettres*[5]—and, though there is no suggestion

---

[1] There is a certain amount of general information in Souancé, *Histoire de N.D. des Clairets*, but Thérèse remains a very shadowy figure. The reference in her father's will to the fact that she was a nun already in 1647 and those in the correspondence discussed below are really all.

[2] *TB* 1.   [3] *TB* 7.   [4] *TB* 24.   [5] See Souancé, op. cit.

of scandal or disorder (Val-Richer as Visitor would hardly have turned a blind eye), life at the abbey was no doubt more relaxed than Rancé would have wished. A brief New Year letter in 1673[1] tells us nothing, but in 1679 Rancé replies to a letter from the Abbot of Clairvaux[2] (major superior both of la Trappe and les Clairets) in very uncompromising terms. Thérèse was apparently in such poor health that the Abbot of Clairvaux had been asked ('on le pressoit'), whether by her or on her behalf is not clear, for permission to take the waters. Rancé was consulted, again it is not clear at whose instigation, and replied as he always replied to such inquiries, that a religious should regard the monastery as his tomb, and should never value his life above his salvation. Nine years later he became involved in an exactly similar case, in which the Bishop of Tournai's niece, an abbess, incurred his disapproval by asking, and securing, her uncle's leave to take the waters, and in criticizing the bishop he specifically quotes his earlier reply to Clairvaux about Thérèse.[3] The incident does not seem to have caused any lasting rancour, for in 1680[4] he is discussing with her her health, and that of mutual friends, the marquise de Tourouvre and her mother, and in 1682[5] he writes to tell her that his diocesan, the Bishop of Séez, has died (les Clairets was just over the border in the next diocese of Chartres). It is interesting that on this occasion, and also no doubt on others unrecorded, he wrote to both his religious sisters on the same day. The last sure record of her existence is early in 1683,[6] when he sends her a message of general encouragement. Two hitherto unnoticed letters make it virtually certain that Thérèse died the following winter. Writing to Marie-Louise on 23 March 1684,[7] Rancé comments that he had expected her to be sorry at the news that 'ma sœur' (and hers as well) had died, and in April[8] he thanks an unnamed reverend mother for all her kindness to his dead sister and hopes that he may share in its continuation.

There is a rather odd postscript to the story of Thérèse which hints at a certain coolness, at least momentary, between Rancé and her. In the same letter[9] (to an unnamed friend) where he relates the exchange with Clairvaux over taking the waters, he goes on:

---

[1] *TB* 121.   [2] *TB* 1068 of 26 May 1679 also in Muguet, ii, p. 194.
[3] In *T* 1689 of 9 May 1688.   [4] *TB* 1271 of 22 Jan. 1680.
[5] *TB* 1659 of 23 May 1682.   [6] *TB* 1837 of 21 Jan. 1683.   [7] *TC* II/52.
[8] *TC* II/342.   [9] *T* 1689.

'C'est celle-là même qui vint à une lieue d'ici avec son abbesse...
et que je ne voulois pas voir. Il n'est permis en nulle occasion
d'autoriser ce qui n'est pas bien.' A Cistercian abbess who could
support an application to take the waters, and by implication
approve of an uncanonical family visit, let alone one who encouraged theology and *belles lettres*, could not have enjoyed much
sympathy from Rancé, and since she had presumably chosen
Thérèse as her travelling companion on the occasion of the otherwise unexplained journey, it looks as though she and Thérèse
got on reasonably well. On balance Rancé's relations with his
sister seem to have been normally cordial on personal matters,
rather distant when it came to questions affecting the rule by
which they were both bound.

With the death of Thérèse in 1684, followed by her abbess in
1687, Rancé's relations with les Clairets would no doubt have
lapsed but for the attitude of the new abbess, Françoise-Angélique
d'Étampes de Valençay. For some reason she had conceived an
extraordinary devotion for Rancé, whom she can never have seen,
and allowed nothing to stop her resolve to have him as her superior instead of Val-Richer. Granddaughter of the Montmorency
whom Richelieu (Rancé's godfather) had beheaded, she had been
brought up by a pious aunt at the Visitation at Moulins, where
Mme de Sévigné met her in May 1676,[1] near enough Sept-Fons
for Rancé's fame to have reached her through Beaufort. Her family
held high office in Church and State, and when the aristocratic
abbey of les Clairets fell vacant she was nominated, presumably
as a perquisite of nobility rather than for any specifically religious
reasons. Writing in 1692, Mme de Sévigné[2] speaks of her 'vaga-
bonde depuis trois ans d'abbaye en abbaye, l'a réformée [les
Clairets] et est devenue sainte elle-même.' Her approaches to
Rancé gain in directness what they lack in subtlety. On the
historically justifiable grounds that les Clairets had originally
been under the direction of la Trappe, she persuaded Clairvaux
to transfer the direction of her abbey officially to Rancé: 'vous
voilà donc chargé de la mienne [conduite] devant les hommes, et
je ne sais comment vous prétendez vous en excuser devant
Dieu... Je passe partout pour être votre fille' (13 August 1688).[3]
A month later Rancé most reluctantly accepted the charge, and on

[1] Mme de Sévigné, *Lettres*, ii, p. 95 of 17 May 1676.
[2] Ibid. iii, pp. 817–18 of 22 Nov. 1692.   [3] Copies in *U* 863.

receipt of his letters the abbess wrote back ecstatically, describing how even the sick had hobbled out of the infirmary to join in the *Te Deum* and how everyone had wanted a copy of the letters: 'votre nom seul fait un renouvellement de ferveur.' Val-Richer then made his last canonical visit, the abbess deferring to him on all points save that of having Rancé as her new superior.

His first effective act was to send as confessor dom Jacques de Lanchal,[1] who had originally accompanied Nocey from the Oratory to try a hermit's life near Perseigne. Jacques, son of a Crown official at Alençon, was professed in 1681 at Perseigne, and seems to have kept up close relations with Rancé, probably through his former companion, Nocey. At all events he stayed at les Clairets with Rancé's blessing until his death in 1692, aged 50. His successors included dom Malachie Garneyrin, later founder abbot of Buonsolazzo, then for nearly a year the former Dominican, Antoine Lafarge, and another former Dominican, Grégoire Maupeou. All these men were mature in years and experienced as confessors in their former orders, and it is interesting to read Antoine in 1698[2] refute the charge of Jansenism made against Malachie by the abbess: 'elle a plutôt besoin d'un supérieur pour modérer son zèle que pour l'empêcher de tomber dans le relâchement.' Moderation and charity seem to have been two qualities in which she was conspicuously lacking.

The history of Rancé's visits, to bless the abbess and conduct the visitation, and the consequent controversy, has already been related, and in part answers the question of his influence at les Clairets. In the short term, the provision of sensible and firm confessors can only have done good, and the rapid progress of the reform in the abbey was a good sign after what must be accounted the relatively easy-going rule of Abbess de Fiennes. Unfortunately Rancé's deteriorating health, his abdication, and the strained relations between the abbess and Gervaise soon undid much of the good, at least as far as she personally was concerned. It is significant that her successor (in 1709), Marguerite-Élisabeth de Chavigny, was descended on her father's side from Rancé's uncle Claude, whose great-granddaughter she was, and that her mother was a Bossuet. She came moreover from Sainte-Catherine at Angers, a reformed house of which she had been prioress, so

---

[1] *TC* I/108 of 9 June 1688. See also MS. *Inventaire de la Trappe*, p. 23.
[2] *SG* Suppl. Z f in 40 829.

that the reform initiated by Abbess de Valençay passed into good hands.[1] It is a little odd that after Thérèse's death there seems to have been no mention of her even four years later when Rancé resumed contact with les Clairets. It is also interesting that a contemporary of Thérèse at les Clairets was Mme de Harlay,[2] entrusted as a child to her aunt, Abbess de Thou, and then sent there again from 1659 to 1662 with the intention of succeeding as abbess, only to be forced back into the world by family circumstances. Later, as a Visitandine, she became Rancé's correspondent, but again has nothing to say of Thérèse. Considering the long family connection with the abbey, his contacts among the noble families of many of the nuns, and the proximity of la Trappe, it is only surprising that Rancé's influence should have been felt there so late. Certainly the abbey flourished once he did accept responsibility, so that in 1692[3] he can tell Marie-Louise that there are now so many postulants that there will be no room for a girl she mentions, but for more than thirty years he had paid it little attention. Whether this was because of Thérèse or in spite of her it is impossible to say, but the question merits further study.

Chronologically the next Cistercian house with which Rancé had to do was the abbey of Saint-Antoine in Paris.[4] Here too there had been a family connection, for his paternal aunt, Marie Bouthillier, was abbess there until her death in 1652. She was succeeded by Madeleine Molé, until 1681, and then by Françoise, sister and latterly coadjutor of Madeleine, until 1686. These two were daughters of Mathieu Molé, the powerful *garde des sceaux* (died 1656) and were thus well connected in the world of Parlement and Court. Some time in 1669 Rancé came to hear, apparently through the nuns' confessor, that some of them wanted to move towards a more rigorous life, in accordance with *In Suprema*, but were meeting stiff resistance from the abbess. He wrote in January 1670[5] to encourage the would-be reformers, quoting St. Bernard in support of his exhortation to follow the Rule, and clearly approving their initiative. He had, however, to proceed cautiously, and in a second letter explains that he cannot sign his name 'pour des raisons considérables'. A year later things were no better at Saint-Antoine, but the election of Jean Petit as abbot of Cîteaux gave some hope of improvement. Rancé

[1] On all this see Souancé, op. cit.   [2] *Vis, Lettres circulaires*, Melun, 1714.
[3] *TA* of 11 Sept. 1692.   [4] See *GC* vii, 905.   [5] *TD*, series C, 42–6.

tells the progressive nuns (they seem to have been only two or three) that they are quite within their rights to practise abstinence and other reformed rules, and in case of trouble should apply direct to Cîteaux for permission. Otherwise they must move to a house where they can follow their conscience. By the end of the year he can only tell them to go on trying, and has himself written in firm but respectful terms to their abbess. In 1674 he is still writing to them, but now saying plainly that they can and should leave their abbey, and incidentally chiding them for addressing him as 'Monsieur'. It seems that the story had a happy ending, for, according to Dubois[1] and others, the brother of one of the dissident nuns was shortly afterwards promoted to a bishopric and found her an abbey (not Cistercian) in which she and her followers could live according to their desires. Without names and details the sequel is uninformative, but Rancé's role as monastic reformer, and acknowledged spokesman for the Abstinents, comes out clearly from this episode.

Quite different again is the case of Maubuisson.[2] This royal abbey, not far from Paris, had been ruled (if that is the word) by various ladies of royal blood and notorious profligacy, including members of the d'Estrées clan, when in 1664 Louise-Hollandine, Princess Palatine and sister-in-law of Anne de Gonzague, became abbess. Born in 1622, Louise was converted from Protestantism and brought up at Port-Royal. In 1660 she was professed at Maubuisson, and four years later became the first member of the community for a century or more to be elected abbess, a post she only vacated on her death in 1709. She is often charged with a scandalous life (like her sister-in-law), but the anecdotal footnote so often attached to her seems to belong properly to her d'Estrées predecessor, whose bastards allegedly ran into double figures. However that may be, as abbess she showed herself authoritarian and strict, and at one time formally adhered to the Reform, withdrawing later probably for the sake of greater autonomy rather than more relaxation. Nicole knew her, so did Châtillon, who planned a visit in 1673,[3] and so did many of Rancé's Jansenist friends. A further contact may have been through Saint-Victor,

[1] Dubois, i, pp. 370 seq., tells the story but without mentioning sources (almost certainly in fact dom le Nain).

[2] Vergé du Taillis, *Chroniques de l'abbaye royale de Maubuisson*, gives the bare facts recounted here, but is superficial and little help for this period.

[3] To Le Roy in *U* 745.

one of whose dependent priories at Villers-le-Bel supplied the abbey's confessor over quite a long period. It is rarely possible to state with certainty when a given correspondence, or contact, begins, as so much depends on the accident of survival, but by the end of 1680 Rancé was fully launched on a correspondence with the abbess and the sub-prioress (and possibly the prioress as well). The latter wrote with the knowledge, and perhaps at the instigation, of her abbess, and is typical of a certain excessive scrupulosity all too frequent in religious women. In particular she has difficulty in distinguishing between the immutable and the variable elements in the rule in her anxious quest for perfection. As usual Rancé answered her questions with a letter[1] of eminent good sense, pointing out that such matters as vigils and abstinence can be regulated according to the discretion of the superior, while the interior obligations of the religious life can admit of no dispensation. As for her own case, obedience to a superior 'sans distinction de l'âge et de la qualité de sa personne' and confidence are the surest guides. If confessions are arid, if emotion is dead, she must persevere. He tells the abbess[2] the same thing, and especially not to abstain from the sacraments because response is absent: 'Dieu nous commande de l'aimer, mais non pas de sentir que nous l'aimons.'

Nearly all the surviving letters are in pairs, one to the sub-prioress, the other to the abbess, commenting on advice given to the former and also answering her own questions. The sub-prioress is fortunate in having enjoyed divine grace since she was 12, but is (he tells the abbess) 'une scrupuleuse qui est mieux auprès de Dieu qu'elle ne pense'. Meanwhile she is foolish to think of transferring to another order (probably the Carthusians) where silence and retreat are not so absolute as she thinks. As for the abbess, old as she is, she should not resign until she can see a worthy successor.[3] Six weeks later[4] Rancé hesitates to offer further advice to the sub-prioress, whom the abbess knows so much better, but thinks that she might be excused conferences and recreations if this will help, but not her external duties, because this might simply increase her 'humeur mélancolique'. Not for the first time Rancé counsels a moderation strangely at variance with

---

[1] *TC* 1/2 of 14 Nov. 1680. [2] *TD*, series C, 87 of 12 Dec. 1680.
[3] *TB* 1531 and 1533 of 13 Sept. 1681. [4] *TB* 1555 of 2 Nov. 1681.

the traditional distortion of his character: 'la condescendance est utile et même nécessaire en quantité de rencontres.'

At about this time Rancé's relations with Maubuisson became more formally established, for dom Alain, back from Tamié, went as confessor to the nuns, but not, it seems, to the abbess.[1] By March 1682[2] the sub-prioress has been released from the external duties that had been worrying her and feels much better, and in July Rancé tells her that dom Alain is much more satisfied with her than she supposes.[3] Alain presumably sent regular reports to Rancé, though only one letter to him from Rancé (or possibly two) survives, and Rancé's control over the spiritual life at Maubuisson must have been somewhat similar to that at les Clairets, though he had no canonical status as Visitor and it is not clear under whose auspices a confessor was sent. Thereafter everyone seems to have been much happier. Rancé praises the abbess for her treatment of novices,[4] the sub-prioress praises dom Alain, Rancé praises the abbess to her, and so on. Rather unaccountably after nearly twenty years in office the abbess suddenly decided at the end of 1682 to move her abbatial throne to a less prominent position in the church, and generally to do what she could to obliterate all signs of the honour appropriate to her royal blood as being an obstacle to humility. This caused something of a revolt among the nuns, and Rancé tried to dissuade her from a gesture that was not really essential. Dom Alain evidently had a lot of trouble over this, and Rancé tells him too that the change is unnecessary, but that he is doing a useful job.[5] The last extant letter is in August 1683,[6] and very suitably concludes the series on a note of assurance to the sub-prioress. It is not known when Alain left Maubuisson, where he may indeed have died, nor what the subsequent course of Rancé's relations with the abbey may have been, but this brief excerpt from a much longer story shows a varied selection of relationships over less than three years, with abbess, sub-prioress, and confessor, a princess, an anonymous (but probably noble) nun, and an expatriate Irish monk. It is especially interesting that an abbey—and an abbess—of such prestige, linked neither canonically nor traditionally with la Trappe, should have applied to, or through, Rancé for a confessor when so many alternative directors were available.

¹ *TC* I/95a.   ² *TB* 1620.   ³ *TB* 1698.
⁴ *TB* 1813.   ⁵ *TB* 1825.   ⁶ *TC* II/303.

Last of the four Cistercian houses in this group is Leyme, de Eremo or Lumen Dei, in the diocese of Cahors.[1] This abbey never left the Common Observance, and the connection with Rancé arose directly from the abbess. The diverse spellings of her name do not facilitate research into her biography, but the ascertainable facts are interesting. Anne d'Orviré (or Orvilliers) de la Vieuville (or Viefville) came of an old Picard family and with her sister, Marguerite, entered the Cistercian Abbaye aux Bois,[2] near Noyon, a house traditionally filled with Picard aristocrats. For sixty years (1623–84) the abbess was Marie de Lannoy, latterly assisted by one of the Luynes family, Marie-Madeleine d'Albert de Chaulnes (1684–7), and it was under her supervision that the community removed from Noyon, made uninhabitable by war, in various stages to Paris, where, in 1655, it was established in the Faubourg Saint-Germain. Even in exile the abbey continued to attract girls from Picard and other noble families and supplied superiors to a number of abbeys throughout France. Anne de la Vieuville was elected to Leyme in 1654, and remained there thirty years. She was preceded and followed by a Noailles, and as that family came originally from the Dordogne but later became established near Beauvais (where in the eighteenth century it gave its name to the village of its fief) the Picard connection very likely played a part in Anne's appointment. Leyme was an abbey of some importance, with several local benefices in its gift, and Anne seems to have been an energetic superior. In 1668, at a visitation by the Vicar-General of Cahors, there were twelve professed nuns, one novice, and two lay sisters, a good number by contemporary standards. It is known too that she added two chapels to the church, but for the rest the only source of information seems to be Rancé's correspondence. How they came into contact is not clear: the abbess seems to have known Beaufort of Sept-Fons, whose brother became Vicar-General to Noailles in Paris, and may have been associated with him before, and it also transpires early in the correspondence that a certain 'Mlle' (probably de Vertus or de Goëllo) who is on close terms with Rancé is sending on his letters to Leyme, though Rancé had not at first realized this.[3] Whatever the connection, in 1673 or 1674 the correspondence had already

---

[1] See the very useful article by E. Albe, 'L'Abbaye cist. de Leyme', and also GC i, 190.
[2] See GC vii, 906.   [3] Originals in U 863.

begun, and with more than a score of letters surviving for a ten-year period is an unusually complete series.

The abbess is at first concerned about the progress of the Cistercian reform, and Rancé offers her no comfort at all.[1] If the proto-abbots will not co-operate, he says, she might do better to put herself under her diocesan (Nicolas Sevin). In a characteristic passage he compares the order to 'un vaisseau dans le milieu de la tempête, percé de toutes parts...' and so on, warning her that shipwreck is imminent. Early in 1676 the Abbot of Cîteaux imposed a Visitor on Leyme, whose abbess refused to submit on the question of reform and was duly threatened with excommunication. Naturally distressed at this, she consulted Rancé, who advised her[2] to seek absolution directly from Cîteaux. At the same time he takes up a rumour circulated by Beaufort, who is going round accusing Rancé of Jansenism, and of staying at Port-Royal when in Paris. The latter charge was patently absurd (Rancé always stayed at the Institution de l'Oratoire and had not even visited Port-Royal since his conversion) and the former deliberately mischievous, but Rancé is quite temperate in his refutation. From then on the whole quarrel and reconciliation with Beaufort can be followed from the letters to Leyme, as described in an earlier chapter.[3] The abbess seems to have come to some agreement with Cîteaux; and in May 1676[4] there is no longer any threat of excommunication, though she is proceeding with some measure of reform under Rancé's guidance. He is busy translating the *Us* of Cîteaux, which he eventually sends her, and advises her on a number of points: the practice of proclamation of faults, the importance of excluding all but worthy postulants, and of surrendering the right of nominating to benefices rather than making bad use of it. As at Perseigne, he supports her when she expels an unsatisfactory nun, and in general concludes: 'il n'est guère possible de garder tout à la fois des mesures avec Dieu et avec les hommes.'

Relations with Cîteaux (or the Visitor) do not improve, and in 1678[5] Rancé is denouncing the 'maximes relâchées' of the Visitor and quoting at length from twelfth-century writers to prove that there was never dissension at St. Bernard's Clairvaux: 'il y a très peu de différence entre l'homicide et le murmure.' Now that she

---

[1] *TB* 317.   [2] *TB* 624.   [3] See above, pp. 128–129.
[4] *TB* 670.   [5] *TB* 939.

has introduced abstinence she must carry on to the end, for 'la sévérité est comme le sel'. Soon afterwards the abbess's health begins to falter, and this becomes a recurrent theme of the letters, interspersed with references to Rancé's own increasingly precarious health. Odd incidents stand out: a nun complains to the Visitor of the abbess's severity, and Rancé tells her to avoid excessive punishments; Louis de Noailles is appointed Bishop of Cahors, to Rancé's great satisfaction, but only eighteen months later is translated to Châlons, to be replaced by a prelate unknown to Rancé or the abbess. By 1681[1] failing health and pressure from outside to return nearer home make her think of translation, but Rancé, as always, disapproves. At the same time the prioress, the abbess's sister Marguerite, is nominated to a dependent priory some distance away, and Rancé again disapproves. Yet another awkward nun must be sent away to avoid a bad example; the abbess sadly observes that the education provided for girls in most monasteries is even less Christian than it would be in the world; and her health grows worse and worse. A silence of some months worries Rancé, but in August[2] he answers her inquiry predictably by forbidding her to take the waters, though she may take them at home, and he reassures her about rumours of his own incapacitation. By the autumn she is too unwell to set an example of vigils and abstinence, and the end is only too clearly in sight. They talk of episcopally supervised abbeys, no better off than the others, and Rancé recalls his own experience with Val and Beauvais; she tells him of an English gentleman who has lost everything through exile, and Rancé says he is sorry but 'il ne faut point être chrétien à demi'.[3] New Year greetings for 1683 are exchanged, and then, in a final message before she dies,[4] Rancé tells her that she must leave everything to God; she has wondered how her life will end, but she must just accept what comes. Even so near the end she consults him on a point of discipline, raised some years before, and this time he thinks that proclamation of faults should be practised with discretion, or even suppressed: 'un supérieur est fait pour sauver les âmes'. This was the last word, and exactly a year later her successor was appointed, so that Rancé's letter must have reached Anne only shortly before her death.

It will be seen that the correspondence with Leyme comprises

[1] *TB* 1503. [2] *TB* 1749. [3] *TB* 1779 and 1800.
[4] *TC* II/71 of 8 June 1685.

most of the disparate elements scattered throughout that with les Clairets, Saint-Antoine, and Maubuisson, and though only a small proportion of the letters survive (he probably wrote once a month or so) they give a very good idea of the relationship. Matters of discipline within the abbey, and of discipline within the order, are combined with detailed discussion of mutual acquaintances, like Beaufort or Noailles, of topical issues, like Jansenism, and of personal problems. One is left with the impression of a woman very similar to Rancé himself, courageous, stern, uncompromising, but essentially humane and good, and not at all fanatical or self-important.

Some of Rancé's letters enjoyed an extraordinarily wide circulation even before Muguet published the two volumes of 1701/2, and it must be presumed that this was due more to the recipient than to any intention of Rancé himself. Thus, the long letter on religious duties addressed to the sub-prioress of Maubuisson, another to an unnamed German Cistercian, one to the monks of Saint-Symphorien at Beauvais, and, finally, one sent in answer to a plea from a nun of Gif[1] were all frequently copied and used to illustrate the true spirit of monasticism. The case of Gif is unusual in several respects. This Benedictine abbey in the diocese of Meaux had a very good reputation, and quite close contacts with Port-Royal. In 1667 Anne-Victoire de Clermont de Montglat[2] was professed at the abbey, after spending some years as a *pensionnaire* at Port-Royal, which she had to leave with her sister in 1659, aged about 12. Lame in one hip at the time, but later cured, she was then brought up by an aunt until she came to Gif, where she became novice mistress and sub-prioress. With the death of Madeleine de Cheverny, she found herself in 1675 faced with the abbatial succession. She shrank from the threatened responsibility and wrote, apparently out of the blue, to Rancé to ask his advice. Apart from possible Port-Royal contacts, she may well have been put in touch by M. Ameline, Visitor of the abbey, Archdeacon of Paris, and a friend of Rancé. Rancé seems to have been genuinely surprised that she should consult him on such a point, and did not at once reply, but then answered at length. He begins by expressing his surprise that she should consult a stranger ('une personne qui ne vous est point connue') on so grave

[1] Muguet, i, p. 68.   [2] *GC* vii, 601; see also Moréri, s.v. *Monglat*.

a matter, and then gives eight points requisite, in his opinion, for such an office as she is hesitating to assume. She fears that her strength is insufficient to push through needed reform, she fears her 'présomption dominante', and so on. He talks to her about humility and responsibility in the most concrete and specific terms: she must eat in the refectory, sleep in the dormitory, have no personal attendant among the nuns, not allow them to call her 'Madame', abstain from meat, since her health allows, and above all 'ne déchargez sur personne le soin de la direction, elle n'appartient qu'à vous'. Apparently reassured, she accepted election, and Rancé wrote back to say how glad he was to hear that 'Dieu a soumis votre cœur à sa volonté.'[1] Accordingly she took office on 7 May 1676, and was blessed next year by the Bishop of Périgueux (P. Le Boutz, a former Oratorian).

Her attempts at reform were considerably helped by the death from old age or sickness of a dozen or so nuns within a year, and with the backing of Ameline and with Rancé's moral support she accomplished a good deal. Rancé went on writing (though few letters survive) and, for example, tells her in 1680[2] that dom Claude, a former Celestine, has died at la Trappe, that she must stay where she is, and that he knows well the family of a certain Mlle N. who is now at Gif. In 1682 he speaks warmly of Gif as an orderly and well-run house in a letter to Bossuet;[3] in 1684 he commends the abbey again in a letter to a young woman[4] about to go there; but the abbess was again having doubts. By 1685[5] she is ready to shed the burden unwillingly assumed: 'toutes vos pensées vous portent à vous décharger d'un fardeau qui vous paraît excéder vos forces', but how can she risk the destruction of all she has achieved by the appointment of an unsuitable successor? Next year, her mind made up, she resigned[6] in favour of Anne de Béthune d'Orval, a nun of Reims some ten years her junior, who had a sister at Port-Royal (to whom Rancé wrote in 1683). Strangely enough the story does not end there, because at the request of the new abbess Anne de Montglat became prioress early in 1687, remaining in that office until her death in 1701. She was still not happy, and in 1688[7] Rancé tells her that if resigna-

[1] TB 278.   [2] TB 1306 of 18 July 1680.
[3] TB 1777 of 5 Oct. 1682 and Bossuet, Correspondance, ii, p. 316.
[4] TC I/126 of 10 Feb. 1684.   [5] TC II/186 of 22 Apr. 1685.
[6] Moréri, art. cit.   [7] TC I/134 of 15 Jan. 1688.

tion has not brought her the peace she seeks, this is because the decision was hers, and not God's, and she is being made to suffer for it. A year later[1] she wants to abandon the charge of prioress: 'vous continuez de vous juger avec votre sévérité accoutumée', notes Rancé; but she might well accept a new post offered which 'vous oblige seulement à quelques soins et à quelque vigilance'. When she died she left a reputation for piety, and seems loyally to have supported her successor, who remained in office until her death in 1733.

The case of Gif was particularly well known because Rancé's first letter to the future abbess was full of sound advice, but it is only one of many such for which evidence is usually too fragmentary to be useful. Rancé almost certainly wrote also to Anne de Montglat's successor, and in the same diocese of Meaux the Augustinian abbey of Jouarre is known to have received regular correspondence from la Trappe. Bossuet's great friends and constant correspondents, Mme d'Albert and her sister Mme de Luynes (granddaughters of the famous Mme de Chevreuse), frequently refer between 1690 and 1697 to messages and packets sent to or from la Trappe, through Bossuet, and some may well survive as anonymous copies.[2] It is interesting that at Jouarre Bossuet was very much the director, with Rancé as a distinguished second, while no letters from Bossuet to Gif are known, though as diocesan he must have visited the abbey regularly.

A last example of Rancé's dealings with abbesses is that of Essai, an important Augustinian house near Alençon.[3] From 1638 to 1693 the three successive abbesses all belonged to the family Trotti de la Chétardie, of which the most celebrated member was Joachim (1636–1714) who became curé of Saint-Sulpice (where he had been trained) and director to Mme de Maintenon. His relative, Françoise-Marie, came to Essai from Jouarre in 1638 to find 'ni cloitre ni régularité'. She worked hard to reform the house, setting a personal example of humility, poverty, and simplicity, and died in 1676 with solid achievements to her credit. She was succeeded by her niece, Françoise de Jésus (1629–87), who had also been brought up at Jouarre before coming as a

---

[1] *TC* II/234 of 5 Jan. 1689.

[2] Bossuet, *Correspondance*, iv–v, 21 Dec. 1690–30 July 1697.

[3] See the important and informative register begun by the nuns' confessor (and continued by them) in *Archives de l'Orne*, H. 3, pp. 132 seq. (H 3976).

novice to Essai in 1645; Françoise became coadjutrix in 1659. 'Sa manière de conduire fut la douceur', but she introduced abstinence on Mondays, which must have taken some firmness, even if she also contracted considerable debts ('debita non pauca contraxit', in the words of *Gallia Christiana*),[1] which rather suggests the opposite. Being particularly associated with the ducal house of Alençon, Essai was of special interest to Mme de Guise, and it was at her request that Bossuet blessed the abbess (24 August 1684) after the Bishop of Séez, had, for some reason, refused to do so (the ceremony of abbatial blessing was optional and conferred no canonical status). Her director was M. le Chevalier,[2] sometime curé of Alençon and then archdeacon and director of the diocesan seminary of Séez, who had tried to get Rancé to accept him at la Trappe in about 1670. With all these connections it is not surprising that Rancé should have been her correspondent. She is known to have consulted him on the subject of abstinence, Rancé discussed with her the possible admission of one of the daughters of M. de Tourouvre, who never actually took the veil, the death of their diocesan in 1682, and her own serious illness later the same year.[3] Early in 1683 the most circumstantial of the extant letters[4] deals with the contribution to be made to M. le Chevalier on behalf of missions (presumably to Huguenots) and her intended renunciation of a silver abbatial staff for a wooden one, something Rancé himself had done long before. When she died piously she was succeeded by her sister the prioress, Marie de Sainte-Thérèse (1634–93), who suffered from poor health but did what she could to redeem the debts. The appointment was due to Mme de Guise, who consulted Rancé first, but no more is known of his subsequent role at Essai. None the less, the combined influence of Bossuet, Mme de Guise, and M. le Chevalier are sufficient indications of the way in which, directly or indirectly, he affected an abbey which was moreover near enough to have had many visitors, like Bossuet, who went also to la Trappe.

With the Carmelites of the rue Saint-Jacques, 'les Grandes Carmélites', Rancé's relations are much more personal and at the

[1] *GC* xi, 742–3.
[2] See J. Grandet, *Les Saints Prêtres fr. du XVIIe siècle*, I, pp. 291 seq.
[3] *TC* II/179 of 8 Feb. 1682; *TB* 1734 of 22 Aug. 1682 and 1765 of 10 Apr. 1682.
[4] *TC* II/328 and *TB* 1833 of 14 and 21 Jan. 1683.

same time more what one would expect of a spiritual director in the accepted sense.[1] The exemplary piety of the convent and its smooth running left no room for talk of possible reform or fresh austerities such as came up with the abbeys and superiors just discussed, and the correspondence consists mainly of exhortation, consolation, and affirmations of spiritual solidarity. His first, and principal, contact was, however, of a somewhat different nature, and can properly be described as a close personal friendship, involving a whole complex of relationships not so far mentioned. This was with Mère Agnès de Bellefonds,[2] one of the most remarkable religious of the century. Born in 1611, she at first joined the Court of Marie de Medicis, but then in 1629 entered the Carmelite house where she remained until her death in 1691. Subprioress in 1645, prioress in 1649, she spent sixty-two years in religion, of which more than half were in these two offices (held for periods of three years, renewed to six, with an obligatory break of three years before the next tenure). Her influence on her convent, and on the countless high-born men and women who frequented it, is incalculable and her reputation that of a saint. Her nephew, Bernardin Gigault de Bellefonds, became one of Rancé's closest friends, and their correspondence normally passed through her hands as intermediary. Just when, and in what circumstances, Rancé first met either Mère Agnès or her nephew is not known, but it could have been at any time in his worldly period. By 1672 he was in regular correspondence with Bellefonds, but the earliest identifiable surviving letters to Carmelites date from 1674. As was so often the case with Rancé, and other letter-writers of the period, his letters were meant to be read by friends of the recipient, and were also sent in batches to the same or neighbouring destinations for postal reasons. Thus as well as to Mère Agnès and her nephew, Rancé wrote at various times to sœur Anne-Marie de Jésus, sœur Louise de la Miséricorde, and sœur Émilie de la Passion, and no doubt also to others unnamed. In addition a niece of dom le Nain joined the convent in 1682 as sœur Marie-Anne de Jésus, and is known to have received letters

[1] An invaluable source of information about the members of this house is still V. Cousin, *La Jeunesse de Mme de Longueville*, with its detailed appendices on the Carmelites, covering all the religious mentioned below.

[2] Her reputation and influence come through unmistakably in the invariably respectful and affectionate references to her in the correspondence of a wide variety of men and women. On her nephew, the maréchal, see below, pp. 256–263.

from her uncle, so that links between la Trappe and the Carmelites
were unusually numerous.

Rancé's letters to Mère Agnès, or the few that survive,[1] are
full of news and quite conversational in tone, as befits two friends
with so much in common. While he was in Paris in November
1674 he paid a visit to the Carmelites, and there met Anne-Marie
and Louise, among others, but he was not then to know that this
would be his last visit. On his subsequent abortive trips to Paris
in 1675 he had no time for anything but the business of the order.
It so happens that the earliest extant letter to Mère Agnès refers
to his last flying visit in April, when to his great annoyance he
had to leave Bellefonds alone at la Trappe, and was so disgusted
with the failure of his cause that he never again took any part in
Abstinent affairs, and never again saw Paris. He speaks warmly of
Anne-Marie, and of Louise (recently professed), deplores the
state of his order, and is even more depressed at the threat to la
Trappe where, on top of everything else, heavy mortality is at
last striking. In the next letter it is she who is dissatisfied with
herself, but Rancé offers comfort: 'ceux dont le cœur est droit ne
sauroient ne point souffrir.' A further link is established when we
read that R.P. de Monchy has just left la Trappe and will bring all
the news. By the end of 1676 Rancé is meeting a lot of criticism
from both Molinists and Jansenists, and has begun a correspondence with Brancas, a recent convert and frequent visitor to the
Carmelites, and also related to Bellefonds. Since 1672 Mme de
Longueville had been living at the Carmelites, and they, like any
other community with Jansenist connections, let alone sympathies,
had to face hostile comment from the other side. Soon afterwards
Rancé is in trouble locally; the Bishop of Évreux is spreading
the rumour that Bellefonds and Rancé have fallen out on doctrinal
issues, and the Bishop of Séez, whose letter to Bellefonds Rancé
forwards, is furious. Val-Richer, very friendly with Jesuits, is
allegedly the source of the tale, and Rancé comments: 'vous ne
sauriez vous imaginer jusqu'où va le déchainement des dévots
de Normandie contre moi.'[2] As he had already told her, 'on a cela
de bon avec les Jansénistes que quand on ne dit pas mal d'eux,
ils disent du bien de vous,' and now finds two years later[3] how
right he had been in his assessment of the others: 'j'éprouve tous

---

[1] Copies of a series of seven are in *TD*, series, C, 1–17, from 4 Nov. 1675 to Oct.
1677.
[2] Copy in *U* 3069 of Nov. 1675.   [3] *TD*, series C, 10 of 14 Sept. 1677.

les jours aussi bien que vous qu'à moins d'être livré et abandonné aux passions des Molinistes ils ne gardent point de mesure, et ne font aucun scrupule d'accabler les personnes innocentes.' Unfortunately Rancé has to contend not only with Molinists but also with formerly trusted friends, like Beaufort, whose treachery he discusses with her. It is typical of the interlocking pattern of Rancé's relationships that the Carmelite nun to whom Beaufort divulged Rancé's confidential answer to Le Roy should have been Mère Thérèse de Jésus, as Mlle Tomeran de Remenecourt a former member of Gaston's court,[1] where Rancé might have met her, and a close friend of his correspondent Mme d'Huxelles.[2] Though no more letters to Mère Agnès identifiably survive, there are frequent references to her in letters to Bellefonds and others up to the time of her death.

Another member of the community to whom he wrote, but in much more general terms, was Turenne's niece and the sister of Cardinal de Bouillon, sœur Émilie de la Passion (1639–96), who became a Carmelite in 1658, followed three years later by her younger sister, sœur Hippolyte de Jésus. Messages for the cardinal, condolences on the death of Turenne, and concern for the health of Mère Agnès are the main features of these letters, but they furnish a large number of the spiritual maxims anthologized by various admirers of Rancé.[3] As one would expect, the emphasis is on the transience of earthly affairs, but Émilie had hardly had time to be much of a sinner and the tone is quiet.

A very different person was sœur Louise de la Miséricorde, and one very much more in Rancé's own style.[4] One of the *grandes pénitentes* with whom he seemed to feel a special affinity, she sounds more like the heroine of a romantic novel than a real figure. Louise le Blanc de la Vallière was born at Tours in 1644, lost her father when she was only 10 and moved to Blois, where her mother had taken as her third husband Gaston's *maître d'hotel*. There they stayed until Gaston's death, and at both Tours and Blois had opportunities for meeting Rancé. In 1661 Louise became maid of honour to Henriette-Élisabeth, duchesse d'Orléans, and by July had already come to know the King through

---

[1] See Cousin, *Mme de Longueville*, p. 365.   [2] See letters in *A* 3202.
[3] See BN 19324 *passim*.
[4] See J. Lair, *Louise de la Vallière*, containing her life and her letters to Bellefonds, quoted below.

the intermediary of another former member of Gaston's court, the father of Rancé's later correspondent the duc de Beauvillier. In December 1663 she bore Louis a son, and a little more than a year later another, both of whom died in infancy. By 1667 she had borne him a daughter and a son, who both lived, but she was already the object of Mme de Montespan's malevolent attentions. In 1670 she fell seriously ill and seems to have felt the first stirrings of conversion. Her friend, Anne de Gonzague, claimed that Louise deliberately attended Mme de Montespan, her successor in the King's favours, for three whole years to punish herself. The sudden death of Henriette-Élisabeth the same year further affected her, and on Ash Wednesday (10 February 1671) next year she fled to the convent of the Carmelites at Chaillot, intending to stay at least for a while, but was brought back after only twelve hours. At this stage, or before, Bellefonds, who knew her intimately and was very fond of her, aided by Bossuet, resolved to snatch this brand from the burning despite Louis's indignation, and she was recommended to the Carmelite Père César, formerly of Arras and later Namur. By 1674 her mind was made up: for the sake of her two children she got the court painter Mignard to do her portrait and then entered the Carmelites. Just before she went she wrote to Bellefonds: 'enfin je quitte le monde! C'est sans regret; mais ce n'est pas sans peine; ma faiblesse m'y a retenue longtemps sans goût, ou, pour parler plus juste, avec mille chagrins', and just after: 'il y a deux jours que je suis ici: mais j'y suis si satisfaite et si tranquille que je suis en admiration des bontés de Dieu.' It was at this precise moment that Rancé wrote to her (19 March 1674)[1] and though only a fragment remains, it is significant: 'vivre dans cette pénitence extérieure et se perdre à la fin, ce sont des choses qui ne sont pas incompatibles.'

In June 1674 her solemn clothing took place, conducted by the abbé Pirot, who later became director of the convent; Rancé came to see her in November; and in June 1675 she took her vows, with Bossuet preaching. Throughout this time she was in constant contact with Bellefonds (forty-eight of her letters to him survive), Bossuet, le Camus, and Rancé. After her meeting with Rancé she writes to Bellefonds (7 November 1674) that she and her friend Anne-Marie have had the joy of hearing instructions similar to those given to the novices at la Trappe: 'qu'il aime Dieu au prix

[1] In TD, series A.

de moi!' A year later it is Tréville who brings Rancé back to the parlour, spiritually at least, this time in the form of the *relation* of Charles Denis's death[1] which he read out to the nuns. A mutual friend, M. de Valentiné, goes to la Trappe in 1676; le Camus too comes up in the correspondence; and it is evident that Louise is closely involved with the inner circle of Rancé's friends. Apart from her letters, mostly on spiritual matters, she wrote a book (perhaps as early as 1670) entitled *Réflexions sur la miséricorde de Dieu par une dame pénitente*, which was published in 1680 without her permission, probably at Bossuet's instigation. This too is very much in line with Rancé's own writings on penitence and conversion, though there is no reason to suppose that he had any hand in it. The subsequent course of her life in the convent was marked by recurrent ill health, by concern for the health of Mère Agnès, to whom she was devoted, by the death of her son (1683), her mother (1686), and of most of her fellow nuns (thirty of the fifty she had first known were dead by 1700), but she persevered in her life of penance until her own death in 1710. Only one other of Rancé's surviving letters bears her name, a formal expression of esteem early in 1681, but he certainly wrote to her at regular intervals. Besides, the letters addressed to the Carmelites were common property, and people like Bossuet, Bellefonds, Tréville, Brancas, le Camus, and many others would ensure that his influence was not forgotten.

Her close friend, and another friend of Bellefonds, was sœur Anne-Marie de Jésus,[2] daughter of the duc d'Épernon, Governor of Guyenne, and granddaughter of Henri IV. To the fury of her family, who had hoped to see her marry Casimir, future king of Poland, she abandoned the world in 1648, at the age of 24, and was professed next year at the Carmel at Bourges, soon passing to that of Paris. Long before her death in 1701 she had acquired a reputation for sanctity. Her case was an unusual example of independence in the face of her father's frantic but vain appeals to the Queen Regent, Parlement, and even the Pope, and is known to have inspired Pascal's friend, Mlle de Roannez, in her similar but abortive attempt to take the veil at Port-Royal.[3] The first

---

[1] See Lair, p. 102.
[2] See abbé de Montis, *La Vie de... sœur Anne-Marie d'Épernon*, and article by R. Limouzin-Lamothe in *DBF*.
[3] See J. Mesnard, *Pascal et les Roannez*, pp. 549–50.

mention of her in Rancé's correspondence is in a letter to Belle-fonds (15 August 1674)[1] in which he agrees with her acceptance of God's will; but they certainly knew each other before. Later, when *Sainteté* has just come out, he comments (15 April 1683):'[2] 'sœur Anne-Marie a toujours vécu avec tant de piété et de religion qu'elle n'y trouvera guère de choses qu'elle n'ait pratiquées.' He met her, as we have seen, in November 1674, and wrote, probably just afterwards, with advice on confession and peni-tence in Advent and Lent. Thereafter he remained in touch, either directly or through Mère Agnès, Bellefonds, or sœur Louise. He tells her not to abstain from communion too often, but to think rather of God's mercy; he regrets the controversy into which his name has been drawn (through his letter to Brancas in 1676) and wishes people would leave him alone; he shares her distress at the decay of the Reform; but on the whole the correspondence is not very factually informative, rich though it is in spiritual maxims.

More perhaps than any of the other communities of women so far discussed, the Carmelites may be said to have shared Rancé's spiritual values and individually to have come closest in his intimacy. It is noteworthy that he knew, and enormously admired, the work of St. Teresa; he refers to her often in letters, and even in official writings, usually in the context of her complete dis-regard for the opinion of others. The ties of friendship and a common aristocratic background, further predisposed him in favour of this quite exceptional community, and it is probably safe to affirm that he gained as much (and knew it) from the example of Mère Agnès and her sisters as they did from him.

Of his three sisters in religion, the one of whom Rancé seems to have been most fond, and the only one to outlive him, was Louise-Isabelle.[3] She entered the Annonciades in Paris in 1646, and was to have been professed a year later. Owing to ill health this was not possible, and at her own urgent request, and with her father's approval, she sought and obtained leave to remain in the community with the special status of 'fondatrice' and as such exempt from some of the rigours. On taking this step in 1647 she followed the practice of the order in prefixing the name Marie to

---

[1] *BN* n.a. 12959, f. 19.   [2] Ibid., f. 101.
[3] See above, p. 8, n. 1. Originals and copies of Rancé's letters to her are all at la Trappe.

her own, and was henceforth known as Marie-Louise. At least one letter from Rancé survives addressed to 'Mère Louise-Isabelle,' but meant for Marie-Louise, as she then was, and biographers have hitherto assumed the existence of two sisters, where in fact there are only two names. There is some evidence that his younger sister, Marie, may briefly have tried a vocation at the Annonciades before marrying the comte de Vernassal and dying young, but the full story is still to be discovered.[1] At all events Marie-Louise was still alive in 1704 (attesting a miracle attributed to her brother)[2] and by an extraordinary chance sixty of his letters to her, more than half of them original, survive for the period 1669–94.

Rancé's first sermon was preached at his sister's clothing in 1647, and it must be supposed that he saw a lot of her in the years preceding his own retreat. The superiors of the convent had to deal with him after his father's death over the financial settlement for his sister, and in the ecclesiastical and social circles of the capital Rancé and his sisters had numerous common acquaintances. In the early years brother and sister would have met often enough to make correspondence unnecessary, and it is perhaps a sign of their unfamiliarity with written exchanges that in the earliest extant letter,[3] written between his return from the Pyrenees and his visit to Paris (16 November 1660), he tells her that he is 'scandalisé de toutes les façons que vous faites dans vos lettres, les cérémonies ne sont ni pour vous ni pour moi'. The next we hear is after his return from Rome, when he has become a public figure, and a more suitable recipient of marks of respect than he had been in 1660. At the beginning of the monastic year (10 September 1667, for Holy Cross Day, four days later)[4] he sends his two(?) sisters two carved oaken figures and medals via the prior of la Trappe. Two years later his growing authority in the world of religion is attested by Marie-Louise's formal consultation on a point of her rule. The Annonciades Célestes (so called to distinguish them from another order of Annonciades) were of recent foundation (1604) and had been established in Paris only since

[1] A letter to Favier of 25 Nov. 1691 (Gonod, p. 80) speaks of 'la réception de mes sœurs à l'Annonciade… la cadette s'est engagée après la mort de mon père', and this could refer either to Marie before her marriage in 1658 (though most probably not) or another, unnamed, sister, who presumably died quite soon. The mystery remains baffling.

[2] Statement of 24 Oct. 1704 reproduced in MS. de Sept-Fons, ad fin.

[3] In TD, series A, 1.   [4] Ibid. 7

1623.[1] Their rule was not particularly austere, but included a special fourth vow of total enclosure. To attract more recruits, and thus endowments, some of the nuns wanted to relax this rule, and abolish the grills, but Marie-Louise was not happy about the proposed change and asked her brother's opinion. He naturally rejected any such slackening of the rule, and said so unambiguously,[2] quoting their foundress and two Italian priests who had advised her. He saw no reason to change the rule whereby the grills were opened only three times a year to parents, brothers, and sisters, and thought it a complete fallacy that such a relaxation could save the institution from its very real material worries. Seven or eight years later[3] the same question came up again, no doubt for the same reasons, and Rancé reminds Marie-Louise of what he had said on the subject, suggesting that she refer to his earlier letter if she has kept it. His advice seems to have been followed, and relations between the two communities were formally established when he sent the Annonciades an Act of Association in 1675.

Though he was evidently very fond of his sister, and wrote regularly, Rancé showed the same kind of distance as he did with Thérèse. In 1674,[4] for example, just before a visit to Paris, he excuses himself for not answering her letter, not for any lack of affection, but because he tries not to advise anyone and she has only to follow her rule. Next year (10 April 1675)[5] on returning from what was to be his last visit to Paris, he found a letter waiting for him from Marie-Louise saying that she had been ill, and he expresses regret, but it is clear that he did not visit her on that occasion, and indeed never saw her again. Most of his letters refer to mutual friends, often visitors to la Trappe who could bring first-hand news of Marie-Louise and Paris and go back with messages and pious souvenirs. She passes on books for him, shows his letters to selected friends, and defends him from all-too-frequent attacks.

Health is a constant theme of these, as of so many other letters, and the death of such dear friends as Pinette the occasion for the usual reflections on eternity. The tone is the familiar mixture of

---

[1] See *Dict. d'histoire et de géog. eccl.* on origins and development of the order in France.
[2] Muguet, i, p. 99. [3] Ibid., p. 418.
[4] *TA* 6 of 8 Oct. 1674. [5] Ibid. 4.

outward formality, even sternness, with underlying affection and sympathy, and his spiritual counsels are by no means banal. He tells her not to worry if confessions are not always a success, because for want of preparation 'souvent nos confessions nous nuisent plus qu'elles ne nous servent'.[1] He warns her not to get drawn into controversy (apparently on his account) unless invited to speak, 'mais surtout n'insistez jamais et évitez tout ce qui ressent ou de l'entêtement ou de l'opiniatreté',[2] In the same letter he speaks sympathetically of the trials and 'la léthargie de ceux que se donnent à Dieu'. Later he tells her, after pondering her problem, that she would do better to forget the past, 'il n'y a rien de plus sensible que ces aridités et ces sécheresses dont vous vous plaignez, cependant elles ne laissent pas d'avoir de grandes utilités.' His objectivity can be disturbing; she seems to have thought that he had shown no great enthusiasm for a retreat she was about to make, but he denies this,[3] saying, however, that retreat might be a good thing, though not the most important, for it often happens that people spend ten days being 'réguliers et exacts' only to fall back into the habits they had momentarily interrupted. All in all, this substantial series of letters is as revealing as one could wish, being full of facts as well as being spiritually significant. It should be added that half a dozen or so letters to the prioress, Mère Marie-Luce, survive;[4] they show that Rancé was on cordial terms with her, and at her death in 1689 he speaks warmly of her to his sister, but apart from the question of enclosure, his letters to her are almost entirely of general encouragement and exhortation.

Psychologically by far the most interesting series of letters comprises those addressed to the Visitation at Tours. Like the Carmelites and Annonciades, the Visitandines were of very recent foundation, and the house at Tours dated only from 1633. Fond as Rancé may have been of his sisters Thérèse or Marie-Louise, much though he respected Mère Agnès de Bellefonds, no woman influenced his spiritual life to anything like the same extent as Mère Louise-Françoise at Tours. Like her namesake, Mme de la Vallière, this Louise was a Mary Magdalen figure, but combined a vivid past with the kind of maternal presence that was exemplified by Mère Agnès and was obviously of compelling

---

[1] Ibid. 5 of 26 Dec. 1683.   [2] Ibid. 28 of 14 Nov. 1693.
[3] Ibid. 35 of 2 Feb. 1687.   [4] At la Trappe, in copies, from 1682 to 1688.

importance for Rancé. Born in 1616 at Tours, Louise Rogier de la Marbellière was the daughter of the Lieutenant-criminel of respectable rather than noble stock. In 1637 she met Gaston d'Orléans[1] whose favourite, Rancé's cousin Chavigny, acted as go-between. Next year she was officially recognized as Gaston's mistress and accompanied him to Paris, where she was fêted everywhere. All was not well, however, and at Easter 1639 Gaston learned that Louise was deceiving him with one of his court. She confessed, the man was dismissed, and the result of the reconciliation was a son born the following January. Meanwhile Louise, perhaps under the influence of Gaston's confessor, P. de Condren (later General of the Oratory), was beginning to worry, and though (or because) pregnant spoke of taking the veil. This was in August. By November Gaston had tired of her, and the child never knew either parent. In May 1640 Gaston told Chavigny that Louise really was going into religion, and in 1644 she was professed at the Visitation at Tours, presumably after an agreed transitional period of penitence before clothing. Ten years later Gaston made an attempt to see her again, but she declined, and as a token sent a present of some fruit to Gaston's wife. As for the boy, he was more or less adopted by Gaston's daughter, la Grande Mademoiselle, who secured for him one of her titles, that of comte de Charny, and he had a worthy career of arms.

Louise paid a heavy price, as did Mme de la Vallière, for her three or four years of worldly success, and she stayed more than sixty years in the cloister, dying only in 1707.[2] Rancé was of course too young to have known her at Court, but his connections with Gaston, and Chavigny, must have familiarized him with one side of the story, while as a near neighbour at Véretz he had every opportunity for seeing the other. By 1652 Mère Louise had become superior for the first time; she held that office for two

---

[1] For details of her early life and affair with Gaston see G. Dethan, *Gaston d'Orléans*.

[2] By her express wish almost no details of her long career were contained in her obituary notice (*Vis, Lettres circ.*, Tours, 1707), but occasional facts can be gleaned from other such letters from Tours. Thus in 1701 she had outlived all other former superiors and at the age of 85 accepted the charge of the novices. Two years later (12 Apr. 1703) she herself wrote the obituary of the superior who had just died. At least two nieces came to Tours in her time, and she must have been a person of decisive character and influence to judge from her one surviving MS. letter (previously unknown), in which she protested against the translation of Mère d'Albon, and also from the trenchant style of the few surviving circular letters known to have been composed by her.

further periods of six years each (her obituary, apparently in error, credits her with twenty-four years in all as superior). It is not known exactly when Rancé first came to know her well, but during the critical phase of his conversion (1657–63) she was not in fact, as most biographers seem to suggest, superior of the convent. She was one of those to whom he first turned for help and guidance, as we have seen, and his letters to her (Gervaise claims[1] to have seen 200 and about half that number survive) are the main source for his early biography.

By 1662 or 1663 Rancé's young niece, Louise-Henriette d'Albon,[2] had joined Mère Louise Rogier in the convent at Tours, and he wrote to them both, as well as to a Mère de la Roche, individually or collectively for the rest of his (or their) life. Louise-Henriette, daughter of Rancé's sister Charlotte by her second husband, was about 16 or 17 when she became a nun: she remained at Tours until 1687, when she moved to Riom, where she died in December 1688. Her father, comte d'Albon, came from Auvergne, as did Favier, and in 1658 one of Rancé's visits was to his sister in Auvergne, where he probably met his young niece. Both her sisters married into Auvergnat families, and when Favier retired to Thiers he saw a lot of them, and kept Rancé informed of family news, though he was too old and infirm to visit Louise-Henriette by the time she came to Riom. They did, however, exchange frequent letters of which several survive, more in fact than from any other member of the family.[3] Even before she lost her father in 1679, Louise-Henriette was under strong pressure from her family to move to Auvergne, and this and other factors contribute a sense of tension to her correspondence with Rancé which is both unusual and revealing. Her close association with Mère Louise Rogier over a period of twenty-five years makes it difficult, if not impossible, to disentangle the story, in so far as there is one, of the two women. To these must be added Mère de

---

[1] *Jugement critique*, p. 25. The copies at the Mazarine (1214) and Sainte-Geneviève (Df 49) are duplicates, and though the text is reliable enough, the chronological order is chaotic. In the Arsenal (2106) collection the dates are often completely wrong, and thus the greatest care is needed in attempting to reconstruct the course of events.

[2] Her long obituary (written by Mère Rogier in *Vis, Lettres circ.*, Tours, 1689) is unusually detailed and candid, especially about her stormy early years.

[3] Original letters from Louise-Henriette in *CF* 344 B (mostly published by Jaloustre) and U 738. Letters from Rancé to her in the same MSS. as those to Mère Rogier (and Mère de la Roche) noted above.

la Roche,[1] mentioned above, daughter of a sister of Mère Louise, and a nun from an early age. Brought up at the convent after her mother's death, she was a close friend of Louise-Henriette, and lived to survive her aunt by only a few months.

The numerous letters written up to 1664 are mainly concerned with Rancé's own life, his efforts to find the right path and his monastic début. Early in 1664 Louise-Henriette fell ill, but there is no more news of her until 1666, when Rancé returned from Rome and sent her messages of general encouragement. All seems to be going well, and Rancé tells her (22 June 1666)[2]: 'croyez que vous n'avez rien fait pour lui quand vous vous êtes engagée à son service, mais qu'il a beaucoup fait pour vous quand il vous a choisie par une élection particulière.' From 1664 to 1667 the superior was the very senior Jeanne-Françoise le Vasseur,[3] sister of the founding superior of 1633, and she held office for twenty-one years in all, but in 1667 Mère Louise Rogier was elected again after a twelve-year interval, and was later re-elected for a second triennate. It cannot be coincidence that this change of superior marked a sharp change in Louise-Henriette's conduct and in Rancé's attitude to her. There are very few letters from 1667–9, but early in 1670 Rancé learns that M. d'Albon wants his daughter to move, and that she is not getting on at all well with Mère Louise Rogier, to whom he continues to write about his own affairs. By the end of the following year Mère Louise Rogier has been re-elected superior and things have come to a head. Rancé sends his friend Félibien to Tours to talk to Louise-Henriette (he always disliked writing confidential information if it could be passed by word of mouth) and tells her it is time that she set a better example instead of going her own way. She has apparently been pressing for greater austerity (the Visitation rule had been devised to suit elderly women seeking retreat), but Rancé tells her that humiliation and self-denial will do her more good. She must declare her penitence before the whole community and admit that her superior's conduct had been justified. At the same time Rancé wrote to Mère Louise Rogier to report that Louise-Henriette is ready for reconciliation and rather sadly

---

[1] She was born in 1637, professed 1653, died 1707 (*Vis, Lettres circ.*, Tours, 1708). Just to make identification more confusing she too was Louise—Louise-Elisabeth Robin de la Roche.

[2] *M* 1214, 85.

[3] Details of all houses of the Visitation in *M* 2440 (Tours f. 175, Riom f. 52).

wonders how a friend of more than twenty years' standing (which would put their first meeting in about 1650) could entertain unworthy suspicions of him.[1] All this is very mysterious, but a month later Rancé has seen Félibien again and tells Louise-Henriette[2] he has nothing to add, she must trust her superior, and then everything becomes clear: 'il n'y a nul moyen d'entrer dans P-R. [sic].' It is not at all clear whose idea it may have been that she should do so; her father had many years before belonged to a group that included Jansenist sympathizers,[3] but he had then taken a Jesuit confessor (P. Saint-Jure) and Rancé was as uncompromisingly opposed to the move as were the Visitation authorities.

Rancé may have crushed his niece's revolt, but he did not intend to leave it at that. Writing to Mère Louise Rogier for the New Year 1672,[4] he tells her to treat his niece 'rudement', to keep her away from outside contacts, and to give her the most menial tasks, even to ban her from the altar for a while. Such severity towards a person for whom he undoubtedly felt great affection is most unusual, and not very appealing, but Rancé knew what he was doing. By June of the following year Mère Louise Rogier had finished her second triennate, the new superior was taking office for the first (but not the last) time, and Rancé can write that he is glad to see his niece now 'dans la paix et dans l'union', and on good terms with her superior. A year later he apologizes for not writing very often, but the crisis is obviously past.[5]

Shortly afterwards Louise-Henriette appears in a quite different context, and quite by chance emerges as a person in her own right. In 1677, during the great controversy over fictions, Le Roy, through his secretary Vuillart, wrote a very great number of letters to men and women all over France asking to know their (and, where appropriate, their order's) attitude to Rancé's alleged[6] practice. Among others, Louise-Henriette received such an inquiry, and five letters in her very characteristic hand have been preserved out of what must have been a regular correspondence. She begins (19 June 1677) by praising her new superior

---

[1] *M* 1214, 97 and 99.   [2] Ibid. 102 of 3 Dec. 1671.
[3] See notice in *DBF* and Mesnard, *Pascal et les Roannez*, pp. 822–3.
[4] *M* 1214, 104.   [5] *A* 2106, ff. 72 and 78.
[6] See above, pp. 33–34 and 40–41. Letters in *U* 738.

(elected to fill a vacancy caused by sudden death), Anne-Françoise Royer, 'une personne tout à fait incapable de préoccupation', an admirer of Le Roy and a faithful exponent of the principles to be found in 'les bons livres', which seems to be a reference to those of Le Roy and his Jansenist friends. A person, moreover, so humble that she had done all she could to avoid taking office. Louise-Henriette had been grieved to hear through Vuillart (whose brother, Grécourt, lived just outside Tours) of Rancé's quarrel—'mon saint oncle'—with Le Roy, but has not yet seen her uncle's offending publication. She then quotes examples of Visitation practice, including some from the house at Mâcon of which her aunt was soon to become superior (1684). In view of her experience a few years earlier it is instructive to read that humility is essential for those 'qui sont obligés d'obéir aveuglément à ce qu'on leur ordonne'. The letter is signed 'les trois sœurs', and it appears from later letters that one of the others was de la Roche, Rancé's correspondent already mentioned, while the other could be read as 'de Luce'. In July she writes again, having now read Le Roy's paper. All her anger goes against 'l'infidèle ami de mon oncle' (probably Beaufort) whom she would punish by 'une entière exclusion de son abbaye et de sa confiance, et je ne le croirais pas même après cela assez puni'. Such fiery spirit helps to explain the crisis of 1670–3. She interestingly goes on to ask Le Roy not to attack Mme de Chantal's directives on humiliations directly in his book, because she had given examples from a work normally kept secret, and if Le Roy quoted her everyone would know that the information came from either Tours, Poitiers, or Angers;[1] elsewhere 'on a plus soin d'empêcher qu'on ne lise tous les bons livres qui viennent de vos MM, que d'examiner si on a raison d'en empêcher la lecture.' This allusion throws further light on Rancé's earlier reference to Port-Royal.

The next letter (9 August 1677) shows that Le Roy had been trying to find out who had printed Rancé's answer, but Louise-Henriette had not succeeded in discovering the required information: 'tout est interdit à une nièce'. She thinks that Rancé will never change his mind, and that of all their mutual friends only

---

[1] In 1679 a major scandal blew up over the apparently real Jansenist sympathies of the Angers house, so that it is quite likely that Tours and Poitiers housed similar but more discreet, sympathizers (one from Angers was in fact sent to Tours). See *Vis*, MS., Carton A, and printed *Relation fidèle… d'Angers* G MS. C 3552, ff. 259 seq.).

the Bishops of Alet (who died three months later) or Châlons (who did in fact intervene) could effect a reconciliation. She sadly concludes: 'il en faut revenir là que Dieu permettant que ces sortes de différends arrivants entre ses saints pour leur propre sanctification il faut adorer les ordres de sa Providence sans blâmer personne.' By the same post she sent a letter to Vuillart, saying that she was too distressed to discuss Rancé with Le Roy, but would leave this to Mère de la Roche, 'notre sœur ainée'. Neighbours of Le Roy, the curés of Nangis and Saint-Dizier, have been staying nearby with Vuillart's brother and have made a good impression. Mère de la Roche takes over with strong criticism of Rancé, who has misunderstood Le Roy's dissertation, and passionate defence of Le Roy, 'père des religieuses, et qui se consomme en travail pour leur utilité'. They have written to Tourouvre (near la Trappe) to try to find out more of the circumstances under which Rancé's answer was printed, but for the present Félibien is the prime suspect—all this 'fraternellement et confidemment dans le secret'. All she reveals of herself is that she knows Nangis (near Provins) well. This odd correspondence ends (14 September 1677) with a brief letter from Louise-Henriette to Le Roy, whose *Éclaircissement* she has shown to several people. She cannot understand how Rancé took it so amiss, but everyone approves Le Roy's decision to keep quiet. She is keeping all his admirable letters carefully (none survive) and, as she and her friend Luce (?) are going into retreat, Mère de la Roche will write for them later.

There is no reason to suppose that Rancé ever knew that his niece had written these letters to Le Roy, though he must have known of the latter's contacts with Tours, and these five letters corroborate most unexpectedly the details of character and attitude seen, from Rancé's point of view, in his own letters. Unfortunately, and rather strangely, there is a complete gap in his letters to Tours from 1674 to 1679 and there may well have been some estrangement, but in April 1679[1] he writes to say that God is now leading his niece in smoother paths, though she has certainly had her cross to bear, and by the end of that year he condoles with her on the death of her father. Throughout 1680–2 he writes to his niece, to Mère Rogier and Mère de la Roche. The latter two are getting old and infirm, and he mostly urges de la Roche to take things more calmly and Rogier to persevere. Early

[1] *A* 2106, f. 86.

in 1683[1] his niece shows signs of fresh trouble. She is afraid of waning zeal, and he tells her that pride and self-love are at the root of all our faults; she should seek to cure herself by taking on 'les offices du monastère les plus pénibles et les plus laborieux'.

Meanwhile Mère Rogier, who had been ill in 1682, has recovered and in May 1683 becomes superior once more, and it seems again too much of a coincidence that Louise-Henriette should fall back into unhappiness just at this moment. In September Rancé consoles her[2] and counsels her to 'adorer ses desseins [Dieu] et les accepter avec une soumission parfaite'. God will never abandon her. To the two others he now talks almost invariably about approaching death. By June 1684,[3] after a year of Mère Rogier's rule, Rancé's niece is thinking of a move, but he dissuades her. In February 1685 she falls ill and he tells her[4] not to read 'livres de doctrine... très préjudiciables', a warning no doubt prompted by the Le Roy incident. She still finds the austerities of her rule insufficient, and Rancé thinks she should have followed her confessor's advice in abandoning external penitence. 1686 is something of a turning-point. In March Rancé writes (somewhat prematurely)[5] to Mère de la Roche 'les moments de votre fin approchent' and she must prepare herself for death. No more letters to her are known, but the end was not to come for twenty more years. In May Mère Louise Rogier was re-elected for three more years; in October Rancé tells his niece[6] 'ne vous impatientez pas que Dieu vous laisse sans croix et sans affliction', but let her rather avoid being conspicuous. By the end of January 1687 her long-heralded move has become reality, and she has been elected superior of Riom, succeeding officially in May, despite Rancé's categorical warning against it and the extreme annoyance of her own superior, who had not been consulted.[7]

The last two years of her life are the best documented, for Rancé continued to write to her, and to Favier about her, and she wrote to Favier about her uncle. She found all the difficulties she had expected; Rancé urges her to use patience and moderation, to get her nuns to read Rodriguez and François de Sales, and, if all else fails, to give up the post rather than participate in their

---

[1] *TB* 1854.   [2] *A* 2106, f. 115.   [3] Ibid., f. 128.
[4] Ibid., f. 134.   [5] Ibid., f. 142.   [6] Ibid., f. 143.
[7] See protest in *Vis*, MS., sent to the mother-house at Annecy by Mère Rogier.

iniquities.[1] It is fascinating to see how after all these years (since 1664) he suddenly adopts the same tone with her as he had taken with other superiors: he advises her not to admit one girl, to expel others, agrees that two more have behaved badly, opines that all parental gifts should be common property, and that she should re-read *Sainteté*. To Favier he is full of praise for her firmness: 'je ne crois pas... qu'elle soit si condescendante qu'elle le prétende.' She would dearly like to see Favier, but he is too old to travel. The correspondence also contains agitated discussion about the intentions of Louise-Henriette's sister, Catherine de la Barge, whose daughters were destined for (in Rancé's eyes) unsuitable convents. They were currently staying at the Visitation at Thiers, where their paternal aunt was superior. Rancé's last word to his niece begins: 'Je vois que vos peines augmentent', and he advises her to go back to Tours as soon as she can. Unhappily she could not follow his advice, and a few weeks later she was dead, having complained of a bout of toothache which turned to mortal fever, near her family, it is true, but exiled from what had been her home for more than thirty years.

From 1687 to the end of the following year most of Louise-Henriette's brief letters to Favier concern her nieces, but there are references to her uncle of some interest.[2] She speaks of the delay in publishing Rancé's *Explication*, held up by the bishops, and says: 'Pour moi mon plaisir seroit de voir les livres avant leur correction. La véhémence de ce saint homme ne me déplait point'. When one recalls the opportunity she had had, on her own account as a young nun and later in respect of Le Roy, for experiencing this vehemence, the sentiment is to say the least remarkable. Late in 1688 Favier sends her what she calls 'un riche trésor... Je copierai toutes vos lettres avec plaisir... cela ne peut pas être si tôt fait'. From other evidence[3] this must have been Favier's collection of some fifty letters sent by Rancé, nearly all to him, but by a strange irony she died before she could complete the task of copying, so that it was Favier, the oldest of them all, and Mère Louise Rogier, also loaded with years, who preserved Rancé's letters for posterity, including those to his niece. It is interesting that Louise-Henriette found only Favier and the local Oratorian superior in whom to confide, and with

---

[1] *A* 2106, ff. 145 seq.   [2] All these letters quoted in Jaloustre.
[3] Unpublished and almost illegible draft scribbled by Favier in *CF* 344 E.

their encouragement, and that of her uncle, she makes some progress in reforming her convent, 'tout cela me console un peu dans
le déplaisir que j'ai de me voir chargée d'un emploi qui passe mes
forces.' Even the curé of Riom, superior of the convent (M.
Azan), got into trouble for insisting that a notorious sinner should
ask public forgiveness on her death-bed, and had to go to Paris
to defend himself against charges of rigorism. It seems clear
enough that her rigorist tendencies have not changed over the
years, and that the close association between the Visitation of
Tours and the Oratory, decisive in Rancé's conversion, continued
at Riom. As it happens, the bulk of letters to the Visitation nuns
and to Favier are preserved in copies made at the Paris Oratory by
P. Galipaud, himself once suspected of Jansenist leanings and
one-time member of the house at Riom.[1]

No more is known of Mère Rogier's correspondence after she
laid down the superiority for the last time in 1689, but it must be
assumed that Rancé continued to write to her. About 150 letters
to the Visitation over a period of forty years is a considerable
survival, and the further survival of the letters to Le Roy and
Favier shows better than any other evidence the effect Rancé
had on a personality as passionately uncompromising as his own.
His early harshness is as typical as his later pleas for moderation,
and his niece's letters bear unsolicited witness to the affection
and respect he inspired. Not the least intriguing feature of the
correspondence is the strong circumstantial evidence it provides
of strained relations between the two nuns with whom he probably had more to do than any others.

Another Visitandine with whom Rancé had regular correspondence was Marie-Françoise de Harlay, sister of the Archbishop of Paris. She had, as already mentioned, been sent as a
child to les Clairets, and was sent back in 1659, aged 15 with the
intention of succeeding her aunt, de Thou, as abbess. Obliged
after three years to return to the world, she was in 1665 converted,
and of her own volition entered the Visitation at Melun, where
she died in 1714 after exercising every office save that of superior.[2]
(Her mother, Charlotte-Françoise, widowed in 1670, joined her
in 1678 (aged 55) and stayed till her death in 1704.) Most of the

---

[1] See A. M. P. Ingold, *Le Chancelier d'Aguesseau et l'Oratoire* and *Le R. P. Galipaud
et le Jansénisme.*
[2] See obituary in *Vis, Lettres circ.,* Melun, 1715.

extant letters identifiably addressed to her are later than 1683, but the content is too vague for definite identification to be always possible. On more than one occasion, however, Rancé and her brother used her as an intermediary in sounding the other's opinion.

A full catalogue of religious women and orders who received letters from Rancé would be at least as comprehensive as that of men: the Poor Clares at Alençon ask his prayers to enable them to sink a well;[1] the Prioress of Chaise-Dieu seeks his advice;[2] the abbess of Tard (near Dijon) exchanges Associations; and so on; but the interest of these sporadic exchanges is naturally less than that of the cases discussed above. The outstanding lessons from all these letters to nuns, whether members of his family or not, are the firmness and moderation with which Rancé defended the essential principles of the religious life and dissuaded his correspondents from excess, both physical and spiritual. The fear of death, the toll of illness, the conscience tormented by scruples, or aridity, the clash of personalities in the narrow world of the cloister, the temptation to gossip or distractions as a remedy for boredom—all these problems he knows and answers with consistent concern for the individual and a humanity tempered by total commitment to God's service. Rancé was no stranger to emotions, and freely confided in a Mère Agnès de Bellefonds or Louise Rogier, but he allowed nothing to deflect him from his goal, and expected others to share his ideals.

[1] *TB* 1479 of 19 May 1681.   [2] *TB* 1477 of 11 May 1681.

PART III

RANCÉ'S INFLUENCE IN THE WORLD

10. Prelates

CONSIDERING the fact that Rancé turned his back on an episcopal career at the onset of his conversion and devoted his entire religious life to the cloister, it is remarkable how many and how close were his contacts among clergy of all ranks, whose problems seem to have little connection with his own. On the strength of such evidence as survives he took at least as much interest in pastoral as in monastic questions, and seems to have found more intimate friends outside the cloister than within it. Since these friends were public figures with numerous other contacts, it is often possible to judge from external as well as internal evidence the nature and scope of Rancé's influence.

Unlike the monastic world, of which he knew next to nothing before he entered it, the ecclesiastical world was familiar to Rancé from his earliest youth, first at the Sorbonne, then as a young *abbé de cour*, finally in an official capacity at Tours, with his uncle, at the Assembly of Clergy and at Blois, as Gaston's chaplain. Human nature being what it is, one should not be surprised that his friends of this earlier period should have retained his intimacy, with few exceptions, and that the *amitiés particulières* so frowned upon by all monastic authorities should almost entirely have escaped him. Beaufort is a marginal case, because his early career was so similar to Rancé's own, but it is the exception that proves the rule, since his misconduct discouraged further intimacy, even if a reconciliation was effected. A number of Rancé's contacts were purely formal, expressions of deference or requests for support, but a far greater number were personal, and rank is not a reliable guide to this distinction.

As Richelieu's godson, Rancé was no stranger to prelates; his uncle, and several cousins, were bishops, and he would undoubtedly have followed them but for his conversion. His strained relations with Mazarin have already been discussed, but his friendship with Retz goes beyond politics and bridges the two phases of his career.[1] Their many mutual friends in the *salons*, and

[1] Retz's relations with Benedictines are well enough documented in biographies and correspondence, but no one seems to have taken very seriously his relations

perhaps the fact that Retz conferred orders on Rancé, predisposed them to a personal, as well as an official, relationship. After the Fronde, and up to the time of his retreat, Rancé publicly identified himself with Retz's interests, and it was natural that Retz in his turn should support Rancé and the Abstinents to the best of his ability once his friend had been entrusted with the mission to Rome. All this is still on the public rather than the personal level, but after Rancé's return from Rome a change took place in Retz and in their relationship. In 1669 Rancé paid a visit to Retz at Commercy, and then went on to Châtillon. Always mercurial, but in this case apparently sincere, Retz seems to have discussed with Rancé his plan, formulated more than once, to withdraw to a monastery. In 1673[1] Rancé, writing about the affairs of the Reform, took the opportunity of reminding Retz of his project: 'l'affaire pour laquelle il me parut que vous aviez tant de passion, toute importante qu'elle est, n'est pas plus avancée qu'elle étoit pour lors; cependant tout fuit avec une vitesse effroiable...' All was not lost, however, and two years later Rancé tells Bellefonds (20 September 1675)[2] that Retz 'se prive et perd par une abdication volontaire ce qui avoit fait tout le mouvement de sa vie... M. le Cardinal se donne entièrement à Dieu, et consacre les dernières années de sa vie à la pénitence et la solitude', and that it had taken him ten years to put his original resolution into practice. A few days later (3 October)[3] Rancé mentions to Favier that he saw Retz on a visit to Paris earlier in the year.

By 1677[4] Rancé is still soliciting Retz's intervention in favour of the Reform, but much regrets that several letters have gone unanswered. He says (and it may well be true) that only ill health prevents him going to see Retz, whose support he needs in seeking papal permission to continue the present observance at la Trappe. In August 1679[5] Retz's agitated life came to an end: 'Enfin le pauvre M. le Cardinal de Retz a fini sa course; il est mort avec beaucoup de piété et de résignation à la volonté de Dieu... il lui témoigna l'obligation qu'il lui avoit de ce qu'il ne l'avoit pas pris dans ses dérèglements, mais qu'il l'avoit attendu à pénitence.' According to report, Retz had paid up 40,000 *livres*

with Rancé. Had Retz continued his *Mémoires* one wonders how much he would have revealed of what follows; it certainly assorts ill with the public image he chose to present.

[1] Muguet, ii, p. 47.   [2] *BN* n.a. 12959, f. 29.   [3] Gonod, p. 56.
[4] *TB* 882.   [5] *TB* 1129 of Sept. 1679 to an unknown 'M'.

in what might be called conscience money before he died. An even more remarkable epitaph is to be found in a letter to the saintly M. Du Hamel (27 October 1680),[1] to whom Rancé was much attached. He refers again to the Cardinal's death, now five months past, and to his 'grands desseins de retraite... il y a plus de 14 ans [sc. 1664] qu'il m'avoit ouvert son cœur sur cela et je suis certain qu'il ne jouoit pas la comédie... s'il se fût tourné tout à fait du côté de Dieu, comme il en avoit envie, il auroit fait de grandes choses... je ne puis consentir qu'un homme que j'ai honoré et aimé avec la dernière tendresse soit éternellement malheureux.' Still later, in June 1681,[2] Rancé tells his friend, P. Berziau, of the Oratory, that he will write as requested to the duchesse de Lesdiguières, niece of Retz, 'pour lequel j'ai eu une tendresse et un respect que je ne puis exprimer'.

Even in the flowery traditions of the century this is almost uniquely strong language for someone like Rancé, and indicates a depth of affection without parallel in his extant letters. He cannot have been unaware of Retz's scandalous, not to say blatantly cynical, immorality in sexual matters, nor of the incessant political intrigues; the reference to 'jouer la comédie' is a sufficient indication that he was under no illusions regarding Retz's normally histrionic behaviour; but the most extraordinary observation of all is Rancé's refusal to admit the possibility of Retz's damnation. It is a great pity that only one, purely formal reference to Rancé survives in Retz's correspondence, but in view of the chronology quoted above, something deeper may lie behind the formality. Writing in 1664[3] to Barberini in Rome, Retz commends Rancé, who had just been to see him, 'pour marquer le désir que j'ai de lui être utile et pour satisfaire aux obligations que je lui ai... si grandes...' Without Rancé's letters one might see this as an allusion to Rancé's championship of Retz against Mazarin in 1657, but that debt is evidently too old in 1664 to prompt quite such warm expressions, and it can hardly be doubted in the light of Rancé's disclosures to Du Hamel that the obligations were spiritual rather than political. Anyone familiar with Retz's *Mémoires* will recognize his irresistible desire to prove himself more penetrating, skilful, and wily than his contemporaries, but what is perhaps less obvious is that his often brilliantly entertaining picture

---

[1] *TB* 1239.   [2] *TB* 1481 of 2 June 1681.
[3] Retz, *Supplément à la Correspondance*, p. 86.

of his own wickedness is a carefully contrived mask disguising more natural goodness (and a more tender conscience) than he was prepared generally to admit. His support of Rancé and the Reform was not specially efficacious,[1] but clearly sprang from conviction rather than expediency or mere love of intrigue for its own sake. Rancé was, on his own admission, a poor judge of character, but it is not credible that he could have felt as he did for Retz unless he had found some genuine inner quality in the man to evoke such a response.

Apart from Retz, who is in every way a special case, the only other cardinal with whom Rancé seems to have had personal as well as official relations was the Bernardine (that is, Feuillant of the Italian Congregation) Bona (1609–74).[2] By a strange coincidence his Dauphinois family was related to the Lesdiguières, and as we have just seen the Duchess was Retz's niece and a protector of Port-Royal. As General of the Feuillants (a triennial appointment), Bona lived in Rome and became friendly with Cardinal Chigi, the future Alexander VII. On that pontiff's express request Bona was nominated (not, as was usual, elected) General again in 1657, and then renewed in 1660 to keep him in Rome. He succeeded in winning release from office, but remained in Rome, seeing the Pope twice a week to give advice. It was during this period that Rancé came to know, and esteem, him. Like Alexander, Bona was opposed to laxism and probabilism, but they were no more Jansenist than Rancé. In his various writings on liturgy and theology Bona struck a note appreciated by the Jansenists, again much as Rancé did, and like him took a morally rigorous and theologically traditional approach. The election of Clement IX saw a continuation of pontifical favour for Bona, created cardinal in 1669. He was so faithful to his monastic vow of poverty that his friend Sluse had to provide him with silverware for his official entertaining. On the sudden death of Clement IX in 1669, Bona was a much favoured candidate for the succession— in the event secured by the octogenarian Clement X. Rancé is known to have remained in contact with Bona; he wrote to congratulate him on his promotion, and again in 1673 to solicit his help for the Reform, but on 28 October 1674 he died and

---

[1] Lekai, Rise of Cist. S.O., and Leloczky, Constitutiones et Acta, deal with Retz's support of the Abstinents.
[2] See L. Ceyssens, 'Le Cardinal Jean Bona et le Jansénisme'.

Rancé lost a powerful ally at the Curia. As a considerable scholar Bona was in close contact with the French Maurists, and through them (after the Peace of the Church of 1669) with Arnauld and Nicole, and their friend Floriot. In this, as in so much else, the circle of his contacts in France considerably overlapped Rancé's. In addition Bona's biography, and one of his treatises, was translated into French (1683) by Rancé's friend Du Suel.[1] Their common Cistercian heritage, and much in their temperament, would explain why the two men got on so well together, and but for geographical distance they would probably have become close friends.

Still within the same circle, Bona's great friend Sluse, promoted cardinal only in 1686, the year before his death, was someone whose favour Rancé later cultivated through their mutual friend Nicaise, but it does not appear that Rancé was ever in direct contact with Sluse.[2] Once the two branches of the Cistercian order in France had arrived at a *modus vivendi*, Rancé and la Trappe interested people in Rome no longer from a political but from a spiritual and monastic point of view. In this connection the various biographers make much of the letters of support and good wishes dispatched from time to time to Rancé by members of the Curia, and even the Pope, but it cannot be very seriously contended that these tell us anything significant about Rancé's contacts in Rome. Thus the Brief of Innocent XI empowering the monks of la Trappe to elect a prior should the monastery ever fall back into commend,[3] or the expressions of benevolent concern from Cardinal Cibo when informed by the monks of Rancé's poor health,[4] or the encouragement of Cardinal Casanata, who had received *Sainteté* from Baluze,[5] testify to Rancé's good standing in official esteem, but barely more than that. Similarly, his correspondence with Ranuzzi, the Nuncio,[6] or Cardinal d'Estrées, and probably with Cardinal Bouillon[7] (whose Carmelite sister passed on the letters) concerns such official matters as migration from one order to another, favours requested on behalf of some friend, or approval for his books, so reflecting his personal pres-

[1] *Le Guide du ciel*, together with *La Vie de... Bona*; all very vague.
[2] See letters to Nicaise in Gonod, pp. 101–41 from 1684 to 1687.
[3] See Rancé's answer (in Latin) of 18 Oct. 1677 in le Nain, *Vie* (1719), ii, p. 712.
[4] See letter to Retz in *TB* 882 of 1 Oct. 1677.
[5] *BN* Coll. Baluze 361, f. 90.   [6] *TC* I/20 of 27 Oct. 1677.
[7] None from Rancé survive, but two from d'Estrées and two from Bouillon (who is known to have paid a three-day visit in 1693) are quoted at the end of the *MS. de Sept-Fons* in an anthology of distinguished tributes.

tige, and in that sense influence, rather than the sort of spiritual influence he exercised on Retz. It is true that in assessing Rancé's relative prominence or presumed sympathies on such issues as Jansenism or Gallicanism these official connections cannot be ignored, but they are much less interesting than those involving Retz and Bona.

Going down the hierarchical ladder, bishops play a major role throughout Rancé's life, first exercising decisive influence, later undergoing it. It may or may not be true that, as abbot of la Trappe, Rancé was at one time considered for promotion to the cardinalate (it seems unlikely, and it is hard to see what he would have done with the dignity if conferred), but had he not become a regular he would certainly have been a bishop, and most probably Archbishop of Tours after his uncle. Speculation on what might have been is seldom very helpful, especially when it concerns vocations as sudden and precise as Rancé's, but it is not wholly idle to wonder what would have happened had Victor Bouthillier been a different man, and bishop, or if he had died sooner. As a young man Victor (1596–1670) had spent four years at the Oratory in Paris (1617–21), and as such figures in Batterel's memoirs of the Congregation.[1] but an episcopal career seemed more appropriate to a member of a family already of ministerial calibre. His elder brother, Sébastien, died Bishop of Aire in 1625, and in 1630 Victor was appointed coadjutor to Deschaus, of Tours, succeeding in 1640. His record as diocesan seems to have been perfectly respectable: he founded or favoured new orders in his diocese, like the Visitation or the Oratory, and looked after administration, charity, and building with every sign of reasonable care, but in retrospect his nephew was unenthusiastic about Victor's pastoral qualities. When Rancé first consulted the Bishops of Alet and Pamiers, according to Batterel,[2] they encouraged him to assist his uncle, as he was already doing, but he was unconvinced.

The course of his correspondence with Mère Rogier and Andilly reveals a growing rift with his uncle over a number of issues. Rancé, for example, at one time wanted to hand over his benefice at Boulogne to the Oratorians at Tours to make into a diocesan seminary, but the scandal provoked by Séguenot and his colleagues accused of Jansenism frustrated that project. The only surviving letter from Rancé to his uncle[3] indicates at the very

---

[1] Vol. i, ch. XL.   [2] Ibid., p. 394.   [3] A 6035, f. 290 (copy).

least a failure of communication. Rancé, it seems had been told by
his uncle to go to Paris (in 1658), but had not done so, on the
grounds that the request was not specifically to perform some
service for the Archbishop, and Rancé concludes with the hope
that his uncle realizes 'que le caprice et le bizarrerie n'ont aucune
part dans ma manière de vivre'. A letter of the same period to
Mère Louise Rogier[1] refers to an interview in which the archbishop had spoken 'avec beaucoup de chaleur', and it needs little
imagination to understand how irritated he must have been, not
least by his nephew's insistence on selling or giving away all his
property, including the superb estate at Véretz in which Victor
had always been so interested. When Victor died in 1670, Rancé
commented to Mère Rogier that it was hardly enough to have two
days' sickness 'pour compter avec Dieu de quarante années d'épis-
copat', and later critical references to the behaviour of unnamed
bishops may also have been inspired by memories of his uncle.

If this influence was largely negative, it was more than counter-
balanced by that of four other bishops who played a decisive
part in his conversion. The tale has already been told[2] of Rancé's
successive consultations of the Bishops of Châlons, Comminges
(later translated to Tournai), Alet, and Pamiers. For different
reasons in each case he remained in contact with all of them after
he had made his decision and become regular abbot. After 1664
Rancé had no particular reason to write to Alet until 1670,
when the unexpected arrival and subsequent profession of Paul
Hardy, former théologal of Alet, caused surprise and perhaps a
certain coolness with the bishop. The arrival of Arsène Cordon
in 1672, and then dom Paul's death in 1675, were the occasions for
further letters, and if Alet had not died in 1677 he would no doubt
have intervened in the fictions quarrel, as Louise-Henriette suggested.[3] Rancé always held Alet in the highest regard, and when
friends of his like Barillon and later Tréville (in 1675) went to the
bishop he clearly expected them to share his respect for such a
holy man, but this very holiness—and of course a difference in
years—always kept the two men at a certain distance.

Bishop Pavillon's neighbour at Pamiers, the former Sulpicien
Étienne Caulet, had nothing like the same influence on Rancé,
but enjoyed similar respect. In 1669 Rancé was writing to him

---

[1] M 1214, 2 and 91.
[2] See above, pp. 13–15.   [3] Letters in U 848, TC I/19, and TB 616.

about the way of life at la Trappe, and in 1672 about the possibility of establishing an offshoot of la Trappe in the Pyrenees.[1] In fact the proposal came to nothing, but Pamiers seems to have been very impressed by Rancé's achievements and at least once, in 1675, paid a visit to see for himself. When he died Rancé wrote warmly of him to Gourdan,[2] who was well acquainted with conditions at Pamiers and with the bishop himself through the Victorine Rainssant, reformer of the chapter, who had come back to die at Saint-Victor in 1669. Both Alet and Pamiers also knew dom le Nain, through his family or Saint-Victor or both.

The third of these early contacts was Félix Vialart de Hersé, Bishop of Châlons, like Alet proposed by Louise-Henriette as a mediator in the quarrel with Le Roy.[3] He and Rancé had many mutual friends, including Le Roy and Bellefonds, and Rancé always spoke very warmly of him. He intervened tactfully to heal the breach with Le Roy, and in 1675[4] was asked by Rancé to intervene on behalf of abbé Luthumière, whose seminary at Valognes, near Bellefonds's home, was threatened with closure on suspicion of Jansenism. The bishop fell seriously ill in 1676, and died in 1680, to Rancé's evident sorrow. To these three might be added Henri Arnauld, Bishop of Angers, and brother of Antoine, but though Rancé knew and respected him, he does not seem to have had any great influence, except perhaps through his writings.[5] All four were leading sympathizers of Port-Royal and Alet and Pamiers in particular became men whose friendship could easily be seen as a liability. None the less Rancé never failed to proclaim his admiration and regard for their personal qualities, and fully acknowledged his early debt to all of them.

The case of Gilbert de Choiseul,[6] Bishop first of Comminges and then in 1671 translated to Tournai, is different and more interesting. He came of much more aristocratic stock than his neighbours at Alet and Pamiers, and had many friends and relatives in the *salon* society which Rancé once frequented. They thus knew each other on a somewhat different basis, both before and after the great change in Rancé's life. The bishop also knew

[1] *TD*, series A, 41 of 26 Mar. 1669 and *TB* 92 of 23 July 1672.
[2] *TB* 1326 of 12 Sept. 1680. See also Bonnard, *Hist. de Saint-Victor*, ii, p. 165.
[3] See above, pp. 40–41.   [4] *U* 3061, f. 95.
[5] One copy in *TB* 301 of 1673, but there must have been others.
[6] See article by R. Limouzin-Lamothe in *DBF*, s.v. *Choiseul du Plessis-Praslin* (no. 22).

Le Roy and was inevitably drawn into the controversy. Rancé wrote to him in 1677[1] refusing a public reconciliation with Le Roy, and somewhat tendentiously observed: 'mon crime est d'avoir soutenu la sainteté du désert et les humiliations de la croix.' Only a week later (23 August)[2] Rancé criticized Choiseul to Mme de Saint-Loup for acting on insufficient evidence in condemning him to a 'réparation à laquelle je ne suis point obligé'. If this caused a momentary coolness between the two men it did not last, for five years later Rancé assured the bishop of his faithful friendship.

The other side of the relationship can be seen much later in a correspondence provoked by the bishop giving his consent to his niece, abbess of le Sauvoir, near Laon, to take the waters.[3] Rancé was very loud in his disapproval (though not very exactly informed, for he speaks of the abbess as the bishop's sister instead of niece), and his unknown correspondent passed the letter on to Choiseul, who replied with reminiscences of thirty years ago. According to him, he was the first to tell Rancé that it was more in accordance with the Church's teaching to be a regular than a commendatory abbot: 'à quoi il me répondit qu'il avoit une horrible aversion pour le froc...' Two years passed, and then he met Rancé again in Paris, to learn that the seed sown in 1660 at Comminges had sprouted, so much so that only six weeks later they met again just as Rancé was about to enter the novitiate: 'Là-dessus je lui dis que comme je connoissois qu'il avoit l'esprit ardent il iroit si loin que personne ne le pouvoit suivre. Il m'assura du contraire et qu'il se modéroit—Vous voyez sa modération, qui ne va qu'à faire mourir les gens et ne compte cela pour rien... cette fermeté que je nommerois dureté, une inhumanité, si je ne parlois d'un homme dont j'honore infiniment le mérite, et aime tendrement la personne...' Rancé's reaction to this revealing and candid letter is a little surprising: 'Dieu me garde de contester contre lui. Je le considère comme mon maître et comme mon supérieur par sa qualité... j'ai trop de respect pour lui pour oser le contredire en face.' The last word was with the bishop (13 June 1688): 'Je vous renvoie la lettre de notre excellent ami... Je ne puis me rendre à ses raisons.' A year later he was dead. This incident quite fortuitously throws light on events of the distant

[1] *TB* 855 of 15 Aug. 1677.   [2] *TD*, series A, 89.
[3] Copies in *T* 1689, May–June 1688.

past, and also on the curiously paradoxical effect Rancé had on so many of his friends. Their very real affection for him is much more significant than a respect which could easily have been just grudging. Choiseul must constantly have wished that Rancé would show more moderation, and often urged him to do so, as in the Le Roy affair, but the abbot's singleness of purpose lost him hardly any true friends.

All Rancé's biographers stress his great respect for the episcopal dignity, and the examples so far quoted confirm this, but such respect was not incompatible with antipathy for individual bishops as persons and, on occasion, blank refusal to obey their command. His relations with the Bishop of Évreux, Maupas du Tour, were temporarily strained as a result of gossip about Bellefonds, to whom he later reported reconciliation.[1] The Bishop of Tournai and the Archbishop of Paris (Péréfixe) are only two whom he politely refused when they told him to send back religious from other orders. On the whole, however, it is fair to say that he shows consistent respect for bishops as such, and particularly for the successive occupants of the see of Séez, his own diocese, to whom he sent his very rare candidates for ordination.

Bishop Rouxel de Médavy was translated from Séez to Rouen in 1671, to be succeeded by Jean de Forcoal, with whom Rancé established very close relations, and warm affection, to judge from letters written to such intimates as Bellefonds or his sisters Thérèse and Marie-Louise on the bishop's death in 1682.[2] Rancé had in 1678 been most critical of the comte d'Angennes who, supported by the duc de Montausier, was engaged in a major dispute with the bishop, and in 1680 he wrote to Marcel, curé of Saint-Jacques-du-Haut-Pas, expressing some doubt as to the sincerity of the comte's conversion while he remained at odds with the bishop.[3] As soon as the name of the new incumbent (Mathurin Savary) was known, Rancé wrote via Bellefonds to offer his respects. Savary's successor, Louis d'Aquin, had barely arrived (his election in 1698 was contested) before Rancé fell into his last and fatal illness, and it was left to him to assist Rancé on his death-bed and later pronounce a panegyric, subsequently published.[4]

---

[1] *BN* n.a. 12959, f. 63 of 23 Dec. 1677.
[2] *TB* 1659 and 1661 of 23 May 1682; *BN* n.a. 12959, f. 96 of 8 June 1682.
[3] *BN* n.a. 12959, f. 69 of 6 Oct. 1678, and *TB* 1279, of 24 Apr. 1680, to Marcel.
[4] *Imago R. P.... de Rancé*, mentioned above, p. 57.

Once Rancé's reputation had become widely established, he
received letters and visits from bishops as much as from any
other class of society. One small incident is worthy of record:
on Caulet's death in 1680 the see of Pamiers fell vacant and Pierre
de la Brosse, then Bishop of Léon in Brittany, was summoned to
Court more or less under orders to accept translation. During a
halt at Mortagne the bishop wrote to Rancé[1] to say that he was
going to try to avoid the move (in which he succeeded) but would
not call at la Trappe, near as it was, for fear that his refusal would
be attributed to Rancé, a notorious opponent of episcopal translation. The bishop's scruples do him as much credit as his deli-
cacy, and the episode gives an idea of the almost oracular role
Rancé had come to play. Perhaps the strangest episcopal visit
was that of the Bishop of Lescar, Esclaux de Mesplez, who, as a
widower, had quite canonically taken orders, and then attended
the profession of his son as frère Euthyme in 1692.[2] One of the
last letters dictated by Rancé (23 February 1699)[3] was to Charles
Taffoureau de Fontaine, newly appointed to the see of Alet, who
had asked him for some guidance on his episcopal duties and who
as Vicar-General of Sens had previously sought admission to la
Trappe, but in vain. He was told that a bishop's function is sacred
and his conduct must be irreproachable.

The list of such formal or incidental episcopal contacts could be
prolonged almost indefinitely, but it is more profitable to look
at another group of bishops, of Rancé's own age or younger, who
were by their own account more influenced by him than he by
them. These include his intimate friends Henri Barillon, Bishop
of Luçon 1671–99, Étienne le Camus, Bishop of Grenoble
1671–1707, Lascaris d'Urfé, Bishop of Limoges 1676–95, and,
with some reservations, Bossuet, Bishop (briefly) of Condom in
1670 and then of Meaux 1681–1704. His relations with Harlay,
Archbishop of Paris, Le Tellier of Reims, and Noailles, of Cahors,
Châlons, and finally Paris are similar but less close and less well
documented. Although a whole book has been devoted to the
subject,[4] the relations between Rancé and Bossuet are less easy to
define than the others. It is reasonably clear what Rancé thought
of Bossuet, much harder to see just how important Rancé and his
friendship were to Bossuet in the full and complex pattern of his

[1] *TB* 1397, of 18 Dec. 1680.   [2] Letters to Barillon, *P* ff. 638 and 640.
[3] *TC* II/9.   [4] M. L. Serrent, *L'Abbé de Rancé et Bossuet.*

public and private life. The two men had taken the doctorate at the same time (1654), but it would be misleading to think of them as old student friends. Whatever contact they may have had before Rancé's conversion, to all intents and purposes they began a new acquaintance some time between Rancé's return from Rome in 1666 and the beginning of 1672, when Bossuet (recently appointed Bishop of Condom but almost at once replaced on becoming preceptor to the Dauphin) sent Rancé a complimentary copy of his *Exposition*. The terms of Rancé's letter of thanks[1] do not suggest any degree of friendly intimacy. However, Bossuet by this time had become very friendly with Bellefonds, and it is most likely through him and other mutual friends that the initially formal acquaintance became something more. In 1672 also Anne de Gonzague underwent her dramatic and famous conversion, and Bossuet in his *Oraison funèbre* refers to the part he asked Rancé to play in that.[2] A few months later it was the turn of Mme de la Vallière, and the joint role of Bossuet and Bellefonds meant that Rancé was informed, if not directly involved, in this equally dramatic episode.[3] It is common experience that a cause or principle unites men closely, but never so personally as sharing in the joys or sorrows of mutual friends, and long before Rancé and Bossuet actually met again face to face their relationship had become more intimate, though the stages cannot be accurately plotted for want of evidence.

Like all Rancé's friends, Bossuet was drawn into the quarrel with Le Roy, and wrote in 1677 two letters[4] distinctly favourable to Rancé but essentially urging moderation. Bossuet continued to send Rancé copies of his books; in 1681 it was the *Histoire universelle* that drew Rancé's thanks, and in that same year the possibility of a visit came much closer. Bossuet had planned to come in the summer but had to write (22 September)[5] regretfully postponing the visit because of the Assembly of the Clergy. In July next year he wrote a much quoted letter (8 July 1682)[6] referring to the 'ordures des casuistes' and a few months later he found the long-awaited relief from such preoccupations when at last he made himself free for long enough to pay his first visit to

---

[1] *TB* 40, of 22 Feb. 1672, also in Bossuet, *Correspondance*, i, p. 236.
[2] Dubois, ii, pp. 54–61.   [3] See above, p. 195.
[4] Originals in *U* 741, of 10 July and 5 Sept. 1677.
[5] Bossuet, *Correspondance*, ii, p. 241.   [6] Ibid., p. 257.

la Trappe. The consequences of his visit completely changed the
nature and frequency of their contacts, and arguably marked a
new stage in Rancé's life, because the immediate result was the
publication, urged and sponsored by Bossuet, of the manuscript
of what became *Sainteté*, which Bossuet had seen at la Trappe.

Rancé's reluctance to publish the work was probably not wholly
genuine, in the sense that he clearly believed that it would do a
lot of people a lot of good, but it is virtually certain that encouragement from a man of Bossuet's status made all the difference. It is impossible to determine the role of Maisne in the
affair, except in the light of his behaviour earlier that year, when
he told Favier of his intention to collect Rancé's letters, and what
he did later.[1] In any case the active support of Barillon and le
Camus meant more than that of a mere secretary. However that
may be, for the rest of Rancé's life his public reputation, and that
of la Trappe, became ever more closely associated with *Sainteté*,
and Bossuet similarly threw his weight ever more heavily on
Rancé's side. Correspondence between the two became more frequent and Bossuet's intentions of making an annual visit to la
Trappe were partly fulfilled; up to 1696 he went there nine times
in all, and possibly once more in 1698. When Rancé died, Bossuet
assumed quite naturally the role of literary executor.

Much of the contact between Rancé and Bossuet concerned
Sainteté and the ensuing polemic, but they had many other things
to discuss. The affair of dom Muguet (1684–5)[2] temporarily
embroiled them both with the Maurists; in 1687 one of the canons
of Meaux, Jean-Baptiste de Vitry, first sought admission at la
Trappe, but only in 1690 was professed as dom Dorothée (he
died in 1693); the visits of James II from 1690 on were a further
link, for Lord Perth, James's Chancellor, had been converted by
Bossuet,[3] and his brother, Melfort, accompanied James and
corresponded with Rancé; the frère Chalype incident, also in
1690,[4] partly involved Bossuet, as did the subsequent departure of
the former Huguenot, Armand-Climaque. In 1694 they lost their
mutual friend Bellefonds, and in 1697 Bossuet brought Rancé
into the Quietist dispute against Fénelon.[5] In the last months of
his life (20 June 1700)[6] Rancé wrote to Bossuet about the recent

[1] See above, pp. 43–44.   [2] See above, p. 122.
[3] See A. Joly, *James Drummond, duc de Perth*.   [4] See above, p. 51.
[5] Bossuet, *Correspondance*, viii, pp. 259 seq.   [6] Ibid., xii, p. 266.

visit of a Danish acquaintance of Bossuet named Winslow (or Vinsløv) and rather touchingly added: 'Il ne m'est pas possible de passer toute ma vie sans vous faire ressouvenir de moi.' The last letter from Bossuet came only a few weeks before the end (16 September 1700)[1] and regretted that he had been unable to visit la Trappe again. Until he died in 1704, Bossuet was active in protecting Rancé's reputation and trying to commission a reliable biography.

There can be no doubt that Bossuet and Rancé needed and complemented each other in their experience and aspirations. Rancé's refusal to take sides on the Jansenist question while remaining a moral rigorist was much easier in a monastic context than in the glare of publicity to which Bossuet was constantly exposed. One can see the attraction for Bossuet of such an uncompromising work as *Sainteté*, which upheld fundamental Christian teaching on a practical rather than theoretical basis, admittedly in a limited context. If Bossuet was, so to speak, an impresario for Rancé, Rancé was sufficiently remote from public affairs to be a powerful and objective ally for Bossuet in some of his bitterest controversies, for instance with casuists or Quietists. In the last analysis, however, the explanation of their relationship is undoubtedly personal and spiritual, as the very private exchanges with the nuns at Jouarre or Faremoutier illustrate; Rancé added at Bossuet's own request an element to his direction which recognizably enriched it.[2] Bossuet's usually unsatisfied need for retreat needs no explanation in view of the incessant strain of his public life, but it is worth considering the extent to which he was also affected by the sight of Rancé's authority in the monastery and with monks in general, since authority was always of prime importance in everything Bossuet said and did. How literally he believed in Rancé's formal sanctity is unimportant; what matters is that he recognized in Rancé's person and achievement the living witness of the truth he himself proclaimed with so much pomp and circumstance.

A complete contrast is provided by Rancé's correspondence with Louis Lascaris d'Urfé, Bishop of Limoges.[3] He came of very noble stock, was a marquis in his own right and grandson of a marquis d'Alègre, but led a life of great piety and humility.

---

[1] Ibid. xii, p. 331.   [2] Cf. ibid. iv, p. 289 and many others.
[3] On Limoges see *GC* ii, 543.

Appointed to Limoges in 1676, early next year he took up residence in the diocesan seminary, which he affiliated to Saint-Sulpice, and until his death in 1695 lived the life of an ordinary ecclesiastic rather than a prelate. Before taking up his post he made a retreat at la Trappe, which is said to have affected him profoundly. It is by no means clear just when or why he resumed contact with Rancé, but the first extant letter refers, in 1687,[1] to the sincerity of feelings going back forty years, and it is quite likely that they had not communicated much, if at all, in the previous ten years. To judge from the nine letters preserved from the next two and a half years, Rancé wrote at monthly intervals to begin with, and the bishop seems to have gone through a very testing period of doubt and self-criticism. The second letter (5 October 1687)[2] reveals that he had not been satisfied with himself, but had been much edified by reading *Sainteté* (perhaps the immediate cause of the correspondence). It then appears that he had hoped to visit la Trappe, but had been prevented from doing so. Only just before Christmas does Rancé become more specific in his advice.[3] For some reason the bishop wanted to know how he could best practise penitence, and Rancé told him that the main method was realization of his own shortcomings, though there were external mortifications open to him, like cutting down on his table, his carriages, his furniture, and his social life. A month later[4] Rancé sends the bishop at his request a reasoned statement of a bishop's duties, commenting that it must all be perfectly familiar to him already. In June, and again in July,[5] there is talk of the bishop's pastoral progress through his diocese, and Rancé commends his zeal. The New Year, 1689,[6] brings forth some gloomy comments on the plight of James II and the arrogance of William of Orange, and twelve months later[7] we learn that the pastoral visits are over and that ill health is turning d'Urfé's thoughts to death. The most interesting letter is to an unnamed bishop,[8] almost certainly Limoges, for it is dated 13 May 1688 and fits exactly into the story described above. Rancé writes: 'J'aurois un véritable déplaisir que ma dernière lettre... vous eût empêché de donner à votre peuple des instructions qui

[1] *TC* I/71.   [2] *TC* II/335 and I/83.
[3] *TC* I/35 of 14 Dec. 1687.   [4] *TC* II/98 of 28 Jan. 1688.
[5] *TC* I/109 of 13 June 1688 and II/251 of 19 July 1688.
[6] *TC* I/265 of 6 Jan. 1689.   [7] *TC* II/78 of 6 Dec. 1689.   [8] *TC* II/294.

leur étoient nécessaires', but that the bishop, however dissatisfied
with himself, must not keep silent. He had apparently almost
missed preaching at Easter, a month before. Assuming, as is
reasonable from the evidence, that this letter is part of the same
correspondence, Rancé's influence for the period in question
seems to have been decisive. It is hardly likely that his letters
would have produced such an effect if the bishop were simul-
taneously consulting others, and the specific request for rules
and a way of life coming from a man long renowned for his pious
example suggests that Rancé held a very privileged position in
d'Urfé's esteem. As always, one would like to know more, but
the evidence is not too fragmentary to be convincing.

The case of Étienne le Camus is better documented than that of
d'Urfé[1] but so similar in important respects that it is tempting
to fill the gaps of the unknown from the known. Of a very distinguished family (his brother, Nicolas, became Premier Président)
le Camus was a little younger than Rancé (1632–1707), but from
an early date belonged to the circle of his intimate friends. He
took his doctorate at the Sorbonne in 1650, and as a very worldly
abbé de cour was soon appointed chaplain to Louis XIV, who
thought very highly of him. He was promoted to the see of
Grenoble in 1671, but by that time had been through the same
process of conversion as his two closest friends, Rancé and Henri
Barillon. He was extremely friendly with several of the Oratorians
who played such an important role in the spiritual evolution of
his circle, and kept up a regular correspondence with, among
others, Quesnel, whom he at one time tried to attract to Grenoble
as Vicar–General, and Monchy, who was roughly handled during
a preaching tour in the diocese.[2]

He visited la Trappe in 1667, and again in 1670, and during
this period had a number of friends at Port-Royal, including
Pontchâteau, to whom Rancé wrote in 1668:[3] ' Je ne voudrois pas
que M. le C[amus] désirât d'être évêque... mais il ne faut pas
qu'il s'en éloigne de sorte qu'il s'en exclue.' Once le Camus had
gone to his diocese, he began a correspondence with Rancé which
lasted the rest of his life. Ironically enough, one of his earliest
references to Rancé is in a letter to Pontchâteau written just after

---

[1] See A. Lallouette, *Abrégé de la vie du cardinal E. le Camus.*
[2] See E. le Camus, *Lettres, passim.*
[3] Original in *U* 863.

the visit in 1670,[1] when he complains that Rancé is not eating enough. The subsequent course of their correspondence shows a total reversal of roles. On arrival in Grenoble le Camus, an initially reluctant prelate, at once determined that if he must be a bishop and not a monk he would at least practise Trappist austerities privately. Rancé wrote at his request a letter[2] that became celebrated outlining a suitable way of life. His friend should give up meat (always the basic physical austerity for Rancé), do without table silver and rich hangings, sleep on a straw mattress, wear a hairshirt in Advent and Lent. An hour's prayer during the night is 'une pratique très sanctifiante; elle peut être nécessaire pour vous qui en avez passé de [nuits] toutes entières, et en grand nombre, dans les divertissements du monde et de la cour'. Here, and on other similar occasions, he quotes St. Charles Borromeo as the example of the good prelate, and it must be remembered that even before Rancé went to la Trappe he had seen Pavillon leading just such a life at Alet. Le Camus took these instructions as an actual rule of life, tantamount to vows, by which he felt himself bound, and over the next few years enthusiastically identified himself with Rancé's reforms. In 1673 he praises Sept-Fons and Beaufort as 'copie de l'abbé de la Trappe', and the same year tells Arnauld how much he admires Rancé. They both, like many of Rancé's friends, fear for his creation once he has gone, and le Camus tells Arnauld that he has offered a site in his diocese, as Pamiers did, 'dans une vieille abbaye de nos déserts... des vestiges de cloîtres et les murailles d'une église', in case difficulties overwhelm the community at la Trappe.[3] By 1676 he is reassuring Quesnel that there will always be a refuge in his diocese for the monks, should persecution fall upon them, and at the same time reports to Pontchâteau (5 July) that 'la Trappe séculière est commencée dans le diocèse', with the house and chapel all ready for himself and chosen companions.[4] From 1677 to 1681 le Camus passed on news between Rancé and Tamié (not in his diocese, but Grenoble was on the postal route) and had to endure increasing opposition for his alleged Jansenist leanings. To him, as to others, Rancé declares strict neutrality:[5] 'bienheureux sont ceux qui ne sont d'aucun parti que de celui de J.-C. et de son Eglise...

---

[1] Le Camus, *Lettres*, 7.   [2] *TB* 113, of 23 Dec. 1672 and Muguet, i, p. 397.
[3] Le Camus, *Lettres*, 40 and 51. The momentary possibility of la Trappe and the Grande Chartreuse in the same diocese is, to say the least, intriguing.
[4] Ibid. 128 and 125.   [5] *TB* 1411 of 31 Dec. 1680.

hors de là il n'y a que ténèbres et confusion.' So austere a life, and so much strain, eventually told on le Camus's health, and in 1681 he fell seriously ill. By May 1682 he was out of danger, but his friends were alarmed, blamed his illness, not unreasonably, on his austerities, and got the Pope to order him to take care of himself. Rancé had been through all this himself, and something of a crisis of conscience arose over the irreconcilable demands of le Camus's private vows and his public obligations. Rancé's letters show how torn he felt himself to be: to admit that austerities are wrong in themselves would be to abandon a principle, but equally to compromise his friend's health by recommending a resumption of austerity before complete recovery would be foolish and wrong. Rancé admits[1] that le Camus may have suffered from 'votre rigidité dans le vivre, vos grands jeunes, vos veilles, vos oraisons, ces prédications, cette sollicitude, cette occupation continuelle qui n'admet ni récréation ni plaisir', but that this is no reason for the complete change being urged in some quarters. Let le Camus take eggs, a little wine, less broken sleep, and fewer sermons, even eat meat for a time; 'vous n'entamerez point la volonté que vous avez eue d'observer la vie monastique.' He stresses that this is objective advice, not prompted by his own fear of losing a dear friend, and says 'vous pouvez diminuer vos austérités mais vous ne pouvez prolonger vos jours.' The debate was not so soon resolved, and in August 1682 Rancé writes:[2] 'j'abrégerois mes jours avec plaisir pour prolonger les vôtres', but 'ce seroit une chose fâcheuse de régler sa vie par l'opinion des médecins'. Once his health is back to normal le Camus can resume his vegetarian diet with a little wine and two eggs a day. As late as December[3] le Camus is still worrying about fidelity to his vows, and Rancé reassures him that in case of need a monk would be allowed to rest after the night office, and that a bishop should not hesitate to allow himself such reasonable relief. Le Camus evidently arrived at some working compromise, for the matter was not raised again, and most of the subsequent correspondence with Rancé is about *Sainteté*, of which le Camus was joint sponsor. Unfortunately, very few later letters survive, but in 1692,[4] for example, le Camus offered his services as mediator between Rancé and Mabillon, and he probably did what he could to smooth relations

---

[1] *TB* 1686 of July 1682.   [2] *TB* 1730 of 10 Aug. 1682.
[3] *TB* 1804 of 7 Dec. 1682.   [4] Le Camus, *Lettres*, 349.

with the Carthusians (the Grande Chartreuse was in his diocese).
His promotion to cardinal in 1686 infuriated Louis XIV, who
had wanted the hat to go to Harlay, and royal disfavour caused
him far more distress than the elevation gave him pleasure.

As an example of Rancé's direct personal influence this is much
the most detailed and circumstantial, but d'Urfé at Limoges is
quite likely to have been spurred to emulate it as much as possible,
and the effect on le Camus's colleagues and diocesan clergy must
have been real, even if it cannot be even roughly estimated. Those
who speak of le Camus virtually leading a Trappist existence are,
as these facts show, barely exaggerating.

The other friend of Rancé's youth on whom his influence was
equally marked was Henri Barillon, Bishop of Luçon (his recent
predecessors in the see included Richelieu, a forcibly translated
abbot of Cîteaux, and Nicolas Colbert). Barillon died shortly before Rancé, in 1699, and this may be the reason why so much of
their correspondence is preserved (106 letters running from
1665 to 1698).[1] As well as letters, and a rather vague biography by
one of his chapter (probably du Bos),[2] we are fortunate enough to
have a curious autobiography drawn up as a sort of spiritual
profit and loss account under the headings *Gratiae* and *Peccata*.[3]
Henri Barillon was born in 1639, and was thus the youngest of the
three friends.[4] His father died when he was very young, and he
was educated first with the Oratorians at Juilly, then at the
Collège des Grassins. He and his brother Paul, later ambassador
to England, early became friendly with Rancé and le Camus.
Brought up by his pious uncle, Morangis (Du Hamel's protector
at Saint-Merri), Barillon had many friends and close relatives in
the magistracy and public service and was originally destined for a
career of arms with the Knights of Malta. In 1657, however, he
made a retreat at Saint-Magloire, and another retreat the next
year convinced him that he should enter the Church. He took
the tonsure in 1660 and like so many others went to consult M.
Vincent. In 1662 he followed in Rancé's footsteps and went to

[1] In a copy made in 1752, preserved at Poitiers in MS. Fontaneau 65.
[2] *Abrégé de la vie de M. de Barillon.*
[3] *Vie de M. de Barillon écrite par lui-même*, in BN lat. 18389 (copy), partially published in *Revue de Bretagne et de Vendée*, 2e série, 1862, i, pp. 471–82, and ii, pp. 134–49.
Biographical quotations are from the MS. unless otherwise stated.
[4] M. Prevost has written a particularly useful series of articles on the whole family
in *DBF*.

Alet for some five months, returning to accept from Rancé his priory of Boulogne. All this time he was proceeding through the successive sacred orders and also completing his doctorate at the Sorbonne, becoming priest and doctor within a few days in June 1660. Meanwhile he had joined the large and distinguished company whose spiritual director was M. Marcel, curé of Saint-Jacques-du-Haut-Pas, confessor of so many of Rancé's friends, to whom he entrusted the autobiography mentioned above. A very odd entry in this diary for 2 September 1665 strongly suggests that he was consciously comparing himself with Rancé: 'Mort de Mlle d'Alègre dans une grande jeunesse... Dieu s'en servit pour me donner des sentiments de dégoût et d'éloignement pour le monde.' No one has ever suggested that this young woman, who lived in Morangis's house, had inspired any sentimental attachment in Barillon, but her sudden death brought home to him, as did that of Mme de Montbazon to Rancé, the transience of earthly values.

He himself was not very robust, and was stricken by three months' illness in 1665 and six weeks' in 1666, perhaps the commencement of the kidney trouble that eventually killed him. Just at this time he recorded: 'liaison et amitié particulière avec M. l'abbé le Camus', and in 1671 when there was a wholesale promotion of bishops he was nominated to Luçon on le Camus's recommendation. He made a retreat at the Institution de l'Oratoire, like Rancé before him, before his consecration in 1672, and then 'Dieu m'inspira d'aller passer quelques jours avec M. l'abbé de la Trappe. Ses sentiments, ses avis et le bon exemple de sa maison me furent un sujet de grande édification et de consolation dans mes découragements.' Not very much is known of Barillon's personal austerities, and as far as diet was concerned he could hardly have led the sort of life that le Camus did without leaving some record of it. His biographer emphasizes his pastoral care, his close attention to the training of his clergy, his generous donation of episcopal revenues to diocesan needs, but if these are expected and even standard characteristics, one or two others are a little more personal. There is nothing specifically Rancéen in his practice of having St. Charles's *Life* read aloud at table every two years, but the following 'résolution' has a distinctly Trappist ring:[1] 'Je dois au milieu de l'accablement des affaires extérieures

[1] *Abrégé*, p. 69.

tâcher de me faire une solitude intérieure dans mon cœur, pour
être retiré et appliqué à Dieu.' His thoughts on retreat are systematic; an annual retreat of eight to ten days, a monthly one of a
day, and, if possible, one hour every Saturday was his principle.
On his episcopal office he has a memorable phrase:[1] 'Une mitre
bien portée vaut bien un cilice, et un bâton pastoral bien soutenu
vaut bien des coups de discipline.'

From his arrival at Luçon in 1672 to his death he was tireless
in visits, organization of seminaries, and, a special problem in his
diocese, dealing with Protestants, both pulling down their
churches and trying to win them over with charity. Family and
diocesan affairs took him to Paris for several months in 1678–9
and again in 1682–3; on the latter occasion he managed to spend
ten days with le Camus as well as a week at la Trappe. His first
bad attack of nephritis struck him in 1684, and thereafter he was
never free from pain. He visited Grenoble and la Trappe again
in 1687, and only a few months after being reunited with his
brother Paul, after a separation of eighteen years, had to go back
to Paris to assist at Paul's death-bed, returning via la Trappe.
His last visit to Paris was in 1698, when he was operated on for
the stone, but died on 7 May 1699. Bound by ties of friendship to
both le Camus and Rancé, maintaining regular correspondence
with both of them, Barillon was probably under more continuous
influence from Rancé than was anyone else.

Their copious correspondence, of which only Rancé's letters
survive, is a commentary on these basic biographical facts. The
numerous deaths occurring in Barillon's family are a recurrent
theme, but Rancé's close interest is so evident as to make the
frequent condolences seem more than a dry formality. In 1678
Barillon's brother, Morangis, was Intendant at Alençon, and
Rancé writes that they both agree that a visit would not infringe
the obligation of residence to which a bishop should rightly give
absolute priority.[2] In fact Barillon was obliged as just mentioned,
to be absent in Paris for long periods at a time, often prolonged by
illness, but he was never away from his diocese for pleasure.
After 1682 *Sainteté*, and its sequels, is a constant topic of their
correspondence, with Barillon acting as go-between with Bossuet
and le Camus, and in the years around the Revocation of the
Edict of Nantes progress in converting Huguenots provides a

---

[1] Ibid., p. 93.   [2] P, f. 765 of 13 Jan. 1678.

counterpoint to these questions of publication. Rancé, like his friends, was always opposed to violence and is glad to learn that kindness pays at both Luçon and Grenoble where 'on n'a point vu... de ces gens qui portent la terreur avec eux et cependant tout s'est soumis'.[1] News of mutual friends, like Pinette and Monchy, and requests for favours to be rendered through official channels, exchange of men seeking admission to la Trappe or being sent on to Luçon after failing, regular visits by clergy from Luçon on their way to or from Paris—many small details of this kind add up to a notably intimate relationship in which no aspect of daily life is neglected. After James II was expelled from England, and then from Ireland, the situation of Paul, former envoy to the exiled monarch, came to the forefront, but his illness and death robbed his homecoming of any joy for his brother and Rancé. Rancé was convinced that he too was going to die soon, and the combination of personal and political gloom is depressing indeed. Paul is still taking 'kinkina' but gets no better; Rance is tortured by rheumatism, exacerbated by a hard winter 'qui n'est pas moins malfaisant par ses humidités que par ses froideurs';[2] Henri is regularly laid low by his nephritis; and only a few days after Rancé was on his feet again, after a long illness provoked by a fall, Paul was dead. Towards the end Rancé was writing every week, answering bulletins from Henri and their common friend M. Marcel.

Rancé's intense interest in the campaign against William of Orange is hardly surprising by ordinary standards, but it is in fact inconsistent with his professed indifference to external events. He must have felt this himself at one point, for he wrote to Barillon:[3] 'quand Dieu aura rendu la paix à toute l'Europe et que les armes du Roi seront triomphantes... je rentrerai avec plaisir dans l'ignorance où j'étois avant ces derniers mouvements.' There is a good deal about the various disputes with Benedictines, Carthusians, and so on, and about the reconciliation with Mabillon. One of the oddest subjects mentioned is that of a boy of 8 or 9, nephew of a local priest, 'qui a toutes les manières ecclésiastiques' and whom Rancé recommends to Barillon for his *petit séminaire*.[4] Another interesting piece of information is contained in a friendly, but very respectful letter to Barillon from

---

[1] *P*, f. 622 of 29 Nov. 1685.   [2] *P*, f. 634 of 2 Jan. 1690.
[3] *P*, f. 638 of 19 Jan. 1692.   [4] *P*, f. 648 of 11 Oct. 1694.

Zozime, Rancé's newly appointed successor.[1] Since Rancé's resignation, Zozime says, he has neither sent nor received letters without Zozime's permission, 'son exactitude va même jusqu'au scrupule. Il me menace de venir au premier jour dire ses coulpes en chapitre.' Growing infirmity reduced the volume of Rancé's correspondence, but a useful scrap of information comes from a letter reporting the visit of Barillon's nephew, whom Rancé praises as having 'des principes de vertu qui m'ont surpris.. toutes les qualités d'un parfait honnête homme' and to whom he promises he will write every three months.[2] In practice this is probably what he did with many of his correspondents, but so explicit an arrangement is not mentioned elsewhere. The last letter of the series (15 January 1698) is sad:[3] Rancé has not written for a long time, has been in the infirmary for three years with one arm useless, and unable to walk without support, but he has still enough energy to send his friend *Maximes chrétiennes* and *Conduite chrétienne*. That autumn Barillon was operated on, but died on 7 May 1699. He had many friends, of whom le Camus was as close as Rancé, but it seems clear from all the evidence that both bishops looked to Rancé as their spiritual master, however much he deferred to their rank and practical experience.

By his position at Court and at the Assembly of Clergy Bossuet differed from his colleagues at Limoges, Grenoble, and Luçon who had forsaken worldly values to the utmost degree allowed by their duties and status, but he was at one with them in recognizing the same principles of sanctification and discipline. There is nothing vague about Rancé's contacts with these men, no mystic or speculative theology, but hard facts about duties and daily routine, progressive realization of a common ideal, in a very real sense the fusing of the monastic spirit with the active ministry. Perhaps the most remarkable feature of Rancé's association with all these prelates, and many others, is the extraordinarily small number of days, or hours, spent in direct contact in relation to the influence exercised. The sheer concentration of spiritual force, undiluted by any external distractions, represented by Rancé and la Trappe is the explanation of this phenomenon, and it needs to be seen in the context of an overpowering desire for retreat on the part of those least able to enjoy it.

[1] P, f. 655 of 5 Jan. 1696.   [2] P, f. 656 of 11 Oct. 1696.   [3] P, f. 658.

11. Secular Clergy and Oratorians

ALTHOUGH Rancé naturally knew far more priests than prelates, it is not so very surprising that his closest friends should have come from the numerically smaller class to which he himself was destined by birth and education. No special explanation of his relations with parish priests or diocesan clergy is required; they came to la Trappe for retreat and advice as do their successors today, in numbers at which one can only guess, but among those whose contacts are documented some very marked patterns can be seen. Whether such patterns are reliable indications of a broader picture, or simply due to the accident of survival, can best be decided in the light of all the evidence, but as an exercise in the reconstruction of human relationships it is well worth examining a limited number. For formal reasons the priests of the Oratory will be studied separately from the other clergy, but very similar considerations apply to them.

The central, though not chronologically the first, figure in one of these patterns is M. Du Hamel.[1] A disciple of Saint-Cyran, he was ordained in 1641 and went to Saint-Maurice, Sens, next year, where Mathieu Feydeau (1616–94) came under his direction. In 1644 he moved to Saint-Merri in Paris, as Hillerin's successor; this was the parish of the Roannez and, for a time, the Pascals. At Sens he had shown more zeal than judgement in his administration of the sacraments, enjoining public penance on some, abstention from the altar on others, and is indeed referred to in the preface to Arnauld's *De la fréquente communion*. With such a record he was an easy target for Jesuit and other critics of Jansenism, but at Saint-Merri he enjoyed the protection of Barillon's uncle, M. de Morangis, and of M. de Bernières among others, and won a well-deserved reputation for charity, piety, and austerity, if not for moderation. Then in 1651 he chose exile rather than what he regarded as the betrayal of signing the Formulary, and was sent to Langres, Quimper, Bellême, and various other places before his friends prevailed on him to sign in 1661, in

[1] See S. Treuvé, *Vie de M. Du Hamel* and also Mesnard, *Pascal et les Roannez*, especially p. 110.

which year he briefly returned to Saint-Merri before exchanging
his parish for a stall in Notre-Dame. Meanwhile M. Cordon, his
former curate at Saint-Merri and then curé at Saint-Maurice, had
caused something of a stir by entering la Trappe, where he was
known as dom Arsène, in 1671.[1] At this point Du Hamel took
over again at Saint-Maurice, and after himself paying a visit to la
Trappe, followed the sort of modified Trappist regime adopted
by, for example, le Camus, abstaining wholly from meat and fish,
and only occasionally taking eggs. By now he was fully under the
influence of Rancé 'en qui il trouvoit une très-grande conformité
pour toutes choses, et surtout pour l'austérité et la pénitence qui
étoit la vertu bien aimée de M. Du Hamel', as Treuvé, his biographer puts it. In 1680 the militant Feydeau, still exiled at
Bourges, tried to persuade him to recant over the signature, and
Du Hamel at once consulted Rancé: 'il ne faut pas s'étonner s'il
ôta à M. Du Hamel le scrupule qu'il en avoit.'[2]

By now Du Hamel, approaching 70 and in failing health began,
in close consultation with Rancé, to cast around for a successor at
Saint-Maurice. One candidate, we learn, has too poor a voice to
sing High Mass, but has other good qualities, no one seems ideal,
but in the end Du Hamel persuaded his nephew to forsake the
Sorbonne for Sens. Only half a dozen of Rancé's letters to Du
Hamel are preserved, from the last three years of his life, but
they are interesting. The first contains the remarkably warm
tribute to Retz, recently deceased, quoted above;[3] later the question of succession is discussed; and then in 1681 Du Hamel paid a
visit. In 1682 he came again, with Pinette, and fell so ill that he
was in bed at la Trappe for two months. He himself wanted to die
there, but his family insisted on taking him back to Nainvilliers
(near Pithiviers) where he died on 13 November 1682. In his last
illness he was unable to make his communion even on Sundays
and feast days, but Rancé comforted him with the thought:
's'éloigner de Dieu par l'ordre du Seigneur c'est s'en approcher.'[4]
Less than a week before the end, Rancé wrote Du Hamel a letter
which he just had time to read in the last moments of his life. So
ill and so old, he had run his course, and Rancé's last words to
him[5] offer real consolation: 'Car quoique nous désirions extrême-

---

[1] See *Relation* i.   [2] Treuvé, *Vie*, pp. 163–4.
[3] *TB* 1239 of 27 Jan. 1680.   [4] *TB* 1668 and 1727.
[5] *TB* 1793 of 7 Nov. 1682 (reproduced in Treuvé).

ment le rétablissement de votre santé, nous savons cependant qu'il vous est beaucoup meilleur d'être vivant parmi les vivants que non pas vivant parmi les morts.' As a tangible token of his affection he bequeathed his watch to Rancé. A little more than two years later his friend dom Arsène was also called to his rest.

Du Hamel and Cordon illustrate very well one aspect of Rancé's relations with formerly active Jansenists. The whole problem is so complex that it requires separate treatment in a later chapter, but it can be said now that what drew such men to Rancé was what had drawn them to Saint-Cyran or Arnauld—a strongly personal attraction based on moral and spiritual excellence, not dogma. Du Hamel's early relief work among prisoners and the poor (with Père Bernard) gave a distinctive stamp to his ministry, and at Saint-Merri, for instance, he worked closely with the Dames de Charité to relieve the needy. Like Cordon, his collaborator, Du Hamel came to desire private peace rather than public victory, and under Rancé's direction they both found it.

Another in the same affiliation is Mathurin Quéras,[1] also a doctor of the Sorbonne and an early supporter of Arnauld. In 1658 he became Grand Vicaire and director of the Seminary at Sens, whence he had to move on the death of Archbishop Gondrin, protector of many Jansenists, in 1674, to Troyes, where he was prior of Saint-Quentin and where he died in 1695. By the end of 1685 Rancé was in correspondence with him,[2] acknowledging receipt of a book on theology (probably his treatise on *Dépendance des réguliers*), and in 1687 answering a query about two religious who had disappeared and who Quéras had wrongly thought might be at la Trappe, the refuge automatically suspected in such cases, as Rancé drily observes. The tone of these two letters is cordial, but not specially intimate, and one can see that this 'janséniste modéré... fort austère' of Sens had been a natural member of the Du Hamel–Cordon group. He is also known to have been closely connected with some of the Celestines of Sens, and may well have played a part in the mass defection.[3]

The same point could be made negatively of Feydeau.[4] He was a by no means moderate Jansenist, and as curé of Vitry-le-François

---

[1] See article in *Dict. de spiritualité* and also note in Bossuet, *Correspondance*, xii, p. 90.
[2] T 1066, no. 9, ff. 75–6 (originals).
[3] See A 5098, where his name occurs in letters to and from Celestines at Sens.
[4] See M. Feydeau, *Mémoires*.

was a close friend and ally of his neighbour Le Roy. He had played a leading role in the great battles of the heroic period of the movement, had been with Du Hamel at Saint-Maurice and Saint-Merri, and like him had endured exile. In 1673 he was still in correspondence with Rancé, who refers in a letter to Quesnel to an unspecified subject under discussion between them. The quarrel with Le Roy brought Feydeau out strongly against Rancé, and a particularly virulent letter[1] written from Bourges, where he was by now in exile (incidentally the letter is attributed to Feydeau and Fléchier, but is unsigned and appears to be in the hand of neither), should almost certainly be seen in the context of Du Hamel's consultation mentioned above: 'Ah qu'il est bien plus avantageux au salut de conserver l'amour de la vérité [sc. Jansenism] et d'être toujours prêt à la défendre en mangeant de la viande avec M. l'abbé de Hautefontaine que de l'abandonner et la trahir en ne mangeant que des racines et des légumes avec le Père abbé de la T.—il passera, il sera détruit, mais la vérité qu'il abandonne ne passera point, elle subsistera toujours.' There follows the charge that Rancé will only accept novices willing to sign the Formulary.

Not every friend of Le Roy, however, became an enemy of Rancé. Jean Cappé,[2] a native of Vitry, in 1679 became an Oratorian, and with two other priests was put in charge of the diocesan seminary of Châlons, of which he became superior in 1685. In 1679 he supported Le Roy when consulted about fictions, but like his colleague Gardey was on the friendliest terms with the Abbot of Châtillon, whose own friendship with Rancé remained unshaken. This Vitry connection has a further ramification of some interest. In a letter from Châtillon to Cappé (3 August 1677)[3] we learn of the links between Châtillon, Cappé, Gardey, their bishop, and Rancé's friend, Vialart, and finally Treuvé. Châtillon, writing from Paris, refers to a projected visit to Louvain, which, as Treuvé will appreciate, he is only too happy to abandon in favour of one to Hautefontaine. It would be fascinating, and instructive, to unearth more of Châtillon's Jansenist connections, but for the moment it is Treuvé who commands our attention.

Born in 1651, Simon Treuvé[4] entered the Congrégation de la

[1] In U 751 of 27 Jan. 1679.   [2] See U 743.   [3] U 745.
[4] See long article in Moréri.

doctrine chrétienne at Vitry in 1668, but five years later left them
to join Feydeau, still at Vitry, and later spent some time with Le
Roy. After publishing *L'Instruction sur la pénitence et l'eucharistie*
(dedicated to Mme de Longueville) he yielded to the urging of
Vialart and accepted ordination in 1676. In 1679 he went to
Espoisses as chaplain to the comte de Guitaut and then on to the
duchesse de Lesdiguières, Retz's niece and the friend of Port-
Royal with whom Rancé had some acquaintance. From there he
wrote to Le Roy[1] condemning Rancé's recent letter to Bellefonds
for its sentiments on the signature, but praising its moral tone.
He was at this stage certainly on the side of Le Roy and Feydeau,
but in 1684, after a year or two as curate of Saint-André-des-Arts
in Paris, he went to Meaux as a canon, and thenceforth developed
on rather different lines, no doubt under Bossuet's influence. In
about 1690 he published his *Vie de M. Du Hamel*, a by no means
uncritical study which does its subject more credit than the vaguely
hagiographical treatment too often favoured by biographers of
the age, and which gives a very balanced but sympathetic picture
of Rancé and his relations with Du Hamel. This growing appreciation of la Trappe found permanent expression after a visit
he paid with Bossuet in 1697, as a result of which he composed
two sermons on the life of the religious.[2] Despite the bilious
predictions of Feydeau in his letter to Le Roy, it was Rancé, not
Le Roy, who survived to inspire, if not wholly conquer, at least
in spirit, Du Hamel and his biographer. The Vitry circle formed
round Feydeau, the clergy of the Châlons diocese, including the
brothers of dom Paulin de Lisle, who took their cue from Bishop
Vialart, the Hautefontaine circle, which looked to Germain
Vuillart after Le Roy's death in 1684, the friends of Abbot Claude
of Châtillon—all interlock and constantly involve Rancé in the
most unexpected way, as when Louise-Henriette at Tours meets
the curés of Saint-Dizier and Nangis on a chance visit to Vuillart's brother.[3] From the mere fact of association with one or other
of these groups one can never be quite sure what a given person's
attitude to Rancé is likely to be, but one can be sure that there will
be some attitude.

[1] U 772.
[2] This is stated quite plausibly in Moréri, but in fact the sermons in question were
published anonymously, and are, without explanation, attributed to the Oratorian
Claude Masson in the BN catalogue of anonymous works (D 19871).
[3] See above, p. 206.

Following Treuvé's traces at Meaux, we have already seen that another canon, Jean-Baptiste Vitry, was attracted to la Trappe, and finally admitted there as dom Dorothée. If this was most probably due to Bossuet's connections, the case of another of his clergy, M. de Saint-André, is rather more complex. André Chapperon, known as de Saint-André (1654–1740),[1] is a much more important figure in the history of la Trappe than has apparently been realized. For some years, from 1668, he enjoyed the revenues of a canonry at Arras. He took a doctorate at Bourges, and in 1681 attended a synod of Protestants, which suggests early theological competence. About this time, or perhaps a little later, he went to la Trappe, where he spent sixteen months as a secular. It is by no means clear why he left, or indeed why he ever went there, but (according to E. Levesque) he was a cousin of Maisne, whose ascendancy dates from about 1680. He then found his vocation as a parish priest, in the diocese of Meaux, first (1688–98) at Bannost, near Nangis, and then at Vareddes. In 1706 he was appointed Archdeacon of Brie, but was never promoted further. He was reputedly anti-Jansenist, and very much Bossuet's *homme de confiance* where Rancé was concerned. Finding himself at la Trappe at the time of Rancé's death, he was entrusted by Bossuet with the task of safeguarding the mass of papers, many of them highly controversial, and it is virtually certain that he played a leading role in organizing some of the work of transcribing, editing, and collecting documents. By chance only one letter to him from Rancé has been preserved (on Quietism), of 1697,[2] but if it is ever possible to discover or identify other papers, Saint-André will most probably turn out to be a key figure in the last decades of Rancé's life, and after his death.

Mention of Arras brings in yet another connection. François du Suel[3] was trained at the Oratory, and became a doctor of theology, but did not remain in the Congregation. Appointed curé of Châtres (now Arpajon, near Versailles) in 1661, he published a book on St. Philip Neri in 1665, and in 1673 paid a visit of three weeks to la Trappe, with some idea of trying his vocation.

---

[1] See Bossuet, *Correspondance*, ii, p. 330, and v, p. 221, and several letters of Bossuet to Saint-André in late 1700 and 1701 in xii.

[2] Ibid. viii, p. 507, original sold (to BN) at Sotheby's in 1970.

[3] See above, p. 119, and article in *Dict. de spiritualité* by I. Noye.

The result of this was a book which enjoyed considerable popularity (and several editions) and stimulated interest in la Trappe, *Entretiens de l'abbé Jean et du prêtre Eusèbe* (1674). A modern commentator points out that some of the ideas attributed to the abbot in these dialogues on the solitary life are more reminiscent of Bérulle than of Rancé, but there is no doubt about du Suel's enthusiasm and sincerity. In 1676 he left his parish for Arras, where he spent the ten years until his death as canon-penitentiary, thus drawing on both his pastoral and theological experience. He wrote several books on penance and unworldliness of a rigorist flavour, and translated Bona's life into French, as well as his *Guide du ciel*. From Arras he is known to have sent one young man who died a lay brother at la Trappe and another whose fate is unknown, and it is more than possible that he also had something to do with the visit of his canonical colleague Saint-André. What he himself received from la Trappe is clear from his book of 1674 and the few letters surviving from later years. Already in 1678[1] Rancé speaks sympathetically of du Suel's love of solitude, and in 1682 and 1683 of the heavy burden of his office. As penitentiary, du Suel had even more responsibility for those entrusted to him than as parish priest (the office involved cases of absolution removed from ordinary jurisdiction by canon law), and Rancé always laid great stress on the awesome task of the confessor, from which he frequently tried to deter priestly correspondents. Du Suel very naturally yearned for the retreat and peace he had once briefly found at la Trappe, and Rancé more than once offered to welcome him back, not necessarily as a monk. However, like so many of his clerical colleagues, du Suel found it hard to escape from routine for even a short visit, and there is no evidence that he ever returned. A phrase from Rancé's last letter to him[2] sums up a very common attitude: 'Dieu vous fait aimer la retraite et désirer dans le milieu du monde de jouir du repos de ceux qui n'en sont pas.' The Oratory and Bona, rigorism in moral theology, a practical interest in securing recruits for la Trappe, and immense personal regard for Rancé characterize du Suel, and one would expect further research to reveal others at Arras (or Châtres) who first came into Rancé's orbit through his influence.

In the case of du Suel we know a certain amount about the man and his reactions to la Trappe, very little about his circle;

---

[1] *TB* 948 of 15 Feb. 1678.   [2] *TC* II/283 of 14 Aug. 1684.

in that of Louis Marcel we know a great deal about the circle and not nearly enough about the man.[1] As curé of Saint-Jacques-du-Haut-Pas from 1667 to 1704, Marcel was much the most important parish priest associated with the friends of Port-Royal. His penitents, and intimates, included Mme de Longueville, the Roannez, Nicole, the Barillons and he must have known more than any other single person of the inner lives of Jansenist sympathizers. Rancé wrote to him very firmly in 1677[2] to justify himself for signing the Formulary, denying that he had ever supported Jansenius, but insisting that he made no personal distinctions between those admitted since the *paix de l'église* to be Catholics and their opponents who had never been condemned. Such a letter must have formed part of a larger correspondence, and similar discussions with Brancas, Bellefonds, and others belong to the same period, but the few other letters surviving are on quite different topics.

The curé intervened personally in the dispute with Mabillon (in 1692), which suggests that Rancé's friends attempted to enlist his good offices, and letters of the previous year show that throughout Paul Barillon's last illness Rancé was in close touch with both brothers and Marcel.[3] In 1694, to Quesnel's intense annoyance, Rancé wrote Marcel a letter which soon became public property, justifying himself against the bitter attacks provoked by his thoughtless, but innocuous, observations on Arnauld's death in a letter to Nicaise.[4] Rancé and Marcel were clearly on terms of intimacy and mutual respect for a score of years and more, and from what is known of their respective methods must quite frequently have recommended individual men and women to each other. Nothing is known of personal visits, though Rancé cannot have failed to meet Marcel during his early years in Paris, and perhaps subsequently, and it is hardly credible that Marcel never came to la Trappe. The last act which united them is significant. A month after Rancé's death Quesnel was again angered because Marcel held a service in his memory, though he had done nothing for Arnauld, technically his parishioner: 'Voilà ce que c'est que d'être bien à la cour, on y gagne encore des

[1] See Mesnard, *Pascal et les Roannez*, pp. 895–6.
[2] *TD*, series C, 50 of 4 Jan. 1677.
[3] See letters to Marcel of 7 Apr. and 8 Sept. 1692 (Gonod, pp. 389 and 394) and 14 Sept. 1693 in *BN* 19656, f. 200, and letters of the same period to Barillon in *P*.
[4] Quesnel to du Vaucel, 14 Jan. 1695, in *Correspondance*, i, p. 336.

prières après la mort.'[1] With Du Hamel, Marcel is Rancé's most
distinguished friend among parish clergy, and it is not hard to see
what the three men had in common or which friends they were
likely to share.

In general Rancé showed noteworthy respect for priests and the
priesthood. His own reluctance to send monks for ordination
extended to the advice he gave others contemplating the priesthood, and especially the cure of souls. The cases so far discussed
are of men of superior calibre, but by way of light relief one may
add a letter written to the neighbouring parish of Prépotin,[2]
whose curé had complained that some of Rancé's people (not
necessarily monks) had fired on his pigeons. This man can hardly
have been distinguished by either birth or education to have remained in so humble a post, but Rancé replies with exquisite
courtesy. The father and uncle of the curé had been Rancé's
friends, and if the culprit were indeed one of Rancé's dependants
he would do nothing to save him from punishment: 'Si j'estois
de profession à châtier par moi-même une action de la nature de
celle de laquelle vous vous plaignez, je ne manquerois pas d'en
faire le châtiment.' This letter was written in 1681, and at a
somewhat later date there are extant documents[3] relating to different lawsuits between la Trappe and the curé of Prépotin (not
necessarily the same, of course), but for his part Rancé always
respected the office, even if he had no use for the man. Other
priests with whom Rancé is known to have had contact, of
which little or nothing survives, are such men as directors of
seminaries, like Luthumière[4] at Valognes, Anjubault[5] at Mayenne,
le Chevalier[6] at Séez, and many others in positions of similar
influence. These, the diocesan bishops already discussed, parish
priests, and diocesan clergy like du Suel all add up to a poten-
tially enormous reservoir of influence, much of which we can
never hope to establish, but which makes Rancé and la Trappe
a force of exceptional importance for the spiritual life of the
age.

For the record it is worth including a word on Rancé and
missionaries. Because Dubois never checked his sources, the

[1] Ibid. ii, p. 115.   [2] TB 1506.
[3] Details in Tournoüer, Bibliographie, p. 69, no. 325.
[4] See above, p. 220.
[5] See original letter to him from Rancé of 20 Feb. 1686 in BN 24123.
[6] See above, p. 191.

significance of an otherwise slightly comic incident has not previously been realized.[1] About 1689 a missionary *en route* for Asia
encountered a violent storm in rounding the Cape of Good Hope.
He duly prayed for deliverance and, for some unexplained reason,
coupled this prayer with a specific request that he might be spared
to see la Trappe, of which he had heard so much. He was saved,
and on his return to France paid a visit, and recognized in Rancé
the stranger who had appeared at the helm to steer the ship to
safety. Before he set out again on his travels the missionary persuaded Rancé to give him a long letter on the vocation of foreign
missions, and apparently carried this letter on him as a kind of
talisman, handing out copies to his colleagues abroad.[2] In 1691,
this time off the coast of Coromandel, the missionary encountered another storm and, having again invoked Rancé's aid,
was saved.

As it stands, this looks like a typical pious legend, but in fact
the identity of the missionary obliges one to take at least his
reactions rather more seriously. As dom le Nain quite clearly
wrote, his name was Charmot,[3] not Chaumont as the printer,
followed by Dubois, thought. Le Nain specifically says (and this
is not in the printed version) that Charmot 'nous a mandé'[4]
the second incident in a letter written from Rome in 1706. This
fortunately makes identification certain, and the story interesting.
The missionary was Nicolas Charmot,[5] who first went to China
in 1685, and then in 1695 became Procurator for the Missions
Étrangères of Paris in Rome, where he was the leading opponent
of the Jesuits in the affair of the Chinese rites. He was one of the
most prominent Far Eastern missionaries of the time, and when he
died in Rome in 1714 was one of the directors of the Missions
Étrangères. Thus the story, and the contact, are far from being a
mere *fait divers*, though the miraculous element is obviously a
matter of taste.

At a time when so many scholars were in orders, and so many
priests spent all their time on study, it is more helpful to classify
friends and correspondents by occupation rather than status.

---

[1] See Dubois, ii, pp. 179–82.
[2] Two eighteenth-century copies are still in the Grand Séminaire at Quebec.
[3] Carpentras, MS. 625, p. 618.   [4] Ibid., p. 623, in fact 23 Feb. 1706.
[5] See R. Streit, *Bibl. Missionum*, v, 941. Charmot was born *c.* 1655 at Chalon-sur-
Saône. Streit lists a number of letters and other documents relating to Chinese
missions in which he is concerned as author or addressee.

Thus Rancé's relations with J.-B. Thiers (1636–1703), the excitable curé of Champrond and then of Vibraye,[1] belong rather to the realm of polemical than pastoral concerns, and similarly the amply informative correspondence with that arch-gossip Nicaise,[2] or with Favier, do not primarily involve either in his sacerdotal capacity, though this inevitably comes in from time to time. To these one could add Hermant, Nicole, Arnauld, Floriot, even Mabillon, and many others with whom Rancé corresponded on matters of doctrine or scholarship. Obviously such men were scholars and theologians as well as priests, but Rancé's contacts with them were generally limited to the specific issue under discussion, and his influence, if any, was of a quite indirect kind. Much more relevant to the present consideration of his relations with the clergy as such is his long and close association with the Oratory.

As a group the members of the French Oratory are, of course, well defined and immediately recognizable by purely objective criteria, even if it is not always apparent from records that such men as du Suel or Victor Bouthillier for a time belonged. Within the group of the formally constituted Congregation there were, however, other groupings of a more personal nature, not necessarily based on a particular house (Oratorians were very mobile) but gravitating round one or more key figures. One of these, and probably the most important, was not in orders himself but could hardly have been more influential in the spiritual life of the age if he had been.

Nicolas Pinette (1613–94)[3] belongs to that highly distinctive class of men and women in the seventeenth century who rejected all half measures, only abandoning the world and its values when sated with success, not failure, to give themselves up to a new life of equally zealous penitence. Rancé himself, le Camus, Beaufort, Mme de la Vallière, Mme de Longueville, Louise Rogier—the list includes some of the strongest and most attractive characters of the century. Pinette embarked on a career of arms as a promising young courtier, and is said to have felt the first stirrings of conversion in 1640, after an attack of fever in Turin. This did not change him at once, but in 1643 he performed Lenten exercises

---

[1] See above, p. 53.   [2] See above, pp. 49–50.
[3] On Pinette see the very full article by P. Carpentier, 'Tricentenaire d'une fondation oratorienne; l'ancienne maison d'Institution'.

for the first time, and in the same year became treasurer to Gaston d'Orléans. Next year he was campaigning in the North, at Calais and Gravelines, when he met a former friend who had joined the Oratory and become a priest. This time the conversion was definitive; Pinette made a general confession, and did not lapse again. It is interesting, incidentally, that this turning point in his life should come at exactly the same age, 31, as with Rancé a dozen years later.

The circumstances of his conversion made it natural that he should feel a special attachment to the Oratory, and in 1649 he first conceived the idea of endowing a house for their use. The project took precise form when, in 1652, he met Mlle Chouberne, herself a convert and friend of Mlle d'Épernon, the Carmelite, who felt a clear mission to found a house for the Oratory in Paris (she came from Bordeaux). She died in 1655, but, aided by her money, Pinette went ahead with the scheme, so that by 1657 Caulet, Bishop of Pamiers, was able to consecrate the chapel. Next year the Maison de l'Institution was fully endowed and functioning as Mlle Chouberne had wished. Pinette, though a layman, directed its affairs for nearly forty years, and was buried there.

It is not always easy to judge just how wicked a life such converts as Pinette had led. In the nature of things they tended after their conversion to see their earlier life as something quite sensationally bad. Indifference to religion in faith and practice is one reliable criterion in the context of formal Catholic observance, and a general confession invariably marked a return to the fold. More concrete sins, or crimes as they were wont to call them, might involve blasphemy, murder (in duelling or quarrels), gambling, and, of course, sexual delinquency. With the women the latter can usually be assumed to be the proximate cause of conversion, but with the men one can seldom be so sure. In the case of Pinette, however, a conclusive piece of evidence (apparently overlooked by biographers) explains much; in September 1654, just before Mlle Chouberne's death and the purchase of land for the Institution, the Paris Parlement registered the legitimation of François Pinette 'fils naturel de Nicolas Pinette, trésorier général des finances du duc d'Orléans'.[1] So authentic a sinner, so effective a conversion could not fail to inspire hope and

---

[1] *BN* 4495, f. 514.

confidence in those, like Rancé, who were sure of their sinfulness but afraid of backsliding. At any rate Pinette and Rancé became firm friends (in 1682 Rancé tells Caumartin that Pinette is his 'ami intime'),[1] and there is evidence from numerous letters to Marie-Louise, at least from 1682 onwards, that she too shared in her brother's friendship with Pinette, a regular visitor to la Trappe who brought news to and from Paris. It must be remembered that until Rancé's last visit to Paris in 1675 he always stayed at the Institution, and therefore up to that time did not need to write very often as he had opportunity for personal contact with Pinette and his Oratorian friends there.

The network of relationships linking the Oratory and la Trappe has a second focus in the Court of Gaston d'Orléans,[2] and it is remarkable how many links can be traced between the two. Gaston was a great benefactor of the Oratory, and much influenced by his confessor, P. Condren, later General of the Congregation. Rancé did not spend a great deal of time at Blois as domestic chaplain, but such time as he did spend there brought him into contact with members of the Oratory. One such was P. de Saint-Pé (1599–1678), a man with a great reputation for sanctity who had been a close friend of the Pascal family in Rouen from 1646 and was confessor to the duchesse d'Orléans from 1655 to 1666. He left this post when she persisted in her refusal to pay her debts, and went for six years to Notre-Dame des Vertus, Saumur. Until recently very little was known of his contacts with Rancé, but, as one of Pinette's four deputies in the Oratorian assembly, Saint-Pé was obviously no stranger. On his death Rancé wrote a warm letter of condolence[3] to M. le Nain, dom le Nain's father; and a note has now come to light,[4] scribbled in Rancé's own hand, recommending an unnamed ecclesiastic to Saint-Pé for guidance. The tone of these two letters ('un homme saint… qui continue après sa mort à faire des choses extraordi-naires') speaks of sincere respect for a holy and much older man.

A second link between Gaston, the Oratory, and Rancé (in fact chronologically the first) is Mère Louise Rogier. Herself a former penitent of Condren during her brief stay at Court, she

[1] On 25 July 1682, in Denis, *Autographes de Troussures*, p. 419.

[2] On Gaston see Dethan, *Gaston d'Orléans*; on all the individual members of the Oratory the biographies are in Batterel, *Mémoires domestiques*.

[3] *TB* 1072 of 7 June 1679 and Muguet, ii, p. 199.

[4] In *SS*, MS. Amelote, 219.

remained in close contact with the Oratory throughout her long life, sending copies of her correspondence with Rancé for safe keeping to the Paris house. At the time of Rancé's conversion she was friendly with P. Séguenot (1596–1676), superior at Tours from 1655, to whom she sent Rancé in the first instance. He was also much older than Rancé, and soon implicated in the Jansenist controversy which rent the Congregation and led to his long exile. References in early letters to Mère Louise and in one written on his death to Quesnel[1] show how highly Rancé thought of him, but he did not know him at all well. Through Séguenot, however, Rancé was introduced to P. Bouchard (1605–81) in Paris, to whom he made his general confession and who thus played a major role in Rancé's spiritual evolution. The two men remained in touch, though no details of visits or correspondence are known for certain, and in 1680,[2] only a year before Bouchard died, Rancé told Pinette that however few visitors he could now afford to receive, Bouchard would always be one of them. The same letter includes among these chosen few P. Berziau (1620–96), another of Pinette's deputies, and, according to the most recent research, in his quiet way probably as generous a benefactor to the Institution as Pinette himself.[3] Berziau had under his direction Mme de Lesdiguières, to whom Rancé wrote in 1681[4] at Pinette's request (and who at about the same time took on Treuvé as chaplain). Pinette and Berziau worked so closely and so long together that Rancé can be assumed to have shared equally in their friendship.

Together with Bouchard, the Oratorian who played the most important part in Rancé's conversion and became one of his closest friends was P. Pierre de Monchy (1610–86). Of a very noble Picard family, related to the maréchal d'Hocquincourt, Monchy was intimately connected with Barillon, le Camus, and Rancé, and was one of the leading directors of the day. He frequently preached at Saint-Jacques-du-Haut-Pas and knew well all the friends of Rancé connected with that parish. Mère Agnès de Bellefonds at the Carmelites, and Brancas are only two of the people to whom Rancé passed on news of Monchy in his letters. In 1660 Monchy found himself with Rancé at Gaston's death-bed,

---

[1] In Tans, letter 31, of 11 June 1676.   [2] TD, series B, 89.
[3] See Carpentier, 'Tricentaire d'une fondation oratorienne'.
[4] TB 1481 of 2 June 1681.

and thereafter their relations remained intimate. It is not clear why Monchy preferred to act as Rancé's adviser rather than take on the duty of confessor, assumed by Bouchard, but his influence was deep and lasting. So great was the impression he made on le Camus, whom he is said to have converted, that in 1671 he accompanied the new bishop to Grenoble and helped him through his initial doubts and disappointments, but there is evidence that, like le Camus, Monchy was in his turn influenced by Rancé. It seems that he genuinely wanted to enter la Trappe and was only persuaded finally to abandon the plan when told by Rancé that it would be contrary to his vocation as director and preacher. He paid numerous visits to la Trappe, and maintained a regular correspondence with Rancé, so that it is fair to say that he shared many of the benefits of the solitary life, and of Rancé's influence, even if he could not enjoy permanent retreat.

They were both very fond of le Camus, and shared mutual concern over his poor health. In this connection Rancé once wrote to Monchy,[1] whom he very much wanted to see: 'l'amitié n'est qu'un désir et un mouvement du cœur, et on ne cesse point de désirer ceux qu'on ne cesse pas d'aimer.' The last years of Monchy's life were overshadowed by constant ill health, and, as with all too many of Rancé's correspondents, death is a constant topic of discussion. As it happens, the last extant letter from Rancé to him[2] concerns the Chancellor, Le Tellier, who had recently died in Monchy's arms. Just a year later Monchy died peacefully, as Rancé tells Barillon,[3] after ten or twelve hours' final agony. The predominantly sombre note of the letters preserved is by no means the main feature of Rancé's relationship with Monchy, although it was a death-bed vigil that brought them together in the first place. The association was a much more lively and positive one, concerned with people, vocations, spiritual standards in a corrupt age, and so on. They were mutually indebted to each other and complementary in their activity, the one in the cloister, the other in the world.

In the chapter on vocations something has already been said of the special links between la Trappe and the priests of the Oratory, and of the flow of recruits drawn from their ranks or sent on by

---

[1] *TB* 1535 of 9 Oct. 1681.   [2] *TC* II/73 of 8 Nov. 1685.
[3] *P*, f. 628 of 7 Dec. 1686. Full details of Monchy's career in Batterel, *Mémoires domestique*, iii.

them. Empirically speaking, one can discern a close spiritual affinity between the two institutions, and again empirically speaking Jansenists—or Augustinians, to avoid a restrictively partisan label—Oratorians, and Trappists clearly belong to the same spiritual family, as against Jesuits, Sulpicians, and Mendicants, for example. Even so, to start from categories is to invite misunderstanding, for it is with persons that a community or congregation is constructed. Rancé's first firm links with the Oratory came through the personal introduction of Mère Louise Rogier to Séguenot, through personal contacts with Pinette, Monchy, Bouchard, and it was because their influence worked ultimately as it did (together, of course, with that of Andilly, Pavillon, and others) that he went to la Trappe and made it what it became. In modern terms there was a feedback effect, so that members of the body in which Rancé had once sought retreat in their turn came to him and sent others too. It is confusing the issue to look first for theological or partisan motives, though these undeniably played their part later on.

These considerations are particularly relevant to Rancé's contemporaries or juniors, especially as the Oratory became ever more deeply involved in the Jansenist question. All the men so far discussed knew Rancé before or during his conversion, and were all older than he, but the generations can be seen to divide with Pasquier Quesnel (1634–1719). All those who actually came to la Trappe, like Bernard Molac, Charles Denis, and so on, were Quesnel's juniors, and many had come under his auspices. The most distinguished applicant was Malebranche (1638–1715), whom Rancé reluctantly agreed to accept in 1672,[1] after two unanswered letters, but who never came. From the scanty evidence available it seems that Malebranche established continuous relations with Perseigne some two years later,[2] paying regular visits and composing there at least part of the second draft of his *Méditations chrétiennes* in 1682. Such an intellectually distinguished and active recruit would have had difficulty finding his vocation at la Trappe, but it is significant that in the very similar, though much smaller, monastery at Perseigne he found a retreat to which

---

[1] *TB* 48 of 9 Apr. 1672, which does not, however, include the postscript urging absolute secrecy, apparently once preserved in the Bibl. Publique at Orléans and published by J. Doinel in *Revue des questions historiques*, 1876.

[2] See J. Wehrle, 'Malebranche et... Perseigne'.

he constantly returned. It is noteworthy that his well-documented
visit of 1682 occurred at precisely the time when the prior of
Perseigne was most closely following Rancé's guidance, and
when the former Oratorians, Nocey, and Lanchal,[1] had recently
gone there with Rancé's blessing. The conclusion is inescapable
that Malebranche, like his *confrères*, wanted as close an approxima-
tion to la Trappe as his physical and psychological strength would
allow, and it cannot be an accident that he chose the monastery
geographically nearest to la Trappe, though he could have found
many others nearer Paris. That Malebranche continued to esteem
Rancé even after the attack on monastic studies in *Sainteté* is
proved by his somewhat incongruous consultation of him on a
scientific problem in 1689.[2] Increasing absorption in intellectual
problems no doubt answered the most clamant needs of Malebranche's personality, but it does not invalidate the authenticity
of his response to life at la Trappe and Perseigne.

Rancé's contacts with certain Oratorians, such as Bruscoly,
Payen, and Hubert, have already been mentioned.[3] Others whom
he knew were often directors of nuns and others, like P. Aveillon
(1620–1713), superior in Paris, in 1686, about whom he writes to
the Carmelite sœur Émilie de Bouillon, or the various priests
who looked after the Visitation at Tours and later at Riom,
or those invited to Luçon by Barillon, and it would be interesting
to learn more about his standing with members of the Congregation. Batterel in his *Mémoires* and Galipaud, owner or copyist of
the Rancé manuscripts preserved at the Arsenal, Sainte-Geneviève,
and Mazarine libraries, testify to something approaching a cult
of Rancé in the years after his death.[4] None of these contacts with
the Oratory, however, produced an effect quite so far-reaching
as that with Quesnel, and even now it is not easy to assess its full
consequences.

On the purely material plane many, probably most, of the
precious letters and other manuscript documents concerning
Rancé and now preserved at Utrecht would not be there but
for Quesnel.[5] Then, as Rancé's letters to Quesnel show, he was

---

[1] See above, p. 140.

[2] On 29 Aug. 1689, in P. le Brun, *Hist. critique des pratiques superstitieuses*, 2e éd.,
1733, iii, p. 177.

[3] See above, pp. 117–119.   [4] See above, pp. 60 n. 2.

[5] Tans, 'Un Dialogue monologué', gives a succinct but valuable account of
Rancé's relations with Quesnel. Every history of Jansenism inevitably deals with

a prime recruiting and publicity agent for la Trappe for a dozen years or more, but he was also, much later, one of Rancé's most bitter critics, and much of what he said then, being in print, has influenced historians as the manuscript material, published only recently, has not. Quesnel entered the Oratory in 1657, and got to know Rancé at the Institution, where he stayed until 1666. This brilliant and zealous young priest soon formed a close friendship with Rancé and, like Monchy, with le Camus. As we have seen, his brother Guillaume went for a while to try his vocation at la Trappe (1669–70) and he himself had to be discouraged by Rancé from doing the same. Although he was in these early years associated with Arnauld and his supporters, whom he probably met at Saint-Magloire about 1666, after the *paix de l'église* he could, like plenty of his colleagues, hold such views with impunity. In 1676 le Camus thought so highly of him that he invited him to Grenoble as Grand Vicaire, though he did not accept, but in 1678, apparently because of Harlay's (the Archbishop's) hostility, he was sent away from Paris to Orléans. In 1679 Rancé sent him an Association but this was in January, and by the end of the year a sudden chill set in. Already in August 1678 the Oratory was going through an internal crisis, which Rancé commented on with great regret to Quesnel; in November came the letter to Bellefonds; in January 1679 there was trouble over the Benedictine, Fouchières, sent by Arnauld, who within six months had himself been forced into exile; and P. de Sainte-Marthe, General of the Oratory, had capitulated to anti-Jansenist pressure, to the grief of Châtillon among others.[1]

As a respected friend of Rancé, and a leading figure in his order, Châtillon is a guide to the feelings of the much more committed Quesnel, Châtillon knew Sainte-Marthe personally and exclaims to le Roy (30 January 1679):[2] 'Il vaudroit quasi mieux pleurer et se taire que d'écrire ses sentiments sur la lâcheté de cette congrégation et sur la timidité ou les ténèbres de celui que j'estime, que je respecte et qui m'est si cher par tant d'autres endroits.' For him the doctrine of St. Bernard and St. Augustine 'est celle de l'Eglise'. This was not Rancé's style at all; little

---

Quesnel's later career, which is not so relevant here, but the best picture of his earlier life comes out in his own *Correspondance*, and in that of le Camus, as well, of course, as in Rancé's letters to him, published by Tans and quoted below.

[1] See above, pp. 42 and 115.   [2] Original in *U* 745.

more than six months after sending Quesnel the mark of special favour represented by the Association, he writes[1] (22 August 1679): 'Comme je me suis imposé un perpétuel silence sur le sujet duquel vous avez pris la peine de m'écrire [evidently the signature and Arnauld's flight] je ne répondrai rien à votre lettre, sinon que je vous suis fort obligé de ce que la diversité de sentiments n'empêche pas que je n'aie toujours quelque part dans votre amitié.'

A brief acknowledgement next year of a work of Lenten piety, and in 1681 condolences on the death of Quesnel's mother, put an abrupt end to what had been a very cordial relationship. Le Camus too became a much less frequent correspondent of Quesnel, who, in 1684, took the final irrevocable step of joining Arnauld in exile in Brussels. Thereafter, as Arnauld's assistant and successor, Quesnel had no more directly to do with la Trappe, and saw everything from the standpoint of militant Jansenism.

There is nevertheless an epilogue. In 1698 Quesnel met the Abbot of Orval in Belgium, and in 1700 paid a visit of some weeks there. Orval was as close an imitation of la Trappe as possible, and so Quesnel found it:[2] 'Tout y est édifiant... près de 200 personnes, le silence observé religieusement partout... Enfin c'est ici la terre des saints et un lieu bien propre à attendre le Seigneur.' Just a month later, writing again to du Vaucel (10 November 1700),[3] he criticizes the Cistercian abbey of Moulons, near Namur: 'Les lieux réguliers sont beaux; mais ils ne servent qu'à faire gémir d'y voir la régularité éteinte. Quelle différence entre ce lieu et Orval ou la Trappe!' He continues at once: 'A propos de la Trappe, vous avez su la mort de son ancien abbé... Dieu veuille oublier les fautes qu'il a faites contre l'honneur de la vérité et contre le témoignage qu'il lui devait! L'abbé d'Orval ne lui peut pardonner ce qu'il a écrit contre la mémoire de notre défunt [Arnauld].' A few weeks later he comments on the *relation* of Rancé's death:[4] 'Elle est édifiante, la mort conforme à la vie, à la conduite de Dieu et aux désirs de mon cœur.'

It is abundantly clear that Quesnel never ceased to admire Rancé and la Trappe for what they were, but could never forgive Rancé for failing to defend 'the truth', in other words the Jansenist cause for which he, Arnauld, Nicole, and so many others

---

[1] Tans, art. cit., 40.   [2] Quesnel, *Correspondance*, ii, p. 104.
[3] Ibid., p. 108.   [4] Ibid., p. 125.

were prepared to sacrifice homeland and freedom. Doctrinal questions apart, there could hardly be a clearer illustration of the lifelong attraction felt by an incessantly active and restless man for the peace and quiet of the Trappist life. It was as a Jansenist, not as an Oratorian, that Quesnel parted company with Rancé, and his breach made no difference to Rancé's continuing close relations with many other members of the Congregation.

A footnote to the story of Quesnel is provided by the account of a visit paid to la Trappe in April 1684 by P. Bourrée (1652–1722),[1] then superior of the house at Orléans where Quesnel had spent the previous six years and which he was just about to leave for lifelong exile. Bourrée's account is purely descriptive, and laudatory, but since it came at precisely the time that anti-Jansenist measures were being tightened up at Orléans and elsewhere, one can easily imagine some at least of the conversations that took place. Two years later, in September 1686,[2] another unnamed Oratorian (or ex-Oratorian) priest came with a colleague, and left a particularly interesting account of Rancé and the abbey. The fact that the only known copy of this manuscript is preserved with the papers of Pontchâteau and Quesnel at Utrecht suggests at the very least some friendly connection with Jansenists, but proves once more the continuing attraction felt by one generation of Oratorians after another for la Trappe.

[1] *BN* Coll. Moreau 793, t. IV, f. 161.
[2] *U* 3061, wrongly attributed to Pontchâteau; the author speaks of saying mass at la Trappe (Pontchâteau was not in orders) and of having lived in the Oratory with Charles Denis.

12.   The Great: Men

In the tightly knit society of the seventeenth century there is no
class division to be drawn between those aristocrats, men and
women, who remained in the world and their brothers and sisters
who went into the Church. As far as the ties of kinship or acquaintance were concerned, the differences of career or vocation did
little to change the pattern of individual or collective relationships.
As an *abbé de cour* and aristocrat himself, Rancé was on terms of
equal intimacy with those like Henri Barillon, François de Harlay,
or Étienne le Camus, who went on to become bishops, and those
like Paul Barillon and Achille de Harlay who rose to high rank
in the judiciary or diplomacy. In the *salons*, and at Court, sacred
and profane mixed freely; fashion applied as much to sermons as
to plays, indeed, as much to spiritual directors as to poets. In such
a situation it is particularly important to distinguish relationships
of mere civility and compliment from those involving a degree of
genuine personal contact. A certain number of people in all walks
of life were always anxious to get a letter, or if possible an interview, from Rancé, and made the most of such casual acquaintance-
ship as they could thus scrape up. Many genuinely wanted advice
and would have been glad to put themselves under his direction,
but he soon became extremely chary of giving advice, even to
close friends, and normally passed on requests for direction to
parish priests he knew or to Oratorians. Thus a catalogue of his
noble correspondents is more impressive than informative, and
a really significant list would number little more than a dozen
men and women, of whom Mme de Guise, the maréchal de
Bellefonds, and, in the last decade of his life, James II are at once
the most distinguished by their rank and by the intrinsic interest
of the letters addressed to them. It also happens to be the case
that more of Rancé's letters to them, over a considerable period
of years, have been preserved than to any other noble persons.

Just where or when Rancé first met Bernardin Gigault de
Bellefonds is not clear, but whatever other contacts they may
have had, it was certainly through Bellefonds's aunt, Mère
Agnès, at the Carmelites, that a deep and lasting friendship grew

up between the two men, and it was usually to her that each addressed letters intended for the other. Some four years younger than Rancé, Bellefonds came of a family distinguished in Church and State.[1] His father, Governor of Valognes, died when he was 12, and he was brought up under the supervision of one of his aunts, abbess of Rouen, largely by Jesuits. His aunt Judith became Mère Agnès, and another aunt, Marie, married the marquis de Villars. By 1668 Bellefonds had been appointed maréchal, and four years later, in Holy Week 1672, he made his first recorded stay at la Trappe. At that precise moment he incurred Louis's extreme displeasure by refusing to serve under the orders of Turenne, his junior, was sent in disgrace to Touraine, and is said to have considered permanent retirement at la Trappe, though such intentions are somewhat freely attributed to many of his contemporaries at times of crisis. By next year he was back in service again, at Maastricht and Tournai among other places, but in May 1674 he left Court once more, implicated this time in the departure of Mme de la Vallière to take the veil. The death of Turenne in 1675 may have been a factor in the recovery of his fortunes, and at all events he held high command in various theatres of war, finally at Cap de la Hougue, before he died Governor of Vincennes in 1694.

For more than twenty years he maintained a regular correspondence with Rancé, a substantial part of which has survived in the original,[2] and though the tone is invariably formal (Rancé always called him Monseigneur), an unmistakable intimacy lies behind the gracious compliments. Perhaps exceptionally for a courtier and a distinguished soldier, Bellefonds seems to have been consistently devout, and if he ever underwent a spiritual conversion it is not recorded. His evident attachment to his Carmelite aunt, to sœur Anne-Marie d'Épernon, and to Mme de la Vallière (who calls him her director) no doubt explains the stability of his spiritual life and his natural sympathy for Rancé. Bossuet was his close friend, as were Vialart of Châlons, successive

---

[1] In view of his full and varied life, it is strange that so little work has been done on Bellefonds. The *DBF* is quite informative, so is Lair, *Louise de la Vallière*, and these provide the basis of what follows, but there appears to be no study devoted to him.

[2] Dubois had access to it when it was still in private hands, but quite frequently misquotes (or misreads) dates. At some stage E. Levesque acquired the collection, and on his death it passed to the BN (n.a. 12959).

Bishops of Séez (Forcoal and Savary), le Camus, Barillon, and other prelates known for their piety. He made regular retreats at la Trappe, and also at least once at Val-Richer (to Rancé's disapproval) and inevitably became involved in the religious controversies of the day. Abbé François de Luthumière[1] founded a seminary at Valognes, Bellefonds's home town, and soon fell foul of his diocesan, the Bishop of Coutances, for allegedly Jansenist tendencies. As early as 1675 Rancé was consulting with Bellefonds and Châlons to see what could be done to help. Eventually, in 1689, the seminary was closed, but it could hardly have lasted so long without Bellefonds's protection.

At about the same time, that is 1675, Rancé came to know two men whose acquaintance was to involve him and Bellefonds in considerable embarrassment for partisan reasons. The first, and younger, of the two was Henri-Joseph de Peyre, comte de Troisville[2] (also written, and pronounced, Tréville). Born in 1643 he underwent an initial conversion of some kind in 1666, but on the death of Henriette d'Angleterre, to whom he was closely attached, his conversion became definitive in 1670. He was a friend of Mme de Longueville, and perhaps through her, or more likely some Oratorian, wrote to Rancé early in 1673 and received strong encouragement in his design of devoting himself henceforth to religion.[3] At Mme de Longueville's suggestion he went in 1675[4] to consult Pavillon at Alet, whither Rancé and Barillon had gone before, though for him the journey was less unusual since he held an official post at Foix nearby (which he resigned in 1677). From 1674 to 1679 he stayed at the Institution de l'Oratoire, and remained a leading figure in the circles of the devout until his death in 1708, just four years after the King had vetoed his election to the Academy. Bellefonds was in touch with him by 1675 at the latest, and he was a friend also of Mme de Sablé, Mme de la Sablière, and Mme de La Fayette, thus closely connected with many of Rancé's intimates. Not long afterwards, in the summer of 1676, Rancé received a visit from another convert, a distant kins-

---

[1] See copy in *U* 3069 and above, p. 220. See also G. Hermant, *Mémoires*, vol. ii, p. 81.

[2] There is a useful entry in Moréri, see also Mesnard, *Pascal et les Roannez*, pp. 874–5.

[3] *M* 1214, 103, of 23 Feb. 1673.

[4] *TB* 557, Rancé to Mme de Longueville; *TB* 507 of 3 Mar 1675 to Tréville; and *TB* 588 and 616 of Dec. 1675 to Tréville and Alet.

man of Bellefonds, Charles, comte de Brancas,[1] (1618–81), son
of the first duc de Villars and father-in-law of the third. He had
been a close friend of Gaston, had enjoyed the favours of Mme
Scarron (later Mme de Maintenon) for a time, and had supported
Mme de la Vallière against the Queen Mother. Late in the day he
became converted and, like Tréville, was one of those who gave
pious addresses to the Carmelites through the grill. He is said to
have inspired La Bruyère for the portrait of Ménalque in the
Caractères.

Like so many others, the new convert was attracted to la
Trappe and seems to have impressed Rancé favourably, though
in the first letter to Bellefonds which speaks of him Rancé describes him as apparently Jansenist.[2] It looks as though Brancas
had tried to sound Rancé on the Jansenist issue, perhaps assuming
his sympathy in advance, because three unusually long and detailed letters written from August to November make Rancé's
position absolutely clear.[3] In the first of these (13 August 1676)
he deplores the ease with which people attach the label 'heretic'
or 'schismatic' as if they were saying of someone 'il a l'air pâle
et le visage mauvais', and then makes his own profession of complete orthodoxy and submission to the teachings of his superiors. At the end of October he returns to the charge, and
shows how delicate is the balance to be struck by anyone in his
position (28 October 1676): 'Je crains qu'après que je serai bien
lavé des soupçons du Jansénisme, il ne me reste une seconde
affaire, qui sera d'empêcher que l'on ne croie que je favorise le
parti contraire.' The morality of these others, that is Molinists, is
so corrupt that he is horrified to be associated with 'des sentiments que je condamne de toute la plénitude de mon cœur'. He
concludes very realistically: 'vous voyez bien que le parti que je
prends est tout propre à m'attirer tout le monde sur les bras et à ne
contenter personne.' This very long letter (twelve pages) further
indicates that Brancas has discussed la Trappe with Mme de
Guise, whom he would have known ever since sharing her
father's debauched life, and that Brancas and Tréville have together consulted him on the subject of the controversy about
fictions. In this and another letter written some three weeks later

[1] See article in *DBF* by Roman d'Amat.
[2] *BN* n.a. 12959, f. 47 of 27 Sept. 1676.
[3] Originals in *SS* (apparently from Levesque papers).

(21 November) Rancé gives a long and circumstantial account of how Beaufort had betrayed his confidence, and it is clear from similarly detailed explanations given to Bellefonds and the abbess of Leyme, for example, that Rancé was extremely angry and hurt at Beaufort's conduct,[1] but also anxious to exonerate himself by representing his case to as many friends as possible. Passing references in the same letter to the Oratorians Monchy and Amelot confirm that Brancas and Tréville moved in the same circles as most of Rancé's Parisian friends. A year later, in the only other surviving letter to Brancas, Rancé once again affirms his neutrality in the disputes currently dividing the Church and speaks in glowing terms of Mère Agnès, as well as le Camus.

It will be seen that with neither Brancas nor Tréville did Rancé show any hesitation in answering the most searching questions, and indeed showing them an unusual degree of confidence in view of the notorious indiscretion prevalent in Jansenist circles. Their friends were his friends; unlike them, he refused to be drawn into religious disputes, and there seems to have been no question at any time of assuming the role of director. None the less these two very soon involved both Rancé and Bellefonds in a most unfortunate situation.

In his first letter to Brancas, Rancé had defended his action in signing the Formulary like most of his contemporaries, but went on to speak in conciliatory terms of the Jansenists, now, since the Peace of the Church, 'dans la communion et dans le sein de l'Eglise. Elle les regarde comme ses enfants et je ne dois les regarder autrement que comme mes frères... je suis persuadé que les jansénistes n'ont point de mauvaise doctrine.' The indiscretion of some, and the malice of others, had inevitably brought accusations of Jansenism (or even Molinism) against Rancé, and by the end of 1678 nothing less than an official *démenti* could put the record straight. On 27 November Rancé received a letter from Bellefonds inviting such a *démenti*, and at once set to work to produce a long and celebrated statement dated 30 November 1678 of which countless copies were made, and which was even printed separately. In a covering letter,[2] also rather long, he writes: 'je souhaite que celle que je vous envoie soit telle que vous le voulez. J'y exprime toutes mes pensées dans la vérité et sincérité, c'est

---

[1] See above, pp. 128–129 and 186.
[2] Originals in *BN* n.a. 12959, ff. 73–83.

mon cœur qui parle...' He ends this covering letter by saying
that his friendship with Tréville is the main cause of the accusation of Jansenism, which could, of course, be extremely damaging
to both Bellefonds and himself just at the time when new persecution was about to begin. The actual *démenti* is as unequivocal as
possible: 'depuis que je ne suis plus du monde je n'ai jamais été
d'aucun parti que de celui de J.-C. et de son Eglise... J'ai toujours cru que je devois me soumettre à ceux que Dieu m'avoit
donnés pour supérieurs et pour pères (j'entends le pape et mon
évêque)...', and he stresses that he has banned all discussion of
Jansenism at la Trappe. He himself had always followed the
teaching of St. Thomas, though in fact the Jansenists themselves
claimed that their own teaching was the pure doctrine of St.
Augustine, perfectly consistent with that of St. Thomas. Perhaps
the most provocative statement in Rancé's letter is his unrepentant
admission that he signed the Formulary 'sans restriction et sans
réserve'. In a letter written to Bellefonds at the end of January
1679[1] Rancé expresses pleasure at the reception of his published
letter, even though it had not satisfied everyone.

Meanwhile the death of Mme de Longueville in April 1679
proved the final blow against the already precarious Peace of the
Church. Rancé had been attacked at length and in detail a few
weeks earlier for his letter to Bellefonds (in the Jansenist *Réponse...
d'un ecclésiastique...* of 9 February and 8 March)[2] and thereafter
took the greatest care in dealing with any known Jansenist
sympathizer. As he said (24 January 1679): 'la plupart des hommes
veulent des sectateurs et ne peuvent souffrir que l'on ait.. des
réserves quand il s'agit de leurs passions et de leurs sentiments.'
Brancas died at the beginning of 1681, but the damage had already
been done. It is henceforth very noticeable that when new names
crop up in the correspondence with Bellefonds the allusions are
polite and non-committal. Thus the comte de Saint-Géran (1641–
96), related to Bellefonds through his mother and a distinguished
soldier, or the marquis de Lassay, come to visit, exchange compliments, and that is all. Quite often Rancé asks Bellefonds for
services on behalf of some friend:[3] the abbé de Villars, Bellefonds's
nephew, commendatory abbot of Moutiers, is not co-operating as
the Abbot of Clairvaux would like in improvements to the mo-

---

[1] Ibid., f. 83 of 24 Jan. 1679 (the only fully autograph letter of the series).
[2] See *U* 3203.   [3] *BN* n.a. 12959, f. 92 of 23 Apr. 1682.

nastery buildings, and on Clairvaux's behalf Rancé asks Villars to cede part of his abbatial garden. More than three years later[1] Clairvaux has renewed his request and Rancé enlists the support of both Bellefonds and Mère Agnès to try to persuade Villars to be more helpful. Less insistently Rancé recommends the young son of his friend and neighbour, the marquis de Tourouvre, who is serving on board a vessel commanded by Bellefonds's son-in-law, Amfreville.[2] Later it is the turn of Favier, whose nephew is serving in the regiment commanded by Bellefonds's son.[3] Not content with general recommendation, Favier asks through Rancé that the boy should be given moral guidance by his commanding officer, a somewhat circuitous request which it is hard to believe came to anything.

From about 1689 there are frequent references to the various medicines sent by Bellefonds, not only for Rancé but for other ailing monks as well. There is a vivid description of a mishap occurring with a remedy against dropsy,[4] so fermented that 'dans le moment de l'ouverture la liqueur sortit avec impétuosité et donna presque jusqu'au plancher... et continua de sortir... comme d'un tuyau', but fortunately enough could be salvaged for the patient, who was later reported cured. This homely note was, however, soon followed by more weighty preoccupations. Recalled from retirement, Bellefonds was put in charge of the forces assembling in the Cotentin in support of James II, and Rancé took an extraordinarily keen interest in all that ensued. In September 1689[5] Rancé tells Bellefonds: 'je ne puis me remettre des affaires d'Irlande.' In April next year the sudden death of the Dauphine casts a further gloom over the correspondence; in July the Battle of the Boyne removes any lingering hope of James's swift restoration; and on 24 November, shortly after arriving back in France, James paid his first visit to la Trappe. Rancé wrote Bellefonds on 29 November 1690[6] an extremely enthusiastic account of the King and his visit (Bellefonds had had to leave in too much of a hurry for conversation), and almost at once copies of this letter began to circulate widely, arousing very mixed feelings. Later the same year the death of Mère Agnès, old though she was, came as a sad blow, and increasingly bad health

[1] Ibid., f. 111 of 25 Nov. 1685.   [2] Ibid., f. 101 of 15 Apr. 1683.
[3] Ibid., f. 137 of 26 Apr. 1690.   [4] Ibid., f. 123 of 4 July 1689.
[5] Ibid., f. 133 of 5 Sept. 1689.   [6] Ibid., f. 142.

afflicted both Rancé and Bellefonds. Low in spirits, Rancé was still more dejected at the naval disaster of la Hougue, and took it so much to heart that he comments himself on his inability to keep silence. 'Cet évènement m'a causé une douleur sensible,' he wrote in June 1692,[1] 'les conseils de Dieu sont impénétrables, mais se pourrait-il faire que la plus injuste de toutes les causes qui fût jamais triomphât de la meilleure?' In August the death of Bellefonds's son-in-law, Amfreville, on active service was yet another blow in the continuing series of disasters, public and private. Rightly or wrongly Bellefonds had been blamed for the failure of the campaign, and when he died at Vincennes on 5 December 1694 he had had his full share of grief and disappointment.

Even with Favier, whom he knew for longer, Rancé did not cover so complete a range of topics as he did in his correspondence with Bellefonds, and in any case the relationship with his old tutor could never be quite the same as that with a friend of the same age, particularly one so influential in public life. Jansenism and Protestantism, the rebuilding of a monastery and the pious writings of a Carmelite nun, battles and politics—all the preoccupations of the day are discussed in these letters, together with domestic affairs, like medicine or proposed postulants for la Trappe. At every turn of Bellefonds's eventful life, in disgrace or in favour, Rancé shares his friend's feelings and sends texts for meditation or more personal encouragement. It is obviously not possible to assess the influence of one man on the other in such a relationship, nor even the precise role of Bellefonds in introducing such men as Brancas, Tréville, or even James II, but the regularity and duration of the correspondence, and the easy sharing of confidences give more than a hint of an intimacy even greater than that enjoyed with Bossuet, their mutual friend.

Another aristocratic friend of Rancé and Bellefonds is a rather special case in several respects. One of Rancé's first problems when he decided to give up all his worldly possessions was the disposal of the great estate at Véretz, originally acquired by his father. After much difficulty he finally sold it in 1662 to the abbé d'Effiat and his nephew, Armand-Charles, future duc de Mazarin (1632–1713).[2] The latter, son of the duc de la Meilleraye, was imprudent enough to marry Hortense Mancini, niece of Cardinal Mazarin,

---

[1] Ibid., f. 159 of 9 June 1692.   [2] See L. Bossebœuf, *Le Château de Véretz*.

and obliged to take the name Mazarin,[1] but by 1671 his wife had finally abandoned him and went to live in London, where she died in 1699, the close (though apparently platonic) friend of Saint-Évremond. Her sister Marie, it may be observed, did no better, and, abandoning her husband, Prince Colonna, led an equally errant and unedifying life, sometimes in company with Hortense. The initial link between Rancé and Mazarin was thus a business one, but Bellefonds was a mutual friend (and his son married the duc's daughter Marie-Olympe in 1681) so that it was natural that relations should continue on a friendly basis. At the end of 1679 Rancé lost his brother-in-law, the comte d'Albon, and wrote to Mazarin of his edifying death; next year the whole estate of Véretz passed by agreement with Effiat to Mazarin, whom Rancé congratulated on his acquisition. The same letter (2 June 1680)[2] is something of a mystery, for Rancé reports to Mazarin on the recent visit of 'un gentilhomme de Madagascar' sent by the duc to try his vocation at la Trappe. The man's name, his subsequent fate, and indeed his connection with Mazarin remain unknown, and everything about the incident sharpens curiosity in vain.

There is a slight indication that Rancé may have offered Mazarin advice and comfort in his conjugal difficulties in 1675 (the addressee is not named, but the details fit), but in 1682 a new scandal overwhelmed the unfortunate duc, this time involving his daughter Marie-Charlotte. There is mention of a quarrel, now patched up, with Bellefonds in a letter of April 1682,[3] and then in September Rancé wrote to Mazarin,[4] and a week later[5] to Bellefonds, politely declining to give advice on grounds of incompetence, but recommending either le Camus or P. Monchy. Mazarin had apparently solicited the views of three friends, of whom Rancé was one, on the subject of his daughter's marriage, but Rancé refused to be drawn, and as late as May 1683 repeated his refusal (probably to Bellefonds).[6] What had happened was in

---

[1] Nobody has much good to say for Mazarin; Mme de Sévigné and Saint-Simon are contemptuous, but all the evidence suggests that the virtue he most conspicuously lacked was common sense.

[2] *TB* 1293; dom Jean Leclercq published this with a note in *Collectanea*, xxviii, 1966, pp. 68–70, but failed, however, to decipher either the name of Mazarin or that of Véretz.

[3] *BN* n.a. 12959, f. 92.   [4] *TB* 1768 of 13 Sept. 1682.

[5] *BN* n.a. 12959, f. 98 of 21 Sept. 1682.   [6] *BN* 24123, f. 67 of 3 May 1683.

the best traditions of that mercurial family: Mazarin's daughter
had been abducted from the convent at Chaillot by her lover, the
marquis de Richelieu, great-nephew of the Cardinal (the relationship adds a further touch of irony) and the young couple had fled
to England, where, of course, Mazarin's estranged wife was living.
Faced with *fait accompli*, Mazarin first tried ineffectually to assert
his authority and then in desperation turned to three friends
(according to Mme de Sévigné, le Camus, Rancé, and Henri
Arnauld, Bishop of Angers).[1] Inevitably he had to give his consent to the marriage, in 1683, but, as Mme de Sévigné wrote, 'le
moyen de ne pas perdre patience avec un tel fou?' Nevertheless
Rancé did not lose patience, and on 12 March 1684[2] sent Mazarin
the Act of Association requested earlier, commenting 'il n'y a
guère de chose plus fâcheuse à supporter que la situation dans
laquelle... vous êtes à l'égard du monde', but it is divine, not
human, justice that counts. There is no record of further contact
between Rancé and Mazarin, nor even mention of him in letters
to Bellefonds or others, and as Governor of Alsace the duc may
have lost interest in la Trappe. He maintained his reputation for
eccentricity, and Saint-Simon is as scathing about him as Mme de
Sévigné had been, but it is interesting that he should have turned,
albeit in vain, to Rancé for advice in a crisis, and that Rancé
should have persisted in patient friendship despite the defects of
Mazarin's character, which he could scarcely have failed to observe.

Different from any of those so far discussed, Rancé's relationship with James II is in fact unique: first because James was a king,
though dispossessed, with all that meant for the passionately
royalist Rancé, and then, by a fortunate accident, the correspondence with James is the only one of which both sides have been
largely preserved. Over a period of ten years from 1690 James
wrote 38 letters, of which copies still exist, and Rancé 18, together with another dozen or so (plus two to the Queen) recorded
but now lost.[3] There must have been other letters, and in addition

---

[1] See Mme de Sévigné, *Lettres*, ii, p. 917 of 23 Dec. 1682.

[2] *TC* II/262.

[3] Rancé's original letters are all at Windsor, and have been published (not complete in all cases) in *Stuart Papers*. James's widow ordered that authenticated copies
of the letters should be made on his death, and a notebook containing eighteenth-
century copies of James's now lost letters was acquired by Tournoüer (MS 13)
and is now with his papers near Alençon. Internal evidence, and comparison with
Rancé's letters, leave no room for doubt concerning the authenticity of these
copies. See also article by M. L. Serrent, 'Une correspondance inédite...'

James came to la Trappe every year, sometimes with the Queen, for a brief visit.

As already mentioned James came to la Trappe for the first time on 24 November 1690, and on his return to Court (he had his own at Saint-Germain-en-Laye) wrote to Rancé on 8 December proposing formally that they should start a correspondence: the history of France and England showed that 'on peut être saint et grand roi à la fois', and he would value Rancé's advice. It is a little hard to see just how James applied his chosen examples of Edward the Confessor and St. Louis to his own situation, but he was, of course, by no means reconciled to lifelong exile even after the Boyne. Rancé's reply, of 21 December 1690,[1] is just what one would expect of any close friend of Bossuet: it is God's pleasure that kings should go about with pomp and circumstance 'qui les rendent redoutables à leurs ennemis, et qui les fassent craindre, aimer et respecter de leurs peuples, mais il ne veut pas qu'ils s'y attachent, ni qu'ils s'en élèvent'. From then on the letters pursue their somewhat cautious way, with James rather evidently treating Rancé as a person of almost oracular distinction, and Rancé combining diplomatic respect with spiritual frankness as best he can. Secondary figures in the correspondence are the Drummond brothers, James, Duke of Perth, and John, Earl of Melfort; the former of whom was apparently converted in about 1685 after reading the papers attributed to Charles II regarding his own conversion and after correspondence with Bossuet;[2] while the other accompanied James on several of his visits to la Trappe. To these Scottish nobles should be added George Douglas, Earl of Dumbarton, with whom also Rancé was directly in touch. It was, incidentally, most probably through Perth, himself perhaps informed by Bossuet or Barillon, or both, that James first heard of la Trappe. It is therefore interesting that James's second letter to Rancé should enclose the memoirs of Charles II (and of James's first wife, the Duchess of York) which had played such a decisive part in converting Perth. Early in the spring of 1691 Rancé had a bad fall that nearly cost him his life, and James was much mortified at the refusal of Louis XIV to allow him to follow the campaign at Mons, where his presence would have been an unwelcome liability, both personally and politically, but Rancé replied to

---

[1] *SP* p. 59.   [2] See Joly, *James Drummond, duc de Perth*.

James's complaint most diplomatically. In July James received an account of Santéna's conversion,[1] and this prompted some interesting exchanges on the value of moral excellence in Protestants. Rancé is unusually harsh in attributing such virtue to the devil 'imitateur de J.-C.... il a eu ses confesseurs, ses martyres, et il n'y a rien qu'il ne fasse pour jeter les peuples dans l'illusion'.[2]

Almost exactly a year after his first visit, Rancé sent James an Act of Association at the king's request,[3] and for once the question of influence can be tentatively resolved. In acknowledging receipt of the document, James writes (2 December 1691): 'j'ai commencé à communier plus souvent que je ne faisois, me trouvant dans l'état... que vous m'aviez dit qu'il falloit pour cela.' He admits that his first visit had been inspired mainly by curiosity, but that since then 'je songeai plus sérieusement à mon salut'. Obviously the king's regular confessor (the Jesuit, Sanders), and others whom he saw all the time, had more opportunity of influencing him than had Rancé, but precisely because James's experience at la Trappe was so completely different from anything else he knew, and so concentrated in its intensity, it is perfectly reasonable to believe that Rancé played a decisive role in the king's spiritual evolution. Small details reinforce that impression: at one point James asks Rancé how he can make best use of his now frequent bouts of insomnia, for at 4 in the morning it is not 'à propos de me lever pour prier ou louer le bon Dieu'.[4] Rancé's answer has unfortunately not been preserved, but the fact that James should consult him on such a point is significant.

The subsequent course of the correspondence is predictable and rather melancholy, overshadowed as it is by failing health and waning hopes. Early in 1694 James confesses that he sees little or no prospect of crossing the Channel again; a year later the death of his daughter, Queen Mary, is all the more painful to him because her Anglican chaplains falsely assured her that she was innocent of any serious sin, so that she died impenitent. Rancé for his part regularly sends James memoirs and *relations*, answering various spiritual problems and encouraging James to persevere.

---

[1] Known thereafter as fr. Palémon.   [2] *SP*, p. 64.   [3] *SP*, p. 65.
[4] (Alençon) Tournoüer MS., letter of 21 Oct. 1692. The official life by F. Bretonneau, *Abrégé de la vie de Jacques II*, says very little about such problems, and there is some reason to suppose that no one but Rancé knew of them.

After returning from his annual visit, James tells Rancé,[1] 'il est très nécessaire de se souvenir de la Trappe et de tout ce qu'on y a vu et ouy, pour ne se laisser pas entraîner par le mauvais exemple de beaucoup de courtisans.' Not all, however, lead evil lives, and he has just seen at the Camaldules (at Grosbois) the comte du Charmel, a compulsive gambler who had been dramatically converted and had become a friend of Rancé, so much happier now than his former companions.[2] James in his turn sends a *relation* of the edifying death of a converted Protestant named Hales (former Governor of the Tower of London and James's companion in flight), and by a curious coincidence raises a ghost of some twenty years before in reporting the scandalous conduct of the pseudo-Luzancy, whom Rancé had briefly received on Le Roy's recommendation under his real name of Beauchâteau before he crossed to England and a successful career as ecclesiastical confidence trickster.[3] 1696 saw an abortive attempt to mount an expedition from Calais and Boulogne, but 'Dieu qui est le maître des vents... n'a pas voulu qu'il nous ait été favorable'.[4] A consolation prize in the form of the Polish crown, for which his name had been put forward, did not appeal to him, and James seemed resigned to his fate. It is interesting that several of the letters between Rancé and James were delivered by Rancé's nephew (it is not clear which) and that James showed favour also to Rancé's younger brother, the chevalier.

An odd incident at the beginning of 1697 proves that James's interest in religious matters was anything but formal or perfunctory. James had been reading in manuscript Rancé's 'Instructions pour la conduite d'une dame' (Mme de Guise), and had come across a passage which had been wrongly transcribed, 'car de la manière qu'il est on pourroit le tourner en un sens à votre désavantage', and experts whom he has consulted agree 'cela n'étoit pas comme il falloit'.[5] Rancé's answer, fortunately preserved, explains the king's concern: James's copy read: 'il n'est venu que pour ceux qui marcheroient après lui dans les voies qu'il a tracées' instead of 'il n'est venu que pour inspirer et pour apprendre à ceux qui viendroient après lui à marcher par les voies qu'il leur aura tracées'. Neither Creation nor Redemption

[1] Letter of 9 Oct. 1695.   [2] On du Charmel see below, pp. 274–275.
[3] See above, p. 121.   [4] Letter of 12 May 1696.
[5] *SP*, pp. 122–3.

could save all men because not all wished to follow. The first version is clearly Jansenist (or even Protestant), and at a time when James was facing accusations (partly justified) of harbouring Jansenists in his entourage he was as sensitive as Rancé had been to any slur on his Catholic orthodoxy.

Meanwhile James and Rancé were both involved in personal crises. In October 1697 James tells Rancé how William's emissary Bentinck, had vainly tried to secure from Louis James's expulsion before concluding the Peace at Rijswijk in September, but his position had become an inglorious one. In March 1698[1] James looks back on his life, and concludes that he would not have known the truth (of Catholicism) but for his twelve years' exile in Catholic countries, and, though he was formally converted before his second marriage, it took the final disaster to bring him back to a Christian life: 'il me falloit ce voyage [à la Trappe] pour me donner la connoissance de moi-même, et pour me faire mépriser tout ce qui paroist grand dans le monde et ne s'y attacher pas.'

That same year opposition to Abbot Gervaise was mounting; James briefly met Maisne, 'un si honnête homme', with the abbé Boileau when they were between two visits to Court to discuss the Estrées affair; then Gervaise, through Rancé, asked James to take no action on his behalf with Louis. A visit to la Trappe did nothing to turn James against Gervaise, and on his return he wrote to Rancé[2] to say that he had tried to 'disculper le nouveau abbé de ce que son zèle pour l'augmentation de leur réforme en d'autres endroits l'avoit poussé à faire un peu brusquement le pas', but unfortunately the affair of les Clairets 'fait bien du bruit à son désavantage'. By Christmas Gervaise's resignation was public knowledge, and Rancé reassured James in a New Year letter that life at la Trappe has hardly been disturbed by the intrigues of two or three misguided but essentially well-meaning persons.

The last few letters are more and more funereal. Rancé proposes a respectable married couple to look after the temporal affairs of the abbey of Montmartre, given as a present to James by Louis, and no further word survives from him, though James continues to acknowledge letters up to the end of August 1700. For his part, James devotes one letter[3] to gloomy reflections on the recent deaths of the Queen of Portugal, the King of Denmark, and the dowager Duchess of Modena (his mother-in-law), an-

[1] Letter of 15 Feb. 1698.   [2] Letter of 26 Sept. 1698.   [3] 28 Apr. 1700.

other to William's continuing persecution of Catholics though 'je prie comme on est obligé tous les jours pour la conversion de ce pauvre malheureux Prince d'Orange'. His last letter (20 September 1700) is very dispirited: Rancé's ill health prompts James to quote St. John Climachus on death: Maisne has just recovered from a serious illness; Anne (James's daughter) has just lost her 11-year-old son; the only one in better health is William, and he is in Holland; the first Catholic priest has been sent to Newgate under the new penal laws—the prospect is bleak indeed. The news of Rancé's death a few weeks later came as no surprise, but was none the less a hard blow for the exiled king, who was himself dead before a year was out.

The epilogue is provided by Perth, who at the Queen's command wrote two letters to the new abbot, Jacques de la Cour, describing James's end.[1] According to the king, it was to la Trappe and Rancé 'qu'il devoit tout ce qu'il avoit dans le cœur de sentiments véritablement chrétiens'. A second letter (9 October 1701) adds the detail that James always kept by him a cross sent by Rancé 'et la vénération qu'il avoit pour ce saint homme a duré dans son cœur jusqu'à la fin'. The same letter adds a valuable indication of the authenticity of the letters sent by James, for the Queen requests the abbot to have copied without delay the letters sent by her late husband to Rancé and to send her the copies duly marked with the seals of the abbot and of Maisne. Though the originals have perished, the extant copies can certainly be accepted as genuine.

This rather strange correspondence also includes an unsigned and undated document, in James's hand originally, of which a copy survives.[2] Headed simply 'consultation', it betrays an oddly anxious attitude about the hereafter. James asks Rancé, 'sous le secret', whether he should avail himself of the prayers of the Church 'pour tâcher d'obtenir de Dieu d'abréger le temps que je dois être dans le purgatoire... [ou] si ce n'est pas mieux fait d'estre content de tout souffrir jusqu'au temps prescript, et de donner cet argent qu'on laisse ordinairement pour prier pour son âme aux pauvres'. He wonders too whether he should pay the customary alms while still alive or leave payment to his heirs (this sounds slightly mistrustful towards the heirs). Just what

---

[1] Copies in Archives Nationales, K 1717, no. 26.
[2] Included as the last item in the copy.

prompted this gratuitous inquiry, just why he was unable to satisfy his conscience by recourse to the royal confessor, it is impossible to say. It is, however, fair to guess that Rancé advised him to give his money to the poor (as he himself had done) and certain that whatever Rancé said James would try to do it.

James only too clearly suffered from a troubled conscience and in his heart quite probably associated his public failure with his private sins. He was, like so many of Rancé's noble correspondents, a convert, not so much to Catholicism as to Christianity, and it is perhaps for this reason that one senses a much greater degree of tension in this correspondence than in that with Bellefonds, whom James knew well and visited at his Norman home. The solid and practical piety of Bellefonds carried him through adversity and disgrace, not wholly unlike that suffered by James, with no apparent anguish or heart-searching. Bellefonds's retreats at la Trappe no doubt restored his spiritual vigour, as happens with most people, and he may even be said to have needed these periods of reflection and withdrawal; but for James urgency rather than quiet confidence is the note so often struck. It may reasonably be claimed on the evidence just examined that James believed Rancé and la Trappe to have affected his inner life dramatically for the better, and while this view can only be objectively assessed in the context of all the other voluminous evidence regarding James's later years, it is highly interesting and significant in itself.

It is incidentally noteworthy that the last choir monk to be professed in Rancé's lifetime was the 22-year-old frère Alexis,[1] born Robert Graeme of Edinburgh, kinsman of Montrose on his father's side and of Perth on his mother's; the young man died only seven months later. Perth himself came down for the occasion, on 25 October 1700, which was accompanied by the abjuration (from Protestantism) of Colonel Graeme, Robert's father, and followed by Rancé's death two days later. James on his death-bed exhorted the young man's cousin, Murray, also to accept conversion. An elder brother was already a Capuchin, and wrote an edifying account of frère Alexis's life and death which was published later. No other direct Jacobite connection with la Trappe is recorded during the lifetime of Rancé or James, but visitors certainly came, and Bossuet was in close touch with James

[1] See *Relations*, iii and Joly, *Drummond*, pp. 354 seq.

and many members of his entourage, like Perth and Graeme, to whom he no doubt recommended la Trappe.

The full list of noble and influential correspondents of Rancé will almost certainly never be known, because, even if mere exchanges of compliments are disregarded, a very large number of letters on business requiring immediate action went out to various people in power, of whom most were no more than acquaintances, but among them were a few close friends. Legal figures are naturally prominent in this kind of official correspondence, since it was mostly questions of dispute over land, or privilege for publication, or authority to accept recruits from other orders, that obliged Rancé to involve himself in the world of administration. One such correspondent was Louis Le Fèvre de Caumartin (1624–87),[1] who had been Retz's agent before becoming Intendant in Champagne (with Clairvaux included in his jurisdiction). A protracted correspondence with him lasting from 1680 to 1685 over the case of dom Joseph Garreau, former prior of Bugey, then exiled to Fontfroide, and finally allowed to come to la Trappe, shows how time-consuming each individual case could be.

Another of Rancé's correspondents and distinguished friends was Achille de Harlay (1639–1712),[2] brother of François, later Archbishop of Paris, who in 1689 became Premier Président. Letters surviving from the period 1683–9 show that Rancé kept regularly in touch with so valuable a contact, sending him books and soliciting his approval for them. Although the tone is friendly and, by contemporary standards, warm, Rancé's letters to both Harlay and Caumartin hardly go beyond official business. At one time Caumartin, a friend of Barillon, had been intimate enough to visit Rancé in his first retreat at Véretz,[3] and relations with the Harlay brothers, and indeed their religious sister, had also been close, but neither Caumartin nor Achille de Harlay can be said to have been in any sense under Rancé's influence in later years.

[1] See article by M. Prevost in *DBF*. The letters (all originals) seem to be all in private hands, and are recorded in the BN *Fichiers Charavay* and *Autographes de Troussures* (ed. Denis), with a further one preserved in a copy in *TC* II/83.

[2] Seven original letters in BN 17418, 17419, 17420, 17423 for the years, respectively, 1683, 1684, 1685, and 1689.

[3] Rancé to Andilly, 10 Sept. 1658 in *A* 6035, f. 244. It should be mentioned that there was also a Jacques Le Fèvre de Caumartin (? brother) with whom Rancé was transacting legal business in 1663, but his friendship with Louis is not in question (see *Docs. du Minutier Central...*, p. 250).

With other distinguished public figures his relations were personal rather than official, and it seems to be they, not he, who are asking for favours. Paul Barillon,[1] like his episcopal brother, had been a friend from the earliest days, but service as ambassador in London from 1677 until James's expulsion in 1689 made contact difficult. Rancé heard news of him through his brother and mutual friends like Pinette; he sent condolences on the death of his mother in 1682, and showed intense and sympathetic interest throughout the final illness in 1691. Shortly before the end he wrote to urge him to profit from illness to prepare for death as, he is sure, so 'instruit et éclairé' a person will do.[2] Paul was a member of the circle that included La Fontaine, Mme de Sévigné, Mme de la Sablière, and Mme de La Fayette; in London he had known intimately Saint-Évremond and the runaway duchesse de Mazarin, to whom he certainly talked about Rancé; and about 1686 Colbert is recorded as criticizing him for irreligion. For all that, it was almost certainly he who first introduced Perth and James II to la Trappe by showing them the *relations*, and, irreligious or not, he obviously respected Rancé, who in return never wavered in his esteem and affection. Other members of the family maintained contact with Rancé to the end, many of them rendering useful services in their official capacity, like Antoine de Morangis (another brother), Intendant at Alençon from 1677 to 1682 and then at Caen until his death in 1686, and sons and nephews never failed to visit la Trappe to pay their respects.

Another *conseiller d'état* personally influenced by Rancé was Honoré Courtin (1626–1703).[3] He had been with Paul Barillon as ambassador to Cologne in 1673, and in his time had also been ambassador to London. As old age approached, he began to go blind with cataract: moreover he had a son in the Church who 'menait une vie de crapule', to quote the succinct biographer, and can have afforded him little consolation. He was a childhood friend of Rancé, had many contacts with la Trappe, like the Barillons, and in 1686 paid a visit there with his friend and fellow *conseiller* Fieubet.[4] Like so many visitors, he was struck by the promise of peace and inner happiness and considered retreat there,

---

[1] See article by M. Prevost in *DBF* giving details on all the members of the family.
[2] See *P* f. 779.
[3] See article by Roman d'Amat in *DBF*.
[4] The fullest details regarding both Courtin and Fieubet are in the memoirs of M. de Saint-Louis, *AE* 1442, pp. 160 seq.

probably, at that age, as a layman sharing some of the community's exercises. A year later (30 October 1687)[1] Rancé wrote to him kindly, but firmly, saying that God wanted him where he was and that the loss of so many friends should encourage him to prepare for the end.

His companion, Gaspard de Fieubet, fared rather differently. He too had had a distinguished career, serving as Chancellor to the Queen and *commissaire* in Brittany, but on the death of his wife in 1686 he seems to have envisaged the possibility of retreat even more seriously than Courtin. After the first visit of two days he is said to have maintained a regular correspondence with Rancé, but the exact course of their discussions can only be surmised.[2] Quite suddenly, in July 1691, he disappeared from society and Mme de Sévigné is only one who comments on the general amazement when it was learned that he had retired to the recently (1642) founded Camaldolese hermitage at Grosbois, just outside Paris to live, like his friend Saint-Louis at la Trappe, not as a monk, but in seclusion and, in his case, looking after the poor in an almshouse built for that purpose. He is known to have remained in touch with Rancé, and to have paid a visit to la Trappe just before his death in 1694. Nothing is mentioned of the reasons prompting his choice of monastery, but Rancé is known to have played an active part in his final decision, and the initial conversion dates from the visit to la Trappe five years before his retreat.

To the same class of distinguished courtiers or public servants belongs Louis de Ligny, comte du Charmel (1646–1714).[3] He had become an *habitué* of la Trappe a little before 1686, and thereafter remained a lifelong friend. He had been a worldly and popular member of Court, personally acceptable to Louis and a conspicuously successful gambler. Although he did not, like Fieubet, go into formal retreat, his conversion caused a similar stir, and he became something of a repentant prodigal figure. James II, as mentioned above, met him in 1695 at Grosbois (after Fieubet's death) and commented on his evident happiness compared to that of his former worldly companions. He retained a wide circle of acquaintances, including such lay friends of la Trappe as Paul Barillon and Saint-Simon, as well as Gerbais and Marcel, of Saint-Jacques, and in Rancé's last years is constantly mentioned in

[1] Copy in *TC* II/189.   [2] See Saint-Louis, loc. cit.
[3] See Saint-Simon, *Mémoires*, i, p. 561.

connection with the affairs of the abbey, where he made a practice
of spending each Lent. His original conversion, according to
Saint-Simon, was inspired by reading an apology for Christianity
by the Huguenot Abbadie, but, whether this is true or not, he
withdrew to the Institution de l'Oratoire, whence it was spiritually
only a step to la Trappe. Again according to Saint-Simon,[1] 'il
passoit sa vie dans une pénitence dure jusqu'à l'indiscrétion...
c'étoit un homme d'une grande dureté pour soi.'

By a curious chance Rancé's only known contact with the
Camaldules[2] involved both Fieubet and du Charmel. In a letter
to Gerbais of 31 August 1693[3] Rancé says that he is sending 'le
R.P. Majeur' (the title of the superior of the Camaldules) to
Fieubet and du Charmel 'pour lui ôter toute pensée de suivre son
dessein'; he should instead remain in his Congregation and edify
the public. The order had only been introduced into France some
sixty years earlier (it was of earlier foundation than that of Cîteaux,
but had not spread much), and it seems that Grosbois never
numbered much more than half a dozen or so hermits but like
other small, strict orders, became affected by Jansenism. This
reference to the R.P. Majeur would remain mysterious but for
the fact that two years later Rancé wrote to Gerbais again about a
monk who had gone from the Camaldules to Berryer's priory of
Perrecy,[4] where he became professed, and at exactly the same time
(October 1695)[5] Beaufort wrote also to Gerbais defending his
action in taking in two other Camaldules to Sept-Fons, and moreover James II saw du Charmel at Grosbois that same week. The
conclusion is inescapable that du Charmel and Gerbais were acting
on specific instructions from Rancé to prevent the disintegration
of this small community. The involvement of Beaufort and Berryer
is a further example of the extraordinary ramifications of Rancé's
indirect influence.

Like so many able-bodied noblemen of the time, du Charmel
had served in the field, but his conversion struck the courtier
rather than the soldier. Apart from Bellefonds, however, the
number of professional soldiers attracted to la Trappe is large
enough to be significant. The attraction naturally varied in in-

---

[1] Ibid.

[2] For the scanty information available on the French Camaldolese see articles in
Dict. de Théologie catholique and *Dict. d'histoire et géog. eccl.*

[3] *BN* n.a. 12959, f. 202.

[4] *A* 5172, f. 148. On Berryer and Perrecy see above, pp. 154-155.   [5] *A* 5172.

tensity and duration, from the Saténas and Muces who came and stayed to die as monks to the passing visits of, for instance, the maréchal d'Humières, curious to see Saténa as a monk, but it is not hard to see the psychology behind it. A letter to the prince de Soubise makes the point.[1] Rancé had known him very well through his mother, Mme de Montbazon, and remained closely in touch with the whole family throughout his life. In 1677 Soubise wrote to Rancé from the camp at Valenciennes, in itself an interesting detail, a letter of which the contents are unknown, but which can hardly have excluded mention of religion. Rancé wrote back to say that he continues to pray for Soubise's conversion, and that, while dying for one's king (for Louis at any rate) is to give one's life for God, it is wrong to court needless dangers. In other letters to Soubise he harps on the theme of conversion, but the letter to Valenciennes clearly makes the point that men in the continual presence of sudden death need some ultimate reality to grasp at, and this they found in the total and uncompromising renunciation of earthly for spiritual values at la Trappe.

A small group of men illustrates the way the military mind was influenced by la Trappe. When Rancé first went there he encountered such opposition that his life was threatened, and he was only saved from injury, or worse, by the intervention of a local military man, M. le Honreux de Saint-Louis.[2] After distinguished service as a cavalry officer, Saint-Louis found himself in 1684 temporarily unemployed with a severe eye infection, and withdrew, with golden opinions from such great men as Turenne and even the King, to the neighbourhood of la Trappe. At first he stayed with a friend, the commandeur de Laval, at Gournay near Verneuil, but then for some reason tired of a life of pointless hedonism and went over to see Rancé. He soon made up his mind, exchanged one discipline for another, and took up residence in the former abbatial lodgings dating from commendatory days. There he led a life of retreat, but by no means total seclusion (with two horses and three servants), until he died, and met many of those who came, like Saint-Simon, to visit the monastery. He has left a full account of his conversion, which leaves no doubt that the

---

[1] *TB* 819 of 28 Mar. 1677.

[2] See p. 16, above. Apart from his autobiography he left copious spiritual reflections (*AE* 1440–4).

different but equally demanding life of a soldier and a monk met his particular needs.

Not long after the conversion of Saint-Louis his erstwhile host was persuaded to reconsider his own position. Like Rancé's brother, Laval was a Knight of Malta, but unlike him had never taken the spiritual side of his obligations at all seriously. At the same time, or a little later, another Knight of Malta, the commandeur de Mareuil, a friend of du Charmel, was also in touch with Rancé, who began a correspondence with both. At Laval's request he sent a very detailed rule of life,[1] from getting up to going to bed, indicating the various duties appropriate to their calling, such as almsgiving or visiting the sick, as well as war, with instructions for prayer at different moments of the day. By the end of 1688 he commends Laval for his edifying conduct, and bids him to be always ready for the last journey. Laval, in fact, went off to Malta to spend three years of obligatory residence, and on his return to France was prevented from seeing Rancé again by an urgent and fatal operation to remove a stone. His conversion seems to have been genuine and lasting.[2] Meanwhile, in 1689, Rancé wrote to Mareuil,[3] refusing to give any more instructions for fear of finding himself accused of wanting to change everything. These men, it must be remembered, belonged to an international order with long-standing traditions and rules, even if by the seventeenth century membership for many may have involved little more than social distinction. Other Knights of Malta surely figured among Rancé's visitors and correspondents, and his brother must have introduced some at various times, but though no record survives of names other than Laval and Mareuil, Rancé's relations with them, and Saint-Louis, are sufficient evidence of how he advised military men in general and Knights of Malta in particular.

[1] TC II/268 of 2 Nov. 1688 and TC I/27 (s.d.).
[2] Full details in Saint-Louis, loc. cit.
[3] TC II/103 of 16 July 1689. Quesnel also wrote to him in 1681 at Marseilles (U 1085), which is significant.

13. The Great: Women

ALL the men with whom Rancé corresponded could, if they so wished, visit la Trappe and reasonably expect to talk to him. In such cases as those of Bellefonds, James II, Brancas, and Tréville visits were perhaps the most important element in the relationship, but with women the situation, and thus the relationship, was totally different, though it varied considerably as between individuals. Up to 1675 a certain number of Rancé's friends, both men and women, could still hope to see him, at least for a moment, when he came to Paris on business of the order. His break with the world of *salon* society, back in 1657, by no means constituted a break with all the individuals composing that society, and many of them kept up friendships with him which were only interrupted by death. Thus Mme de Saint-Loup, the sisters of Mme de Montbazon, Mlles de Vertus and de Goëllo, Mme de Sablé, and others never lost touch with him. Similarly through them, or other friends, he came to know, sometimes quite late in life, such women as Mme de la Sablière, Mme de La Fayette, or Mlle de la Trémoille, none of whom he appears to have met. After 1675 he made no exceptions, not even for his own sister, Mme d'Albon (nor indeed for Thérèse), much as he would have liked to see her, but where inclination could be sternly repressed, obedience to rank overrode all other rules. When Mme de Guise, the daughter of Rancé's late patron, Gaston d'Orléans, or her sister, the Grand Duchess of Tuscany, asked to see him it was a command, and even the cloister had to be opened for them.[1] Moreover, when such great ladies came, they brought attendants, and it is known, for example, that at least one of Rancé's correspondents was able on occasion to talk to him during such official visits. Over the period of more than a dozen years that Mme de Guise used to come over from Alençon quite a number of noble ladies must have been able to meet Rancé without stretching the rules, or at

---

[1] Canon Law has always recognized this right of royal ladies, and Rancé fully accepted it, explicitly stating his position in a letter to Gourdan of 27 Aug. 1682 (TB 1745). Among those known to have attended Mme de Guise were Mme de Belin, Mme de Vibraye, and Mme de Mornay.

the very least listen to him. In this respect nuns were at a disadvantage compared to their sisters in the world outside, since they seldom had any common fund of experience, past or present, to share with Rancé, and after 1675 could never hope to meet him (and even before that only in Paris), but on the other hand he never shrank from giving them counsel, while he tended to be more cautious with laywomen.

It would be interesting, and convenient, if one could use simple statistics to assess the relative importance of men and women in Rancé's correspondence. Obviously on business matters, on questions of possible vocations for la Trappe, on visits past or future, he was almost exclusively involved with men, but the very fact that conversation was theoretically possible made letters less essential. Even so, the proportions found in the *lettres à imprimer* are probably representative: out of 382 letters, just under 100 each went to religious men and women, rather more than 40 to prelates, and about the same number to women not in religion, while another 100 or so went to other men (it is not possible to be more specific as 'Monsieur' is used indiscriminately for clergy and laity). Thus women account for about a third of letters addressed to seculars (excluding prelates), and perhaps for half or more of all addressed to layfolk. A somewhat similar impression is gained from looking at the principal series of letters to known addressees: Nicaise, Favier, Barillon all provide 100 or more, Bellefonds more than 80; while, except for Rancé's sister, Marie-Louise, and his two Visitation correspondents, Mères Louise Rogier and Louise-Henriette d'Albon, the only woman to receive more than 30 extant letters is Mme de Guise with about 100.[1] Survival is largely a matter of accident, and for some reason the letters to Mme de Guise are all copies, but it is highly probable that no one else did in fact receive more than she did, if only because her rank entitled her in Rancé's eyes to a prompt response. At the same time the preponderance of letters to men by no means indicates any antipathy to women on Rancé's part, nor any inability to cope with their problems; after all, his own spiritual journey owed as much to Mère Louise, and perhaps his aunt Mme Bouthillier, as to any man. The one thing Rancé would

---

[1] The proportions in Muguet are almost exactly equal as between men and women, with Mme de Guise accounting for a third of those to women, but this may be due to deliberate editorial policy.

not countenance was to be used as a fashionable director whose name could be dropped impressively in *salon* circles. On the evidence that survives, Rancé's letters to women, especially the great, show him at his prudent and compassionate best.

If any female correspondent could rival Mme de Guise it would probably be Mlle de Vertus, to whom Rancé wrote perhaps once a month until her death in 1692.[1] She and her sister Mlle de Goëllo constitute an extraordinarily suggestive link with the past, and if the legend of Mme de Montbazon's last hours could have been settled by anyone it was by these two sisters who survived her by thirty-five and fifty years respectively, remaining faithful friends of Rancé to the end. The precise chain of events is extremely difficult to reconstruct, partly because some of the most vital indications are insufficiently explicit and occur so long after the events in question. Marie de Bretagne, who married the duc de Montbazon in 1628, was the eldest of eight sisters, no other of whom married. Françoise-Philippe (1620–84) became abbess of Nidoiseau, near Angers; Madeleine took the veil in a place unknown; Marie-Claire, the youngest (1628–1711), spent sixty-three years in religion and became abbess of Malnoue. Constance, Mlle de Clisson (1617–95) is said to have been of a worldly disposition, and friendly with the Jesuits; Marguerite-Angélique, Mlle de Chantocé (1622–94) is simply recorded as dying at the Petite-Mère Hospital in Paris. There remain Catherine-Françoise, Mlle de Vertus (1615–92) and Anne, Mlle de Goëllo (1626–1707).

In contrast to her older sister, Mlle de Vertus was left on the death of her mother with neither fortune nor husband, and on any material calculation led a life of some adversity. After staying briefly in the household of Mme de Soissons and then Mme de Rohan, she joined Mme de Longueville after the Fronde (about 1653) and stayed with her for a while at Moulins, at the Visitation of which Mme de Montmorency, Mme de Longueville's aunt, was superior (and incidentally grandmother of the Mme de Valençay, who was to become abbess of les Clairets). Here, in August 1654, Mme de Longueville became definitively converted, and eventually, through the good offices of Mlle de Vertus and

---

[1] See article by M. Prevost in *DBF*, s.v. *Avaugour de Bretagne, Claude*, for the bare facts about the family, and also V. Cousin, *Mme de Sablé*, especially pp. 228 seq., and *La Jeunesse de Mme de Longueville*.

Mme de Sablé, found herself under the direction of M. Singlin, to whom she made her general confession in November 1661. At that time Mme de Longueville[1] speaks of Mlle de Monchy, M. le Nain, and P. du Breuil as 'notre petite société... accablée' by the Formulary, and it will be seen that the chronology of her conversion as well as her choice of friends overlap to a remarkable degree with those of Rancé.

Singlin died in 1664 and was succeeded by M. de Sacy; M. de Longueville died in 1663; and after endless trouble with her eldest son, Dunois, who briefly tried a Jesuit vocation before running away to be ordained in Rome (1669), Mme de Longueville suffered the shattering blow of her younger son's death, the comte de Saint-Paul, at the passage of the Rhine on 12 June 1672. After a little hesitation she withdrew to the Carmelites in the same year, and remained there until her death in 1679, under the direction of M. Marcel, curé of Saint-Jacques-du-Haut-Pas. The previous year (1671) Mlle de Vertus had entered Port-Royal under similar conditions, and stayed there until her death, virtually bedridden for the last eleven years of her life. It is rather artificial to attempt to isolate and classify the different influences and friendships which linked Mme de Longueville, Mlle de Vertus, and Rancé; Retz and Mme de Montbazon before the Fronde and after, then Port-Royal, the Carmelites, certain Oratorians, and so on, were all common friends, and it is fruitless to speculate on just who first brought them together.

In June, and again in September, 1672 Rancé wrote letters[2] of condolence to Mme de Longueville, and in 1675 he was still corresponding with her, about Tréville's recent visit to Alet, about Pavillon, whom they both admire, and about an unnamed abbé (perhaps Dunois) whom Mme de Longueville has sent to la Trappe. There is every reason to suppose that the correspondence continued until her death, in the context of Rancé's regular letters to his friends at the Carmelites, and she was one of many who are known to have visited him at the Institution de l'Oratoire when he went there for the last time in 1675, but the relationship between them gives the impression of cordiality rather than intimacy.

The same could be said of the two extant letters to the aged

[1] See Cousin, *Mme de Sablé*, pp. 228 seq.
[2] Muguet, i, pp. 228 and 484, *TB* 557, 579, ?878.

Mme de Sablé (1599–1678),[1] like Mme de Longueville a close friend of La Rochefoucauld. In 1675 and 1677 Rancé wrote to encourage her in her failing health, and told her to abandon worldliness rather than take formal religious vows. If the two letters are not particularly informative, the link that they represent with a well-documented Jansenist circle undoubtedly is, and enables one to fill in with reasonable confidence some of the gaps in the narrative, especially as regards Mlle de Vertus and Mlle de Goëllo. The perverse propensity of documents to survive, according to no apparent rule except to frustrate historians, is illustrated by the fact that only one identifiable letter to each of the sisters has come down from the period before 1681, though the correspondence just mentioned with Mme de Longueville and Mme de Sablé (and others) leaves no room for doubt that Rancé was in continuous contact with them and their circle from an early date.

In November 1675[2] Rancé wrote to Mlle de Goëllo an extraordinarily interesting letter, which throws some light on their antecedent relations. He begins with an unusual apology; mistaking her handwriting for that of another, though he had long been familiar with it, he had sent her inappropriate advice. In the acutely security-conscious world of the age it was quite usual not to sign letters, nor inscribe the name of the addressee (none of Rancé's numerous letters to Arnauld d'Andilly is signed, and all too many of the extant originals to others lack an address), but this opening excuse suggests some break in relations, or perhaps more precisely in epistolary relations, for he may well have met her on visits to Paris up to 1675 and thus had no need of frequent correspondence. He then tells her that she is on the right road, and proceeds with remarks so important that they deserve quoting in full: 'On quitte le monde parce que le monde ne plait plus, ou que l'on craint de ne plus plaire au monde... C'est ce qui fait qu'il y a tant de dévots et de dévotes, et si peu de conversions sincères, que tant de gens font profession de piété, et que le nombre de ceux qui en ont est si petit.' After these words, not surprisingly included in an anthology of his more weighty sayings, he goes on to be more specific: 'Je ne suis point surpris que l'on dise que vous êtes Janséniste; c'est une espèce de phantosme que les gens du monde, et les dévots à la mode, qui veulent à quelque

[1] TB 551, 840.   [2] TB 584, and U 3069, f. 114.

prix que ce soit concilier leurs affaires, leurs intérêts et leurs plaisirs avec la croix de J.-C. opposent aux personnes qui se retirent de leurs sentiments pour suivre les maximes étroites.' She is fortunate enough to have a good confessor (unnamed) 'incapable de se servir de ces règles toutes humaines et de ces condescendances molles, dont usent la plus grande partie des Directeurs, qui flattent seulement les maux et les consciences...' Rancé's phrasing leaves little doubt open as to his, and his correspondent's, attitude to the 'phantosme' of Jansenism.

The following years are sparsely represented by surviving letters, though there is one to Mlle de Vertus, by then permanently installed at Port-Royal under a semi-official rule of life, encouraging her to relax her austerity a little (6 April 1675):[1] 'vous avez assez reçu de Dieu pour remettre quelque chose aux hommes.' From 1680, however, more and more letters survive (1682 is the record year) and an event in 1681 provoked a highly significant response. Marie-Éléonore, eldest daughter of Mme de Montbazon, died after an exemplary career, first as abbess of Caen, then of Malnoue (1629–81). Rancé thereupon wrote letters of condolence to her closest relatives. To her brother, François, prince de Soubise (1630–1712),[2] he wrote exhorting him not to limit himself to grief at the unexpected bereavement, but to take urgent steps towards his own salvation; to her sister Anne, duchesse de Luynes (1640–84) he wrote in rather gentler terms,[3] praying God to make her 'exacte, vigilante et fidèle dans toute votre conduite'; and to her aunt, Mlle de Goëllo, he wrote saying that such an experience should make us think of death.[4] A little more than a year later,[5] however, in the same context, he wrote Mlle de Goëllo a strange and impressive letter full of allusions which cannot all be fully explained, but are clearly of the greatest importance and must be quoted at length. It should be mentioned that the dead abbess was succeeded by her own aunt, Mlle de Goëllo's younger sister, Marie-Claire, only a year her senior and coadjutrix since 1669 (she had entered religion in 1648, aged 20).

Rancé begins:

Votre lettre m'a fait faire beaucoup de réflexions, toutes les choses passées me sont revenues en foule dans la mémoire, et quand je les mets auprès des choses présentes, je ne puis qu'admirer et adorer tout en-

[1] TB 953.   [2] TB 1468 of 21 Apr. 1681.   [3] TB 1475 of 24 Apr. 1681.
[4] TB 1470 of 21 Apr. 1681.   [5] TB 1719 of 23 July 1682.

semble la providence de Dieu, dont les dispositions sont impénétrables, et qui conduit par des voies qu'on ne peut comprendre ceux qu'il daigne regarder des yeux de sa miséricorde, aux fins auxquelles il les a destinés; Je vous avoue qu'il me seroit bien difficile de m'acquitter auprès de luy des prières que je dois à M [*sic*], et que mes obligations en cela me paroissent si grandes que, quoique je fasse, il ne m'est guère possible d'y satisfaire; je n'y puis penser que ce souvenir ne fasse sur moi des impressions profondes, et plust à Dieu que je fusse assez selon son cœur pour être en état des assistances utiles, au cas qu'on ait encore besoin du secours des vivants; Il n'y a personne, Mlle, qui puisse mieux que vous exciter sur cela mes sentiments, puisque comme vous le dites, vous avez été témoin des désirs de l'un et des résolutions de l'autre; je suis trop persuadé que rien n'échappe à la sagesse de Dieu, qu'elle règle jusqu aux moindres évènements, et j'aperçois son ordre dans celui-ci avec autant d'évidence qui si je le voyois écrit de sa main.

On a purely linguistic basis it is hard to be sure just what he means by 'l'un… l'autre', though on the most obvious interpretation it would refer back to the opening antithesis between past and present. Again the undisclosed identity of 'M' is a puzzle, and though the copyist on the next page twice expands the abbreviation in the margin, once as 'votre nièce', the second time as 'Mme de Malnoue' (that is the dead abbess), it is not completely certain that the earlier 'M' refers to her, and if it does, the nature of the immense obligations cannot be explained by any known fact of Rancé's biography. The specific references to the past, and to Mlle de Goëllo's own position as witness of these decisive events, strongly suggests that the first anniversary of the abbess's death had recalled that of Mme de Montbazon, whose twenty-fifth anniversary had fallen in the same month (she died on 28 April 1657). Like her daughter the abbess, she had died comparatively young (45 to her daughter's 52), after a very brief illness (only three days in the case of the abbess, about the same with her mother), and the depth of Rancé's feeling and the onrush of memory would be perfectly well explained if Mlle de Goëllo had herself made the comparison in writing to him of her niece's death. Whatever interpretation one cares to put on this enigmatic letter, it is abundantly clear that Mlle de Goëllo played a much greater role in Rancé's life than is suggested by the fortuitous survival of no more than four letters identifiably addressed to her.

The letter goes on with reflections reminiscent of Pascal in their attitude to human attachments to other transitory creatures: 'cependant nous nous attachons à nos amis comme s'ils devoient être immortels, et quand il arrive que Dieu nous les ôte, ils nous laissent autant de regret en nous quittant que si nous n'avions jamais dû les perdre.' Mlle de Goëllo had, it seems, been deeply attached to her niece (it must be remembered that there was only a difference of three years in their ages), but Rancé presses on to the inexorable conclusion: 'quoique vous ayez trouvé en Mme de Malnoue tout ce que vous me mandez, je suis persuadé qu'il y avoit un vide dans votre cœur qu'elle ne remplissoit point, et en un mot la créature qui ne doit et ne peut être contente que de la possession de Dieu seul, ne trouve rien hors de lui qui soit capable de la satisfaire.'

After this he develops the argument very much *ad feminam*:

quand vous penserez par quels changements, et par quelles révolutions vous êtes devenue ce que vous êtes, vous devez être pénétrée de reconnaissance. Car il est vrai que rien ne pouvoit être plus opposé aux pas que vous avez faits pour votre salut, et à l'ardeur avec laquelle vous désirez d'être à Dieu, que cette négligence et cette langueur dans laquelle vous aviez passé vos jours, et il se peut dire qu'il ait fondu des montagnes de glace avant que de vous donner une étincelle de son amour.

He concludes with a lengthy encouragement to her not to be hard on herself but to take comfort from the fact that God 'n'a pas été chercher si loin pour vous abandonner après vous avoir trouvée.'

By a strange coincidence the only other extant letter to Mlle de Goëllo is another one of condolence for her younger niece, the duchesse de Luynes, who died in 1684. After this there is no sure trace of her, though she outlived Rancé, except for a hint from Mme de Sévigné of the sort of life she led. On 15 February 1689 Mme de Sévigné dined with her,[1] in the company of the abbé de Polignac (probably the future cardinal), the abbé de Rohan (her great-nephew) and the abbé David, and reported that she 'adored' Mme de Grignan. Such a party with its emphasis on noble abbés suggests a sedately comfortable piety, without excess or drama, but in the absence of further information about her that is as far as one can go.

Just when the letters to Mlle de Goëllo fade out those to her

[1] Mme de Sévigné, *Lettres*, iii, p. 347. She incidentally spent the rest of the evening with Mme de La Fayette, Pomponne, and Paul Barillon.

sister begin to fill the gap. A set of four letters, all signed originals, dating from 1676 is very probably addressed to Mlle de Vertus;[1] and the last of these seems to refer to Mlle de Goëllo and tie up with the letter written to her a year before. Rancé says that when in Paris (therefore before April 1675) he had sent his correspondent's sister to an Oratorian 'très homme de bien, pas fort connu', and that her whole life hitherto had been spent in 'une négligence et... inutilité prodigieuses'. Since it transpires that his correspondent has just been dangerously ill and is living in a religious house, it seems reasonable to identify her as Mlle de Vertus. If this is so she can in turn be linked with Leyme, to whose abbess she has been, unknown to Rancé, transmitting his letters. If Mlle de Vertus is indeed the correspondent, these letters tell us a little more about Mlle de Goëllo's conversion. From 1682, however, identification is certain, and nearly a score of letters cover the next ten years up to Mlle de Vertus's death.

Sickness is inevitably the main topic, for Mlle de Vertus knew herself to be incurably ill from about 1681, and Rancé constantly praises her courage and tries to console her. Her doctor was the saintly M. Hamon[2] (who had visited la Trappe but whose ministrations Rancé had vigorously declined in 1677) and she is told simply to follow his instructions. Not for the first time one is surprised at the almost trivial points on which Rancé's advice was sought, and apparently taken, by persons living under another's formal rule and direction.[3] He tells her for example (28 March 1685):[4] 'Le caphé [sic] est un soulagement si commun que vous pouvez en user sans façon... Plus vos œuvres sont petites, plus il faut que vos intentions soient grandes.' Most of the time, of course, his counsel bears on weightier issues: God's justice and mercy, preparation for death, fortitude in suffering. He tells her: 'Dieu veut être importuné, c'est par la persévérance que nous obtenons ses grâces, particulièrement quand il est si pénible, qu'il semble que c'est à nos dépens que nous le servons.' Early in 1687 Hamon's death adds to her burden, and Rancé writes:[5] 'On ne peut

---

[1] In *U* 863, addressed simply 'Mlle'.

[2] The beloved physician of Port-Royal. See M. Catel, *Les Écrivains de Port-Royal*, pp. 199–223.

[3] Dubois, ii, pp. 342–8, quotes extensively from these letters, the originals of which were then owned by the Hecquet family at Abbeville, but they can no longer be traced, and neither the copies at la Trappe nor Dubois's excerpts provide a complete text.

[4] *TC* II/65.   [5] *TC* II/167 of 2 Mar (?May) 1687.

être plus touché de la perte que vous avez faite du pauvre M. Hamon... il était bon pour les âmes que pour les corps... Ne vous lassez point de baiser la main qui s'appesantit sur vous... la plus grande bénédiction que Dieu puisse répandre dans une âme qu'il exerce et qu'il fait souffrir est celle d'aimer ses souffrances.' The praise of Hamon, perhaps the most universally loved of the Messieurs, is noteworthy at this date. It is also interesting that Rancé's correspondence with the equally doomed Mme de la Sablière began just a fortnight later. In May 1687[1] Rancé sent Mlle de Vertus the latest *relations*, *Saint-Dorothée*, a piece on humiliations, and a wooden spoon and crosses made at la Trappe. In August he writes with total candour:[2] 'Je vois bien qu'il ne faut pas espérer de voir jamais votre santé rétablie, vous devez vous regarder comme une victime qui est déjà mise sur l'autel et toute prête d'être immolée.'

Sometimes she asked specific advice about her rule of life. On one occasion she had been obliged to receive a number of visitors, very reluctantly, and Rancé comments in evident reply to her question (4 November 1685):[3] 'la conduite que vous tenez de ne pas approcher de la communion lorsque vous vous êtes trouvée le jour précédent dans quelque dissipation considérable est très louable, mais il ne faut pas être souvent dans ces nécessités... il est utile de s'en éloigner quelquefois, mais c'est afin de s'en rapprocher avec plus de sainteté.' Some years later she is still worried about her sacramental discipline, and his answer is as eminently sensible as always:[4] 'Je ne vois pas qu'il y ait rien qui puisse vous empêcher d'approcher des saints mystères aussi souvent que vous le faites: vos souffrances et la séparation du monde dans laquelle vous vivez sont des préparations véritables.' She had to endure three more years' suffering before she died, and Rancé wrote a generous tribute to her patience and heroic endurance to her doctor, Hecquet.[5] Considering that she lived more than twenty years virtually as a religious at Port-Royal, the attachment, and perhaps dependence, of Mlle de Vertus with regard to Rancé is remarkable. What one cannot even guess at is the role of her dead sister, Mme de Montbazon, in this relationship, but from the indications already discussed in letters

---

[1] *TC* I/40 of 20 May 1687.   [2] 29 Aug. 1687, quoted by Dubois.
[3] *TC* II/195.   [4] 2 Mar. 1689, quoted by Dubois.
[5] 21 Nov. 1692, quoted by Dubois.

to Mlle de Goëllo it seems in the highest degree likely that these two sisters (and perhaps some of the others as well) held a uniquely important place in Rancé's affections.

Although Mme de la Sablière was in touch with Rancé for barely six years, and never met him, their correspondence has so many points of similarity with that conducted with Mlle de Vertus that a comparison can hardly be avoided. Marguerite Hessein (1640–93)[1] was born into a Huguenot family, and when she was not yet 15 married her cousin, also a Huguenot, Antoine de Rambouillet (no connection with the famous family of that name), sieur de la Sablière. They had three children, then in 1667 Antoine became secretary to the King, and next year the marriage broke up. Marguerite moved in with her brother, Pierre, and established a *salon* attended by such eminent men as Fouquet, Lauzun, and Paul Barillon. From about 1673 La Fontaine stayed with her, and in friendly mockery of her Cartesian sympathies dedicated to her the fable 'Des Deux Rats'. Mme de Sévigné became a close friend a year or two later, and in about 1676, for a year or so, Mme de la Sablière formed an intimate, but apparently platonic, liaison with the marquis de la Fare, an epicurean and memorialist of some repute.

Some time before 1680 she became converted to Catholicism, probably by Rapin; in 1679 her estranged husband died; and in 1680 she set up house in the rue Saint-Honoré. Convert though she was, the Revocation came as a sore trial; her brother, Pierre, had also accepted conversion, but her uncle, and protector, Antoine Menjot (friend of Mme de Sablé) would not, and two of her children went into exile rather than abjure. By then she knew that she was seriously ill, and moved to a house near the hospital for Incurables (in the parish of Saint-Sulpice), with the aid of Tréville, a friend of hers. The death of her director, Rapin, at the end of October 1687 forced her to look for another, but a year later her new confessor (possibly the Carmelite, Père Césaire) also died. It is only from this period that her relations with Rancé begin, and by a unique accident copies of sixty-one of her letters (mostly to him) survive, but only one of his, though extensive passages are quoted in her replies.

It seems that she originally wrote to Rancé in March 1687 with

---

[1] For all that follows see Menjot d'Elbenne, *Mme de la Sablière*. He used a copy lent by the Musée Condé at Chantilly and another which he had purchased himself.

no specific intention, then, on Rapin's death, wondered whether the director who had done so much for the similarly ill Mlle de Vertus would also help her, but Rancé refused. For some reason she wrote direct to Maisne, and on his advice tried Rancé again, this time successfully. Maisne's part in what ensued is uncertain; she wrote at least sometimes to him direct, and it is thought by the modern editor of the letters (a collateral descendant of Menjot) that he may have taken an unauthorized copy of all she wrote for his own ends. On the evidence of the letters themselves there seems no doubt as to their authenticity. It is quite likely that Tréville first gave her the idea of writing, and quite certain that it was not Rapin, never a detectably enthusiastic admirer of Rancé and la Trappe.

Her first letter concerned her difficulties over confession, always a stumbling-block for former Protestants, and a year later (28 April 1688)[1] she was still worried on that point, but quotes Rancé's words of some eight months earlier: 'prenez sur vous ce que vous pourrez, mais ne vous inquiétez pas sur ce qui ne sera pas en votre pouvoir, car Dieu ne vous le demande pas. Le principal est de conserver la paix, n'y ayant rien de plus nécessaire ni qui donne plus de force.' In June she moved to a less expensive house, and spent more and more time at the Incurables, whose superior later became her confessor. On the strength of two initials there is a legend that La Fontaine may have planned a visit to la Trappe:[2] 'Je trouve le désir que LF avait de vous aller voir fort refroidi', and while there is no inherent reason why he should not momentarily have been curious to go where his poetic friend Santeuil was attracted ten years later, there is absolutely no supporting evidence for this pleasant conjecture. More relevant is a letter of the same month (June 1688) saying that her confessor knows nothing of her relations with la Trappe. By the end of the year she has lost this confessor and now only leaves her house to visit her sister and Harlay, *procureur-général* and another link with Rancé. She now makes her communion every Sunday and feast day, confessing beforehand, but her confessor gives her absolution only once a month, which she finds rather often.

The next few months pass uneventfully: Rancé sends her *Saint-Dorothée*, the *relation* of dom Muce, and an account of his visit to les Clairets; she tells him of a pet bird she has lost, and he re-

---

[1] Menjot d'Elbenne, op. cit., p. 279.   [2] Ibid., p. 281.

minds her of Saint John's legendary partridge when she wonders
if keeping a pet is compatible with strict renunciation. His line is as
always clear and reasonable:[1] 'vous aurez banni toutes les in-
utilités de votre vie lorsque vous vous serez réduite aux seules
visites auxquelles la nécessité ou une bienséance qui sera selon
Dieu voudra bien que vous donniez quelques moments.' By
1692 she speaks openly of her illness, cancer of the breast, but
asks Maisne (it is not clear why she should have written to him at
all) to respect absolute secrecy regarding it and burn her letters,
which of course he did not. Rancé's only surviving letter is from
these final months (28 May 1692).[2] In September yet another link
is identified: abbé Têtu, returning from la Trappe, has seen a letter
there addressed to her and is very angry, presumably from
jealousy or simply at being kept in the dark.[3] One of the last
letters[4] exclaims, 'Que je suis heureuse! je ne vois plus que
l'éternité devant moi', and on the feast of the Epiphany 1693 it
was all over.

For once the effect of Rancé's letters is better documented than
his reaction to appeals for help, and if the case of Mme de la
Sablière is unusual, perhaps unique, in terms of her background
and conversion, Rancé's treatment of her physical and spiritual
sufferings is remarkably like that shown to Mlle de Vertus during
precisely the same period. None the less the two series of letters
are by no means interchangeable, and there is enough material
addressed to particular problems to prove that the inevitably
repetitious formulas of consolation constituted only part of
Rancé's extraordinary reputation as a director.

One more link with the world of literature and the *salons* is
attested by only two extant letters, but one of these has become
celebrated, partly for its content, partly because it is addressed to
Mme de La Fayette. Like Mme de Longueville and Mme de
Sablé an intimate friend of La Rochefoucauld (though the nature
of the intimacy was very different in each case), Mme de La
Fayette was probably recommended to Rancé by Tréville, who
seems to have been tireless in his self-appointed role of amateur
director to all who would listen. Some time in 1686, when she
was already 52, she apparently consulted Rancé on some unrecorded personal problem, and took the opportunity to ask him
why he had left the world. It is most unlikely that she was the

[1] Ibid., p. 313.   [2] TC II/223.   [3] Ibid., p. 331.   [4] Ibid., p. 333.

first person to put such a question, and rather odd that at her age
she should do so—she was, after all, in her twenties when Mme
de Montbazon died and when she came to Paris two years later
was soon familiar enough with *salon* society to have heard all the
gossip then—but she did, and for some quite unaccountable
reason Rancé answered her (22 October 1686),[1] in strictest confidence (not respected) and with the comment that he had never
told anyone before. His answer is very simple: 'Vous me de-
mandez les motifs qui m'ont déterminé à quitter le monde. Je
vous dirai simplement que je le haissais parce que je n'y trouvais
pas ce que je cherchais.' He had at first thought of retreat to
Véretz, but realized that this 'état doux et paisible' was not God's
will for him and so took the decisive step. Another letter written
two months later[2] adds no more than a general desire to help her,
with a reference to the ubiquitous *Saint-Dorothée*, and concludes
with remarks about Mme de Saint-Loup similar to those about
Tréville in the earlier letter: 'Il ne faut pas tout à fait croire Mme
de Saint-Loup quand elle est sur mon sujet, elle est pleine de
charité et fait ce qu'elle peut pour rehausser ses amis.' Mme de La
Fayette died the same year as Mme de la Sablière, and Rancé
probably went on writing to her until then, but no more is
known of their correspondence. It is incidentally interesting to
note that Mme de Sévigné, who knew all these people, and Mme
d'Albon too, never wrote to Rancé as far as is known, any more
than did La Rochefoucauld, whose three most intimate women
friends (and most intimate male rival, Retz) were all correspondents of Rancé.

Mention of Mme de Saint-Loup[3] takes the chronology back far
beyond these very late associations with Mme de La Fayette and
Mme de la Sabliére to the early days before Rancé's conversion.
She is in fact one of the first friends to appear in his correspondence, and the reference to her in the letter just quoted suggests
that Mme de La Fayette may not have been the first person with
whom she had played the role of Rancé's unauthorized publicity
agent. Born Diane Chasteignier de la Roche-Posay (*c.* 1625–98),
she had married the financier Nicolas le Page, who acquired an
estate at Saint-Loup whence he took his title. Like so many others
in the aftermath of the Fronde, she turned from a life of scanda-

---

[1] *BN* 24123, f. 62.   [2] Ibid., f. 63.
[2] On Mme de Saint-Loup see Mesnard, *Pascal et les Roannez*, pp. 729–30 and 894.

lous dissipation to be converted in 1656, thus following closely the spiritual chronology of Rancé and Mme de Longueville. In 1658,[1] when Rancé was still at Véretz, he wrote to Mère Louise Rogier: 'Mme de Saint-Lou [*sic*] sort présentement de chez moi; c'est une femme dont le cœur est fort à Dieu, et qui constamment a des intentions les meilleures du monde. Elle y a passé un jour tout entier. Vous jugez bien qu'ayant chez moi la personne que j'y avois je n'ai pas pu me dispenser de la recevoir.' The impression of excessively well-meaning importunity is the same thirty years later. Early in 1672 she lost her husband, and it is almost certainly to her that Rancé wrote two very sobering, even sharp, letters, printed simply as 'à une dame veuve qui vouloit se retirer seule au fond d'une forêt.'[2] In answer to two letters from this lady he observes, 'les desseins de cette nature ne conviennent plus à notre temps.' His advice fell on deaf ears, and he tells her in a second letter that if she had taken notice of what he had already written she would have saved herself a lot of trouble. He goes on with devastating common sense: 'Il n'y a rien de plus agréable que de se figurer une solitude affreuse, une forêt sombre, une caverne, une grotte, un rocher, une cellule, je dis pour ceux qui veulent se retirer du monde; ce sont des idées qui frappent et qui plaisent'; but the reality is very different from this romantic fantasy, and it is no good seeking in the cloister a mere refuge from worldly preoccupations. The letter ends in the same calmly objective way: 'gardez-vous bien de considérer ce que je vous dis comme des oracles, ne vous figurez pas que Dieu vous parle par ma bouche.' Both the proposition and Rancé's reply, as well as the recent widowhood, fit so well what is known elsewhere of Mme de Saint-Loup that the identification deserves serious consideration. Even if the recipient should turn out to be someone else, Rancé's treatment of an all too familiar type of pious lady merits remark.

Mme de Saint-Loup in fact withdrew in 1672 to a home less wild, but perhaps even more dangerous, than a forest, and in her house in the Faubourg Saint-Jacques sheltered Arnauld and Nicole among others. At just this time Anne de Gonzague, Princess Palatine, was undergoing a sensational conversion under Bossuet's aegis, with long-range assistance from Rancé,[3] and

---

[1] M 1214, 5.   [2] Muguet, i, pp. 215 and 441.
[3] See *Oraison funèbre* of Anne in Bossuet, *Oraisons funèbres*, p. 146.

there is some indication that Mme de Saint-Loup was already acting as intermediary, as she certainly was a few years later. Mme de Saint-Loup had also become quite friendly with Mme de Longueville, and the circle around the duc de Roannez (like her from Poitou) to which Pascal had once belonged. Her natural impetuosity, and devotion to the Jansenist cause, made her a correspondent of whom Rancé was somewhat wary.

In 1676, when he had been drawn into discussion about Jansenism with Brancas among others, she wrote to him, apparently on the same subject (the Signature). He replied (6 December 1676)[1] diplomatically but firmly: 'Il y a vingt ans que je n'avais tant pensé ni tant parlé de l'affaire de laquelle vous m'écrivez... mes réflexions n'ont fait que me confirmer dans ma première opinion... Je garderay une fidélité inviolable à mes amis, mais il y a des choses sur lesquelles l'amitié ne doit pas s'étendre.' He goes on to say that he still retains 'toute la tendresse et l'estime dont il est digne' for their mutual friend (probably Arnauld or Nicole, her director), for he has 'une bonté de cœur et une extrême fidélité pour ses amis'. The conclusion is unequivocal: 'si j'étais en votre place, je préfererais la prière aux conversations'. Unabashed she returned to the charge, and in January 1677[2] Rancé writes to say that he has burnt her letter and asks her to burn his. In the past three months, he says, he has had to think more about the subject than in the previous fourteen years (that is, since he became a monk)—presumably a reference to the correspondence with Brancas—but only the Church's authority will make him change his mind. She seems to have been trying to persuade him that a cause promoted by a saintly friend (probably Pavillon, of Alet) must be right: 'je le considère comme un grand saint, mais Dieu n'a point donné toutes lumières à tous ses saints... M.N. est un saint et un évêque, et moi je ne suis ni l'un ni l'autre, le rang que je tiens dans l'église de Dieu est celui d'un pécheur.' His only wish is to remain obedient to the Pope, and not await his dying moments to proclaim his submission, like, for example, Pascal. It will be seen that Rancé's basic good sense and moderation were stimulated by the excessive zeal, and indeed silliness, of someone like Mme de Saint-Loup.

In July, well-meaning as ever, she sent M. Hamon to la Trappe with the mission of giving Rancé medical advice, but he was not even admitted to the refectory, although Rancé held a high opinion of him personally:[1] 'le règlement principal de notre maison de n'appeler jamais de médecin quelque maladie qui arrive à nos religieux, et de nous contenter du chirurgien.' There were no more medical missions to la Trappe. Only a month later she had started another hare, this time intervening in the interminable quarrel with Le Roy. Rancé then defends himself against what he conceives to be the ill-considered action of the Bishop of Tournai, and begs her not to raise the matter again.[2] There is silence then for a while, at least no letters survive, until 1680, when he wrote her a letter of which more than one version circulated (in copy) and which became rather well known.[3] Endlessly agitated and agitating, she complained that she could not find the peace she sought. Rancé once more is consistent, firm and tactful: 'Je ne puis me dispenser de vous déclarer une chose... C'est que je ne saurois croire que l'engagement que vous avez pris dans les affaires du temps vous convienne, ni qu'il soit conforme à la volonté de Dieu... Vous êtes femme, pécheresse et pénitente, ce sont des qualités qui vous obligent à procurer l'oubli du monde...' Since the death a year earlier of Mme de Longueville she had become self-appointed champion of the newly persecuted Jansenists, and he tells her that in thus engaging in religious controversy she is 'comme assise au milieu des Docteurs', a posture quite unbecoming to her situation. As he says, 'il ne faut pas s'étonner si vous ne trouvez pas en vous ce fond de paix et de tranquillité que vous y cherchez', and he tells her to go back to her country house, in Poitou, as soon as she has completed her business.

It is most unlikely that such sound advice had any lasting effect, but at least things seem a little calmer eighteen months later. He is glad to see a friend of thirty-five years' standing (that is, since 1647) in such a frame of mind, and in May 1682 he bids her abandon herself to God in the tempest.[4] In the same letter he thanks the Princess Palatine for a friendly message, and asks Mme de Saint-Loup to thank her for a gift of incense when she has the opportunity. They certainly went on corresponding to the end (1698), for Rancé refers to her over-enthusiastic friendship in the

---

[1] *TB* 843 of 4 July 1677.   [2] *TD*, series A, 89 of 23 Aug. 1677.
[3] One copy in *U* 723, others in *TB* 1158 and Gonod, p. 407.
[4] *TD*, series A, 91 and 92.

letter of 1686 to Mme de La Fayette quoted above and, again, assures Mme de Guise of Mme de Saint-Loup's loyal attachment to her in 1692. In such an eventful life Mme de Saint-Loup made it her business to get to know as many distinguished people as possible, especially among those sympathetic to Port-Royal, and while her good intentions are not in question, she was one of the several friends who did Rancé much more public harm than good, and sorely tried his patience by her lack of balance and discretion. All the more interesting is it, therefore, to see how admirably he dealt with such a person.

Other friends have left less trace, but are known to have been very close. Among his nearest neighbours were Antoine de la Vove, marquis de Tourouvre,[1] and his wife Marie de Remefort de la Grélière (or Grillière), whose mother was eventually obliged by failing sight to move from the family home in Poitou to join her in Tourouvre. The seventh of their nine children was called Jean-Armand (1674–1733) after Rancé and died Bishop of Rodez; another (either Antoine or Jean-Alexandre) was in the navy and recommended in 1673 to Bellefonds in a letter from Rancé;[2] and a daughter, Marie (1668–1726), was thinking of a religious vocation when Rancé commended her to the Abbess of Essai nearby, and apparently still making up her mind in 1685 when he tells his sister, Marie-Louise, about it;[3] in fact she never entered religion, and never married either, and died after a life of good works for the local poor. Bellefonds knew the family, and called on them on his way to or from la Trappe, so did Mme de Guise, and probably many other eminent visitors.

As they lived so near, Rancé did not need to write very often, unless they were away in Paris, but fragments of one or two letters (about backbiting and tolerance) survive, and at least one whole one. This, of 8 March 1677,[4] was written when the marquise had either just produced or was about to produce her ninth child, and contains interesting advice on how to bring up children (the eldest was by then 15). Three of the children had recently been ill, and from the context the family was in Paris; the children must not be taught to sing or play cards, and they must not go to the theatre or

---

[1] Mme Montagne, an erudite historian of Perche, living at Tourouvre, has been kind enough to supply otherwise unknown facts about the Vove family on which she is an expert. I am most grateful.

[2] *BN* n.a. 12959, f. 101 of 15 Apr. 1683.

[3] *TB* 1426 and *TA* 7 of 21 Aug. 1685.   [4] *TB* 603.

gamble. To attend the theatre with a clear conscience, says Rancé, one must either be obliged to go (presumably by social necessity) or 'que l'on soit tellement mort à ses passions qu'elles n'en soient plus touchées'. In 1680 the marquis is mentioned in a letter to Marcel, at Saint-Jacques-du-Haut-Pas,[1] in connection with a dispute between the Bishop of Séez and M. d'Angennes, and Thérèse at les Clairets, not far away, hears in 1680,[2] somewhat prematurely, that the marquise is even more ill than her mother, but is preparing for a Christian death, which came only thirty years later (even her aged mother lasted until 1690). In 1683[3] Mme de la Grélière was in such poor health that Rancé told Maupeou (his future biographer, curé then of Nonancourt nearby) that she must not go through Lent without meat, and that eggs are not enough, and three years later[4] he consoles her for her lack of sight, owing to cataract, by speaking of the clearer spiritual vision she could attain. From the scanty evidence that survives, one can see how close an interest Rancé took in the whole family, who in turn are known to have been very kind to him and his monks, both in his early days at la Trappe and later in his illness.

A good idea of Rancé's standing and methods as director can be gained from his extant letters to Jeanne-Françoise de Garand, marquise d'Alègre (1658–1723).[5] This young woman, whom Rancé can never have met, married in 1677 Yves d'Alègre, later maréchal, a member of a family related to both Colbert and the d'Urfés (including Rancé's friend the Bishop of Limoges). Not long after her marriage she was converted from a notably dissolute life and became the friend of both Bossuet and Fénelon, the former of whom most probably put her in touch with Rancé. He seems, at the beginning at least, to have written quite frequently, perhaps once a month or so, and it is interesting to see how specifically he deals with her problems as a newly wed aristocrat of 24, compared, for example, with those of the excitable widow, Mme de Saint-Loup. He tells her (20 July 1682)[6] that her decision to lead a life of piety will inevitably arouse criticism from those around her, but there is a middle way: 'vous n'avez pas peine à vous maintenir dans une bienséance qui n'ait rien de choquant, de blasmable et qui convienne néanmoins à la piété dont vous

---

[1] *TB* 1279 of 24 Apr. 1680.   [2] *TB* 1221 of 21 Jan. 1680.
[3] *TB* 1849 of 11 Feb. 1683.   [4] *TC* II/85 of 14 Aug. 1686.
[5] See *DBF* and note in Bossuet, *Correspondance*, iv, p. 333.   [6] *TB* 1713.

faites profession... Il faut être juste et ne point être extrême...
Dieu ne veut pas que les chrétiens disputent, mais il veut bien
qu'ils résistent.' He does not object to her taking the waters for
her health, and explicitly says: 'vous ne pouvez ne point donner
quelque chose à ceux avec lesquels Dieu veut que vous viviez,
vous suivez en cela son ordre.' With the ardour of a neophyte
she was not satisfied with half measures, and at the end of the
summer Rancé had to speak out again. She had complained of her
dependent state as a wife and found it uncongenial, but she must
submit:[1]

Ce mouvement qui vous fait souhaiter que Dieu vous délivre afin que
vous ne soyez plus partagée... a besoin d'être modérée... Vous êtes
jeune, il y a si peu que Dieu vous a touchée, ce que vous avez fait
jusqu'à présent pour son service et pour votre salut est si peu de chose...
vous ne devez point aspirer à des choses qui ne sont pas faisables.
Enfin faites les biens qui vous conviennent.

In November 1682 her zeal had still not abated:[2]

Je connois par votre dernière lettre que vos dispositions sont presque
toujours les mêmes; vous servez Dieu, et vous voudriez que ce fût
d'une manière plus parfaite... Prenez sur votre esprit et sur votre cœur
ce que vous ne pouvez prendre sur votre chair et sur vos sens, et
croyez que la mortification secrète et intérieure est incomparablement
plus grande au jugement de Dieu que non pas celle qui est extérieure,
qui frappe les yeux et qui tombe sous la connaissance des hommes.

It cannot be too strongly emphasized that, for all the celebrated
and extreme austerities of la Trappe, this was the spiritual
principle to which Rancé remained consistently attached. She
seems to have settled down to a much calmer mood, for three
letters of 1683 and one of 1685 concern fairly neutral questions—
the dispute over fictions, the death of a mutual friend, and so on—
and it is reasonable to suppose that Rancé's moderating influence
had been effective.

This list of noble ladies could be prolonged considerably, but
the salient facts are clear enough from what has already been said:
Rancé was at his best with those whose worldly background he
had known so well in the past, but who, like him, had been converted to a more profound piety. The prestige conferred by claim-
ing him as a director is a factor that cannot be ignored, but his

[1] *TB* 1761 of 6 Sept. 1682.   [2] *TB* 1792 of 15 Nov. 1682.

firmness, moderation, and simple charity are what produced the real spiritual effect and kept his correspondents faithful to him.

Apart from Mme de Longueville, with whom his relations were rather brief, and fairly formal, and perhaps Anne de Gonzague, with whom his contacts are only vaguely recorded, all these noble women enjoyed his correspondence and advice as a pure favour. With Mme de Guise the situation was quite different, and indeed unique, for no one else, except James II, not even intimate friends like Bellefonds, could demand and expect a prompt answer as she could and did. The very frequency (and, of course, survival) of Rancé's letters to her means that a much wider range of topics is discussed, but respectful as it is, his spiritual advice to her is exactly the same as to all the others.[1]

Elisabeth d'Orléans, Mlle d'Alençon (1646–96), was the second of three daughters of Gaston d'Orléans by his second marriage to Marguerite de Lorraine, and grew up in an atmosphere of bitter hostility from Mlle de Montpensier, her half-sister, la Grande Mademoiselle, only child of Gaston's first marriage and a thorn in her flesh throughout a long life of rivalry at close quarters. In 1667 she married the young duc de Guise, Louis-Joseph (1650–71) her kinsman, and was thereafter known as Mme de Guise. Marie, Mlle de Guise, her husband's aunt, had been her most powerful protector against Mlle de Montpensier and remained her loyal friend until she died in 1688. Mme de Guise was not destined to be happy: she lost her husband from smallpox when he was only 21; their only child, the last duc de Guise, died in 1675 before he was 5; and her mother-in-law, Mme de Joyeuse, never very stable, became quite mad and lingered on at the abbey of Essai until two months after her daughter-in-law died. By the time she was 30, therefore, Mme de Guise had had more than her fair share of difficulties, and the necessity of spending half the year at Court or sharing the Luxembourg Palace with her half-sister did nothing to brighten her remaining years. The rest of the time she stayed at Alençon, where she exercised author-

[1] See Saint-Simon, *Mémoires*, i, pp. 283 seq. His facts are reliable enough, his judgements less so. In 1702 Muguet published 24 of Rancé's letters to her in the second volume, and Gonod published 28 of them from an eighteenth-century copy. 44 more survive in a probably nineteenth-century copy in *BN* n.a. 12960; 6 are known at la Trappe; so, even allowing for duplicates, there are about 100 but no originals. As so often happens, the BN collection is not in order and '7' in dates is often confused with '8', but it is not too hard to correct this.

ity over all her subjects very much in the feudal tradition. With his usual malice, Saint-Simon describes the formal superiority she asserted over her husband during their brief marriage, and the haughty way in which she treated her diocesan Bishop of Séez, but even he acknowledged her piety and good works. The proximity of Alençon, Rancé's links with her father, and her evident need of a forceful personality as director very naturally led her to la Trappe, and for his part the fervently royalist Rancé was only too glad to have Henri IV's granddaughter as his spiritual daughter and temporal protector, for her rank brought her into daily contact with the King, her cousin, when she was at Court.

Her contact with Rancé must go back a very long way,[1] and she is known to have called on him during his last visit to Paris in 1675. It is likely that his formal assumption of the charge of directing her dates from about this time when, widowed and childless, she withdrew more and more. She often came to la Trappe, staying just outside the enclosure in the former abbatial lodging for a night or two, but the earliest surviving letter is from November 1682. Thereafter the harvest is copious, amounting to more than a hundred, sometimes a week or less apart, though mostly very brief. In addition Rancé composed for her his *Instructions chrétiennes* and *Conduite chrétienne*, and many of his letters to her were subsequently published in whole or in part. Their mutual friends were numerous, including her dame d'honneur, Mme de Vibraye, a correspondent of Rancé and protector of Thiers, his over-zealous defender, Rancé's niece, Mme de Belin,[2] successive abbesses of Essai, the Tourouvre family, and so on, and through her Rancé undoubtedly got to know and influence scores of others.

The first letter is typical; on her way from Alençon on the poor winter roads Mme de Guise had had what could have been a fatal accident near Tourouvre, so Rancé tells her (19 November 1682)[3] to profit from the lesson and devote herself even more ardently to God's service. There then comes a complete series of forty-four letters, almost all from 1686 and 1687. Many of them

---

[1] He must have known her to some extent during the brief time that he was chaplain to her father, but his conversion would then have interrupted whatever contacts they had had.

[2] On Mme de Belin see following chapter. The only extant letter to Mme de Vibraye is *TC* I/130 of 1685, but they must have been in contact through Thiers and, of course, when Mme de Guise visited.

[3] *TB* 1798.

concern routine exchanges, about his health or hers, gifts of souvenirs made at la Trappe (wooden spoons, forks, crosses), or books, pious exhortations, and the like, but there is also much of more specific interest. After the Revocation in 1685, and to some extent just before, Rancé's friends, particularly Barillon at Lucon and Bellefonds, discussed the Huguenot problem with him, and Mme de Guise's high sense of responsibility naturally led her to consult him too. Early in 1686[1] Rancé had written to Bellefonds (then at Valognes): 'les convertis de ce pays sont extrêmement durs, ils sont assez éloignés de nous et ne viennent point jusque dans notre détroit, à la réserve d'un gentilhomme de nos voisins qui n'est pas moins Huguenot après son abjuration qu'il l'étoit auparavant. Bellême et Alençon sont deux villes qui se sont signalées entre toutes les autres pour leur opiniâtreté.' It is in the light of this judgement that one should read his remark of a few months later to Mme de Guise, very concerned at the obduracy of her own town of Alençon:[2] le fruit des missions [n'est] pas tel qu'on le pourroit attendre... il me semble qu'après l'abjuration il eût été beaucoup plus utile de les instruire et de les disposer avec beaucoup de douceur à approcher de la sainte table que non pas de leur en faire une nécessité.' Rancé's rejection of the official 'compelle intrare' policy was more than justified by events, but it is noteworthy that he spoke out so clearly to one who was in a position to follow his advice.

In 1687 another team of missionaries tried their hand at reducing heresy at Alençon, but Rancé sounds distinctly reserved at their prospects of success (16 March 1687):[3] 'Il est certain qu'il seroit à souhaiter qu'on n'eût qu'un même esprit... Il faut espérer que la mission sera utile et que les vérités étant éclaircies sans cet air de contestation qui d'ordinaire les rend odieuses, elles entreront avec plus de facilité dans les esprits et dans les cœurs.' Again it is instructive to see how far removed from the grotesque distortion represented by the 'Thundering Abbot' sobriquet is the authentic portrait of Rancé the man of peace, whether with Protestants or Jansenists. Violent in his own defence, he was all against the use of violence with others. In May 1687 Mme de Guise is still preoccupied with the same problem:[4]

---

[1] *BN* n.a. 12959, f. 115 of 25 Feb. 1686.
[2] *BN* n.a. 12960, f. 12 of 11 June 1686.
[3] Ibid., p. 35.   [4] Ibid., p. 30 of 26 May 1687.

J'ai bien cru que V.A.R. ne trouveroit point dans les nouveaux convertis toutes les dispositions qu'elle y avoit souhaitées: le temps, la
douceur et le soin que l'on prendra de les instruire pourra les faire
revenir de leurs préventions, mais il y a grande apparence qu'en les
pressant trop on leur nuit plus qu'on ne leur sert. L'esprit de l'homme
va quelquefois plus vite que celui de Dieu, et souvent ce qui empêche
le succès de ce que l'on entreprend pour son service est qu'on prévient
ses mouvements au lieu de les suivre.

And so the sad story drags on. In August[1] he hopes that the
new mission expected in October will be more successful than
those which have gone before, 'car je m'assure que tout le pays
en a grand besoin, je veux dire les anciens catholiques aussi bien
que ceux qui en font depuis peu une profession extérieure.'
Whether the people of Perche were any less devout than others of
the time it is hard to say, but it is obvious enough that the standard
set by those of the old religion was the ultimate factor in deciding
the reactions of reluctant converts. In September emigration
could already be seen as a serious problem. Rancé, of course, was
not concerned with its social or economic consequences, solely
with the fact that emigrants could never be won from their errors,
and he sadly comments:[2] 'Chacun a fait à sa fantaisie; les uns ont
usé de la modération, les autres de rigueur, et ainsi les maux
augmentent de jour en jour au lieu de diminuer.' Unlike his great
predecessor St. Bernard, Rancé was not called to take a direct
part in the conversion of heretics (or if called, refused), but such
phrases as that just quoted make one wonder if he would not have
been a more effective missionary than some of the professionals.

During this period, 1686–7, the other great preoccupation of
Rancé was the King's serious illness at the end of 1686. His
sincerity is patent when he reiterates his anxiety, and with the
official announcement of Louis's recovery in January 1687 he had
a special *Te Deum* sung. A less urgent problem was that of a
successor to the abbess of Essai,[3] a post to which the lords of
Alençon had always nominated. With the death in 1687 of the
administratively incompetent Abbess Françoise de Trotti something had to be done to restore the temporal fortunes of the abbey,
and, after consulting Rancé, Mme de Guise had the sister of the
late abbess appointed.

---

[1] Ibid., p. 39 of 31 Aug. 1687.   [2] Ibid., p. 45 of 24 Sept. 1687.
[3] Ibid., p. 43. On Essai see above, pp. 190–191.

By 1688 a new preoccupation appears in Rancé's correspondence, as he constantly reverts to the fate of James II. Early in
1689[1] Mme de Guise asks him for some rules to follow in Lent,
and after giving her guidance about this he goes on: 'On voit un
Roi détrôné, chassé de son pays, une grande Reine [Marie-Louise
d'Orléans, Queen of Spain] morte... qu'est-ce que cela dit davantage sinon qu'il n'y a point de véritable grandeur sur la terre...
les choses d'ici bas... ne sont plus rien qu'un éclair, qui paroit et
disparoit en un instant, parce qu'il n'a ni matière, ni solidité, ni
consistance.'

Unfortunately nothing survives from 1690 to 1691, but by
another happy chance a series of twenty-seven letters for the
whole of 1692 and 1693 had been preserved, and is widely known
through Gonod's publication of it in the last century.[2] The progress of Louis's campaign continues to engage Rancé's attention,
and his letters are interspersed with comments on such events as
the capture of Namur (1692) and the siege of Rheinfeld (1693),
and a sour observation on perfidious Albion: 'les Anglais n'ont
ni fidélité ni bonne foi'. Another topic is the dispute with Mabillon, in which Mme de Guise played a decisive role, eventually
bringing the two men together in a meeting of charitable reconciliation.[3] Mostly the letters deal with individuals known to
them both: the death of M. de Nocey, the hermit of la Trappe,
the attempts of the widowed Mme de Mornay to settle down at les
Clairets despite bad health, and her sister's doubtful vocation,
Mme de Guise's kindness to Mme de Belin, and so on. The death
of la Grande Mademoiselle elicits some favourable comments, not
least on Mme de Guise's stoic acceptance ('désintéressement')
at her half-sister's failure to leave her a penny.[4]

Some personal remarks are not without interest but show a
generally sombre mood:[5] 'V.A.R. a grande raison de dire que le
déguisement est presque général, et si on avoit tiré le masque,
on verroit bien les difformités auxquelles on ne s'attend pas. La
grande piété du Roi devroit convertir tout son royaume...' The
accents of Pascal, or La Bruyère, are clearly echoed here. On her
own conduct he is always specific:[6] 'C'est à vous à régler vos
communions selon les dispositions où vous vous trouverez.'

---

[1] *TC* I/64 of 8 Feb. 1689.   [2] See Gonod, pp. 287–337.
[3] See above, pp. 53–54.   [4] Gonod, p. 322 of 12 Apr. 1693.
[5] Ibid., p. 289 of 4 Feb. 1692.   [6] Ibid., p. 296 of 7 Apr. 1692.

Later he advises her to make her communion on St. John's day, 1693, rather than on the preceding Sunday, and in September approves her deferment of communion for reasons of health, and in the last letter of all[1] he tells her not to worry about giving up her breviary in her failing state of health. He adds: 'le caractère qui distingue ceux qui sont à Dieu de ceux qui n'y sont pas, c'est de pardonner et d'oublier; et le propre d'un véritable chrétien est d'être sans souvenir, sans mémoire et sans ressentiment.' The reference may well be to her half-sister, and Mme de Guise's lifetime of estrangement from her. The rest is silence, for no more letters survive.

Mme de Guise died in 1696, of cancer, as piously as she had lived, and at her own request was laid not in a royal tomb but as an ordinary religious in the church of the Carmelites of the rue Saint-Jacques.[2] Rancé's firm and gentle guidance evidently brought her comfort in a life of considerable loneliness and disappointment, and behind his invariable tone of respect one discerns a very real human affection.

[1] Ibid., p. 334 of 7 Dec. 1693.
[2] A typical tribute was the published *Oraison funèbre de Mme de Guise*, by the Capuchin Jérothée de Mortagne, whose order had been charged after the Revocation with converting Huguenots in the Alençon area.

14. Family

RANCÉ's relations with those members of his family who stayed outside the cloister were by no means as impersonal as Dubois, for one, seems to think, nor is it really true to say that he shows any lack of interest when discussing their problems with third parties, especially Favier who knew them all. At the same time he strenuously rejected requests to use his influence for what he regarded as unworthy motives, and only very reluctantly offered advice even when it was sought. Despite these reservations, certain episodes in his family dealings are very fully documented and throw much light on the society of Rancé's day.

His elder brother, Denis-François, died so early that he can have had little influence on subsequent events, and his younger brother, Henri, embraced a career of arms which took him abroad for much of the time.¹ The only letters known to survive of those addressed to him show a warm affection and sympathy for the dangers and uncertainties of a military life, but little else.² It is not even known whether, or how often, they met in later years. He occasionally comes up in correspondence with others: seeing the Pope on his way back from Sicily in 1677,³ meeting James II twenty years later; but he remains a rather shadowy figure until we reach Saint-Simon's recollections⁴ of him in extreme old age (he was well over 90 when he died and had apparently grown to resemble Rancé quite remarkably). On one occasion Mme d'Albon tried to get Rancé's support for establishing their brother, then, in 1680,⁵ no longer young, in a less

¹ Henri (1629–1726) is mentioned as having recently visited la Trappe in 1667/8 in a descriptive letter by one F.F.P.A. (a Maurist) *Description... de la Trappe*, 1670, p. 8, included in the 1683 edition of Félibien, *Description*, p. 71, but that seems to be all. It is a mystery where Dubois (i, p. 8) got the idea that his name was Philippe-Charles; he always signed Henri and is never referred to in any other way in legal documents.

² A brief autograph of 23 May 1669 in the Tournoüer collection, *TB* 1841 of 7 Feb. 1683, and *TC* I/45 of 15 Feb. 1686.

³ Mentioned in a letter to Retz of 1 Oct. 1677 in *TB* 882.

⁴ Saint-Simon, *Mémoires*, vi, pp. 202–3. He did not meet him until 1718 (he had long been at Marseilles) and then only briefly, but the likeness to the late abbot astonished him.   ⁵ *TB* 1353.

dangerous occupation, and specifically to secure him a benefice, but this Rancé flatly refused to do on the grounds that Henri did not have any ecclesiastical training or status.

One of his sisters, Marie, married in 1658 François de Chalvet-Rochemonteix, comte de Vernassal,[1] and died in 1665, when Rancé was still in Rome. After causing much trouble over the succession, her husband followed her in 1673. There is no trace of any correspondence with either of them, though business matters were discussed acrimoniously and at length, according to other letters; they left two sons and a daughter, who briefly comes on the scene.[2]

In 1674[3] this niece is the subject of discussion with Marie-Louise, and seems to be considering a religious vocation. Six years later she wrote to Rancé, giving news of herself and her two brothers, one (Maximilien) already Chevalier, in terms which suggest that she had been responsible for their upbringing since their mother's death and also that Rancé had not had much, if any, communication with her before. He says[4] that he feels all due affection for the children of his late sister but goes on: 'cependant quelques sentiments que j'aye pour eux, je ne puis leur servir de rien. L'estat où je suis m'oste tous les moyens de leur estre utile.' He will, however, recommend his nephew, the Chevalier, to Bellefonds who, out of friendship, is likely to do something. Twenty years later he speaks of a nephew carrying letters between James II and himself, and it is presumably this same Chevalier, who rose to be lieutenant-general in 1734, and died last of his line in 1755, having outlived his soldier son.[5] As for his niece's own vocation, all he can do at present is to pray for guidance for her. In September 1680[6] he sent her a very typical letter, again offering support but no specific advice: 'quitter le monde c'est se tirer du milieu d'une tempête dans laquelle il est presque impossible d'éviter le naufrage', but she should be very careful before choos-

---

[1] See *MC* XLII. 169 (Ferret) of 11 Aug. 1670, giving date of contract as 27 Apr. 1658, 'passé devant Carpet au baillage de Forez'.

[2] The family name was Chalvet de Rochemonteix, seigneurs de Vernassal. See J. B. Bouillet, *Nobiliaire d'Auvergne*, ii, pp. 93–5. See also *BN*, pièces originales, 2520 *Rochemonteix*, and Archives Nationales, *Insinuations au Châtelet*, y 226, XV, 71 of 1 Feb. 1670 (f. 77ᵛ). On the death of François de Vernassal, his sister, Gillette, became guardian of the minor children, and, to judge from the documents just cited, it must have been a very litigious family.

[3] *TD*, series A, 11, of 23 Jan. 1674.   [4] *TB* 1245 of 29 Jan. 1680.

[5] See Bouillet, loc. cit.   [6] *TC* I/26 of 3 Sept. 1680 and Gonod, p. 67.

ing her cloister. He wrote to Favier by the same post (like most of Rancé's relatives the Vernassals lived in Auvergne), making similar comments. Next year in another letter to Favier[1] he expresses his sympathy for her in 'une si grande incertitude', for she is still awaiting a real call; and with that we lose trace of her and her family. Favier would certainly have kept in touch, but makes no reference to them in any extant letters to Rancé so far as one can judge.

The other sister, Claude-Charlotte, was older than Rancé by a year or two (perhaps four or five even) and died in 1697. His relations with her and her family were constant and close, and on the death of their mother she may to some extent have taken over the maternal role. Married through the Queen's favour to René Faudoas d'Averton, comte de Belin,[2] she lost her mother and her husband (murdered by his brother-in-law) within the space of four years, when she was only a young girl (1638 and 1642). From this first marriage she had a son 'le petit baron', who did not live, and a daughter Antoinette, who married a cousin, Emmanuel, in 1655 and was known as Mme de Belin.

In 1644 Claude-Charlotte married again, Gilbert d'Albon, comte de Chazeul,[3] a member of a family of Lyonnais origin, related to the maréchal de Saint-André and apparently known to both Rancé and Favier already in 1642. He became a favourite at Court, and was eventually appointed chevalier d'honneur to the duchesse d'Orléans. He was a man of conspicuous piety, a friend of the marquis de Liancourt among others, and at one stage (about 1650) he was to be found in circles friendly to Port-Royal, but he took a Jesuit confessor, P. Saint-Jure, and his Jansenist sympathies do not seem to have lasted very long. He joined the Compagnie du Saint-Sacrement, and was one of those, like the ducs de Mazarin, Luynes, and Roannez, who pointedly refused to accompany Louis to Metz in 1665 and was branded by Colbert in a confidential report as a *dévot*. Later, with Brancas and others, he was active in the campaign against *Tartuffe*. A sister of his, Perronnelle-Claude, who married in 1642, took the veil on being

[1] Gonod, p. 68 of 25 May 1681.
[2] See article by M. Prevost in *DBF* s.v. *Averton*.
[3] See article by J. Balteau in *DBF* and also Mesnard, *Pascal et les Roannez*, pp. 822–3. By following up cross-references in P. Anselme and De la Chesnaye Desbois some of the family's history can be reconstructed, but there are still a lot of gaps because information about daughters is seldom adequate.

widowed and joined the Visitation at Mâcon, where another member of the family, Marie-Hélène, was superior from 1684 to 1690. The Albons had an estate in Auvergne, not far from Vichy, and a house in Paris, so that the young Rancé had ample opportunity for meeting them as he finished his studies and embarked on his career in the Church. Favier, probably because he too was an Auvergnat, was always on close terms with the Albons, to whom he had been tutor, as he seems to have been with the Vernassals, and never ceased to be involved in the family's affairs, which is incidentally how the relevant documents have come to be preserved.

On his father's death in 1650, Rancé became head of the family; two sisters, Thérèse and Louise-Isabelle, were already in religion, and a third, perhaps Françoise, or even Marie before her marriage, was very shortly to follow; his only surviving brother was a Knight of Malta, so that his two brothers-in-law were the persons with whom he had most dealings in business matters. The Albons soon started a family, and produced three daughters in rapid succession: Claude-Catherine, Louise-Henriette, and Marie-Claire. In 1658, the year after his conversion, Rancé is known to have paid a visit to the Albons in Auvergne at a time when he was still intending to work out a rule of life at Véretz, under Andilly's guidance and in close contact with Mère Louise Rogier at Tours nearby. At the time of this visit none of his nieces can have been more than 13, but by a curious chance the most critical period of his life coincided with the decisive moment in that of Louise-Henriette. By 1661 Rancé had made up his mind to sell Véretz, which necessitated protracted negotiations with his brothers-in-law, and in a letter of December that year describing to Mère Louise Rogier his difficulties in disposing of the estate he sends warm greetings to his niece, who had been sent in about 1652 to be educated at the convent at Tours. By the end of the following year both uncle and niece had made up their minds, one to enter the Visitation, the other to become a Cistercian. Rancé's biographers suggest, very plausibly, that the sight of the young girl's sacrifice may have contributed decisively to his own final step. The choice of Tours, as against Riom or Thiers, nearer home, or Mâcon, with her aunt, is stated in her obituary notice to have been determined by the presence there of her great-uncle, the Archbishop, and Rancé, while her profession was specifically

approved by her father and great-uncle.[1] The story of Louise-
Henriette has been told in an earlier chapter; her father's later
attempt to bring her nearer home, her own defiant wish to go to
Port-Royal, and her often strained relations with Mère Louise
Rogier suggest that whatever influence Rancé had did not go
unchallenged.

There are several indications that it was not a very happy family.
A letter to Favier of 1 November 1670[2] speaks of the elder
daughter as being on good terms with her parents, but in a way
which strongly suggests that this was not always the case. This
niece, Catherine, must have married François de la Barge[3] at about
the same time that her uncle and sister were being professed, and
her subsequent history is by no means tranquil. Her husband came
from near Thiers, and like all the others she remained in close
touch with Favier and, through him, with Rancé. M. d'Albon no
doubt approved the match, for shortly after his death the third
daughter married, and Rancé goes out of his way to reassure his
widowed sister[4] that even if the husband (Gilbert d'Hostun,
comte de Verdun) was not the one preferred by the late M.
d'Albon, he might have changed his mind if he had lived. There
is a further clue to Rancé's relations with his brother-in-law in a
single surviving letter, informative in its silence (22 October
1677).[5] Rancé finds it 'assez extraordinaire qu'étant à Dieu autant
que vous y êtes... nous ayons si peu de commerce ensemble', and
continues with some very impersonal remarks about recent attacks on himself, the difficulties of introducing reforms, and so on.
Other members of the Compagnie du Saint-Sacrement, notably
Brancas, were close friends of Rancé, and his lack of contact
with M. d'Albon is almost certainly due to differences of personality (and memories of legal wrangles over succession) rather
than of belief. It was incidentally at exactly this time that Mme
de Sévigné met the Albons at Vichy and later went out to dine at
their home[6]—a further indication of the society to which they
were accustomed. When M. d'Albon died, Rancé wrote to Maza-

---

[1] On Louise-Henriette see above, pp. 202–209. The details are taken from her
obituary in *Vis, Lettres circ.*, Tours, 1689.

[2] Gonod, p. 38.

[3] On the La Barge family see Bouillet, op. cit. i, pp. 153–4.

[4] *TB* 1353 of Oct. 1680.

[5] Or possibly 22 Oct. 1678 in *A* 2106, f. 83.

[6] Mme de Sévigné, *Lettres*, ii, p. 361 of 27 Sept. 1677.

rin of his Christian death and, of course, to his sister and niece
with the usual condolences. There is no reason to question
Rancé's respect for his brother-in-law's piety, but this did not
extend to his business acumen. The endless financial complications consequent on Rancé's monastic profession had sorely tried
Rancé's patience, but Albon remained heavily in debt, if we are
to believe a letter to Favier of 1674,[1] and left no male heir to
restore the family fortunes.

Meanwhile M. d'Albon's stepdaughter, Mme de Belin, now
ten years widowed, was beginning to take stock, and at the
beginning of 1677 Rancé wrote to her one of his typically hortatory letters, telling her to waste no more time but to accept
conversion. She was by then approaching 40, and by the end of
the year Rancé, visibly exasperated by her attitude wrote:[2] 'vous
vous contentez de penser et de vouloir... Quand Dieu s'est lassé
de parler aux hommes il garde avec eux un éternel silence'; she
must act before it is too late. How far she heeded his advice cannot be ascertained, but in 1693 (to Mme de Guise) and in 1694
(to Marie-Louise) Rancé speaks of her sympathetically. By then
her health was poor, but she enjoyed Mme de Guise's favour
and had presumably taken some positive step towards the conversion contemplated earlier. It is odd that he never refers to their
family relationship, although they had often been together at
Véretz in the past. Living at Averton (Mayenne) she had more
opportunity than his Auvergnat nieces for visiting la Trappe in
the train of Mme de Guise, but no details of such visits are known.

Not much more than a year later Mme d'Albon too seems to
have come to some kind of spiritual cross-roads, though it
would be inappropriate in her case to speak of conversion. In
early 1679[3] Rancé writes to say how pleased he is to hear of her
intention of giving herself more fully to God but that he would
have been even more happy to have heard this from her own
mouth. It must be remembered that up to 1675 he had had a
chance of seeing her whenever he was in Paris, and only now did
separation appear final. In December 1679 she lost her husband,
and by the following autumn the marriage of her youngest
daughter Marie-Claire left her alone. Only a few weeks after

---

[1] Gonod, p. 52 of 24 Apr. 1674.
[2] *TB* 780 of 14 Jan. 1677 and *TB* 891 of 2 Dec. 1677.
[3] *A* 2106, f. 7 and Gonod, p. 66 of 3 Feb. 1679.

M. d'Albon's death a serious quarrel blew up between the widow and her eldest daughter, Mme de la Barge. Under the circumstances it was most probably over questions of succession, for nothing more readily strains family relations, and M. d'Albon's chronic indebtedness left his then only son-in-law in an unenviable position. At all events Rancé wrote in January 1680[1] to his niece, noting with regret that she is on bad terms with her mother, but also recommending Favier (who lived at Thiers) as an adviser for the rule of life which she ought to adopt. It looks very much as though she too, like her mother and half-sister, were going through some spiritual reappraisal. Some time in 1680 or 1681[2] Rancé told Louise-Henriette that if he saw Mme d'Albon (which apparently he did not) he would try to effect a reconciliation. Whatever had happened, it seems clear in the light of subsequent events that, on the death of M. d'Albon, widow and daughters independently turned to Rancé for help and guidance. In October 1680[3] he heard from his sister that the marriage frowned upon by M. d'Albon was settled, and he told her once more how much he would like to see her, but it would be too much to expect her to make a special journey to la Trappe just to see 'une personne qui n'en vaut pas la peine'. Early in 1681[4] he told both Favier and Louise-Henriette that he did not approve of 'ces mariages prétendus' in the context of his sister's relations with Mme de la Barge, and again, though the details are obscure (it could by the date refer to the eldest la Barge girl), Rancé has obviously begun to play an active part in family affairs. In 1682[5] he has still not seen his sister, and wishes he could so that he could relieve her of some of the cares of those obliged to live in the world. He probably never saw her again, but he was active on her behalf, for in 1690[6] he wrote to M. le Nain in Paris to thank him for help in a lawsuit in which she had been engaged. Much as he disliked material problems in general and litigation in particular, he clearly made an exception for his sister.

No more is known of the relations between Mme d'Albon and her eldest daughter, but the last chapter in this family saga is the most illuminating. For a long time pressure had been put on Louise-Henriette to move from Tours nearer home, as was perfectly normal in her order with its system of triennially elected

[1] TB 1203.   [2] TB 1422.   [3] TB 1353.   [4] A 2106, f. 96.
[5] TB 1724 of 30 July 1682.   [6] 2 June 1690, original in Tournoüer collection.

superiors, but Rancé had steadfastly opposed such a move. The
death of her father in 1679, the marriage of her younger sister in
1680, and finally the re-election of Mère Louise Rogier in 1683
must all have contributed to Louise-Henriette's decision to allow
her name to go forward in 1686 for election to Riom with effect
from the following May. Reluctant as she was (and fully justified
by events), she must have felt a duty to be near her mother and,
perhaps, her sister who is known to have engineered the appointment, to the intense annoyance of Mère Louise Rogier.[1] At
exactly the same time the tentative steps towards conversion
first mentioned in 1680 seem to have led Mme de la Barge to
specific action, for her uncle writes in December 1686:[2] 'Je loue
Dieu de ce qu'il vous met au cœur de penser à vous plus que vous
n'avez fait à présent.' She had been ill for some time, and was by
now about 40, always the crucial age for Rancé's correspondents,
but has a good confessor and has just made her communion,
apparently as a specific step in conversion. All the same, Rancé
is not entirely reassured and expresses doubts to Favier some
months later.

In May 1687, however, Louise-Henriette arrived in Riom to
take over her new charge and everything came to a head.[3] She
could not go over to Thiers to see Favier and he was too infirm
to visit her (or even Mme de la Barge), and we can thus follow the
course of events from the correspondence between all the interested parties. As soon as she could get away from home, at the
end of September, Mme de la Barge went to stay for a fortnight
with her sister (and not, incidentally, with her mother, who is
never mentioned and must have been elsewhere). She brought
with her one of her daughters, referred to as 'ma nièce de Tours'
(a secondary title of the la Barges taken from a village a few miles
away and nothing to do with Louise-Henriette's recent domicile).
This girl was to spend some time boarding with her aunt to give
her a taste of religious life before going on to the Cistercian
house of l'Esclache, recently transferred from the country into the
town of Clermont, as soon as the dowry could be collected. The
plan was vague at first, and Louise-Henriette simply tells Favier,
'nous avons ma nièce de Tours qui devient un peu dévote... Je ne

[1] See above, p. 207.   [2] TC II/270 of 1 Dec. 1686.
[3] The story can mostly be followed in Jaloustre, *Précepteur auvergnat*, but for some
reason he omitted to publish one or two of the letters in CF 344.

sçay ce qu'il plaira à Dieu d'en faire...' Nothing much happened during the first six months, but then the crisis broke. Mme de la Barge had two other daughters, one referred to as 'Bellisme' (another secondary title), the other unnamed. While one daughter was with her maternal aunt at Riom, the other two had been sent to the Visitation at Thiers, where in May 1688 their paternal aunt had been elected superior (she had served two earlier terms before they came and had been one of the founders.)[1] In April Louise-Henriette is not very impressed by her niece 'de Tours', 'qui a estrangement l'esprit du monde', and in June 'sa complaisance pour moi n'ira pas jusqu'à la faire changer sur son entêtement'. At the same time we first hear that the two other girls are destined for the Benedictine house of Courpières, only a few miles from their home. Louise-Henriette obviously disapproved of Courpières, and almost at once wrote a secret letter to her niece de Bellisme inviting her to come to Riom if she really wanted to become a nun. She must also have written direct to Rancé, or asked Favier to do so, because a month later Rancé wrote a memorable letter to Mme de la Barge which made a tense situation even more dramatic.

Louise-Henriette's opinion of the situation is highly relevant, for her words or a paraphrase of them must have reached her uncle and prompted his response. Writing of her niece de Tours she tells Favier (9 July 1688): 'On se fait religieuse parce qu'on ne pourroit être grande dame à Paris, parce qu'on prétend à quelque abbaie, que les religieuses de l'Esclache ont de l'esprit, et l'esprit du monde, et qu'elles sont toutes filles de qualité, qu'on n'y a ni assujetissement, ni austérité, ni communauté régulière, excepté l'office.' A month later she says: 'Ma sœur me dit... que ma nièce ne fera jamais tant de mal dans la religion que dans le monde, parce qu'elle prétend que le cloitre et la grille la mettront à couvert de tout devant le monde.' It is not hard to detect the influence of Rancé on his fiery niece.

Acting on information and opinions of this kind Rancé, as he says himself, broke all his resolutions about non-interference (not for the first time) and sent Mme de la Barge what she herself described as 'une verte réprimande' (26 July 1688):[2] L'intérêt que je prends à votre salut et à celui de vos filles m'oblige de vous

---

[1] *Vis, Histoire de la Visitation de Riom* and M 2440 on Riom and Thiers.
[2] *TC* I/184.

avertir que vous attirez la colère de Dieu sur votre personne et sur toute votre famille si vous les engagez dans la profession religieuse sans être assurée que Dieu les y appelle.' She must exercise the greatest care in choosing the right cloister or 'vous rendrez vos filles malheureuses pour jamais'. The effect of this intervention was devastating; the distraught mother wrote to Favier (28 September 1688):[1] 'J'aimerois mieux mourir que de leur laisser prendre l'habit à Courpières' and adds the irresistibly convincing feminine touch: 'Les habits de mes filles sont achetées pour leur faire prendre l'habit. Je suis dans une perplexité à faire pitié.'

A week or two later she wrote to Favier again, and it is this last, undated, letter which sets the whole incident in its context.[2] She asks Favier to give a letter secretly to her children, clearly without the knowledge of the superior, their paternal aunt. They still want to go to Courpières (Rancé was too remote to frighten them as much as present terrors) and their father had resolved to take them there on St. Martin's day (11 November), with the support of his sister. The latter had now changed her mind and wanted them to stay at Thiers until Christmas; Mme de la Barge had meanwhile forced them to write to their father (an extraordinary reflection on relations within the family, for Thiers, the château of la Barge, and Courpières are within a circle of some five miles radius) and would still like to send them to Courpières, 'car je ne les aime où elles sont que par la régularité de l'ordre, at après la manière dont on les y a traitées, qui recommencera dès que ma belle-sœur ne sera plus supérieure [1694] je voudrois de tout mon cœur qu'elles en sortient.' Then comes the echo of her uncle's terrible warning; she asks Favier to help them harken to God's voice in making their choice, 'que je n'aye point de compte à rendre au Seigneur au dernier jour si terrible'. She and her husband beg their friend, now 80 years old, to help them, and she ends 'si je croyois qu'elles vouloient demeurer [à Sainte-Marie de Thiers] religieuses et que cela fût sûr je serois en repos...'

The whole situation reads like a first draft of Diderot's *La Religieuse*; obviously the one point on which M. de la Barge admitted no discussion was *whether* his wretched daughters should take the veil, though he might grudgingly debate *where*. The

---

[1] Jaloustre, *Précepteur auvergnat*, p. 30.   [2] *CF* 344 B, f. 116.

sequel is not known, though these two do not seem to have married and probably did go to Courpières in the end.

This was not all, however, for Louise-Henriette still had her niece de Tours, and had by no means finished trying to influence her two other nieces, through Favier, directly by letter, and through a certain M. Montagnier.[1] All we learn of the two at Thiers is that Mlle de Bellisme has apparently yielded to argument; but there is more detail about Mlle de Tours, who seems to have inherited the headstrong character of both mother and aunt. 'Elle ne fera pas ici de fort grands progrés dans la piété, car c'est un esprit... d'une vivacité étonnante', which, in view of Louise-Henriette's own early record, is not without its irony (the very word is used in her own official obituary). Meanwhile the girl could still not go to l'Esclache until the money was forthcoming, because the abbess, her aristocratic kinswoman Mme de Montmorin de Saint-Hérem (died 1692), needed it for her building programme. In September the girl 'n'est pas si docile, mais elle ne paroist pas si empressée qu'elle estoit pour aller à l'Esclache.' One of her best friends, the prioress, has just been promoted abbess of another house and she is thinking again. By the end of November, after more than a year wrestling with her niece's will, Louise-Henriette seems to have won. A P. Soanen (probably an Oratorian) has spoken to her mother about the girl, now described as 'plus sage', and she has promised to give up the idea of l'Esclache. It must be remembered that throughout this time Louise-Henriette had been acutely lonely and unhappy, and often sick, in her attempts to reform the house to which she had unwillingly been sent, and had by now decided, or at least been advised by Rancé, to return to Tours on completion of her triennate in 1690. As there is no word of her mother in any of the letters, she must be assumed to have left Auvergne for good, and was certainly no longer a factor to be reckoned with. However, just as all three nieces seemed on the point of following Louise-Henriette's advice, based on that of her uncle and Favier, she suddenly died on December 1688 attended by Mme de la Barge and one of her nieces, and in fact the letter of November just quoted is the last she left. There is a brief epilogue, for three years later Rancé wrote to Favier (3 September 1691)[2] that his niece (sc. great-niece) de Tours was still hesitant about a vocation, and

---

[1] Jaloustre, *Précepteur auvergnat*, pp. 29, seq.   [2] Gonod, p. 77.

if the other two had been still a problem by then he would surely have said so. The last mention of the family is in 1716, when Marie-Jeanne de la Barge, perhaps Mlle de Tours, did homage, presumably on the death of her father, and the line died out.[1]

The whole story throws into sharper relief Rancé's problem in dealing with the numerous cases of girls with uncertain vocations; it highlights the extraordinary authority he continued to exercise over members of his family, none of whom he had seen for twenty years or more; and it shows too, in the most interesting way, how years of correspondence with her uncle had made Louise-Henriette speak with his voice. The attitude of the la Barges towards the religious life, with their emphasis on amenity and congenial company, if possible within easy reach of home and under the rule of some relative, and no attention at all to spiritual values, shows more graphically than any amount of polemic just what Rancé, and Louise-Henriette, were fighting against, and, as already mentioned, makes it easier to see how Diderot's scurrilous novel came to be written and enjoyed. Certainly in any assessment of Rancé's influence this chapter on his immediate family should be seen as reflecting in microcosm what he constantly tried to achieve in a broader field.

[1] Bouillet, loc. cit.

PART IV

CONCLUSIONS

15. Rancé and the Jansenists

VERY frequently in the course of this study the question of Rancé's relations with the Jansenists, and his attitude to their doctrines, has come up, and since it is this more than any other single question that has bedevilled the whole issue of his biographies for nearly three centuries, some attempt at clarification has to be made. As Dubois rightly observes, the problem is partly one of chronology—Jansenism meant different things at different times—partly one of distinguishing between persons and doctrines, but, in his obsessive concern to clear Rancé of any compromising contacts with these dangerous heretics, he goes to such lengths that the exactly contrary thesis of the Jesuit Le Lasseur (1876)[1] seems hardly more absurd. If one starts with the pre-conceived notion that all Jansenist sympathizers are trying to wreck the Church by perverting its doctrine, and that those who appear harmless are just successful hypocrites, then a grand conspiracy theory inevitably results, as both Dubois and Le Lasseur in their opposite ways show. Let it be said once and for all that there were Jansenists, especially in the early eighteenth century, who were prepared to do most things to justify their cause, and that posthumous enrolment of Rancé among their elect was part of their programme, but in trying to exonerate Rancé, too many of his non-Jansenist friends have actually suppressed material which puts him in a more favourable light than that of whitewash. The sum of evidence now available all goes to show that Rancé neither attacked nor defended Jansenists or Jansenism as usually understood, he offered a viable alternative of which not enough has been written.

The chronology of his contacts and some comments on them will probably help most to resolve the question. Dubois very reasonably marks three periods—before, during, and after the Peace of the Church, 1668–78 (more or less). In 1657 Rancé had lived through the long debate provoked by publication of the *Augustinus* (1640), culminating in the condemnation of Arnauld (1656). Odd hints in letters of this early period to Favier show

[1] F. Le Lasseur, 'Rancé et le Jansénisme'.

that he took the interest in the debate natural to any student of theology. Later his *salon* friends played with Jansenism as they had played with the Fronde, but some were genuinely convinced that Arnauld's cause was right. When it came to giving his signature to the Formulary of 1656 Rancé did so as a matter of obedience, not at all on the abstruse merits of the case. His position in 1657 is best described as neutral on the Jansenist side.[1]

His conversion led him to take the next logical step. By definition he had chosen the narrow way, and, short of becoming a monk at once (a solution which we know he rejected out of hand until 1662), the circle on whose periphery he had long found himself was the obvious answer. His aunt, Mme Bouthillier, was an old friend of Andilly and of Mère Louise Rogier. The Oratorians, to whom the latter sent him, included du Breuil, soon to be exiled for Jansenist obduracy, and they in their turn approved his recourse to Andilly. The bishops he consulted, Châlons, Alet, Pamiers, were closely associated with Port-Royal, and as one friend sent him to another he naturally formed in these crucial years friendships which meant more to him than casual contacts in society. Thus when Favier was given Saint-Symphorien, in 1662, it is no surprise to read that he was accused of being a Jansenist, and in any case, under Bishop Choart de Buzenval, Beauvais was a major centre of Jansenist activity. Rancé's weeks with Le Roy at Véretz in 1659 led to yet another network of contacts later on. By his reading, directed by Andilly, and his contacts Rancé was intimately, but passively, involved, with the friends of Port-Royal and if he had followed the advice of Alet, to become a bishop, rather than that of Comminges, to become a regular abbot, he would have been forced into active support. However, his decision in 1662 to renounce not only preferment but also the world in which he had so far lived necessarily implied a renunciation of all partisan activity not directly connected with his monastery.

From 1662 to 1666 he was too busy preparing to become a monk, then in the novitiate, then in Rome to have much time for friends, however old, but on his return it was not long before he found that the passive role of a private person is very different from that of a superior. He was identified with the cause of Cistercian reform, that is, an actual way of life, led by actual men

---

[1] On all this see above, pp. 9–10, and the early letters in Gonod.

and women, and in so far as the austerity he preached and practised fulfilled a spiritual need similarly fulfilled by Port-Royal (a
Cistercian foundation, one should recall, only recently granted
autonomy), it is entirely natural that a very similar clientele sought
la Trappe for brief retreat or even for life. By 1667 he was in
touch with Pontchâteau, a former solitary, who came to stay,
and had renewed contact with Andilly, while at the same time
Benoît Deschamps, Jacques Puiperrou, and Pierre le Nain took
the habit, all closely associated with Jansenism—Rigobert's
arrival in 1665 from Hautefontaine seems to have had purely
monastic motives.[1] The fact that these three found a true vocation
at la Trappe must have had a lot to do with subsequent applications
from like-minded men. Up to the Peace of the Church, then, Rancé
had forsaken none of his old friends as friends, he had simply
given up all partisan allegiance active or passive, in favour of an
increasingly publicized willingness to accept any religious suitable
for la Trappe whatever their theological persuasion, on the strict
understanding that no reference to doctrinal matters would ever
be made within the monastery. This attitude could be called
passive benevolence, and it remained constant throughout his
life. If strict neutrality means the exclusion of known Jansenists
he was not neutral, but such a definition is scarcely helpful.

The period of the Peace of the Church followed so soon that
the question of strict neutrality became somewhat academic in
theory, though in practice battle lines were being drawn up for
the next round of open warfare. A stream of visitors came in the
next few years, including most leading Jansenists. In 1669 Tillemont came to see his brother, dom le Nain, and Guillaume Quesnel, brother of Pasquier, came to try his vocation. From the
same year dates the beginning of a correspondence with Quesnel
which lasted until 1681. Quesnel, who had met Arnauld and
Nicole at Saint-Magloire (and Rancé in his early days at the
Institution), and many of his colleagues, including Monchy,
Bruscoly, Saint-Pé, and others, provided an important source of
recruitment, and a large body within the Congregation of the
Oratory became identified with the Jansenist cause, and in any

[1] See B. Neveu, *Pontchâteau*, and the same author's *Un Historien à l'école de Port-
Royal* (on dom le Nain's brother, Tillemont). Benoît's brother was gardener at Port-
Royal; Jacques and other Celestines were in contact with Jansenists at Sens and
elsewhere (see above, pp. 159–161).

case against the Jesuits.[1] In 1670 or 1671 Rapin paid a visit, and went on to Perseigne, where he took malicious satisfaction in reporting that 'M. de la Trappe se faisait grand tort de se lier avec ces Messieurs, qu'il faisait plus de mal à l'Eglise que les Jansénistes, pratiquant par effet ce qu'ils avaient enseigné.[2] This highly partial testimony is interesting for its recognition of the essential difference between la Trappe and Port-Royal, between practice and theory. Du Hamel[3] came for the first of several visits in 1671, and in 1682 fell so ill at La Trappe that he almost died there. Arnauld himself came in 1673, and was much edified.[4] Other visitors or correspondents included Hermant,[5] Sacy,[6] Nicole,[7] Floriot,[8] and they, and many others, sent books for Rancé's opinion (he actually seems to have read some of them and had quite a debate with Floriot). All things considered, it looks as though Rancé's Jansenist friends felt that his growing prestige would do them more good if they represented him not as an ally, but as a benevolent neutral, or at most fellow-traveller, in moral values.

From about 1675 Rancé's letters show a somewhat changed attitude. A key phrase comes in a letter of November 1675[9] to Mlle de Goëllo, and so excellently sums up his present and future attitude that it is worth quoting again: 'Je ne suis point surpris que l'on dise que vous êtes Janséniste; c'est une espèce de phantosme que les gens du monde, et les dévots à la mode... opposent aux personnes qui se retirent de leurs sentiments pour suivre les maximes étroites', and he goes on to condemn the majority of directors who use 'ces règles toutes humaines et ces condescendances molles'. His opposition to the laxists, and Molinists, was shared by a wide range of clergy from Bossuet down ('les ordures des casuistes') who were free of Jansenist connections, and his remark only underlines the inadequacy of using moral theology alone as a criterion in this debate. At exactly the same time he wrote to Mère Agnès de Bellefonds,[10] whose

[1] See above, pp. 117–119 and 251–255.

[2] Copy of letter by Benoît Luce, of Perseigne, in PR 415.

[3] See above, pp. 256–258.   [4] Arnauld to Le Roy, Lettres, ix, p. xx.

[5] Rancé wrote to him in 1672 (Muguet, i, p. 231), in 1673, and 1674 (Denis Autographes de Troussures).

[6] Letters in 1672 (Muguet, i, p. 383) and 1673 (TB 277).

[7] Letters in Nicole, Lettres, i, pp. 559 seq., from 1679 to 1689.

[8] Letters in Morale... du Pater, 1745, vi (separate pagination after p. 74).

[9] See above, pp. 282–283. TB 583.   [10] TD, series C, 1.

nephew, the maréchal, was being accused of Jansenism: 'On a cela de bon avec les Jansénistes que quand on ne dit pas mal d'eux, ils disent du bien de vous... pour les autres, à moins que l'on épouse leurs passions... ils vous considèrent comme leur ennemi'. These remarks to Mlle de Goëllo and Mère Agnès, together with Rapin's report, should be enough to prove that by 1675 Rancé was, and had long been, regarded with disfavour by the Jesuits and their friends, but they also show that even at that time, when Jansenists were legally tolerated, he specifically dissociated himself (and, by implication, his two correspondents) from belonging in any sense to the party.

This explains his extreme annoyance with Beaufort next year (1676) for upsetting his relations with Le Roy, but also for spreading rumours of his Jansenist sympathies.[1] It is wholly typical of his consistent attitude from now on that in the same year, 1676, he should accept a monk sent by Arnauld (frère Maxime, who finished up at l'Étoile),[2] receive a visit from Caulet, Jansenist Bishop of Pamiers, who offered him a site for a monastery in his diocese if ever needed[3] and write a long letter to Brancas[4] reiterating his continuing loyalty to old friends, deploring the freedom with which accusations of heresy are bandied about, but reaffirming his total submission to his lawful superiors in the matter of the Signature. Two letters to Mme de Saint-Loup of a few months later[5] restate his position with even more emphasis: it is twenty years since he had given the problem of the Signature so much thought, but 'mes réflexions n'ont fait que me confirmer dans ma première opinion... Je garderay une fidélité inviolable à tous mes amis, mais il y a des choses sur lesquelles l'amitié ne doit point s'étendre.' In his second letter he tells her to burn the previous one and goes on to say that only the Church's authority can make him change his mind, 'celle de M.N. [probably Alet] ne peut rien sur moi... je le considère comme un grand saint, mais Dieu n'a point donné toutes lumières à tous ses saints.' Nor does he want to wait until his dying moment to declare his submission to the Pope (perhaps a reference to Pascal).

As if to prove the point, he welcomed a visit from Hamon in

[1] See above, pp. 128–129.
[2] Fr. Maxime's very interesting letters to M. le Nain are in the Tournoüer collection.
[3] Visit reported in TB 611.   [4] In SS.
[5] TB 752 of 6 Dec. 1676 and 785 of 20 Jan. 1677.

1677,[1] and explained his position in a letter to Marcel, at Saint-Jacques.[2] So many and such unequivocal actions and statements should have convinced even the most obstinate, but somehow those most closely concerned would not, or could not, admit that it was possible not to be against them without being for them. The letter to Bellefonds of November 1678[3] was only the public announcement of what he had been saying for years to his friends.

Even the end of the Peace did not alter Rancé's attitude, though it certainly altered that of some, by no means all, Jansenists towards him. The flood of hostile comment provoked by Le Roy's circular included bitter remarks from Feydeau and others that Rancé had betrayed what he knew to be the truth, but Feydeau's old colleague, Du Hamel, as late as 1682 wanted to die at la Trappe.[4] Quesnel was annoyed at Rancé's refusal in 1679 to re-open discussion on the Signature, but next year sent him *Jésus-Christ pénitent*.[5] Arnauld was disappointed that the Vannist dom Henri de Fouchières was rejected for his intransigent Jansenism, but paid a generous tribute to Rancé when *Sainteté* came out and Larroque attacked him.[6] Quéras and Nicole were still in perfectly amicable contact with Rancé in 1688, and perhaps later, and about the same time dom Paulin de l'Isle illustrates the consistency of Rancé's admissions policy. Writing to his brothers on 22 May 1686[7] he quotes from *De la fréquente communion* by 'un grand homme de nos jours', and reveals that he is also reading, among others, St. John Climachus, Cassian, and Rancé as he waits for the end of the probationary period imposed by his superiors before they would release him for la Trappe. Next year he had at last been allowed to go, and later became novice master, though his sympathies were hardly in doubt.

The episodes of Maupas (1692), 'voilà M. Arnauld mort' (1694), and Beaupuis and Tillemont (1696)[8] all irritated certain militant Jansenists, but they were so touchy that they would have been irritated by anything. Against these incidents may be set Rancé's continued friendship with Tillemont's father, M. le

---

[1] As a person, not as a doctor: to Mme de Saint-Loup in *TB* 843 of 4 July 1677.
[2] *TD*, series C, 50 of 4 Jan. 1677.   [3] See above, pp. 260–261.
[4] See above, pp. 237–238.   [5] Published in Tans ,'Dialogue monologué'.
[6] Arnauld, *Lettres*, ix, p. xxxviii 'à un homme de bien inconnu'.
[7] Lambert, *L'Idée d'un vrai religieux*.   [8] See ch. 3 above.

Nain[1] (who helped Mme d'Albon in a lawsuit), his new friendship with Berryer[2] (from about 1688), who died an appellant against *Unigenitus*, and his lifelong friendship with such friends of Port-Royal as Mlle de Vertus, Mme de Saint-Loup, and many others.[3] At the end, in 1698, attempts were made to discredit dom Malachie Garneyrin (who died abbot of Buonsolazzo in Tuscany) for allegedly Jansenist conduct at les Clairets at a time when he was proposed as replacement for Gervaise,[4] but by then these were routine calumnies employed by any enemy of la Trappe.

To this chronology one might add Rancé's long and friendly association with superiors who were openly favourable to Jansenism. Apart from Hautefontaine, where personal factors had already clouded the issue before Le Roy died, there was Châtillon, whose abbot, Claude le Maître, was a close friend of both Le Roy and Nicole and lived until 1693, following Rancé's advice in the reform of his house; there was Charles Benzeradt of Orval (died 1707), who gave a home to Pontchâteau and Nicole and whose house later became a centre for militant Jansenism, but who also modelled the conduct of his abbey on that of la Trappe; there was Maubuisson, whose royal abbess, Louise-Hollandine (died 1709), had been brought up at Port-Royal, was a friend of Nicole and Châtillon, and in 1682 accepted dom Alain as confessor on Rancé's recommendation.[5] Rancé's close and cordial relations with these and other superiors (Abbess de Montglat of Gif was another product of Port-Royal) have been discussed in earlier chapters, and were at all times independent of partisan or doctrinal issues. He had, it is fair to say, a special relationship with Jansenists, in that they were always welcome at la Trappe, even as monks, provided they kept silence on all contentious issues. When he wrote to Leyme[6] (and to others), 'je n'ai jamais été d'aucun parti que de celui de Jésus-Christ et de son Eglise' he meant exactly what he said. Like an even more famous Frenchman, he belonged to all because he belonged to none. If it is argued that associating with persons of known Jansenist views is equally reprehensible whether or not active propagation of those views is permitted (Le Lasseur's thesis), if all heretics are bad, and must be either converted or liquidated, then Rancé must be

---

[1] Rancé also wrote to him on his loss of sight.   [2] See above, pp. 154–155.
[3] See ch. 13 above.   [4] See letter of fr. Antoine in *SG* Suppl. Z f in 40 929.
[5] See chs. 7 and 9 above.   [6] *TB* 624 of 1676.

found guilty. If on the other hand it is argued that shouting slogans is not the only way of expressing an ideal, and that some of the most admirable aspects of French Catholicism in the seventeenth century were preserved, admittedly with others less admirable, by Port-Royal and its friends, then Rancé stands out as the man who more than any other brought out the best in individual Jansenists and made of their convictions something of lasting spiritual value in the monastic context.

As for Jansenist doctrine, it is not difficult to be specific. On the moral issue, as we have seen, Rancé remained implacably hostile to laxists, and always practised and recommended 'les maximes étroites'. On the issue of obedience, represented by the Signature, he never wavered, and was as staunch an upholder of hierarchical authority as Bossuet; it is probably fair to add that while he remained totally submissive to the Pope he had unmistakable Gallican sympathies. On the theological issue of grace he more than once professed his acceptance of St. Augustine's doctrine (however understood) but in general avoided any speculative theology in his writings, published or private, and, very probably, in conversation too.[1] There is not the slightest evidence that he held any but strictly orthodox views. Finally on the sacraments there is a wealth of evidence extending from 1676 to 1691 for a completely consistent line. Among others who consulted him on sacramental discipline are sœur Anne-Marie, the Carmelite, the Abbess (or perhaps prioress) of Maubuisson, Mère Harlay, the Visitandine, Mlle de Vertus, and James II. To every one of these he urged frequent communion, preceded by confession, and he advised them to stay away only for some grave reason, like a troubled conscience or perhaps some social obligation which had prevented adequate preparation. Communion on Sundays and feast days for the laity, more often for religious, was his rule. To one priest (dom André, in 1682)[2] he recommends that he should only abstain from saying mass 'par esprit de religion', in other words never as a deliberate deprivation. The record is clear enough.

In conclusion some evidence from dom le Nain is relevant.[3] In documents written or signed by him, preserved at Troyes (with

[1] See dom le Nain's signed statement in T 2183, ff. 33 seq. and copy in U 3069, ff. 44 seq.
[2] TC II/155 of 6 Sept. 1682.   [3] See note on le Nain, above.

a copy at Utrecht), he makes a number of statements concerning Rancé's attitude to Jansenism as it affected his own *Vie*, then in manuscript. In 1704 he wrote to Bazin, a friend of Gerbais and curé of Saint-Hilaire in Paris, that Rancé had always dissented from Arnauld and his friends on the subject of the Signature. In 1706 he signed 'cartons' for insertion into his manuscript at the insistence of a committee including Berryer, Saint-Simon, and the Bishop of Chartres, but later told Bazin that he wanted to disown the amendment, and left an alternative to be used after his death. The burden of this extensive addendum is as follows: 'Notre Révérend Père a varié, je l'avoue, les Molinistes étaient sans cesse à ses trousses les dernières années de sa vie, il a un peu changé.' He goes on to explain that Rancé 'n'a jamais eu grande liaison avec les Jésuites... on ne voit point en toute sa vie qu'il y ait eu rien de commun entre lui et ces pères... Je parle pour ce qui touche leurs personnes, car pour ce qui est de la morale rien n'a été plus éloigné de la sienne que celle des Jésuites. Que si l'on le considérait de ce côté-là, on trouverait... qu'il était un véritable Janséniste... En un mot la Trappe est le renversement de la morale des Jésuites.'

If this only confirms what the evidence cited above suggests, what follows is more critical. On grace, says dom le Nain, Rancé always declared that he embraced the opinions of St. Augustine, 'et il était si persuadé que M. Arnauld suivait pas à pas ceux de ce grand docteur... qu'il déclarait [dans une lettre] qu'il n'avait point d'autres sentiments sur ce qui touche la grâce que ceux de M. Arnauld, dont il parle avec beaucoup d'estime.' Dom le Nain adds that Rancé signed purely out of obedience, without concern for 'fait' or 'droit'. *Pace* Dubois and others, even this (if true, which it probably is) does not make Rancé more of a Jansenist than such a solid Augustinian as Bossuet.

Finally le Nain again confirms the evidence examined above: 'Si l'on faisait le dénombrement de ses principaux amis depuis la Signature, on les trouverait tous ou presque tous Jansénistes ou amis de Jansénistes.' It should be added that dom le Nain affirms in the same document that Rancé absolutely forbade discussion of these matters at la Trappe.

It will be seen that both the Jansenists and their opponents were equally unsuccessful in compromising Rancé, though the change in the final years mentioned by dom le Nain would explain a noticeable hardening of attitude from 1692 on when-ever militant Jansenists were involved. It will be seen too why dom le Nain's *Vie* so offended some of Rancé's friends; his re-fusal to waver on the Signature infuriated the Jansenists, his open condemnation of Jesuit morals and preference for Jansenist company infuriated the anti-Jansenists. Rancé's loyalty to his friends and steadfast neutrality need no apology. No other course was open to a man of honour—or consistent with faith and charity.

16.   Spiritual Lessons

THE key to Rancé's personality, teaching, and influence lies in a
series of antitheses typical of his century between love of self and
love of God, between this world and the next, time and eternity,
conflict and peace. Since antitheses in real life involve conflict,
it is not surprising that the need to reconcile contingent situations with absolute truths frequently led Rancé into what looks
like inconsistency, but so often difficulties of interpretation are
more apparent than real, deriving as they do from the simple fact
that life is inexhaustibly complex and even within the Christian
house there are many mansions. Monks at la Trappe, monks and
nuns elsewhere, men and women in the world may all be offered
the same ideal, but it never occurred to Rancé for a moment to
propose the same means of execution for all. A major source of
misunderstanding about Rancé is the failure to distinguish between what he saw as the categorical demands of perfection
appropriate to each calling and the entirely legitimate differences
between callings. He always stressed the primacy of interior dispositions, but was wise enough to demand that these, which
should be much the same for all Christians, be translated into a
rule of life to provide framework and expression for what might
otherwise remain vague aspirations. Of all these interior dispositions the first and most vital is rejection of *amour propre*. In
his commentary on the Rule (1689)[1] Rancé quotes with approval
St. Bernard's dictum 'cessit voluntas propria et non erit infernus'.
But *amour propre*, self-will, cannot just be rejected to leave an
empty space; the consequence of stopping at that is apathy and
inertia. As they are overcome they must be progressively replaced
by a real desire, and not just a passive willingness, to accomplish
the will of God. Once this state of mind has been achieved, peace
replaces conflict. The acceptance must be total, 'Dieu ne veut
point de partage', but then 'une paix profonde' will succeed
'l'agitation du monde'.[2]

Thus far Rancé's instructions are simple and applicable to all,
however hard in practice. At what one might call the hinge, or

[1] *Règle de saint Benoist*, p. 14.   [2] To Mme de Saint-Loup, *BN* 19324, p. 17.

transition, from one pole of the antithesis to the other comes conversion, and the interpretation of this critical moment is not so easy. In two different senses it involves an attitude to death. First, in extinguishing *amour-propre*, one must die to the self and the world; second, once liberated from these earthly bonds, the spirit must live for eternity. For Rancé this meant positively welcoming physical death. Neither of these concepts is as simple as it seems, and though the bare statement of such ideas is commonplace, there are implications of a special and controversial character. Here in particular in the dividing line between what Rancé regarded as desirable and necessary for those who elected a religious life and for those who remained in the world, or in some ecclesiastical life outside the cloister. In broad terms the end was the same for all, the means of attaining it vastly different. All must practise penitence and prayer, all must be humble, but each in a manner appropriate to the context of his daily life. The performance of particular acts is in itself meaningless, and thus a comparison, for instance, of life at la Trappe with that tolerated in someone like Retz or Bellefonds misses the point. In his unpublished *Explications sur la Règle* Rancé writes unambiguously:[1] 'la vie monastique quelque austère qu'elle soit n'est qu'un pur judaisme si la préparation intérieure du cœur n'est jointe aux dispositions extérieures'. His constant theme is that the proper dispositions will make us want to offer the works of penitence best suited to our calling.

Some quotations illustrate Rancé's thought, and consistency, on this matter. To the Carmelite Mme de la Vallière he wrote:[2] 'Encore que l'austérité de la vie ait de grandes utilités ce n'est point précisément cette sévérité que Dieu demande de nous. C'est l'intérieure..' To dom Cornuty, then novice master at Foucarmont:[3] 'Les moines sont faits pour pleurer leurs péchés, et leur obligation principale est d'édifier le monde par la sainteté de leur vie et non par l'éminence de leur doctrine.' But to Mme de Saint-Loup, who stayed in the world, though in a constant flurry of pious agitation, he wrote in exactly similar terms:[4] 'La pénitence n'est que la conformité de notre cœur à celui de Dieu,

---

[1] *BN* lat. 17134, f. 26.
[2] 19 Mar. 1674, quoted in *BN* 19324, a copious anthology of Rancé's sayings arranged alphabetically under subject headings.
[3] Muguet, i, p. 415.   [4] *BN* 19324, p. 508.

elle demande une totale abnégation de nous-mêmes, elle ne consiste pas seulement à pleurer, mais à pleurer ce que Dieu veut.' The significance of the last words is further explained in two other remarks, the first to Simon Gourdan, Rancé's devoted disciple at Saint-Victor:[1] 'Il faut mesurer les épreuves aux forces ... Ce n'est pas un moindre inconvénient de faire ses voies trop étroites que de s'en faire trop larges,' and the second to the reforming abbot of Orval:[2] 'La discrétion... exempte de tout relâchement... est une vertu plus grande que la pénitence.' Finally a most revealing phrase, to the Abbess of Gif, links penitence, discretion, and humility:[3] 'Il y a des personnes qui n'ont pas assez d'humilité pour souffrir leurs propres faiblesses.'

It follows from this that feats of austerity performed for their own sake may have a certain value as psychological or physiological evidence of human endurance, a kind of penitential Olympics; but such acts, by encouraging pride, may ultimately lead to a spiritual state worse than that of the inveterate worldling who at least knows that he is sinning. 'L'amour-propre se trouve partout, et souvent dans les humiliations l'orgueil se rencontre comme dans les actions de vanité.'[4]

Such remarks as these could be quoted profusely, and all with perfect consistency show that an essential element of dying to self is the humility which prevents us glorying in our own inadequate offerings to God. Whatever excesses Rancé may have committed in the course of polemic, he was not arrogant about the austerities of his monks and himself, even if his strictures on the relative laxity of others may sometimes suggest this. It necessarily follows that such complete submission to the will of God rules out any attempt to hasten, or provoke, one's own death. To be indifferent to life, and to long for eternity, may in one sense be a death wish, but a wish for life after death which is quite the opposite to a desire to end it all. On physical death and its aftermath he writes bluntly to Mme de la Vallière:[5] 'La vie quelle qu'elle soit ne seroit pas supportable si on ne savoit qu'elle doit finir'; and to dom Ferrand:[6] 'Le chrétien est bien à plaindre quand il ne vit pas dans l'attente de l'éternité'; and again,[7] 'Ma passion dominante est de m'ensevelir tout vivant dans notre désert

[1] Ibid., p. 195.   [2] Ibid., p. 195 (and Muguet, ii, p. 93).
[3] Ibid., p. 197.   [4] To Louise-Henriette in TC II/259 of 21 Nov. 1685.
[5] BN 19324, p. 426.   [6] Ibid., p. 215.   [7] Ibid., p. 592.

comme dans un sépulcre attendant que Jésus-Christ vienne pour
m'éveiller de mon sommeil.' In a slightly different context he
expresses very succinctly how Christ had come to fill the void of
self and also to point our way to eternity. Writing to the Carmelite Émilie de Bouillon he says:[1] 'Jésus-Christ tout seul...
mérite qu'on s'attache à lui. Il est le seul ami de tous les temps et de
tous les siècles.' The direction of Rancé's spiritual thinking and
teaching is unmistakably Christocentric, but the Passion is by
no means the only aspect emphasized, and Christ's person and
message are presented in a well-balanced way.

Still in the realm of spiritual theory, rather than rule of life,
Rancé takes particular pains to correct any tendency to subjec-
tivity. Faith, humility, and obedience are three primary weapons
in the Christian armoury, and prayer the indispensable means of
forging them. Obedience is demanded of all, though naturally
the formal requirements are very different for those living under
rule ('regulars') and others. All the same it is interesting to see
Rancé telling the duchesse de Luynes:[2] 'Dieu n'a point dit qu'il
faut sentir pour faire son salut, mais bien qu'il falloit faire ses
commandements.' Inevitably many of his correspondents, religious and lay, wrote to him seeking advice on the 'aridité' or
'sécheresse' of their spiritual life, and such remarks as those just
quoted provide an effective antidote to those who set up their
own responses as a criterion for measuring the mystery of divine
purpose.

Advice to the Visitandine Mère de la Roche (niece of Mère
Louise Rogier) makes the same point in a slightly different way:[3]
'Si vous ne pouvez trouver Dieu ni dans vos lectures ni dans vos
prières, il faut que vous le cherchiez par la fermeté de votre foi.'
The injunctions to obey God's commandments and to persevere
in faith are both linked with another of Rancé's favourite themes,
common to all Augustinians in the century, of the 'Dieu caché'.
To the same nun he writes: 'Dieu forme des orages sur la tête
de ses élus, mais il les dissipe aussitôt', and 'Quoique Dieu ne
retire pas les yeux de sa miséricorde de dessus les personnages
qu' il aime... souvent il se cache.' A letter to Mme de Saint-Loup
amplifies this idea, and shows the intimate connection in Rancé's
thought between all these spiritual phenomena:[4]: 'Le soin que

---

[1] Ibid., p. 33.   [2] Ibid., p. 59 (and *TB* 874).
[3] Ibid., p. 62 (and *A* 2106, f. 100).   [4] Ibid., p. 256.

Dieu prend de faire naître des occasions pour vous humilier est une marque que vous lui êtes bien présente.' The painful effect of humiliation is not only good for us, but necessary, and none of the counsel offered by Rancé can be followed while the smallest vestige of *amour propre* remains. He tells an unidentified lady:[1] 'Nous voulons bien que tout meure en nous pourvu que l'amour-propre y vive, ce qui est un mécompte dont les suites sont ir-réparables.'

After all these comparatively general instructions it is perhaps easier to set specific rules of life in a more appropriate context. Those like Bellefonds who suffered disgrace, or, like Mme de Guise, were afflicted with tragic bereavement, or the incurably ill, like Mlle de Vertus and Mme de la Sablière, had by force of circumstances started on the road to humility and mortification. They needed the comfort and encouragement that Rancé afforded them in generous measure. If, like Retz or some of Rancé's female relatives, they hovered indecisively on the brink they were urged in sometimes peremptory terms to cast themselves in, trusting to God's mercy, and Rancé became impatient only when good intentions remained too long at the verbal stage. Very exceptionally he would answer requests to send a full rule of life, for example to the Commandeur de Laval, who, it must be remembered, was bound by vows as a Knight of Malta;[2] but more often he recommended people to a good confessor, invariably someone opposed to casuistry and often a member of the Oratory.

If the preceding chapters have given ample evidence of Rancé's common sense and moderation, this is no way implies any readiness to compromise on the principles which he regarded as binding on all Christians, whatever their station in life. Similarly, as has been seen, his teaching on sacramental discipline is exactly the same for all, and his teaching on prayer only varies in detail. Layfolk are not engaged in the *opus Dei*, but in *Conduite chrétienne*[3] (1697) he describes four types of prayer suitable for them: mental prayer, short and frequent prayers 'comme une flèche enflammée', vocal prayer, and active prayer (almsgiving and the like). This, 'la respiration de l'âme', inevitably varies in frequency according to each individual's vocation, but is in essence the same for all.

When we come to monks and nuns the essentials remain the

[1] *TC* II/231 of 5 June 1684.   [2] See above, pp. 276–277.   [3] p. 145.

same, but since they all live under rule, no variations of detail can be permitted. Moreover the humility which is enjoined on all must, in the case of religious, not be left to the hazard of circumstance but must be supplied in the form of prescribed exercises. Obedience means that each religious must abdicate his own will, not just in general to God's will, but specifically to that of his superior. The superior should in theory bow to the rule of his order as represented by Visitors, General Chapter, or immediate superiors, but in practice this turned out to be a weak link in the chain of Rancé's thought. The advice given to Visitandines, like his niece, who fretted after more physical austerities than her rule provided for, or to Gourdan, whose zeal outstripped that of his *confrères* and superiors at Saint-Victor, shows Rancé firmly opposed to any deviations from the norm legally prescribed in each case and, at least in his niece's case, even to transfer, on the grounds that restlessness could too easily be a symptom of spiritual self-indulgence. He never gave the impression that he regarded, for instance, Visitandines or Oratorians as less holy and perfect people than Cistercians; on the contrary, all the evidence confirms his recognition that he and his monks formed a tiny minority of whom more austerity was expected and who were doing a quite different job from the rest, but were not on that account to be considered superior. The title *De la sainteté et des devoirs de la vie monastique* cannot be split; the fundamental duty of monks and nuns is to lead a holy life, and this they can only do if they obey the rule laid down by their founders and successive chapters. This is the crux of the problem, for no rule, however explicit, can legislate for all contingencies, maybe centuries ahead, and such a rule as that of St. Benedict has constantly to be adapted in detail even if the principles remain unchanged.

It would be true to say that with minor exceptions all Rancé's quarrels arose from his interpretation of the Rule, or the ancient Cistercian usages based on it. He continually and vehemently denied that there was anything personal in the rule as he administered it at la Trappe, and to this end appealed to the great monastic saints, Benedict, Bernard, Basil, and his favourite John Climachus. The potent mixture of conviction springing from conversion with belief that such incontrovertible truths must obviously accord with the teaching of the saints could hardly lead to flexibility or an open mind, and so often it is clear to

the observer, as it was not to Rancé, that his passionate defence
of Climachus is in fact self-defence. To be fair, some of the
practices particularly associated with Rancé's rule at la Trappe,
notably that of systematic humiliations, come straight from
Climachus,[1] and Rancé could hardly have evolved it in the
absence of such weighty support. His frequent references to the
Thebaid, repeated by so many of his correspondents, show a yearn-
ing for the heroic age of primitive monasticism, going back beyond the gentler origins of Benedictine institutions, and it would
be a mistake to omit from consideration of his spirituality this
curiously anachronistic element.

In 1657, when Rancé's conversion began, the Fronde had been
over only six years, and what has been called the feudal ethos[2]
of the defeated Frondeurs was seeking an outlet in a similarly
heroic approach to religion, in which Rancé's case is only one of
many. His worldly youth corresponded to the years of Corneille's ascendancy, of Descartes's uncompromising dualism and
ideal of *générosité*. *Polyeucte*[3] is the perfect example of the Cornelian
hero in a religious context, and it is not too fanciful to see in
Rancé and la Trappe a mirror image of Cornelian *gloire*, with the
cult of the absolute represented by total self-denial offered for
the greater glory of God. However that may be, this moral
context is indispensable to an understanding of many of Rancé's
less attractive features: the unquestioning obedience he exacted
was not to him as a person but as the abbot entitled, indeed obliged, to expect it according to the rule. His ruthless humiliation
of his monks, his ban on any links with family or friends, his
passionate defence of la Trappe as the custodian of divinely
sanctioned values prompt comparison with similar attitudes in
secular society.[4] There is no reason to suppose that he ever saw
himself as anything but an unworthy follower of the great
monastic saints, but he unquestionably believed that such conduct
as that just described was an integral feature of their sanctity.
Perhaps, more dangerously, he also believed that criticism and
calumny was the natural fate of saints, so that any suggestion

---

[1] See John Climachus, *Scala Paradisi*, Cologne 1583, pp. 55–6 (also in Migne, *PG*,
lxxxviii, especially *gradus* iii) for examples of conduct approved and copied by Rancé.

[2] P. Bénichou, *Morales du grand siècle*.

[3] *Polyeucte* was written in 1641 or 1642.

[4] The most extreme example would probably be Corneille's *Horace*, but he was
not the only apostle of *gloire*, and Louis XIV's absolutism suggests other parallels.

that he might be wrong proved inevitably counter-productive. There are enough unattractive, not to say unlikeable, saints in the Church's calendar for questions about Rancé's own sanctity to be somewhat misleading, but it is a simply verifiable fact that the few people who have troubled to read all he wrote invariably share the belief of those who enjoyed his friendship in his lifetime that he was a great and good man.

If instead of talking about Rancé's sanctity one inquires what, if any, reflection of Christ he offered, the answer is as usual different according to the emphasis laid on public and private conduct respectively. He was not one to turn the other cheek; he had to force himself (with occasional conspicuous lapses) to be humble; he showed apparent insensitivity in his treatment of men and women as humanly fallible as himself; but against this he always claimed that effective surgery necessarily involves some degree of pain. He was endlessly forgiving and compassionate to the penitent sinner, even to the backslider, tireless in relieving the needs of the poor or in consoling the sick. His life, like his spirituality, if the two can be meaningfully separated, illustrates the tensions so typical of converts compensating, or over-compensating, for misspent years. Like Paul, Augustine, or Pascal he knew the old Adam too well to take any chances in himself or with others, and the unease he inspires in so many readers is the product of this violent, but fruitful, tension. A very characteristic aside to a Carmelite nun expresses one aspect:[1] 'Il est bon de mêler son espérance d'un peu de crainte.'

Undoubtedly another aspect of this same tension is his almost febrile insistence on activity, the compulsive need to be busy, filling up every moment of the day with some well-defined task. A very common criticism of Rancé as a monk is that he allowed too little time for private prayer and pure contemplation, that he shows little awareness of the mystical side of religion and to that extent impoverished spiritual life. In his own case it seems abundantly clear that his restless energy drove him to such activity that there was little time (perhaps an hour or two a day) for meditation, but it must be said that he undertook his vast correspondence as a duty he could not refuse. Similarly, many of the interviews or business matters with which he was charged were the inescapable consequences of his position. All the same,

[1] BN 19324, p. 163.

he was clearly different from, for example, St. Bernard, who was certainly no less active but whose mystical spirit was not thereby repressed. Rancé's letters, especially to nuns, are so full of warnings against introspection that one can be sure that he regarded this as a very real danger in the contemplative life. Even before the Quietist controversy at the end of the century, in which he was momentarily involved, there was more than enough evidence available to convince any superior of the necessity to direct the thoughts and prayers of his religious in positive and safe directions. Seeing visions and dreaming dreams was all very well, but it too easily led to undesirable extravagance. For all that, it cannot be said that Rancé was opposed to all forms of mysticism. Everything baroque, sentimental, or fantastic was anathema to him, but his apocalyptic streak, his incessant preoccupation with eternity and the beatific vision to come, his very real reverence for Christ in the Eucharist belie the accusation that he was indifferent to the mystical strain in religion, let alone hostile to it. His distrust of the subjective element in all spiritual discipline must be balanced by his rejection of mere formalism and his insistence on interior dispositions.

Epilogue

ALL that has gone before reveals in some detail the extent of Rancé's contacts, the broad lines of his teaching and aspects of his personality, but he remains an elusive figure, full of contradictions and mysteries, so long as one tries to assess him in isolation from la Trappe. Ultimately the only possible answer to questions about his sanctity or significance must be sought in the community with which he so totally identified himself. His letters and books make no sense unless they are set in the context of the life from which he daily drew inspiration, and which in turn set the strictest bounds on his experience. If la Trappe had not lived up to his exigent demands Rancé would have been literally a voice crying in the wilderness, a hollow man, and if his enemies (and even some of his friends) had been right his monastery would have drifted back into mediocrity when he died. In the last analysis, influence cannot be measured by the number of letters written or received, by interviews granted or disputes publicized, though these are partial indices. In terms of achievement, or crude productivity, the balance may not look very impressive: his books were successful only for a time, and are now unread, his letters have had to be rediscovered, most of the monks and nuns to whom he wrote are mere names, their monasteries mostly in ruins, as for his more distinguished friends, literature has preserved Retz and Bossuet, one or two others flit across the pages of Saint-Simon or Mme de Sévigné, but even Bellefonds rates only passing mention in the history books. Rancé refused to found any other monastery, refused to start a new order or congregation, even his grave (or what the Revolution left of it) has never been a target for pilgrims.

How then is one to measure his stature and achievement? There are two parts to the answer, one in his own day, the other in the continuing present. He influenced his contemporaries first through the legend created about him, which infuriated some and enthralled others, but also, and more importantly, because he proved to all who would look or listen that his ideal actually worked. However hostile, no visitor denied the reality of life at la Trappe, and for many this represented the perfection of a monastic spirit for which they yearned. Moreover the community was a manifestly happy and united one, even at the end weathering the storm of the Gervaise episode despite Rancé's virtual impotence to intervene. The Jansenists failed to annex him, he could not be tempted away from his abbey to higher dignities; right or wrong he never went back on his decision of 1663 to live and die at la Trappe. If it is absurd to claim that well-run orders like the Carthusians or Maurists benefited in any way from their disputes with him, it is certainly not absurd to ascribe some of the success of Sept-Fons, Orval, and Tamié directly to his influence (all three were incidentally revived after the Restoration of 1815 and still survive), while the quality of life in other houses of both men and women (Châtillon, Perseigne, Maubuisson, Leyme) was also directly affected over known periods and in known ways by his influence. Outside the cloister one can only guess at the full extent of his influence on known correspondents and others, but his close and lasting friendship with the Oratory and Marcel at Saint-Jacques, as well as with Bossuet and other prelates, must be noted. This quiet influence is less dramatic than the strident notes of controversy but it is also more positive and less painful.

The other side of the answer begins with his death. La Trappe's only colony, Buonsolazzo, near Florence, was founded in 1705[1] after unavailing attempts by the Grand Duke of Tuscany to persuade first Rancé and then Gervaise to send an outpost from la Trappe. Under dom Malachie Garneyrin (Rancé's choice as successor to Gervaise) the new community overcame enormous obstacles to prosper for a while, but as links with la Trappe slackened, so the experiment began to fail. Events at la Trappe worked out very differently. Rancé is often accused of harsh, ferocious, unreasonable rule at la Trappe, and if this had really been so it is hard to see how the community would ever have survived, let alone increased. Within twenty or so years after his death there were few monks left who had known him (the last, a lay brother, died in 1765, aged 83, but Gervaise, who of course died in exile, in 1751, seems to have been the last choir monk to have known him) but under successive sensible abbots the abbey

---

[1] The story is well told by F. Michel, *Buonsolazzo, 1704–23*.

continued to flourish.[1] The spirit which had originally transformed the crumbling stones and seedy religious of 1662 into a prosperous abbey of a hundred or more sustained the community without flagging until the Revolution of 1789. No one has yet produced adequate, indeed any, economic or social arguments to explain away this spiritual phenomenon, which made la Trappe in 1789 comparable in population only to Clairvaux and Cîteaux. Everyone had been wrong except Rancé.

What then took place is highly relevant both to an assessment of Rancé's effective long-term influence and also to the Romantic legend, with its correspondingly distorted counterpart, which still prevails.[2] Dispersed like all religious communities by the Revolution, that of la Trappe embarked under the leadership of dom Augustin de Lestrange, then novice master, on an odyssey probably unequalled in monastic history. As many of them as were permitted first took up temporary residence at Val-Sainte, near Fribourg in Switzerland, until driven out by the approaching French armies. There dom Lestrange drew up a revised, much stricter, set of rules which Rome provisionally authorized but never ratified. The inescapable realities of total poverty, near starvation and appalling accommodation had to be met, and somehow incorporated into a routine which enabled some kind of spiritual life, including divine office, to continue day by day. Rigours which would have been inconceivable in the settled conditions at la Trappe became the prerequisite for survival as the ragged band trudged from one insecure refuge to the next. It is sometimes held that dom Lestrange's rule came nearer to Rancé's true intentions than that which had actually been observed at la Trappe. While it is true that Rancé frequently regretted his failure to match the standard set by the Desert Fathers, it is also true that only an emergency situation could justify dom Lestrange's greater austerity, but in the event fully did so.

[1] It should be noted that successive abbots attended General Chapters at Cîteaux and played a full part in the order at large. See Canivez, *Statuta*, vii for 1738 (p. 659), 1769 (p. 757), 1771 (p. 779).

[2] This chapter of Cistercian history is still obscure in some respects and controversial in most. It is treated fully and sensibly by P. Jean de la Croix-Bouton, *Fiches cisterciennes, Histoire de l'Ordre*, 1957, pp. 409 seq., but the story in a sense is far from complete and even now there is disagreement within the order.

At different times small groups of monks were sent to Italy, Spain, Canada, England (Lulworth), as well as the Low Countries and Germany where they stayed, but the main body somehow kept together, continually joined by Cistercian fugitives, including nuns, on their journey through Austria, into Poland, and as far as Russia proper. They were regularly split up and reunited, but at last the Restoration of 1815 enabled them to return to France. Already in 1794 dom Lestrange had been granted the authority of abbot,[1] and was thus the senior superior of the French Reformed Cistercians in dispersion. Other abbeys were flourishing, notably Darfeld in Westphalia (whence Port-du-Salut,[2] the first French revival, was founded in 1816) and Westmalle in Belgium, both governed independently by constitutions closer to those of Rancé than those of dom Lestrange, but the community of la Trappe was the only one of its order in France to return to its original house as a community. Obviously, after twenty-five years of exile membership had changed, but continuity was unbroken and its superior was the same. It must be remembered that up to 1789 Reformed Cistercians were out-numbered by those of the Common Observance, and that the system of filiation to proto-abbeys under the primacy of Cîteaux was as it had been since the twelfth century. All this was swept away, none of the proto-abbeys was reoccupied and Cîteaux itself was restored to the order only in 1898. Since then it has been mother-house only to the Reformed Cistercians throughout the world and they continue to thrive, while the Common Observance, quite healthy elsewhere though much less numerous, counts only a handful of monks in France in three or four houses.[3]

As a result of the complete disintegration of the original Cistercian system, the Reformed abbeys remaining in Western Europe grouped themselves into congregations, before being finally amalgamated at the end of the century, and for most of the nineteenth century la Trappe was *de facto* or *de jure* mother-house. This is how the popular identification of Trappist and Cistercian came about and inevitably coloured all subsequent

---

[1] The last regularly elected abbot, dom Pierre Olivier, died 7 Feb. 1790.

[2] Port-du-Salut was actually founded 21 Feb. 1815 and in deference to dom Lestrange, absent in America, la Trappe was not reoccupied until 6 Dec. 1815. Dom Laprade had in fact adopted Rancé's constitutions as early as 1806 (La Croix-Bouton, op. cit., p. 426).

[3] For modern comparative statistics see Appendices in Lekai, *The White Monks*.

appreciation of Rancé, credited more than a century after his
death with foundation of a congregation for which even the
word did not exist before the Revolution.[1] By custom each new
house founded in the nineteenth century was known as la Trappe
with the appropriate place-name, and the original house was then
distinguished as la Grande Trappe. The spectacular extension of
monastic life in general and of Trappists in particular after the
Restoration, the flood of first-class recruits (a normal post-war
phenomenon), the heroic, and uncompromising, personality of
dom Lestrange, and the epic adventures of his community all
fired imagination and struck an immediately responsive chord
in Romantics like Chateaubriand. This was the context in which
his *Vie de Rancé* was composed, and in which Dubois was later
commissioned to write (in fact to edit) the authoritative life of the
man now regarded as founder of a world-wide order. It is not
surprising that opinion both within and without the order reacted
sometimes sharply against certain aspects of Trappist life and
against the legendary Rancé as then known. Moreover, revival of
interest in Jansenism increased, if anything, the distortion of
Rancé's nineteenth-century portrait.

One feature of the revival needs mention. When the Cistercians
first returned to France, to Port-du-Salut from Darfeld, the Pope
specifically authorized Abbot Laprade to follow Rancé's Constitutions, rather than the emergency rule of dom Lestrange, more
vigorous than prudent. It was indeed on that basis that expansion
took place, and if the heroism of dom Lestrange saved la Trappe
in wartime, dom Laprade (a novice of la Trappe, be it noted, in
1789) was no less authentic a Trappist and ensured peacetime
prosperity by his decision to follow Rancé's rule. Inasmuch as this

---

[1] In 1794 Valsainte was made an abbey 'de l'Ordre de Cîteaux et de la Congrégation de Notre-Dame de la Trappe', whereafter (but not before) it is correct to speak
of Trappists (La Croix-Bouton, op. cit., p. 437). In 1834 the French congregations
were united, with the abbot of la Trappe as Vicar-General assisted by analogy with
the former system by four proto-abbots from new foundations, but in 1847 there
was a new split, with la Trappe and Sept-Fons respectively leading congregations,
and final union was only achieved on 8 Oct. 1892. With the restoration to the order
of Cîteaux as mother-house in 1898 the mention of 'Notre-Dame de la Trappe'
became unnecessary, and on 30 July 1902 more than a century of Trappist history
was ended when the order was officially renamed Ordo Cisterciensium Reformatorum (O.C.R.) or Ordo Cisterciensium Strictioris Observantiae (O.C.S.O.), which is
how modern members of the order sign themselves. It may be noted that the old
title 'dom', once used by all choir monks in orders, is now only given to abbots in
the order.

was adopted in preference to the milder rule of the former Abstinents it is not unreasonable to regard Rancé as posthumous founder of the Trappists.[1] Even those who exclude Providence as a factor relevant to the explanation of historical events have to accept the pragmatic argument that what Rancé began in 1664 still lives on, and 300 years later can fairly be compared with the first great Cistercian flowering, of which he always claimed to be the faithful heir.

It is only honest to admit that in this century at any rate modern Cistercians, even those of la Trappe, have shown some reservations, amounting to hostility, towards Rancé and his work. The ignorance and distortion of which he has been the victim partly account for this, so too does the far-reaching upheaval in monastic affairs since Vatican II. It is not very helpful at this moment in time to press the claims of a Rancé relevant to our age. It is, however, legitimate to answer the question of his stature and achievement by pointing to la Trappe, by comparing the fortunes of that community with those of others, older and richer, by setting him in the context of an age as spiritually unstable as our own, and by pondering the wisdom and firmness he brought to perennial problems like sickness, despair, or bereavement. He will now never be canonized, and it is insulting to his memory to whitewash his faults. So much impatience, so much anger, suspicion, or wounding criticism are human, but regrettable, but when his critics have made capital of his impetuous and turbulent nature, it is pleasant to turn back to sturdy virtues like friendship, compassion, and faith. He was a leader, not a driver of men, a solitary, but not alone.

There is no last word: he had the faults of his virtues, he served God according to his lights, and brought men and women, known and unknown, to faith and hope. He gratuitously offended men as good as himself, or better, like Mabillon or dom le Masson, but meeting always brought about reconciliation. He talked and

---

[1] By a strange irony in 1847 la Trappe, which favoured the most rigorous application of the rule (that of Valsainte was rescinded in 1843), found itself head of the *Nouvelle Réforme* as against the *Ancienne*, headed by Sept-Fons, who were known as 'rancéens' because they wanted to go no further than he had. What Rancé would have made of this use of his name as a specific index of moderation it is hard to say. Modern Cistercians tend to bypass the disputes of the seventeenth century and go right back to their medieval origins in reconsidering their future, but the monks of la Trappe remain notably loyal to Rancé's memory and as more is known of him his real role is increasingly appreciated.

wrote too much, and too imprudently, but he ardently sought silence and peace in the cloister and gave to others what he could not enjoy himself. Above all, he inspired and gave love, and without this saving charity none of his work could have endured.

Bibliography

A. MANUSCRIPT SOURCES

THE situation regarding MSS. of Rancé's letters is exceedingly confused, and until research has gone a good deal further only provisional
statements can be offered. In very rough terms well over 2,000 identifiably different letters of Rancé survive, some 500 of which have been
published in whole or in part. Some 500 survive in the original (about
250 of them being included in the number of those published) and more
than 1,000 are known only in copies made either in Rancé's lifetime or
shortly after his death. Most of the few letters written in his own hand
are unsigned, and belong to the earlier part of his life, before he became a monk. In later years he so seldom wrote himself that he usually
comments on the fact when he does (on 18 July 1672 he tells Le Roy
'après une page d'écriture il n'y a plus rien de lisible' and on 24 Jan.
1679 apologizes to Bellefonds for writing in his own hand because his
secretary is ill). Normally he signed and dated letters dictated to his
secretary (after October 1694 he could not even do that), but unfortunately one of the worst features of his handwriting is the figures
(7 and 8 being particularly hard to distinguish), so that copyists very
often get the date wrong. Moreover, for reasons of security, or in
order to exclude matter judged to be without spiritual interest, editors
and copyists did not hesitate to omit not only the formal opening
phrases of letters, but also references to persons and events, often
contained in postscripts, which are interesting in themselves and would
have made identification much easier. In many cases no addressee is
given at all in copies, often no date, and sometimes, even when they
have been given, they have been heavily erased at some later stage.
Add to these difficulties the duplication of copies, often with incorrect
and inconsistent names and dates, the division of some letters and
amalgamation of others, and some measure of the problems involved
may be imagined. While there is no reason to question the authenticity
of copies, it is almost certain that the majority of them omit something.
When in 1905 Tournoüer published his Bibliography he was aware of
all these facts, but for some unaccountable reason did virtually no
collation between MSS. in different places, and not always between
MSS. at la Trappe. Consequently it would only compound confusion
to refer to his numbering and identifications, which abound in errors,
duplications, and omissions. Further letters, and other MSS., are certain

to turn up, especially in private collections. A notable omission from
the list of sources is Rome, where, it can hardly be doubted, letters from
Rancé and about la Trappe must exist, but so far elude discovery. For
the present, however, the picture of MS. sources is more or less as
follows.

For convenience, all MSS., including the few not by Rancé but
relevant to this book, are included, but duplicate copies of MSS. listed
in the main collections have not been mentioned unless there is some
strong reason for doing so.

La Trappe

Nearly 1,000 different letters, including 40 originals, are kept in the
archives at la Trappe. They are classed in four series, in very varying
condition:

1. *Original*—36 to his sister, Marie-Louise, 1 to the abbess of les
   Clairets, 1 to Arnauld d'Andilly (1662–95)

2. *Lettres à imprimer*—381 letters from Rancé and 4 to him, in copies
   made about 1700, almost all in a single hand. The series runs
   from November 1662 to February 1683, and consists of 4° sheets
   originally paginated from 1 to 1864, but now with numerous
   gaps, especially at the beginning. 906 pages remain in all, and,
   making allowances for what looks like an early change in pagination, about 300 (or more) letters have been lost. It is most
   probable that this series was compiled under dom le Nain's
   supervision (but not in his hand) and that the gaps represent
   letters used for his, or other, lives of Rancé and not replaced.

3. *Lettres de piété*—Now contains 531 letters from Rancé, from 1660
   to 1699. This series, in folio (with 5 exceptions), includes work
   by thirteen different hands, four of which account for some 420 in
   all. The copies are divided into two series: I with 186 letters, II
   with 343, each sewn into seven 'cahiers' (the discrepant numbering is the result of losses). At least 13 are duplicates, 65 exist
   in *lettres à imprimer*, 8 in *lettres diverses*, and 5 in the *lettres originales*,
   thus giving about 440 different letters. They are not so carefully
   copied as the previous series, are full of erasures and other marks,
   and show only sporadic signs of classification, either by addressee
   or chronology. Dom le Nain also annotated this series, and it
   should probably be regarded as the first, rough draft from which
   neater copies would have been made.

4. *Lettres diverses*—Most of the copies in this collection are on folded
   12° sheets, with one letter following another on the same sheet.
   As a result, removal of a given letter often leaves only the begin-

ning or end of those before and after it. Almost all the copies are in the same hand as that of series 2 above, and from the very complex and multiple systems of numbering on the letters, three, or perhaps four, separate sets, each running up to 100 more or less, can be distinguished. 88 letters from Rancé, 23 of them fragments only, survive, and 2 from dom le Nain, who added his annotations to this series too. They are very neatly copied, apparently in chronological order by sources (the supplier of the original is twice noted), but each set starts afresh, the period covered corresponding exactly to that of series 2 (1660–82), for which this was most probably a trial run. There is no duplication between the two. Despite its fragmentary nature this is an interesting and valuable source. 26 other copies are kept in the same collection, 24 in 4°, 2 in folio, but all but 2 are duplicated elsewhere and offer little interest.

It will be seen that these three collections of copies form much the most important source of Rancé's correspondence, and although in two of the series the work of copying was interrupted at 1682 and 1683, the gaps that can be calculated show that for that period alone some 500 or 600 letters must once have been copied but are now lost.

Other valuable documents are also kept in the archives, which are not completely reclassified. Among the MSS consulted are:

Mémoires sur la réforme de Sept-Fons (copy dated 24 Nov. 1759 of an original MS. composed *c.* 1709)

Relations de la Trappe (account of a visit paid in 1687 by an ecclesiastic from Périgord; a letter of 1687 from fr. Arsène de la Croix to his brother at Cîteaux; a copy of the *Règlements*)

Registre mortuaire, 1667–1792 (MS. 308.1)

Inventaire (a large volume showing among other things documents still held at la Trappe in 1761, including some of Rancé's letters, but none of those listed above, and a copy of those from James II)

MS. de Sept-Fons (*Vie de Rancé*) (copy (3 vols.) made in 1901–3 at la Trappe of the original MS. lent by Port-du-Salut, and now apparently mislaid. Despite numerous errors of transcription a valuable check on Dubois)

Paris

Bibliothèque Nationale:

MS. fr. 9363   Original letters from Rancé, Maisne, and others to Nicaise, 1680–1700. Gonod published 128 of them,

MS. fr. 9363 but inadvertently omitted one or two and attributed to Rancé some signed by Maisne

17418, 17419, 17420, 17423 7 original letters from Rancé to Achille de Harlay, 1683–9

17755 4 original letters from Rancé to Nicole, and 1 copy to Bocquillot, 1687–9

19324 *Extraits des lettres et autres ouvrages de M. de Rancé* (732 pp. in 4°). Copy, from Saint-Germain-des-Prés, by several hands, made after 1702. Uniquely valuable because someone has annotated the extracts from letters with the addressee's name, thus identifying many otherwise unknown correspondents. The volume is an anthology, arranged alphabetically by subjects, of Rancé's spiritual teaching.

19656 6 original letters and 2 copies from Rancé to or about Mabillon, 1682–93

24123 *Portefeuilles du P. Léonard de Sainte-Catherine*, containing numerous documents on la Trappe, including 4 original letters from Rancé and some copies (not all dated or identifiable).

25080 1 original letter and meditation from Rancé

25538 1 original letter from Rancé

25557 1 original letter from Rancé

Nouvelles acquisitions fr. 12959 77 original letters and 1 copy from Rancé to Bellefonds, 1672–93, and 4 originals to others

12960 44 copies (nineteenth-century) of letters from Rancé to Mme de Guise, 1683–7

MS. lat. 17134 *Declarationes in Regulam*, a contemporary copy in Latin and French of Rancé's draft for his later published work on the Rule.

18389 *Vie de M. de Barillon écrite par lui-même*, copy of autobiography deposited with M. Marcel at Saint-Jacques

Collections Baluze, 361 Original letters, including 4 from Rancé, to and from Baluze, Casanata, Muguet, 1690–2

Pièces originales, 2520 Information on Rochemonteix family (other documents in this genealogical series add little to published sources)

Collection Moreau, 793, t. IV *Lettre de M. Bourrée touchant l'abbaye de la Trappe*, 20 Apr. 1684.

Fichiers Charavay Important index of sales in the main specialist houses (not only Charavay) of letters etc, up to about

1900. Many of the extracts are incomplete, and dates are often inaccurate, but for some of the letters in private hands this is the only knowledge available (see Index RAI–RAZ)

In 1970 the BN acquired by purchase at Sotheby's some of the Phillipps Papers, including Vol. IX, MS. 14324, with 1 original letter from Rancé to M. de Saint André of 1697 and a copy of an important letter to M. Boi[leau] of 1697. These will eventually be catalogued with the *nouvelles acquisitions fr.* no doubt.

Bibliothèque Mazarine:

MS. 1214	Copies of 106 letters from Rancé, mostly to Mère Louise Rogier, Louise-Henriette d'Albon, and one or two others, 1658–74
1241	*Dissertation sur les fictions*, by Le Roy; *Response*, by Rancé; *Éclaircissement*, by Le Roy
2440	*Registre des supérieures... de la Visitation* (before 1700)

Bibliothèque Sainte-Geneviève:

MS. Df 49   Duplicate of Mazarine MS. 1214
Suppl. ZZ f in fo. 316   Original letter from Rancé to Noailles, Archbishop of Paris, 1698
Suppl. Z f in 4° 829   Original letters to Noailles, 1698, from Maupeou, fr. Antoine, and prior of la Trappe

Bibliothèque de l'Arsenal:

MS. 2106	Bad copies of some of the letters in Mazarine 1214, with about 50 more to Favier as well as the others
3202	2 copies of letters from Rancé to Mme d'Huxelles, 1677, 1691
3824	Account of fr. Candide Chalype
5098	Extensive original correspondence and other documents from Celestines, including 1 original letter from Rancé to P. Ronat at Sens, 1672
5145	*Histoire des Célestins en France*
5172	29 original letters from Rancé to Gerbais, and 3 to others, 1693–7; 11 from dom le Nain and many others, all to Gerbais, concerning la Trappe
5346	Copy of letter from Rancé to Bossuet, 1693
6035, 6037, 6038, 6626	*Papiers Arnauld*: 43 original letters from Rancé to Arnauld d'Andilly, 1 to Archbishop of Tours (copy), 1 from Andilly to Rancé, 1658–73; 1 Rancé to Pomponne, 1691

Archives du Séminaire de Saint-Sulpice:

MS. Amelote 219   1 original letter from Rancé to P. Saint-Pé, 1671
no number (ex Levesque papers)   1 original letter from Rancé to dom
                Robin Couturier, 1671; 3 to Brancas, 1676; 1 to
                Bellefonds, 1679

Archives du Ministère des Affaires Étrangères:

France, MSS. 1440, 1441, 1442, 1443, 1444   Le Honreux de Saint-
                Louis, memoirs and other reflections on what he
                learned of the spiritual life from Rancé and la Trappe

Archives Nationales:

M 825   1 Original letter from Rancé to an unknown priest
Insinuations au Châtelet, y 226, vols IX–XV   Various entries concerning
                Rancé and his family, 1648–72

Minutier Central:

XLII. 169 (Ferret)   Affairs of Henri de Rancé and marriage date of his
                sister Marie
LI. 229 (Richer) Testament of Denis Bouthillier de Rancé
LI. 516, 518, 521 (Cousinet)   Negotiations for entry into Annonciades
                of Louise-Isabelle Bouthillier
N.B.   Details of other documents concerning Rancé are given in
Documents du Minutier Central concernant l'histoire litt., Paris, 1960, pp.
249–52, but the above had not been discovered.

Bibliothèque de la Société de Port-Royal:

MS. 47   4 copies of letters from Rancé to Pontchâteau, 1667–8
    415   Copy of extract of letter from dom Luce at Perseigne
                to Pontchâteau, 1675

Ventes Charavay:

   The periodic catalogues sent out by this specialist house of autograph
letters have included at least 3 original letters of Rancé in recent years,
and give such accurate details, and full extracts, that they must be
seriously examined as a source. Letters sold in 1959 (to M. de Montholon, 1682), in 1967 (to Andilly, 1660), in 1970 (to Caumartin, 1680).
These remain, of course, in private hands.

Alençon

Collection Tournoüer:

                This priceless collection includes 12 or 13 original
                letters from Rancé to various people, many from dom

le Nain, and numerous other documents relating to la
Trappe. The most important item is the eighteenth-
century copy of 38 letters from James II to Rancé.
A typed catalogue exists both at Alençon (Archives
de l'Orne) and la Trappe, but the conditions under
which these papers may be inspected are unclear.
Fortunately they were on loan to la Trappe during one
of my visits, but are now held in private hands near
Alençon.

Annecy

Monastère de la Visitation, Archives:

> The largest extant collection of *Lettres circulaires*
> from different houses of the order is preserved here,
> and provides obituary and other information on
> Mères Rogier, d'Albon, de la Roche, de Harlay, and
> others connected with Rancé. Among MSS. may be
> mentioned the only extant signed letter from Mère
> Rogier, a history of the house at Riom, and letters
> concerning Jansenist troubles at Angers 1679–80.

Carpentras

Bibliothèque Municipale:

MS. 625–626 Dom le Nain, *Vie de Rancé*, a copy made very shortly
before or after le Nain's death, and essential for correcting the printed version.

627 *Vie de dom Malachie Garneyrin*, monk of la Trappe
under Rancé and first abbot of Buonsolazzo

Clermont-Ferrand

Bibliothèque Municipale et Universitaire:

MS. 344 A 52 original letters from Rancé, mostly to Favier,
published by Gonod

B 14 original letters to Favier, 11 from Louise-Henriette,
1686–8, most published by Jaloustre

D 18 original letters to Favier, 2 from Maisne, 1682
(published by Jaloustre), and one from Félibien, 1664

E 1 draft letter from Favier (to Rancé?) and a list in his
hand (barely legible) of 50 letters from Rancé then in
his possession, 1660–87, of which 17 remain un-
accounted for.

Grenoble

Bibliothèque Municipale:

MS. 633   *Vie de dom le Masson*, General of the Chartreux
948   *Correspondance de dom le Masson*, 1675–1703
964, 5. III   *Histoire des intrigues de la Trappe*
C3552–4   Copies of letters and printed documents concerning Rancé's dispute with the Feuillants and many other ecclesiastical affairs

Luçon

Archives de l'Évêché:

22 original letters from Rancé to Henri Barillon, 1 from abbot Zozime (all included in copies at Poitiers, q.v.)

Marseilles

Bibliothèque Municipale:

MS. 1276   Copy of letter from Rancé to M. de la Quère of N.D. des Anges, 22 May 1696, and long reply by la Quère (or Laquerre) on death of Arnauld

Poitiers

Bibliothèque Municipale:

MS. Fontaneau 65   Copies made in 1752 of 106 letters from Rancé to Henri Barillon, 1 to Paul, and 4 other pieces. By consistently reading '7' for '8' the copyist has got the letters badly muddled, but the order can be established from internal evidence. (See Luçon, above.)

Reims

Bibliothèque Municipale:

MS. Pinchart, VII, 1145   Copies of 14 letters and other documents sent to Noailles, Archbishop of Paris, by Gervaise and others concerning his resignation, 1697–8

Archives Municipales:

MS. Tarbé, XV, 139   Original letter from Rancé to P. Chartonnet, of Sainte-Geneviève, 1694
140   Original letter from Rancé to Gerbais, 1695

Rouen

Bibliothèque Municipale:
MS. Montbret y 23, 29 *Liste des religieux de la Trappe, Necrologium*
       1667–1733

Troyes

Bibliothèque Municipale:
MS. 1066 2 original letters from Rancé to Quéras, 1685, 1687
    1689   Copies of letters between Rancé, Bishop of Tournai,
                and a mutual friend, 1688
    2183   2 copies of letters from Rancé to Arnauld, 1674, 1676;
                account of Maupas affair; important dossier—each
                page signed by dom le Nain—on his book and Rancé's
                attitude to Jansenism
    2240   2 original letters from Rancé to Nicole, 1673, 1675,
                1 to Collège des Bernardins, 1675

Utrecht

Fonds d'Amersfoort, Port-Royal (deposited in Rijksarchief; see
Inventaire, by Bruggeman and van de Ven):
MS. 483 6 original copies from Rancé to P. Bruscoly, 1677–8
    723   Copies of 6 letters from and 5 to Rancé
    738–774   Original letters, classified alphabetically, of letters
                sent to Le Roy, mostly about the fictions dispute;
                738, 4 from Mère d'Albon; 745, 7 from abbot of
                Châtillon; 749, 4 from abbot of l'Étoile; 767, 12
                from Rancé, 1672–8
    812   x   *Remarques sur la vie de feu l'abbé de la Trappe par M. de*
                Maupeou
    848   2 original letters from Rancé to Alet, 1670, 1672
    863   Various letters to and from Rancé; 1 original to
                Pontchâteau, 1668; 1 to Mme ——, 1673–4 to Mlle
                [de Vertus?] 1676
    913   Copy of letter from Rancé to Arnauld, 1679
    970   5 original letters from fr. Bernard Molac to Quesnel,
                1670
    1078   5 original letters from Urbain le Pannetier, prior of la
                Trappe, to Quesnel, 1671
    1168   43 original letters from Rancé to P. Quesnel, 1669–81
                (published by Tans)

1797	Abbé Louail, *Relation d'un voyage... à Mayenne et à la Trappe*, 1693
3061	*Voyage à la Trappe*, 1686 (with Pontchâteau papers, but not in fact by him)
3069	Copy of Troyes 2183, dossier le Nain
3201	*Esprit de l'abbé de la Trappe. Sentences de la Trappe*, copied by Mlle de Théméricourt, 1693
3202	*Response aux lettres d'un ecclésiastique touchant la déclaration de la Trappe...*, 1679
6094	Original letter from Rancé to dom Jounel(?) 1695

Windsor Castle

Royal Library:

MS. Stuart Papers 58–121   18 original letters from Rancé to James II, 1690–9 (published in *Stuart Papers*, Vol. I, pp. 59 seq. ed. F. H. Blackburne Daniell, London, 1902)

Florence

Bibliotheca Laurentiana:

MS. Ashburnham, Papiers Huet   Original letter from Rancé to P. D. Huet, Bishop of Avranches, 1696

Quebec

Bibliothèque du Séminaire:

MS. S. 19   Eighteenth-century copies of letter from Rancé to a missionary [Charmot], 1689

There are numerous entries under 'Rancé' in libraries all over France, but on investigation all have turned out to be duplicates, often inferior, of one or other of the letters listed above, all of which I have actually read, except for those in private hands, for which I have had to rely on extracts.

B. PRINTED WORKS

Only works actually consulted have been listed, many more proved so unhelpful that they have not been mentioned. (A full Trappist bibliography up to 1900 will be found in Tournoüer below.) The edition quoted is that which I have used, not always because it is the best, but the only one available or simply the most accessible. In the case of some very rare books the BN *cote* is given. Where only one volume of a set has been used this has been indicated.

1. *Reference books, bibliographies, periodicals*

P. Anselme, *Histoire de la maison royale de France*
Archives départementales de l'Orne. série H
Archives départementales de la Sarthe, série H
Bibliotheca Missionum, ed. R. Streit, vol. v, Aachen, 1929
Bibliothèque générale des écrivains de l'Ordre de Saint-Benoît, 4 vols. (includes Celestines), Bouillon, 1777
J. B. Bouillet, *Nobiliaire d'Auvergne*, 7 vols., Clermont-Ferrand, 1846–53
J. Bruggeman and A. J. van de Ven, *Inventaire des pièces d'archives fr. se rapportant à l'abbaye de Port-Royal des Champs (ancient fonds d'Amersfoort)*, La Haye, 1972
dom L. H. Cottineau, *Répertoire topo-bibliographique des abbayes et prieurés*, 2 vols., Mâcon, 1939
Dictionnaire de biographie française (to G)
Dictionnaire d'histoire et de géographie ecclésiastiques
Dictionnaire de la noblesse, de la Chesnaye Desbois
Dictionnaire des ordres religieux, H. Hélyot (ed. of 1847)
Dictionnaire de spiritualité
Dictionnaire de théologie catholique
Documents du Minutier Central concernant l'histoire litt. (1650–1700), Paris, 1960
Gallia Christiana
L. le Clert, *Notice généalogique des Bouthillier*, Troyes, 1907
Moréri, *Grand Dictionnaire historique*, 10 vols., (ed. of 1759)
H. Tournoüer, *Bibliographie et iconographie de la Trappe (Documents sur la Province du Perche*, 4e série, 2), Mortagne, 1905–6.
Part III was left uncompleted and has now been published as Part III of the original title but renamed *Iconographie de l'abbaye de la Trappe et de l'abbé de Rancé (Cahiers Percherons* 39), Mortagne, 1973
F. van der Meer, *Atlas de l'ordre cistercien*, Paris, 1965
Villars, Henri de, *Procez-Verbal de l'Assemblée générale du clergé de France... 1655–6*, Paris, 1656

Apart from articles listed below, the following periodicals are essential for Cistercian studies:

Analecta cisterciensia
Cîteaux
Collectanea Ordinis Cisterciensium Reformatorum.

2. *Works by Rancé* (excluding those of doubtful attribution, but including those published anonymously or without his authority)

Constitutions de l'abbaye de la Trappe, Lepetit, 1671

Règlements de l'abbaye de ND de la Trappe... avec des réflexions et la Carte de visite faite à N.D. des Clairets (also includes *Carte de visite* of the Abbot of Prières at la Trappe in 1676 and 1678), Delaulne, 1718

Requeste présentée au Roi, Langlois, 1673

Éclaircissement sur l'état présent de l'ordre de Cisteaux, Coignard, 1674 (BN Ld¹⁷.74)

Lettre à un ecclésiastique [Le Roy], Viret, Rouen, 1677

Relations de la vie et de la mort de quelques religieux de la Trappe, 5 vols., Desprez, 1755 (the first ed. appeared in 1677; this, the last, is obviously not all by Rancé, but has been quoted as being the most complete)

De la sainteté et des devoirs de la vie monastique, 2 vols., Muguet, 1683 (Gregg reprint, 1972)

Éclaircissement de quelques difficultez que l'on a formées sur le livre de la sainteté.... Muguet, 1685

Les Instructions de saint Dorothée. Muguet, 1686

La Règle de saint Benoist, traduite et expliquée selon son véritable esprit, Muguet, 1689

Response au traité des études monastiques, Muguet, 1692

Instructions sur les principaux sujets de piété et de la morale chrétienne, Muguet, 1693

Conduite chrétienne adressée à S.A.R. Mme de Guise, Delaulne, 1697

Maximes chrétiennes et morales, Delaulne, 1698

Conférences ou instructions sur les épitres et évangiles, Delaulne, 1698

Lettres de piété écrites à différentes personnes, 2 vols, Muguet, 1701 and 1702

Lettres de A.-J. le B. de Rancé, ed. B. Gonod, Paris, 1846

'Lettre à un évêque pour répondre... aux difficultez de dom Innocent le Masson' (20 July 1689) in *Nouvelles de la République des Lettres*, mai-juin 1710, pp. 488–519, 628–61

'Lettre au R.P. Malebranche' (29 Aug. 1689) in P. le Brun, *Histoire critique des pratiques superstitieuses*, iii, p. 177 2e éd. Amsterdam, 1733

'Lettres à Floriot' (1673/4) in Floriot, *Morale chrétienne... du Pater*, vi (separate pagination after p. 74), Bruxelles, 1745

'Lettres au R.P. Mabillon' (11 Sept. 1689 and 15 Sept. 1699) in *Ami de la Religion*, 128, 1846

'Lettres inédites' (à M. de Montholon, 1682) in *Bulletin du Bibliophile*, 1872, pp. 387–8

'Lettres à Pasquier Quesnel' in J. A. G. Tans, 'Un Dialogue monologué' *Augustiniana*, xiii, 1963

Other letters may be found in the biographies or published correspondence of Arnauld, Bocquillot, Bossuet, Gourdan, le Camus,
Mabillon, Nicole, Retz, Santeuil as listed below.

3. *Works on Rancé and la Trappe*

Abbé de l'ordre de Cisteaux, *Lettre... à l'abbé de la Trappe*, s.l.n.d.
  (BN Ld[17].184)
A.D.P.C.E., *Lettre au R.P. de Sainte-Marthe*, s.l., 1693
Aquin, Louis d', *Imago R.P. A.-J. B. de Rancé... Récit... en forme
  d'épitaphe*, s.l., 1708
Arnaudin, A. d', *Vie de dom le Nain*, Paris, 1715
Aubry, Lucien, O.C.S.O., 'La conversion de M. de Rancé' in *Col-
  lectanea*, xxv. 3, 1963
—— 'A la recherche du vrai portrait de Rancé' in *Cîteaux*, 1972
  (and offprint at la Trappe)
Bremond, Henri, *L'Abbé Tempête*, Paris, 1929
  (English version, *The Thundering Abbot*, London, 1930)
Charency, comte H. de, *Histoire de l'abbaye de la Grande Trappe* (*Docu-
  ments sur la Province du Perche*, ii, 6), Mortagne, 1896
Chateaubriand Henri de, *Vie de Rancé*, 1844
  (Best modern edition in *Textes litt. fr.*)
Denis, dom Paul (ed.), *Lettres autographes de Troussures*, Paris, 1912
Desmares, see Félibien
Didio, Henri, *La Querelle de Mabillon et de l'abbé de Rancé*, Paris, 1892
Dimier, Anselme, O.C.S.O., 'Note au sujet des conférences de la
  Trappe' in *Collectanea*, xxv. 3, 1963
Dubois, abbé, *Histoire de l'abbé de Rancé*, 2 vols., Paris, 1866
Dubois, Louis, *Histoire civile, religieuse et litt. de... la Trappe*, Paris, 1824
Du Suel, François, *Entretiens de l'abbé Jean et du prêtre Eusèbe*, Paris, 1674
[Félibien des Avaux, André and/or Desmares, P.], *Description de
  l'abbaye de la Trappe*, Paris, 1671
F.F.P.A., *Description de l'abbaye... de la Trappe... tirée de la lettre d'un
  religieux bénédictin*, Rouen, 1670 (This brief description, twelve
  pages long, was reprinted in the 1683 edition of Félibien's work;
  pp. 71 seq.)
F.G.A.D.E., *Lettre au R.P. abbé de la Trappe*, s.l.n.d. (BN Ld[17].185)
Gervaise, dom Armand-Fr., *Défense de la nouvelle histoire de Suger avec
  l'Apologie pour feu M. l'abbé de la Trappe*, Paris, 1725

Gervaise *cont. Jugement critique mais équitable des vies de feu M. l'abbé de Rancé...*, Londres (Troyes), 1742

Lambert, abbé, *L'Idée d'un vrai religieux... dom Paulin de l'Isle*, Châlons, 1723
  (The only copy I have been able to trace is in Versailles, Bibl. Mun, o.75. g.)

Lancelot, dom Claude, *Mémoires*, 2 vols., Cologne, 1738
—— *Narrative of a Tour... to Alet*, London, 1813
  (This very free paraphrase of part of the above is by Mary Schimmelpenninck and incorporates much material on la Trappe, one of the first English books to do so)

La Roque (or Larroque), Daniel de, *Les Véritables Motifs de la conversion de l'abbé de la Trappe... ou les entretiens de Timocrate et de Philandre...*, Cologne, 1685

Leclercq, dom Jean, O.S.B., 'La Joie dans Rancé' in *Collectanea*, xxv. 3, 1963

Lekai, Louis, S.O.C., 'The problem of the Authorship of Rancé's "Standard" Biography' in *Collectanea*, xxi, 2, 1959

Le Lasseur, F., S.J., 'L'Abbé de Rancé et le Jansénisme' in *Études religieuses... de la Compagnie de Jésus*, x, 1876

Le Nain, dom Pierre, *La Vie du R.P. A.-J. B. de Rancé*, 3 vols., Rouen, 1715; 2nd ed., much altered, Paris, 1719

Luddy, Ailbe, O.C.S.O., *The Real de Rancé*, London, 1931 (a rather ineffectual answer to Bremond)

Marsollier, abbé, *Vie de dom A.-J. B. de Rancé*, 2 vols, Paris, 1703

[Masson, Claude], *Deux retraites de dix jours... avec deux discours sur la vie des religieux de la Trappe*, Lyon, 1697
  (BN D 19871 contains only the *discours*, attributed by Moréri to Treuvé; perhaps Masson wrote only the missing *retraites*)

Maupeou, Pierre, *La Conduite et les sentiments de M. l'abbé de la Trappe* (against La Roque), Paris, 1685
—— *Vie du T.R.P. A.-J. B. de Rancé*, 2 vols., Paris, 1702

Mensaros, Aurèle, S.O.C., 'L'Abbé de Rancé et la règle bénédictine' in *Analecta*, xxii, 1966

Pacome, frère, *Description du plan en relief de l'abbaye de la Trappe*, Paris, 1708

Pezzoli, Denise, 'Le Discernement des vocations monastiques par l'abbé de Rancé' in *Collectanea*, xxii. 1, 1960
—— 'L'Abbé de Rancé et l'esprit de la pratique eucharistique' in *Collectanea*, xxiii, 2, 1961
—— 'L'Abbé de Rancé. Textes sur la discrétion' in *Collectanea*, xxv. 2. 1963

Presse, dom Alexis, O.C.S.O., 'L'Abbé de Rancé a-t-il voulu fonder
    une observance particulière?' in *Revue Mabillon*, xxi, 1931
[Sainte-Marthe, P. Denis de] [*Quatre*] *Lettres à M. l abbé de la Trappe où
    l'on examine sa response au traité des études monastiques*, Amsterdam, 1692
Serrent, M. L., *L'Abbé de Rancé et Bossuet*, Paris, 1903
—— 'Une Correspondance inédite de l'abbé de Rancé et de Jacques
    II d'Angleterre' in *Revue des questions historiques*, lxxxviii, 1905, pp.
    570–80
Sol, abbé, *Notre Dame de Saint-Bernard de Comminges*, Toulouse, 1923
    (Details of Rancé's part in setting up this shrine, with interesting
    quotations from his letters)
Tans, J. A. G., see under section 2, above
Tillemont, S. Le Nain de, *Lettre de M. de Tillemont*, Nancy, 1705
Vandenbroucke, dom F., O.S.B., 'L'Esprit des études monastiques
    d'après l'abbé de Rancé 'in *Collectanea*, xxv. 3, 1963
—— 'Humiliations volontaires; la pensée de l'abbé de Rancé' in
    Collectanea, xxvii. 3, 1965

4. *Cistercian history*

Albe, E., 'L'Abbaye cistercienne de Leyme' in *Revue Mabillon*, 2e
    série, xxiii, 1926
Beaufort, dom Eustache de, *Lettre*, Paris, 1702
Buffier, Claude, S.J., *Vie de M. l'abbé de Val-Richer*, Paris, 1696
Burnier, E., *Histoire de l'abbaye de Tamié*, Chambéry, 1865
Canivez, J. M., O.C.S.O., *Statuta Capitulorum Generalium Ordinis
    Cisterciensis*, vols, vii and viii, Louvain, 1935–41
Défense des règlements... pour la réformation de l'ordre de Cisteaux, Paris,
    1656 (BN Ld¹⁷.43)
Denais, Joseph, *L'Abbaye de Chaloché*, Angers, 1873
Drouet de Maupertuy, *Histoire de la réforme de Sept-Fons*, Paris, 1702
Éclaircissement sur les differends qui concernent la réforme, s.l.n.d. (BN Ld¹⁷.
    75)
Examen du Chapitre général... en 1672, Paris, 1673 (BN Ld¹⁷.71)
Fleury, G., 'L'Abbaye cistercienne de Perseigne, 1145–1790' in *Revue
    historique et arch. du Maine*, iv, 1878 (Mamers)
Garin, J., *Histoire de l'abbaye de Tamié*, Paris/Chambéry, 1927
[Gervaise, dom Armand-Fr.] *Histoire générale de la réforme de l'ordre de
    Cîteaux en France*, Avignon, 1746
La Croix-Bouton, Jean de, O.C.S.O., *Fiches cisterciennes*: *Histoire de
    l'Ordre* (not commercially available), Westmalle, 1957
Lamy, Firmin, *L'Ancien Sept-Fons (1132–1789)*, Moulins, 1937
Le Bail, dom Anselme, O.C.S.O., *L'Ordre de Cîteaux*, Paris, 1947

Lekai, Louis, S.O.C., *The White Monks*, Spring Bank, Wis., 1953

—— *The Rise of the Cistercian Strict Observance in XVIIth century France*, Washington, 1968

(This book resumes the substance of a number of articles published in various journals, notably an authoritative bibliography of Cistercian pamphlets of the period)

Leloczky, J. D., S.O.C., *Constitutiones et Acta Strictioris Observantiae Ordinis Cist.* (*1624–87*), Roma, 1967

Luddy, Ailbe, O.C.S.O., *The Cistercians*, Dublin, 1952

Martelet, Bernard, O.C.S.O., 'Dom Eustache de Beaufort' in *Collectanea*, xxv. 4, 1963

Michel, Félix, *Buonsolazzo 1704–23*, Marseille, 1960

Nguyen-Dinh-Tuyen, T., S.O.C., 'Histoire des controverses à Rome... 1662–66' in *Analecta*, xxvi, 1970

Réjalot, dom Thierry, O.S.B., 'Le Jansénisme à l'abbaye d'Orval, 1674–1764' in *Annales de l'Institut arch. du Luxembourg*, lxiii, 1932

—— 'Correspondance de l'abbé Ch. de Benzeradt... avec le P. Mabillon' in *Annales...*, lxv, 1934

Response aux dernières objections des premiers abbez de l'ordre de Cisteaux, s.l.n.d. (BN Ld¹⁷.85)

Souancé, vicomte de, *Histoire de Notre Dame des Clairets*, Vannes, 1894

Vergé du Taillis, O., *Chroniques de l'abbaye royale de Maubuisson*, Paris, 1947

Zakar, P., S.O.C., *Histoire de la Stricte Observance de l'ordre cistercian 1606–1635*, Roma, 1966

5. *Friends and contacts of Rancé*

Arnauld, Antoine, *Lettres*, 9 vols., Nancy, 1727–43

[Barillon, Henri de] 'Vie de M. de Barillon' in *Revue de Bretagne et de Vendée*, 2e série, i, pp. 471–82, and ii, pp. 134–49, 1862

Batterel, Louis, *Mémoires domestiques pour servir à l'histoire de l'Oratoire*, ed. A. M. P. Ingold, 4 vols., Paris, 1902

[Besoigne, J.], *Vies des quatre évêques... M. d'Alet, M. d'Angers, M. de Beauvais, M. de Pamiers*, 2 vols., Cologne, 1756

[Bocquillot] *Vie de L. A. Bocquillot*, Paris, 1745

Bonnard, Fourier, *Histoire de l'abbaye royale de Saint-Victor*, 2 vols., Paris, 1904–8

Bossuet, J. B., *Oraisons funèbres*, éd. de la Pléiade, 1936

—— *Correspondance*, ed. C. Urbain et E. Levesque, 15 vols., Paris, 1909–12

Bretonneau, F., S.J., *Abrégé de la vie de Jacques II*, Paris, 1703

Caillemer, E., *Lettres... à Nicaise*, Lyon, 1885

Carpentier, Paul, 'Tricentenaire d'une fondation oratorienne; l'ancienne maison d'Institution' in *Dans l'amitié de l'Oratoire*, nouv. série, 7, nov. 1958, and 8, mai 1959

Catel, Maurice, *Les Écrivains de Port-Royal*, Paris, 1962

Ceyssens, Lucien, O.F.M., 'Le Cardinal Jean Bona et le Jansénisme' in *Benedictina*, x, 1956

Chartreux, Un, *La Grande Chartreuse*, 10e éd., Paris, 1964

Cloyseault, C. E., *Bibliothèque oratorienne*, ed. A. M. P. Ingold, 4 vols., Paris, 1880

Cousin, Victor, *La Jeunesse de Mme de Longueville*, 2e éd., Paris, 1853

—— *Mme de Sablé*, Paris, 1854

Dethan, G., *Gaston d'Orléans*, Paris, 1959

Doinel, Jules, 'Un Épisode inconnu de la vie de Malebranche' in *Revue des questions historiques*, xx, 1876

[Du Bos, C. F., or Dupuis, G.] *Abrégé de la vie de M. Henri de Barillon*, Delft (Rouen), 1700

Feydeau, M., *Mémoires*, ed. A. Jovy, Vitry, 1905

Floriot, see Section 2 above, *ad fin.*

Gervaise, dom Armand-Fr., *Vie du vénérable Père Simon Gourdan*, Paris, 1755

Grandet, J., *Les Saints Prêtres Français du XVIIe siècle*, ed., Latourneau, 3 vols., Angers/Paris, 1897

Hermant, G., *Mémoires*, 6 vols., Paris, 1905–10

Ingold, A. M. P., *L'Oratoire à Luçon*, s.l.n.d. (BN 80 z 9892)

—— *Le Chancelier d'Aguesseau et l'Oratoire*. Paris, 1879

—— *Le R. P. Galipaud et le Jansénisme*, s.l.n.d. (BN Ln^{27}.32351)

Jaloustre, Élie, *Un Precepteur auvergnat de l'abbé de Rancé*, Clermont-Ferrand, 1887

Jérothée de Mortagne, O.S.F.C., *Oraison funèbre de Mme de Guise*, Alençon, 1696

Joly, A., *James Drummond, duc de Perth*, Lille, 1954

La Grande Chartreuse, see Chartreux

Lair, J., *Louise de la Vallière*, Paris, 1881

[Lallouette, A.] *Abrégé de la vie du cardinal E. le Camus*, Paris, 1720

Le Camus, Étienne, *Lettres*, ed. A. M. P. Ingold, Paris, 1892

Le Masson, dom Innocent, *Explication de quelques endroits des anciens status des Chartreux*, La Correrie, 1690

Louen, C. A. de, *Histoire de Saint-Jean-des-Vignes*, Paris, 1720

Mabillon, dom Jean, *Traité des études monastiques*, Paris, 1691

—— *Réflexions sur la response de M. l'abbé de la Trappe au traité...* Paris, 1692

—— *Ouvrages posthumes*, ed. V. Thuillier, 3 vols., Paris, 1724

Menjot d'Elbenne, vicomte, *Mme de la Sablière*, Paris, 1923

Montis, abbé de, *Vie de la vénérable sœur Anne-Marie de Jésus... d'Épernon*, Paris, 1774

Namer, G., *L'Abbé Le Roy et ses amis*, Paris, 1964

Neveu, Bruno, *Un Historien à l'école de Port-Royal*: *Sébastien le Nain de Tillemont*, La Haye, 1966

—— *Sébastien Cambout de Pontchâteau*, Paris, 1969

Nicole, Pierre, *Lettres*, 2 vols., Lille, 1718

Quesnel, Pasquier, *Correspondance*, 2 vols., Paris, 1900

Rapin, René, S.J., *Mémoires*, 3 vols., ed. Aubineau, Paris, 1865

Retz, Paul Gondi, cardinal de, *Correspondance* in *Œuvres*, vii, Paris, 1887

—— *Supplément à la Correspondance*, Paris, 1920

—— *Mémoires*, éd. de la Pléiade, 1956

Saint-Simon, duc de, *Mémoires*, 7 vols., éd. de la Pléiade, 1953

[Santeuil, J.-B. de,] *La Vie et les bons mots*, 2 vols., Cologne, 1742

Tans, J. A. G., *Pasquier Quesnel et les Pays-Bas*, Groningen/Paris, 1960

[Treuvé, Simon] *Vie de M. Du Hamel*, s.l.n.d.

Varin, P., *La Vérité sur les Arnauld*, 2 vols., Paris, 1847

Wehrle, J., 'Malebranche et l'abbaye de Perseigne' in *Province du Maine*, xxxvi, 1928

6. *General*

Adam, Antoine, *Histoire de la littérature fr. au XVIIe siècle* 5 vols., Paris, 1956

—— *Du mysticisme à la révolte. Les Jansénistes du XVIIe siècle*, Paris, 1965

Bénichou, Paul, *Morales du grand siècle*, Paris, 1948

Bluche, F., *Magistrats du grand conseil au XVIIIe siècle*, Paris, 1966

Bosseboeuf, L., *Le Château de Véretz*, Tours, 1903

Clark, Ruth, *Lettres de Germain Vuillart à Préfontaine (1694–1700)*, Genève, 1951

John Climachus, St., *Scala Paradisi*, Cologne, 1583 (also in Migne, *Patr. Graeca*, lxxxviii, pp. 581 seq.)

Mesnard, Jean, *Pascal et les Roannez*, 2 vols., Paris, 1965

Moorhouse, Geoffrey, *Against All Reason*, London, 1969 (includes complete English text of Cistercian Rule of 1964)

Sévigné, Mme de, *Lettres*, 3 vols., éd. de la Pléiade, 1953

This section could be almost indefinitely extended, and I have included only those books either referred to in the text or to which I owe essential information.

Index

The spelling of proper names in the seventeenth-century printed sources is very inconsistent, and in the MSS. chaotic. Particular difficulty arises with the many names incorporating the definite article. The style used throughout the book, and followed in the index, aims at self-consistency, but cannot claim to be authoritative, and cross-references have been used wherever confusion seemed otherwise likely to arise. Apart from the usual abbreviations the following have been used for convenience: *C.* Cistercian, *C.R.* Canon Regular, *T.* monk of la Trappe. All the dioceses mentioned in the index are those appropriate in the seventeenth century.

Bold figures indicate principal references.